BUSINESS and SOCIETY

BUSINESS and SOCIETY:
Economic, Moral, and Political Foundations

TEXT AND READINGS

Thomas G. Marx

**General Motors Corporation
and Wayne State University**

Prentice-Hall, Inc., Englewood Cliffs, NJ 07632

Library of Congress Cataloging in Publication Data
Main entry under title:

Business and society.

   Bibliography: p.
   Includes index.
   1. Industry—Social aspects—Addresses, essays,
lectures.   I. Marx, Thomas G., (date).
HD60.B88 1985   306 ′.3   84-17961
ISBN 0-13-107566-7

Editorial/production supervision and
   interior design: Susan Adkins
Cover design: Lundgren Graphics, Ltd.
Manufacturing buyer: Ed O'Dougherty

Printed in the United States of America

10 9 8 7 6 5 4 3 2

ISBN 0-13-107566-7   01

Prentice-Hall International, Inc., *London*
Prentice-Hall of Australia Pty. Limited, *Sydney*
Editora Prentice-Hall do Brasil, Ltda., *Rio de Janeiro*
Prentice-Hall Canada Inc., *Toronto*
Prentice-Hall Hispanoamericana, S.A., *Mexico*
Prentice-Hall of India Private Limited, *New Delhi*
Prentice-Hall of Japan, Inc., *Tokyo*
Prentice-Hall of Southeast Asia Pte. Ltd., *Singapore*
Whitehall Books Limited, *Wellington, New Zealand*

CONTENTS

v

PREFACE

I'm invariably asked on the first day of class what it's like in the real business world. I always answer that I thought this was the real business world. Surely, endless safety, health, noise, pollution, and fuel economy standards; advertising, hiring, and product regulations; age, sex, and racial discrimination charges; criticisms of immoral business conduct; protests against investments in South Africa; antitrust investigations; and political pressures to open one plant and close another are not the real business world. Isn't the real business world discounted cash flow, return on investment, capacity utilization, growth-share matrices, and Theories X, Y, and Z? While there may be some confusion about the precise nature of the real business world today, it is increasingly clear that there is only one business world in terms of global competition for consumers' dollars, francs, marks, and yen. And there is increasingly only one world for the fulfillment of society's economic, social, political, and moral needs.

This global integration of the world's economies and social integration of human needs have profound implications for future business-society relationships. Business has largely underestimated and misinterpreted the significance of growing global economic and social integration. These economic and social changes will not lead simply to additional external constraints on traditional business product decisions. Business has been slow to grasp the real issues stated clearly by Michael Novak: "... it is not the products themselves that are under attack but the system that produces them and the character and credibility of their producers. ... The business class is engaged for the first time, in a profound and broad intellectual struggle."[1] The challenge to business is to integrate society's total needs into a global business policy decision-making framework in which social goals become a positive, contributing factor to economic success, rather than simply a bound on acceptable behavior. The restoration of business credibility and the legitimacy of business control over the allocation of the majority of the nation's resources demands such an integration. Legitimacy in an increasingly complex, integrated world can no longer reside in simple compliance with externally imposed constraints.

Walter Bagehot observed over a hundred years ago: "The characteristic danger of great nations, like the Romans and the English, which have a long history of continuous creation, is that they may at last fail from not comprehending the great institutions which they have created." To avoid this danger, we must understand the intellectual foundations supporting the great economic, moral, and sociopolitical institutions of democratic capitalism. For only then can we confidently restructure these institutions to meet our changing needs without destroying the solid foundations upon which they rest.

The purpose of this book is to promote a better understanding of these institutions and the complex and changing interrelationships among them. This is a book about business and society—about the relationships among the social constituencies and the relationships among the social institutions which define the role of business in modern society. Thus, while this is a book about markets, competition, and economic efficiency, it is equally a book about civil liberties, justice, political power, individual rights, and moral obligations. Together, these relationships provide the basis for the organization of business and society.

A guided tour through a book of carefully selected and well balanced readings is the most effective way to explore the foundations of these relationships. Much effort was expended in selecting the readings to ensure that they addressed the fundamental business-society issues with which the book is concerned, and that the most compelling arguments in support of opposing viewpoints were presented. The reader will find few straw men in these readings, or arguments which can easily be dismissed. Anything less would be a disservice to the reader. An appreciation of the complexity of these issues is the first lesson to be learned. The authors represent an outstanding collection of intellectual leaders from academia, business, government, labor, and the consumer advocacy movement. Their collective expertise spans economics, ethics, political science, the law, management practice, and business policy.

Passage through the original articles in which these relationships are intensely debated is an exhilarating, sometimes exasperating, experience as the reader participates in the intellectual struggle for a better society. Textbooks amply describe the business, moral, and political institutions which dot the social landscape. They cannot, however, unearth the intellectual foundations upon

---

[1]Michael Novak, *The American Vision* (Washington, D.C.: American Enterprise Institute, 1978), pp. 37–38.

which these institutions are constructed. The dust from such heavy intellectual excavation would cloud the most direct route through the vast social landscape which the textbook must traverse. But such probing is essential to the assessment of the claims upon the nation's resources by competing social constituencies; to the recognition and evaluation of the full range of alternative institutional relationships for meeting society's needs; and to the comprehension of the economic, moral, and sociopolitical implications of alternative business policies.

This book is organized into three parts. Part I examines the relationships among business and its social constituencies, and more particularly, how authority over the allocation of the nation's resources is shared among these constituencies. Part II analyzes the relationships among business, social, moral, and political institutions. Ours is a world of institutions. The individual finds his greatest economic, political, and ethical expression through institutions, and it is through these same institutions that the claims of competing constituencies are formulated, legitimatized, and pressed upon society. Finally, Part III describes business's efforts to respond to the growing integration of society's broad and often conflicting goals, and provides several specific examples of attempts to do so. Together the eleven chapters provide a comprehensive framework for analyzing the foundations of business-society relationships, and for integrating these relationships in a comprehensive business policy decision-making framework.

This partitioning is a considerable pedagogical convenience. The book, however, is concerned with the integration of inextricable economic, moral, and political issues which the business policy decision maker must address. The text accompanying each chapter places the individual readings in the context of these inextricable issues, and the interrelationships among them in the several chapters.

It is at this time uncertain how successfully business policy decision makers will integrate these complex relationships in the "real world," and in what forms business institutions will appear on the social horizon. It is difficult to measure the importance of competing social goals and to measure the impact of changing relationships on the efficacy and form of business organization. However, the key to these measurements may have been provided by Protagoras in the fifth century B.C., when he told us that man is the measure of all things. Perhaps herein lies the only real world. The bottom line is essential in all business decisions, but profit is a means and not an end in and of itself. Profits have to be translated into human and social terms. Lord Keynes told his fellow economists that they are "the trustees, not of civilization, but of the possibility of civilization."

I, of course, owe a great intellectual debt to the many authors whose writings appear in this book. My thinking has also benefited greatly from my association with the General Motors' economics staff these past five years, especially from Brent Upson and the chief economist, Marina Whitman. I am also indebted to Nathan Borofsky and Michael Whitty for their assistance on this project, and to Gloria Pearson and Linda Avenia who typed more drafts of the manuscript than I care to recall. Finally the preparation of this book demonstrated clearly to me the importance of the most basic institutional relationship of all. Without the support, endless patience, and personal sacrifice of my family, none of this would have been possible. To Arlene, Melissa, and Thomas, and to the family, which is the true foundation of American society, this book is devoted.

Thomas G. Marx
West Bloomfield, MI

BUSINESS and SOCIETY

CHAPTER 1
INTRODUCTION

Business policy has been adequately defined as *"the study of the functions and responsibilities of senior management*, the *crucial problems* that affect success in the total enterprise, and *the decisions* that determine the direction of the organization and shape its future."[1] The most crucial problems that management faces today arise from rapidly changing relationships between business and society. These changing relationships have profound implications for the future direction and organization of the private business sector, and for the functions and responsibilities of executive management.

It is through these policy decisions that business allocates the majority of the nation's resources, and it is the social legitimacy of business' control of these resources which defines the proper role of business in society. All legitimate exercises of control, power, and authority in a political democracy must be firmly rooted in fundamental principles of public accountability, and ultimate public control. This legitimacy can be provided for business decision making by either market or political controls which ensure the necessary public accountability. The appropriate mix of these market and political controls provides the blueprint for business' relationships with the social constituencies and institutions with which it interacts. The legitimacy of business' societal relationships thus turns on such issues as: Who is to participate in these decisions; to whom are these decision makers accountable; what economic and social decision-making criteria

---

[1]Roland Christensen and others, eds., *Business Policy,* 5th ed. (Homewood, Ill: Richard D. Irwin, 1982), p. 3. (Emphasis in original.)

are to guide their decisions; and for what private and public purposes are the nation's resources to be employed?

The most fundamental business-society issue for the years immediately ahead is the most appropriate—the most efficient and equitable—mix of market and political controls over business policy decision making. At the polar extremes, pure market control is the hallmark of laissez-faire capitalism, while pure political control over the nation's resources is the economic definition of socialism. We are not, however, concerned here with the theoretical struggle between the great "isms," but with the practical problems of defining business relationships with stockholders, consumers, employees, local communities, and the general public which will meet society's changing needs.

Every fundamental business-society relationship, and every proposal for reforming these relationships to meet changing social needs and expectations is ultimately a question of the social legitimacy and appropriate mix of market and political controls over the use of the nation's resources. Corporate governance, consumer rights, industrial democracy, and community obligations are all questions of social legitimacy and control in business' relationships with its constituencies. Social responsibility, ethical business standards, and government regulation all represent new institutional relationships which change the mix of market and political controls over business decisions. The business policy decision-making process thus provides the primary nexus between business and society, and the basic organizing framework for analyzing business-society relationships. It is essential to a successful search for more positive business-society relationships to understand the economic, moral, and sociopolitical foundations upon which these relationships are built.

GLOBAL ECONOMIC AND SOCIAL INTEGRATION

Following World War II, the U.S. was light-years ahead of the rest of the world, economically, socially, and politically. Business and society could prosper with little regard for events outside U.S. geographical boundaries. Business and social policy decisions were domestic matters, international trading skills were neglected, and the competitive impact of social regulation ignored. These light-years, somehow, have faded faster than anyone ever imagined, and the U.S. is now facing a formidable international competitive challenge requiring a rapid transition to the realities of a global economy.

The economic prosperity of the postwar period and increasing satisfaction of private demands for material goods and services naturally stimulated public demands for a safer, cleaner, healthier environment; greater leisure and job satisfaction; and a heightened concern for social justice, fairness, political equality, and morality. These emerging social priorities were also viewed as domestic policies. But what were considered U.S. social issues in the 1960s and

1970s are now, like business policies, rapidly acquiring global dimensions. The global integration of product markets has substantially increased the (international) market control of business decision making just as society was expanding its political control of these decisions in the mistaken belief that the unrivaled productive capacity of the U.S. could simply be redirected towards the fulfillment of a broader social agenda.

The result has been a direct clash of market and political controls over business decisions and the nation's increasingly scarce resources. This has accelerated the integration of economic and social issues as society has attempted to make the much more difficult (costly) and less controllable trade-offs between competing economic and social priorities. Demands for a cleaner, healthier, safer environment and workplace are no longer satisfied without important implications for international comparative advantage. A safe factory is one thing, an empty factory is another. Social problems of unemployment, family dislocation, declining infrastructure, depressed communities, and frustrated expectations generate political pressures with global economic repercussions ever as important as tighter monetary policy or currency reevaluation. These sociopolitical issues spill out into the world economy, not uncommonly in calls for political controls over international market competition, as each nation attempts to protect itself from short-run wrenching changes without denying itself the long-run benefits of dynamic economic growth.

International competition is competition not only among firms and industries, but also rivalry among competing economic and social systems. International competition from foreign rivals, often benefiting from institutional relationships more favorable to savings, investment, productivity, and technological development, makes effective business-society relationships even more essential to the realization of society's broad range of private and public goals. Among a nation's most important competitive assets are the institutional relationships it creates for resolving social conflict and for allocating its resources among private and public goals.

Ethical codes of conduct, antitrust laws (which can no longer define markets by political boundaries), and social regulation have all taken on global dimensions with the economic and social integration of the world's markets, and the increasing importance of transnational corporations. The United Nations has ushered in an explosion of international regulations extending from the ocean floor to the heavens (including "An Agreement Covering the Activities of States on the Moon and Other Celestial Bodies"). These regulations are not designed simply to constrain business conduct, they are intended to increase the less-developed countries' political control over the world's (solar system's) resources, and to reduce the developed nations' market control over these resources. These international regulations raise fundamental questions about the legitimacy of private property rights, and the distribution of wealth between rich and poor nations (three-fourths of the world's population consumes one-fourth of the world's resources). Business policy decision making is thus also becoming part of a global process of economic and social integration in which the world's social constituencies and national and international institutions compete on a global scale for political and market control of the Earth's resources.

Changes in the fundamental relationships between business and society stimulated by our own past success, and forced upon us by external competitive challenges will require changes in the way business policy decisions are made—in the way the nation's resources are allocated. The continued legitimacy of business' control over the allocation of these resources lies in a successful response to society's changing economic, moral, and sociopolitical goals within an integrated, global decision-making framework.

MARKET CONTROL

The traditional legitimacy of business policy decision making resides in the market control of these decisions. An informed assessment of alternative business-society relationships, and the implications of greater substitution of political for market controls over the allocation of the nation's resources requires a thorough understanding of the differences between market and political control processes. An evaluation of the relative economic and social merits of market and political controls are, explicitly or implicitly, at the root of every important business-society issue. Different assessments of these relative merits support the arguments for greater or lesser reliance upon market or political controls. The market and political control models are only sketched here to provide an organizing, analytical framework for the many business-society issues which surface throughout the readings. The next ten chapters fill in each of the boxes in the market and political control models illustrated in Figures 1–1 and 1–2.

The classical market decision-making control model is illustrated in Figure 1–1. Control over business policy decision making is exercised by stockholders who derive social legitimacy from fundamental Lockean private property rights ("The labor of his body, and the work of his hands, we may say, are properly his"), and by consumers and employees who exercise the political freedom to choose the goods they want to consume and the careers they want to pursue. Stockholder control is exercised directly through the elected board of directors which represents stockholders in the market control model. Consumers, employees, and stockholders also exercise market control over business decision making through product and labor markets and the market for corporate control (corporate takeovers). Government regulation of various market failures (monopoly, externalities such as pollution, or inadequate information) provides the remaining necessary social legitimacy for the market control model.

Decision making in the market control model is closed and hierarchical. Direct participation in the decision-making process is closed to outside constituencies, including those most affected by these decisions. Consumers, labor,

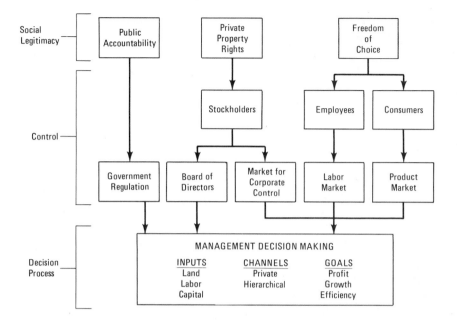

FIGURE 1-1   Market Control Model

and other social constituencies exercise only market control over these decisions, which is control through "exit": Dissatisfied stockholders sell their stock; dissatisfied customers purchase their goods from other firms; and dissatisfied workers find employment elsewhere. These constituencies have no "voice" (political vote, debate, persuasion complaint, or protest) in these decisions.[2]

Decision making in the market model is hierarchical. Information is internally processed up through the hierarchy with analysis, review, and debate bounded by shared values, common goals, institutional memory, and internal reporting and reward systems. Policies are determined at the top with the basic goal of allocating the firm's resources to maximize stockholders' wealth. The company's use of public resources (e.g., the environment and social infrastructure) or effects on social goals may be constrained by government regulation, but are not explicit considerations in the market decision-making model.

The social legitimacy of the market control model is increasingly challenged on several scores. The effectiveness of stockholder control over business decision making, and thus the legitimacy of stockholder property rights, is questioned in light of the extensive "separation of ownership and control" which characterizes the modern corporation. The effectiveness of consumer and employee market control through the exit option is increasingly doubted in a

---

[2]For a detailed analysis of the relative advantages and disadvantages and efficiency implications of "exit" and "voice" controls see Albert O. Hirschman, *Exit, Voice, and Loyalty* (Cambridge, Mass.: Harvard University Press, 1970).

society of large industrial organizations, and where individuals increasingly value economic and social stability. Increasing social interdependencies, sophisticated technologies which test the market model's assumption of informed (free) consumer choice, and the acceleration of demands for economic and social justice which accompany rising living standards increasingly bring into question the market model's ability to reconcile private resource use with broader social objectives.

POLITICAL CONTROL

The remarkable growth of regulation since the middle 1960s represents the initial social response to growing dissatisfaction with the market control model. These regulations have further limited businesses' use of public resources and mandated a wide variety of public goals (e.g., equal employment opportunity). They have significantly affected product, marketing, and production decisions. They have not, however, fundamentally transformed the market control model. Regulation is an external constraint on what the firm can do, just as production capacity limits the amount of goods the firm can produce. Growing recognition of the limits of externally imposed constraints on business decision making have generated pressures for more fundamental reforms of the internal decision-making process—not to limit what the firm can do, but to change what the firm intends to do.

The initial response to the recognition of these regulatory limitations was a call for corporations to exercise greater social responsibility. Social responsibility is an effort to reform the internal business decision-making process through voluntary (with a substantial amount of "voice") adoption of public goals and responsibilities by business. More recent proposals mandate changes in the internal business decision-making process—social responsibility enforced. These proposals suggest a political decision-making control model as illustrated in Figure 1–2.

Legitimacy in the political control model rests squarely on public accountability which parallels the legitimacy of the political authority vested in elected representatives. The restructured board of directors represents the company's numerous stakeholders—consumers, employees, stockholders, local communities, and so on, which in total represent the general public. Stockholders, consumers, and employees still exercise some market control over the firm's decisions (market control is decreased because the company's stakeholders are less concerned with profit maximization and thus less responsive to market demands) but markets no longer provide the primary control nor social legitimacy for business decision making. Indeed, market controls become a source of conflict and aggravation to stakeholders pursuing a more socially orientated agenda (e.g., consumers who exit because of the higher product cost of meeting environmental goals).

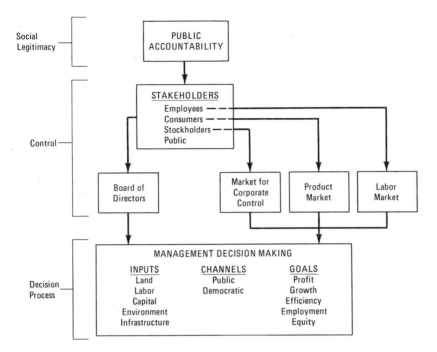

FIGURE 1-2   Political Control Model

The decision-making process in the political control model is democratic rather than hierarchical, and open to direct participation by all constituencies who are given a voice in decisions which affect them. Competing constituency interests are balanced through public debate, persuasion, and negotiation rather than market competition, that is, voice supplants exit as the primary control mechanism. These internal changes in the business decision-making process result in explicit recognition of business' use of public resources and explicit pursuit of a broader mix of public and private goals since these are internalized in the political control model—what the firm intends to do is fundamentally changed.

MARKET AND POLITICAL DECISION MAKING

The future will see if market and political controls mix better than oil and water (if not, alchemy will be an important requirement for future business leadership). The confounding of market and political controls, goals and decision-making processes within the modern business organization has broad and profound implications for the efficiency of resource use. It is necessary to understand the fundamental differences between market and political decision-making processes to access these implications.

The basic differences between market and political decision-making processes are summarized in Figure 1-3:

FIGURE 1-3   Market and Political Decision-making Processes

MARKET	POLITICAL
• Direct	• Indirect
• Individual	• Universal
• Proportional (to expenditures)	• Egalitarian (one-man, one-vote)
• Exit control	• Voice control

There are important differences in the way market and political preferences are expressed and enforced. Individuals express their preferences for private goods directly in the marketplace, whereas preferences for alternative social goods are expressed only indirectly through elected representatives. Individual market decisions are also not binding on others. My decision not to smoke or wear a seat belt does not prohibit others from doing so. Political preferences are universal. A majority decision to prohibit consumption of a risky product is binding on all.

Market preferences are also weighted by the individual's income and financial stake in the decision. The preferences of those with greater financial interest, and thus with greater incentives to spend the time and make the effort to become well informed, carry more weight than the preferences of those with little financial interest and little incentive to be well-informed. Those with no financial interest have no effect on market decisions. This is in marked contrast to political decisions where the egalitarian, one-man, one-vote rule gives equal weight to the preferences of those with no interest in nor knowledge of the issues being decided. However, the weighting of preferences by wealth is also morally objectionable to many, and in extreme circumstances, to most.

It follows from these differences that market decisions reflect individual preferences more accurately, utilize information more efficiently for more informed decision making, and allow greater freedom of individual choice. This is the basis for a strong preference for market decisions in the absence of significant market failures requiring collective choice. In these circumstances, political choice may be necessary, but it is important to recognize two important biases in political decision making.

Political decisions exhibit a strong bias for the status quo which conflicts with the requirements of dynamic economic efficiency. This bias reflects the political influence of entrenched special interests relative to economic newcomers.

One lost job is worse, politically, than two (ten) jobs not created. This bias appears in favor of incumbent managements facing takeovers in Chapter 2; the protection of local communities from competition in Chapter 5; and the protection of established companies from social regulation in Chapter 9. There is also a strong political bias for social programs which bestow large benefits on small groups of appreciative voters and spread the (undetectable) costs over large segments of the society. Alternative programs which provide individually small benefits for large segments of the population are neglected, even if they produce greater total social benefits.

There are also important differences between market and political control mechanisms. Political preferences are enforced through voice—voting, legislation, regulation, protest, debate, and persuasion. Voice control is the hallmark of political democracy, and its absence in the market control model (individuals have no voice in the decisions which affect them) strikes many as undemocratic. Market control is exercised through exit. The effectiveness of market controls over business decision making thus depends upon the availability of reasonably close substitutes which make exit a viable option: Dissatisfied customers must have alternative goods to purchase; dissatisfied workers must have alternative employment opportunities; and dissatisfied stockholders must have alternative investment options. The essence of monopoly is the absence of close substitutes—the absence of exit control.

Exit and voice are substitute control mechanisms. Voice is not effective after the individual has exited. Voice is also a much more costly control mechanism because it requires greater time, knowledge, communications skills, and active involvement by the individual. Thus, voice is used primarily as the availability of exit declines. These factors largely explain the absence of voice in the market control model which presumes an effective exit option available to all. We utilize the full range of voice options to control the local power company because there is no exit control (no close substitute). We do not voice our objections to the policies of the local grocery store, we simply exit. Thus, if effective exit options are available, the absence of voice may simply be efficient rather than undemocratic. Conversely, the extensive use of voice in national politics reflects the absence of close substitutes for the U.S. We are much more inclined to exit at the local level, rather than protest, because states are often reasonably good substitutes for each other.

The substitution of political for market decision-making processes thus introduces inefficiencies from less-accurate expression of individual preferences, less utilization of information, and biases for the status quo and special interest groups, in addition to the loss of individual freedom of choice. These disadvantages must be netted against the not inconsiderable gains from collective choice in market failure situations when assessing the efficiency and social legitimacy of alternative means of controlling the allocation of the nation's resources.

ORGANIZATIONAL CHANGES

The ability of business to adapt its decision-making process to changing social relationships in a way which preserves its social legitimacy without jeopardizing its productive capacity is uncertain. However, some perspective on the remarkable adaptive properties of the private market system is provided by the dramatic changes in the business decision-making process ushered in with the decentralized, multidivisional organizational structures in the 1920s. These earlier organizational responses to control loss and goal adherence problems have many parallels with the current decision-making problems facing business.

Through the early 1920s, centralized, functionally departmentalized organizations were the dominant business form (Figure 1–4).[3] As these organizations grew larger and more diversified with the development of a national market, they experienced serious control loss and goal adherence problems: The former from the magnification of hierarchical levels; the latter from increasing divisional interdependencies and the augmentation of the central office with operating executives to meet the demands of more complex strategic planning. The loss of control at the top increased as it became necessary to transmit, compress, and operationalize larger amounts of diversified data across successive hierarchical levels. This organizational phenomenon is captured in Anthony Downs' "Law of Diminishing Control" which states: "The larger any organization becomes, the weaker is the control over its actions exercised by those at the top.[4]

Goal adherence problems increased as operating executives were called to the central office to augment strategic planning and resource allocation decisions which became more complex as divisions expanded and became more interdependent. These operating executives displayed partisan interests toward their own functional departments at the expense of overall corporate goals. Their primary interests, skills, training, and rewards lay with the performance of their functional responsibilities, not with their contributions to overall corporate profitability.

The decentralized, multidivisional organizational structures introduced in the early 1920s at duPont and General Motors, and now the dominant organizational form for large multiproduct firms, was a direct response to the problems of control loss and goal adherence encountered by functionally organized companies. The multidivisional organizations replaced the functional departments with semiautonomous operating divisions (profit centers), and created a separate central office team freed from operating responsibilities and supported by an independent staff (Figure 1–5).

---

[3]This section is based extensively on the pioneering organizational research by Professor Oliver E. Williamson, and is adapted from Oliver E. Williamson, *Corporate Control and Business Behavior: An Inquiry into the Effects of Organization Form on Enterprise Behavior,* © 1970 (Englewood Cliffs, N.J.: Prentice-Hall, Inc., 1970), pp. 120–21. Adapted by permission of Prentice-Hall, Inc., Englewood Cliffs, N.J.

[4]Anthony Downs, *Inside Bureaucracy* (Boston: Little, Brown, 1967) p. 143.

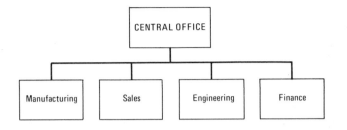

FIGURE 1-4 Functional Organization

Source: Adapted from Oliver E. Williamson, *Corporate Control and Business Behavior: An Inquiry into the Effects of Organization Form on Enterprise Behavior*, © 1970 (Englewood Cliffs, N.J.: Prentice-Hall, Inc., 1970), p. 116. Adapted by permission of Prentice-Hall, Inc., Englewood Cliffs, New Jersey.

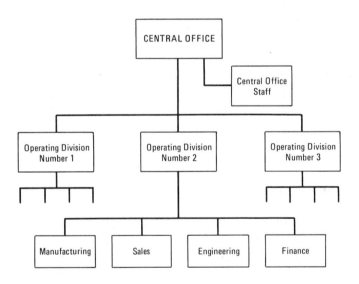

FIGURE 1-5 Multidivisional Organization

Source: Adapted from Oliver E. Williamson, *Corporate Control and Business Behavior: An Inquiry into the Effects of Organization Form on Enterprise Behavior*, © 1970 (Englewood Cliffs, N.J.: Prentice-Hall, Inc., 1970), p. 116. Adapted by permission of Prentice-Hall, Inc., Englewood Cliffs, New Jersey.

The division of the firm into semiautonomous self-contained units mitigates control loss by reducing the amount of communications across hierarchical levels. Subgoal pursuit is reduced by eliminating operating executives from the newly structured central offices which are staffed by executives who have the time, motivation, and commitment to pursue overall corporate profitability. The independent central office staff eliminates top management's information dependence upon operating divisions.

The political control model is in many ways a response to similar problems of control loss and subgoal pursuit in the modern business unit at the macro, or societal level. Think of society as the central office for overall policy decision making, and business firms as society's functionally departmentalized organizations. Business firms pursue narrow "functional" goals of private profit maximization rather than overall societal (central office) goals.

From this perspective, it is apparent that proposals for greater political control of business decision making are in response to perceived losses of social control over business units which have grown and diversified, just as central offices lost control over their functional divisions at the turn of the century. Business adherence to overall social goals has also decreased with growing social interdependencies (which magnify the effects of business decisions on social goals) just as departmental goals deviated from overall company profit objectives in functionally organized companies.

The changes in the internal control of management decision making called for by the political control model also parallel the changes which transformed functionally organized companies into multidivisional organizations. The proposed internal reforms of business decision making can be interpreted as a response to severe control loss problems encountered with externally imposed regulations. Regulatory monitoring and enforcement require the transmission of vast amounts of complex data between business and the regulatory agencies. The proposed internal political reforms would reduce the amount of necessary communications between business and the regulatory agencies by transforming business into semiautonomous, self-contained social decision-making units just as the multidivisional organization transformed functional departments into private profit centers. Regulatory goals would be internalized, eliminating the need for external monitoring, enforcement, and complex communications. Proposals for public directors and additional outside directors are attempts to eliminate the operating biases of business executives from social strategic planning decisions to achieve greater business adherence to overall social goals. Independent auditing committees and greater public disclosure are efforts to reduce society's dependence on its operating units for vital social information.

Business is adapting its decision-making process to the requirements of changing business-society relationships just as it adapted to changing economic relationships in the 1920s. Top executives are increasingly being detached from internal company planning responsibilities to address broader social issues. The rapid growing public affairs offices provide these executives with independent expertise on a broad range of social issues, serving the same function performed by the central office staff for corporate policy makers in the multidivisional organization. These changes alone, however, are not likely to provide all the necessary organizational restructuring. Recall that departmental executives in the functionally organized firms could not address companywide goals when their self-interest lay with departmental performance. How much less corporate executives can be expected to address social goals when their rewards lay with traditional company profit performance. More fundamental organizational change will be required, for which the remarkable adaptive history of business organization is a source of great optimism.

TOMORROW'S BUSINESS LEADERS

Fundamental changes in the internal business decision-making process cannot proceed without important implications for future business decision makers. The requirements for effective business functioning in a political decision-making process are far different from those required for successful performance in the market control model. In the political control model, decision makers must be prepared to debate issues publicly, and must rely upon persuasion, negotiation, and compromise to balance competing demands among social constituencies. They must be prepared to have their views and decisions openly criticized, facts disputed and motivations questioned far more stridently than ever occurs within closed business decision-making channels. They must also have a much broader knowledge of society and the role of their corporation in society. A recent memorandum from the chairman of General Motors Corporation underscores the implications of global economic and social integration for future business leaders: ". . . knowledge of and experience with the international aspects of our business will become an increasingly important requirement for top leadership positions, as will the requirement that top management be knowledgeable of business and social matters outside the boundaries of General Motors and the automobile industry." It is no longer adequate for successful business performance to have only an effective, domestic business strategy. Successful business performance in the future will require the integration of global economic strategies with the realization of broader societal goals.

CHAPTER OUTLINE

This introduction provides a basic analytical theme for the readings, and an organizing framework for the many specific issues raised in these readings. Part I addresses the changing relationships between business and its constituencies which are not now clearly defined, even for stockholders, as society gropes for modifications to the classical market control model. Chapter 2 explores the effectiveness and social legitimacy of traditional stockholder control of management decision making in view of the "separation of ownership and control" characteristic of modern business. The legitimacy of private property rights is challenged for the ownership of stock shares as opposed to physical plant and equipment. A perceived absence of effective stockholder control and social legitimacy has stimulated numerous proposals for political control of business decision making.

In the market control model, consumers exercise ultimate control over the mix of goods to be produced through their individual decisions in the marketplace. Chapter 3 examines the effectiveness of these controls, and whether freedom of individual choice legitimizes consumer sovereignty. If not, resources must be reallocated consistent with collective social values.

Is the authority granted in the employment contract subject to effective market control? Dissatisfied with the effectiveness of market controls, organized labor advocates greater industrial democracy which would increase its political control of business decision making by putting labor representatives in the board room. A fundamental issue raised in Chapter 4 is whether industrial democracy is really democracy. Would it provide legitimate social control and public accountability for business decisions, or simply increase labor's control over society's resources?

Business relationships with host communities analyzed in Chapter 5 are not even recognized in the market control model (Figure 1-1). Are business-community relationships simply the sum of individual transactions with stockholders, consumers, and employees in the marketplace, or is there a "general social purpose" to which business also has a responsibility? Dissatisfied with their market control over business, communities attempt to exercise greater political control by limiting business' ability to "vote with its feet."

Part II is concerned with basic institutional relationships between business and society—with social responsibilities, ethics, politics, regulation, and government. Business goals and responsibilities are instrumental in every business policy decision. The evaluation of the effects of business decisions on stockholders, consumers, employees, local communities, or if these effects are considered at all, is a reflection of the firm's goals and responsibilities. Chapter 6 is concerned with the market's ability to reconcile private and social goals, and the alternative public controls which some argue are necessary to accomplish this reconciliation.

It is the Talmudic belief that the first question asked in the hereafter is: "Hast thou been honest in business?" Chapter 7 is concerned with basic moral relationships which permeate all business-society issues. Ethical conduct standards, social responsibilities, and the claimed moral "rights" of consumers, employees, and communities all have important effects on the allocation of the nation's resources. Similarly, moral criticisms of self-interest pursuit for private gain and income inequality in a market system could have substantially greater effects on the allocation of the nation's resources than changes in corporate governance, industrial democracy, or government regulation.

Chapter 8 examines the complex political relationships between business and government. Political controls can constrain business but can also be a substantial benefit, and are often sought by as well as imposed on business. Some argue that government's dependence upon business for the production of society's goods and services leads to undemocratic business control of political decision making, while others maintain that market limitations on the centralization of political power are essential to the preservation of political democracy.

The business of regulation turns to the regulation of business in Chapter 9. Political control of the market model has expanded with the growth of social regulation from the middle 1960s. At the same time the deregulation of several industries has resulted in greater reliance upon the market control model. The readings in Chapter 9 review the scope and functions of government regulation, and the potential for improving the allocation of the nation's resources through greater reliance upon market incentive controls rather than "command and control" regulations.

Part III surveys business' attempts to adapt to changing social demands and expectations. Public affairs offices are the most visible signs of organizational adaptation. Chapter 10 calls for these offices to play a pioneering role in the development of future business-society relationships appropriate for an increasingly integrated society. The final chapter reviews the efforts of several companies to respond to changing business-society relationships, and to incorporate economic, moral, social, and political goals within comprehensive decision-making strategies.

CHAPTER 2
STOCKHOLDER RELATIONSHIPS

Any exercise of economic or political control over society's resources must be legitimate in a political democracy, that is, those who exercise such power must be accountable to the public for their decisions. In the classical market model of business decision making, managers who allocate resources are accountable to the owners of those resources. Business decision makers are constrained by market forces to seek the maximization of stockholders' wealth. The legitimacy of stockholders' control of the use of these resources resides in fundamental private property rights perhaps best articulated by John Locke: "Every man has a property in his own person. This nobody has any right to but himself. The labor of his body, and the work of his hands, we may say, are properly his. Whatsoever then he removes out of the state that nature hath provided, and left it in, he hath mixed his labor with, and joined to it something that is his own, and thereby makes it his property."[1] In *The Federalist Papers, No. 10,* James Madison makes the protection of different and unequal faculties among men for acquiring property the first object of government.

Challenges to the classical business-stockholder relationship, legitimized by political theories of private property, are based primarily on observations that stockholders today do not, at least directly, exercise control over the use of their property. It follows from this view that business managers are not accountable to the owners of the resources they are controlling, and thus their control of these resources lacks social legitimacy. The appealing notion of share-

---

[1] Peter Laslett, ed., *Two Treatises of Government,* (Cambridge: Cambridge University Press, 1960), pp. 305–6.

holder democracy is invalidated, and the legitimacy of stockholder claims based on private property rights is also rendered suspect.[2]

This "separation of ownership and control," and the implications for corporate governance—who should control corporate decisions if the owners do not—have their origins in *The Modern Corporation and Private Property,* published by Adolph A. Berle and Gardiner Means in 1932. Berle and Means observed that ". . . the owners of passive property, [corporate stock] by surrendering control and responsibility over the active property, [plant and equipment], have surrendered the right that the corporation should be operated in their sole interest,—they have released the community from the obligation to protect them to the full extent implied in the doctrine of strict property rights."[3] In a similar vein, Professor Schumpeter argued that the mere ownership of stock does not generate the same moral allegiance as the ownership of physical property:

> The capitalist process, by substituting a mere parcel of shares for the walls of and the machines in a factory, takes the life out of the idea of property. It loosens the grip that was so strong—the grip in the sense of the legal right and the actual ability to do as one pleases with one's own; the grip also in the sense that the holder of the title loses the will to fight, economically, physically, politically, for "his" factory and his control over it, to die if necessary on its steps. And this evaporation of what we may term the material substance of property—its visible and touchable reality—affects not only the attitude of holders but also that of the workmen and of the public in general. Dematerialized, defunctionalized and absentee ownership does not impress and call forth moral allegiance as the vital form of property did. Eventually there will be *nobody* left who really cares to stand for it—nobody within and nobody without the precincts of big concerns.[4]

From their observations, Berle and Means concluded that corporate management was subject to neither market nor political control. There are no political control mechanisms by which management can be effectively ousted for poor performance, and no market controls since dissatisfied stockholders merely sell their stock. Thus management is able to operate the business in its own interests. Berle and Means concluded, however, that this system worked fairly well because of management's good sense of responsibility.

The perceived lack of management decision-making legitimacy raises two social options. The first is to restructure business-stockholder relationships to restore stockholder control. The second, if stockholder control is not possible or perhaps not desirable, is to make corporations accountable to all of the constituencies affected by their decisions. Proposals for additional outside directors on corporate boards, cumulative share voting, and independent auditing

---

[2]Private property rights are questioned from a moral perspective by John Rawls in Chapter 7.

[3]Adolf A. Berle and Gardiner C. Means, *The Modern Corporation and Private Property,* rev. ed. (New York: Harcourt, Brace Jovanovich, Inc., 1968), pp. 311–12.

[4]Joseph A. Schumpeter, *Capitalism, Socialism and Democracy,* 3rd. ed. (New York: Harper & Row, Pub., 1950), p. 142. (Emphasis in original.)

committees to oversee management decision making represent efforts to restore stockholder control. It is not certain, however, that additional outside directors would restore the classical management-stockholder relationship. Outside directors might be more concerned with social welfare than the maximization of stockholders' wealth, thus increasing the gap between management and stockholders.

Proposals for public directors (perhaps government appointed) represent efforts to make business accountable to its various constituencies and the general public. Public directors represent a radical departure from the traditional role of directors as stockholders' representatives. Public directors would legitimize management decision making by instituting political controls and direct accountability to the public through elected representatives. Such proposals were prominently promoted by Arthur Goldberg when he was on the Board of TWA in 1972.

Berle and Means' basic observations are essentially correct. There is an extensive "separation of ownership and control" in the modern corporation which precludes direct owner participation, and dissatisfied investors do simply sell their stock rather than voice their objections to wayward management. Indeed, it is the separation of ownership from control, and the ease with which stock can be disposed which makes possible the huge accumulation of capital needed to fund modern enterprises of efficient scale. However, in 1932 Berle and Means did not see the connection between the sale of stock and the market control model. They did not see that merely selling stock is the classic market exit option which exerts profound control over corporate management. The sale of stock by sufficient numbers of dissatisfied investors depresses its price. This signals opportunities for other companies to acquire control of the firm, restore performance to levels consistent with stockholder expectations, and realize substantial capital gains from rising stock prices. Thus, the sale of stock coupled with the market for corporate control exerts substantial market control over incumbent managements to operate the firms in the owners' interests.

The efficiency of the market for corporate control (takeovers, mergers, tender offers, and proxy fights) is critical to the discussion of corporate governance, and a central theme of all three readings. The assessment of the efficiency with which this market operates is the basis for alternative views of business decision-making legitimacy and proposals for new business-stockholder relationships.

Mark Green, like Professor Galbraith (Chapter 6), views corporations as public institutions because of the enormous power they wield over society. Indeed, Green sees corporations as "economic governments" coexisting with political government. The difference is that political government is held accountable by a constitution and elections. There are no elections and no accountability for the "economic governments." Green states: "The key issue of corporate governance reform is *who* should make or shape these decisions—a handful of executives or executives *and* a representative board that is open and responsive to the views of a company's many stakeholders?'' [Emphasis in original.] Green is not confident that the imposition of additional external regulatory controls on corporate decision making would be effective. Instead, he advocates federal chartering which would fundamentally change control of the internal decision-making process. The proposed Corporate Democracy Act would give greater "access and voice" to stockholders who now merely sell their stock when disgruntled. It would require a majority of independent directors to restore the power of the board; require greater information disclosure; implement plant closings restrictions to protect local communities (an issue discussed in Chapter 5); protect the civil liberties of employees (discussed in Chapter 4); and provide criminal sanctions for illegal corporate conduct. Federal chartering is necessary because competition among the states for incorporation fees has only resulted in the "law for sale" (also discussed in Chapter 5).

As Green recognizes, this is a funamentally different approach to corporate control. It is not an extension of external regulatory controls to limit what the corporation can do, but an attempt to reform the internal corporate decision-making process to promote self-regulation, and to make business more democratic.

Ralph Winter asks, however, why private profit-making corporations should be democratic (a basic issue which surfaces in several subsequent chapters). He answers his own question when he labels them *private,* rather than public, corporations. Winter argues that stockholders do not want democratic controls over management. They prefer simply to sell their stock—an effective exit control mechanism as long as there is an efficient market for corporate control.

Winter is also critical of the plant-closing provisions of the Corporate Democracy Act which he likens to protectionist trade policies (quotas and tariffs) which isolate U.S. business from foreign competition. Plant-closing legislation is designed to prevent communities from competing for business. Whether it is productive and ethical for communities to compete for business is examined in Chapter 5. Winter, however, notes the political bias for the status quo, or in political terms, the preference for programs benefiting small groups of identifiable voters. Political decision makers are anxious to protect communities from the adverse effects of plant closings at the expense of other (unidentifiable) communities which would benefit from plant relocation. He argues that efforts to improve corporate performance should be directed at accelerating mobility, not frustrating it. Similarly, he advocates the removal of state antitakeover laws which impede the ability of the market to discipline inefficient incumbent managements. Such laws also reflect a political bias for the status quo—the political power base of incumbent management.

Richard West states that proponents of corporate governance seek political control of business decision making because of the perceived ineffectiveness of the market for corporate control. He concludes that the market for corporate control may be ineffective because of businesses' efforts to obtain political protection (federal and state regulations which increase the cost, time, and risk of corporate takeover attempts) from takeovers. One response advocated by Winter would be to resist such pleadings and to remove existing political impediments to corporate takeovers. Absent this, in a classic case of regulation begetting regulation, it may ultimately become necessary to impose controls on corporate governance to counteract controls on corporate takeovers.

One reason advanced by business interests for protection from corporate takeovers is to protect communities from plant closings by distant firms which acquire control of local companies. Would the same business champions of the local community support the Corporate Democracy Act provisions against plant closings by local firms? Would they support advance notification of plant closings as they support advance notifiction of tender offers?

West also discusses the use of "shark repellants" by incumbent managements to discourage corporate takeovers. These may take the form of charter amendments which require large majority votes to approve mergers, or which require the board to consider the social impacts on employees, customers, and the local community before approving a corporate takeover. Should not corporate boards, which display such a high level of social responsiveness when facing a takeover, also display the same level of social consciousness when deciding to close a plant, install pollution control equipment, or dispose of hazardous wastes?

West concludes: "It just may be that Berle and Means were on the right track after all; they simply were a little early." Business cannot have it both ways. Business decision making must be subject to legitimate control in a political democracy, the same as all other exercises of authority. Efforts to circumscribe market controls are an invitation for political controls. This is the first of numerous illustrations of what Milton Friedman and others mean when they say businessmen are their own worst enemies:

> The two chief enemies of the free society are intellectuals and businessmen, but for opposite reasons. Every intellectual believes in freedom for himself, but is opposed to freedom for others. He thinks that, in the business world, because of the chaos of competition and waste, there ought to be a central planning board to establish social priorities. But he's horrified at the thought of a central planning board to establish social priorities for writers and researchers. The businessman is just the opposite. He favors freedom for everybody else, but when it comes to himself, that's a different question. He ought to get special privileges from the government, a tariff, a subsidy or what have you[5]

[5]Milton Friedman quoted in John F. Webster, "Corporate Governance and Legitimacy," in *Public Policy and the Business Firm*, Conference proceedings compiled by Rogene A. Buchholz, (St. Louis: Center for the Study of American Business, 1980), p. 92.

THE CASE FOR CORPORATE DEMOCRACY
Mark Green

Whereas the American political agenda of the 1970s focused extensively on the size and abuses of *big government,* the agenda of the 1980s should focus on the size and abuses of *big business.* It is curious how partisans of the latter can ridicule the inefficiencies and unresponsiveness of federal bureaucracies yet somehow ignore similar problems with corporate bureaucracies. Who governs our giant corporations and how they in turn govern us—economically, politically, biologically—should be preeminent issues in a society whose democratic values require that major institutions be accountable to their various constituencies.

To be sure, there are laissez faire "theologians" who argue that the "free market" is a perfectly self-regulating mechanism, that corporations are merely pass-through devices that respond automatically to the "votes" of autonomous consumers in the marketplace. In fact, corporations are entities run by real people who make two kinds of judgments. First, they decide whether or not to obey the law—which apparently is a difficult choice for many of them. Second, because the law is society's statement of what constitutes *minimally* acceptable behavior, they make choices within a huge area of lawful discretion—where to locate a plant, whether to fight or cooperate with a unionizing effort, what to produce and how to price it, what legislation to support or oppose, whether to participate in the community or to pollute it. The key issue of corporate governance reform is *who* should make or shape these decisions—a handful of executives, or executives *and* a representative board that is open and responsive to the views of a company's many stakeholders?

This fundamental issue of unaccountable corporate power warrants federal legislation for several interrelated reasons:

State chartering has failed. It makes as much sense for states to print money or passports as to issue the legal birth certificates of corportions that market products interstate, if not internationally. The result of this historical anomaly, in the words of Harry First, is a kind of "law for sale" (*Pennsylvania Law Review,* 1969). States lure companies into their jurisdictions, and thus generate incorporation fees, by adopting corporation codes that are excessively pro-management. Because Delaware is the worst state in this regard, it gets the most business: about one-fifth of all Delaware state revenues comes from incorporation and annual fees; and about half of the Fortune 500 are incor-

Mark Green, "The Case for Corporate Democracy," *Regulation,* 4, no. 3 (May–June 1980), 20–25. Copyright 1980 American Enterprise Institute. Reprinted with permission.

porated in tiny Delaware, including Exxon Corporation, for example, which has 160 times the annual revenue of its legal parent. Because other states try generally to imitate Delaware's performance rather than act more responsibly, there is already a kind of federal chartering law—but one drafted in Wilmington, not Washington.

Corporate illegality is extensive.   As examples of antitrust violations, chemical dumping, product hazard cover-ups, consumer fraud, foreign pay-offs, and other economic crimes proliferate, it becomes increasingly apparent that management-directed illegality is prevalent rather than aberrational. "The people who call the shots don't bear the risks," concludes law professor Christopher Stone in his book *Where the Law Ends.* The unblinkable documentation of illegal practices should inspire lawmakers to design a new system of internal governance backed up by workable sanctions in order to encourage lawful behavior. When, for example, there was extensive congressional and press attention on labor racketeering in the late 1950s, the result was a Landrum Griffin Act for labor unions. Today we need a kind of Landrum Griffin Act for our largest corporations—to deal with the problem of corporate "racketeering" in the 1980s.

Our largest corporations are private governments.   Edmund Burke's observation that the large companies of his time were states disguised as merchants is relevant today. One definition of government would be an entity that can tax, take life, and coerce citizens. But what is price-fixing but corporate taxation? What is the willful marketing of defective products but the needless taking of life? What is industrial air pollution or the poisoning of a waterway but coercing citizens to suffer the results of other peoples' transactions—that is, compulsory consumption? In other words, our largest firms exercise extraordinary influence over the citizens of our country and other countries.

Thus, the traditional distinction between the public and private sectors should give way to a new concept about the role of the large corporation—namely—there are two forms of government in the United States, the political government and the economic government. The political government is held roughly accountable to its citizens by means of the Constitution and elections. But the economic government is largely unaccountable to its multiplicity of constituencies—shareholders, workers, consumers, local communities, taxpayers, small businesses, future generations. Ironically, under the Fourteenth Amendment, corporations are accorded the rights of people but not the obligations of governments—although our giant companies are far more like huge governments than they are like real people.

THE CONTENT OF THE CORPORATE
DEMOCRACY ACT

Representative Benjamin Rosenthal (Democrat, New York) and seventeen colleagues introduced H.R. 7010, the Corporate Democracy Act, in April. Its provisions would establish minimum governance standards for the 800 largest U.S. nonfinancial corporations (those with $250 million or more in assets). The goal is not more regulation but more *self-regulation* so that these "private governments" give greater access and voice to their affected stakeholders.

Title I: Directors and Shareholders. By requiring such things as a majority of "independent" directors, cumulative voting, shareholder nominations, and specific committees to oversee law compliance and to receive complaints from interested constituencies, this title seeks to restore the influence and independence of the board of directors.

Almost all students of board activities—from William Douglas in the 1930s to Myles Mace in the 1970s—conclude that directors do not select the top officers, do not establish company objectives, strategies, or policies, do not possess the information necessary even to make such judgments, and rarely if ever dissent from managerial initiatives. Consider, for example, the Penn-Central board before that firm's derailment. "The board was definitely responsible for the trouble," recounted outside director E. Clayton Gengras. Its members "took their fees and . . . just sat there. That poor man from the University of Pennsylvania [University President Gaylord P. Harnwell], he never opened his mouth. They didn't know the factual picture and they didn't try to find out." Although Penn-Central was desperate for capital, for example, the directors paid out nearly $100 million in dividends just before the company filed for bankruptcy.

Shareholders, too, are relatively powerless. Because management controls the proxy machinery, because shareholders cannot nominate candidates for the board, because individual shareholders are overwhelmed by the bloc votes of institutional investors, the corporate structure typically permits only a ceremonial role for shareholders. The great theory of shareholder democracy, or "people's capitalism," comes down to a few shrill voices at a spring rite called an "annual meeting" which is often held in a distant, difficult-to-travel-to city. Ultimately, disgruntled shareholders sell their shares rather than attempt to throw out inept management. Corporate executives cannot have it both ways—they cannot point to shareholders as the legitimizing constituency of the corporation and also acknowledge privately, as many have in business sessions I have attended, that shareholders are merely interested in dividends, not governance.

Corporate directors are almost invariably chosen by written proxies, with management so totally dominating the process that corporate elections have come to resemble the Soviet Union's euphemistic "Communist ballot"—a ballot that lists only one slate of candidates. As is noted in the 1979 staff summary of the Securities and Exchange Commission's corporate governance hearings, "Accoring to Professor Seligman [of Northeastern Law School] shareholder democracy has collapsed. . . . Since 1967, incumbent managements have been re-elected 99.9 percent of the time. In the last five years, not one management slate in any of the 500 largest industrial firms was even challenged."

The institutional irrelevance of directors and shareholders is not ordained by economic imperatives. Managers can be required to share power more equitably and efficiently with directors and shareholders. Even a few conscientious, non-management-controlled directors or shareholders, asking the right questions and given adequate authority, can make it less likely that a Penn-Central, a Kepone, a Youngstown (Ohio), or a Chrysler situation will recur.

Title II: Corporate Disclosure. This part of the bill requires that affected companies disclose in simple fashion such information as worker injury data, employee hiring data by facility, profits abroad, and the effective federal tax rate.

John O'Leary, the former deputy secretary of energy, explained to a congressional committee in mid-1979 why the Department of Energy made an agreement with oil firms to keep certain information on supplies secret. "The companies simply don't like the public peering over their shoulders," he said. This sentiment accurately reflects the traditional corporate view toward data disclosure—the less of it the better. But any effective strategy for bringing about greater corporate accountability to affected constituencies must be grounded in greater corporate dissemination of economic and social information. Such information enables shareholders and workers to know what demands to make, helps communities deal more knowledgeably with their business citizens, and informs press and public opinion—which are thereby better equipped to influence corporate policy. Enlightened executives have become well aware that unless they open their books more widely, the threat of increased and more sweeping regulation will grow. Besides, it seems a matter of simple justice, for example, that workers be allowed to know what detectable carcinogens are present in their work places and that community residents be informed of the distribution by race and sex of the work force in local establishments.

That some companies have disclosed full and precise data in these areas demonstrates that the information is neither confidential nor prohibitively costly to gather and report. That significant numbers of firms still refuse to disclose such information indicates that it will not be made consistently available unless required. The information requirements of the proposed act undermine neither customer privacy nor a firm's ability to protect proprietary secrets. Moreover, they are so simple that the information in question can be reduced to a few pages in company annual reports—as companies that already have adopted these standards have demonstrated. The result is a *corporate self-audit,* understandable to shareholders and lay people generally.

Title III: Community Impact Analysis. In an effort to help communities prepare for a plant closing or relocation by a major local employer, this title imposes prenotification requirements and allows the U.S. secretary of labor to conduct a local inquiry into why the change occurred and how best its local costs might be offset.

Bureau of Labor Statistics figures indicate that, overall, the New England, Mid-Atlantic, and Great Lakes regions lost 1.4 million manufacturing jobs between the mid-1960s and mid-1970s. Major cutbacks—both plant closings and partial transfers of work to other areas—have occurred in steel, clothing, textiles, rubber, auto parts, and electronics.

These basic corporate shifts take place for a variety of reasons—the search for nonunion regions, declining industries, outdated facilities, automation, access to new markets, energy costs, and availability of transportation. No sound economy can be wholly static, of course, and few would argue that the answer to economic dislocation lies in mechanisms that seek only to preserve the status quo. But a plant closing or relocation can be devastating to a community, in part because its effects ripple far beyond the employees directly involved. In the Youngstown case, for example, the *additional* loss from the steel shutdown, beyond the 5,000 jobs lost in steel itself, has been estimated at 11,200 jobs— including 1,413 in wholesaling and retailing, 372 in office supplies, and even 35 in auto repair.

These effects are exacerbated when the closings involve dominant local employers and occur unexpectedly. Without warning, the community's tax base shrinks, leaving schools and municipal services underfinanced and leading to layoffs of municipal employees, while demands on public service increase; unemployment skyrockets before anyone can plan to bring in new industry and jobs; and small businesses that had depended on the closed establishment as a customer are left without a market.

Critics of a "community impact analysis" say that it is up to private enterprise to decide where and when to locate or relocate, not government. This may be true, but it is not the issue. The proposal is not to require government approval for a move but rather to insist that employers give advance notice to the affected communities and employees in order to minimize the financial and emotional costs to those least able to bear them. Because some moves can lay waste a town's life-support system, it is entirely appropriate—regardless of whether the corporate decision makers consider themselves members of a purely private entity—that such private decisions be exposed to greater public scrutiny. As even the *Wall Street Journal* has acknowledged, "a company may have a responsibility not to leave its employees or its hometown in the lurch."

Title IV: "Constitutional" Rights of Employees. This title would protect employees from retaliation for the exercise of their constitutional rights of speech and assembly.

An airline pilot with over twenty-five years experience lost his job for blowing the whistle on a serious defect in the Lockheed 1011 aircraft. A worker in upstate New York who participated in a political demonstration was fired by his employer, who held the opposite view on the issue. What did these two workers have in common? Both were nonunion employees in the private sector who, under present law, had no meaningful legal recourse against dismissal.

This problem is neither conjectural nor infrequent. Cornelius Peck has projected from statistics on adjudged "unjust dismissals" in the unionized sector that thousands of such discharges occur annually in the nonunion sector, with no opportunity at all for redress (*Ohio State Law Journal,* 1979).

About one-third of the U.S. work force is protected against unjust dismissal or discipline for political beliefs or activities, either under collective bargaining agreements negotiated by unions or, in the case of government workers, under civil service laws and regulations. But better than two-thirds of the work force is not protected. These nonunion, nongovernment workers are subject to the archaic common-law rule of "servant at will." And under this rule, the employer is no more bound to the employee than the employee to the employer: either can break out of the employment relationship for "any or no reason." In short, the majority of American workers have the right to be fired—in the term of art used in court—"for good cause, for no cause, or even for morally wrong cause," without being the victim of a legal wrong.

The United States is one of the few industrialized nations that does not provide legal protection against unjust dismissals. France, West Germany, and Great Britain, for example, have developed not only extensive bodies of law to protect the worker's right to his or her job but also procedures to ensure that protection is provided as promptly, inexpensively, and fairly as possible. The Corporate Democracy Act would mandate that employees not be disciplined or discharged for exercising their political or other constitutional or civil rights, or for "corporate whistle-blowing." And it would protect employees against discrimination, discipline, or discharge for refusal to grant sexual "favors" to managerial employees.

Title V: Criminal and Civil Sanctions. This title provides for various penalties and sanctions designed to deter the existing level of corporate crime and to compensate its victims.

Business crime is as old as business. There were prohibitions against monopoly in common-law England. Lord Bryce's *The American Commonwealth* (1888) and Henry Demarest Lloyd's *Wealth against Commonwealth* (1899) examined that era's business corruption, with Lloyd noting that the Standard Oil Corporation "has done everything with the Pennsylvania legislature except to refine it." Widespread stock fraud led to the 1933 and 1934 securities acts. The 1960s saw the great electrical machinery bid-rigging case and the Richardson Merrell Company's marketing of MER 29 even though the firm had evidence of health risks. And today the apparant prevalence of "corporate crime"—a subcategory of "white collar crime"—involving managerial direction of, or participation or acquiescence in, illegal business acts—has raised the issue of the adequacy of legal sanctions. Why has the law failed to deter "crime in the suites?" What new sanctions or governance structures can persuade companies to obey the law? The *New York Times,* in an editorial bristling with indignation, has concluded: "The only effective remedy is to change the incentives and penalties that now shape [illegal] decisions. . . . Otherwise irresponsible decisions will continue to poison not only the physical environment but public confidence as well" (May 1, 1979).

SETTING STANDARDS FOR CORPORATE CITIZENSHIP

The provisions of the proposed Corporate Democracy Act are both reformist *and* realistic, for with few exceptions they have been adopted already by some company or state or Western country. The act would apply only to the largest 800 or so nonfinancial corporations—only to those "private governments" that have little in common with small and medium-sized businesses. It is based on the procedural mechanism of *federal minimum standards,* so that whatever the act does not require is left to existing state incorporation statutes and authorities. A standards rather than a regulatory approach has obvious and prestigious precedent: for example, the 1933 and 1934 securities acts, Title VII of the 1964 Civil Rights Act, the Food and Drug Administration rule that all drug companies establish quality control units. "We have largely federalized the law of antitrust, equal employment and securities," comments Professor Harvey Goldschmidt, of Columbia University's Law School; "the federalization of corporate law is long overdue."

Ultimately, then, the issue is not big government versus freedom. The "freedom" to pollute or to market hazardous products or to retaliate against whistle-blowing workers is not quite the freedom our founding fathers had in mind—not, at least, if your perspective is that of the families around Love Canal who were not free *not* to ingest Hooker Chemical Company's toxic residues. Nor is it overregulation versus productivity. Chrysler and U.S. Steel are in trouble because of their own mismanagement, regardless of how much they may "scapegoat" regulation from Washington.

Nor, finally, is the issue capitalism versus socialism. Rather, it is autocracy versus democracy. For decades the abuses within the American economy have been addressed by remedial regulation affecting the *external* relationships of the corporation: don't pollute, don't fix prices, don't deceptively advertise. The Corporate Democracy Act of 1980 aspires to reform the *internal* governance structure of our largest corporations so that—consistent with a market economy—companies would exercise their power and discretion more democratically and accountably. It is a response to the demonstrated limitations of state corporation laws, of regulatory laws, and of criminal laws to deter corporate abuse.

If preliminary comment is any barometer, however, this approach will be the target of rhetorical overkill by the big business community. An overwrought *Business Week* characterized federal corporate chartering as a reminder of "Mussolini's Corporate State." Business partisans organized a "Growth Day," held on the same April 17 that "Big Business Day" undertook a variety of activities to spotlight the effects of corporate power and to promote the Corporate Democracy Act. "Growth Day" advocates said their target was "zero-growth zanies." Richard Whalen attacked "self-appointed vigilantes" who oppose corporate crime, as if it were somehow illegitimate to try to detect and deter the kind of illegal conduct that has been so massively documented. John Riehm of the U.S. Chamber of Commerce charged, apparently without reading the proposed legislation, that "the advocates of corporate chartering would turn over the control of our economy almost completely to Washington." A Chamber of Commerce "Special Report," calling the bill the "Corporate Destruction Act," warned that it "would end the private enterprise system as we know it in America today." Herbert Schmerz, the leading Mobil Co. publicist, said the bill was a "thinly veiled beginning of the socializing of American industry."

Such obvious distortions demean the importance of the issue of corporate governance. One would have thought that genuine conservatives concerned with human liberty, the entrepreneurial spirit, vigorous economic competition, and lawful conduct would care deeply about those big businesses that deny freedoms to others, that acquire rather than innovate, that seek to frustrate competition, and that violate the law. And one would have thought that the big business community would have learned to restrain its impulse for "Chicken Little" rebuttals—an impulse that has led it to oppose nearly every social advance of this century, from child labor laws to auto safety regulation. Instead of dogma, business critics might want to consider a dialogue. "It is not creative minds that produce revolutions," wrote H.G. Wells in *The Salvaging of Civilization,* " but the obstinate conservation of established authority. It is the blank refusal to accept the idea of an orderly evolution toward new things that gives a revolutionary quality to every constructive proposal."

WHAT'S *NOT* IN A NAME
Ralph K. Winter

I once had occasion to note that proponents of a new government agency to "represent" consumers had blundered in changing the name of the proposed tribunal from the "Consumer Protection Agency" to the "Agency for Consumer Advocacy." Not only was the latter title less catchy, but it was also more (although not completely) accurate. Any degree of accuracy, of course, was fatal to the proposal because it called attention to its merits.

The creators of the "Corporate Democracy Act" have not made the same mistake. The title they have chosen has nothing whatsoever to do with the merits of their proposal.

Briefly stated, H.R. 7010 would (1) mandate federal eligibility requirements for members of corporate boards, impose liability for certain acts upon those directors, and expand the mandatory prerogatives of shareholders; (2) require corporations to comply with stipulated disclosure requirements; (3) impose heavy penalties on corporations that desire to move corporate operations from one locale to another; (4) give tenure to all employees of corporations; and (5) create a variety of penalties to be imposed on corporations and their executives for violating federal and state law.

Obviously, the catalyst that binds together this amalgam of diverse regulatory measures is not democracy, but a generalized anticorporate animus. And the title, "Corporate Democracy Act," is intended not to describe the bill but to shut off debate.

Accepting the bill's title at face value, however, a fundamental question may be asked. Why should business corporations, which claim only to be profit-making enterprises for private investors, be subjected to regulation in the name of democracy,* while organizations that boldly proclaim themselves to be "consumer advocates" or "public interest" groups would not be? It makes little sense to argue that Athlone Industries of Parsippany, New Jersey, must be "democratic," while the Nader conglomerate should be run autocratically and in secret. It can hardly be said that the source of funds for the Nader groups over the past decade is of no interest. This is not, I hasten to add, to argue that "public interest" groups ought to be subject to such regulation. They ought not—but because it is bad law rather than because the alleged principle of democratization does not apply.

While there is no space here to conduct a detailed technical analysis of the Corporate Democracy Act, its text is so technically deficient that at least that fact must be noted. Some of the bill's terminology is so general that the precise effect is in doubt. For example, is an airplane "a product . . . [which] may cause death or serious injury . . . "? Nor is its effect on existing law in areas such as a director's duty of care clear. In fact, it seems to have been drafted by persons whose knowledge of existing law is sparse. For example, the bill seems to assume that corporate political contributions to candidates for federal office are legal.

Ralph K. Winter, "What's *Not* in a Name," *Regulation,* 4, no. 3 (May–June 1980), 26–29. Copyright 1980 American Enterprise Institute. Reprinted with permission.

*Indeed, one should also ask why some corporations are apparently excluded from coverage by the bill. As introduced in the House, it applies only to "manufacturing, mining, retailing and utility corporations." It would not seem, for example, to apply to the broadcast media, a rather odd exemption in light of the claim that this legislation is necessary to reduce the influence of large corporations on American social, political, and economic life.

SHAREHOLDER POWER—
A SHOPWORN IDEA

Such relative refinements aside, however, the proposed legislation is fundamentally wrongheaded in what it seeks to achieve. So far as shareholder protection is concerned, the "problem" to which the bill is directed is an artificial creation of those who chronically favor contraction of the private sector. Proponents of the proposal want us to believe that Mark Green and the Building and Construction Trades Department, AFL-CIO, are the champions of private investors. The only senator to come to the rescue of shareholders is Howard Metzenbaum (Democrat, Ohio), while in the House of Representatives their protector is Benjamin Rosenthal (Democrat, New York), both of whom are among the most persistent critics of profit making in the private sector. That investor protection is a goal of the corporate democracy bill simply cannot be taken seriously.

Both the theoretical basis and the practical need for federal entry into this new field are illusory. The former consists of the antique notion that the chartering of corporations represents the conferral of some sovereign prerogative, which the states are bestowing improvidently. In fact, however, states "grant" nothing. A corporate character is no more than a private contract recorded in a state office for the protection of third parties. The state plays exactly the same role as it does in the case of home mortgages, for which it provides a statutory code of general provisions and a place to record private contracts.

As for the asserted practical need for federal intervention: That consists of the discredited notion that Delaware and other states tilt their corporation codes in favor of management and against shareholders. Even on its face, such a proposition is implausible. Investors need not purchase common stock at all, much less stock in Delaware corporations. They can invest their funds in bonds, partnerships, individual proprietorships, short-term paper, real estate, stock in foreign corporations, or even indulge in present consumption. Nor do underwriters have to participate in stock issues by Delaware corporations or brokers have to recommend such stock. It is simply absurd to think Delaware can monopolize international capital and that Saudi sheiks are forced to sacrifice their petrodollars to greedy managements freed by Delaware law to bilk stockholders. If Delaware were in fact to tilt its laws toward management, the sole result would be to impair the access of corporations chartered there to the capital market. It is simply inconceivable to think that underwriters and investment counsellors would not impose heavy burdens on stock offerings made under a corporate code unfair to shareholders. States that offered better gains to shareholders would in fact get the most corporate charters. If anything, competition for charters leads to corporate codes that optimize the shareholder/management relation.

Limiting management discretion to act without formal shareholder approval is a shopworn idea that collides, each time it comes by, with the same harsh reality: shareholders do not want more "power." Shareholders generally have neither the time nor the desire to participate in management; when they are dissatisfied they prefer simply to sell their stock in the company. Indeed, state law frequently will not respect shareholder votes that ratify management conduct precisely because those votes are meaningless. Shareholders understandably view themselves as investors—like bondholders, but with a more volatile stake in the firm. In fact, one of the great contributions of the corporate form has been to permit the separation of equity investments from the responsibilities of control.

Existing voting rights in common stock play a critical function, because they blend the investment market with a market for control that permits takeovers. If management is inefficient, earnings will suffer and the price of stock will fall. This will create incentives for attempts (by way of merger, tender offer or, less frequently, proxy fight) to replace management through a shareholder vote and thereby reap a capital gain from the increased efficiency of the firm. The market for control thus gives management good reason to keep the corporation's stock price relatively high, a goal consistent with the well-being of shareholders. The provisions of the Corporate Democracy Act are irrelevant to this aspect of voting rights—the only aspect that significantly matters.

Of course, the recent flap over shareholder "power" has nothing to do with investor welfare. Rather, it is an attempt to construct legal procedures which allow small groups that have failed to achieve their goals through the democratic political process to continue to pursue those goals by embroiling management in time-consuming and highly publicized disputes. Although sizable numbers of shareholders are almost never involved, management's desire to avoid controversy often caps such movements with success in affecting corporate conduct.

The bill's attempt to strengthen shareholder "power" is not just meaningless. It would also be harmful. Shareholder votes are often cumbersome and require considerable legal advice given at the highest rates. Moreover, the bill seems to outlaw the use of different classes of stock; such a restriction, by reducing the flexibility of terms on which new investors can be admitted, would impair a corporation's access to capital markets. Finally, opening up the mechanisms of corporate governance to political zealots who have failed to win support for their causes would weaken the institutions and processes by which political majorities govern.

The attempt to strengthen the board of directors is an error in other ways. The bill would reduce the number of persons eligible for membership on boards by limiting the number on which one person may serve. The authors of the legislation no doubt regard financial experience and technical knowledge as of little importance, if not positively harmful, and foresee no problem in finding qualified people. In fact, the pool of people qualified to perform the functions of a strengthened board is necessarily limited so that, to limit it even further, might affect corporate performance adversely.

A strenghtened, active board, moreover, is hardly more "democratic" or "independent." Deeper involvement in the ordinary affairs of corporations would require that directors spend more time and receive higher fees. The "independent" directors would thus become management in all but name.

MORE BURDENS AND DANGERS

The Corporate Democracy Act also purports to give "affected communities" better information on the impact of corporate decisions. What this means, it turns out, is the imposition of financial penalties on firms that decide to shift the locale of certain corporate activities. Not only would such corporations have to continue to pay local taxes and wages to laid-off employees for a period of time but they would also have to give two years' notice of the move. Such notice would in most cases drastically impair the ability of the firm to operate efficiently during the intervening years.

This aspect of the bill is, of course, outright protectionism—the functional equivalent of a tariff and just as detrimental to consumers. The "affected community" to which the corporation was going to move and the potential employees living there are left out in the cold, and the cost reduction that would benefit consumers is prevented. Economic mobility is in the society's interest and, if individual hardship requiring remedial aid results, the proper remedy is not a protectionist law penalizing that mobility but transitional government aid.

So far as corporate disclosure is concerned, there is already an enormously burdensome tax imposed by the federal government in the form of paperwork. If anything, investors want less of this, not more. The bill's wholesale reporting requirements would produce only increased costs, a mountain of unread material, and socially useless litigation. Expansion of reporting requirements should occur only in connection with an articulated governmental policy administered by a relevant government agency. In that way, the overall burden of disclosure requirements could be more easily identified and taken into consideration. Calls for public reporting on every matter that happens to occur to corporate critics will inevitably increase costs without corresponding benefits.

The Corporate Democracy Act also prohibits the discharge of any employee except for "just cause." On a rhetorical level, that seems simple justice. As a legal proposition, it is disastrous. In effect, every employee would be given tenure and, to justify a discharge, serious misconduct or deficiency would have to be proven in legal hearings entailing vast amounts of time and expense. The fact that better workers might be available would be irrelevant. The model for this provision is the civil service—which, these days, is generally not thought of as a model for anything else. In some parts of the country, where tenure provisions like those contained in the bill protect public school teachers, private schools paying much lower salaries than their public counterparts have much better teaching staffs because they have the unlimited power to hire and fire.

The bill also provides a variety of expanded penalties for violation of vaguely defined state or federal laws. This wholesale approach has great danger, because its impact cannot possibly be assessed. Hundreds of laws might be affected—which ones cannot be identified in advance, given statutory language whose lack of precision is exemplified by "an offense resulting in . . . damage to the natural environment." In truth no one can assess the impact of such provisions until years of litigation have passed. Since there is an easy and sensible alternative—varying the penalties available under particular existing laws—this part of the legislation has absolutely nothing to recommend it.

THE LOVE CANAL OF THE NEW CLASS

The proponents of the Corporate Democracy Act have done a disservice to the nation. Instead of focusing on real problems and suggesting remedies tailored to those problems, they have adopted a wholesale, punitive approach accompanied by strident rhetoric ("crime in the suites") designed to appeal to base emotion. The very real problem of proliferating state anti-takeover statutes designed to insulate the managements of local firms from the market for corporate control is disregarded in favor of calls for more power to shareholders who do not want it and will not use it. The problem of reducing the destabilizing effects of economic mobility on individuals is ignored in favor of attempts to restrict the mobility itself. What may be a need for more corporate disclosure is lost in demands for the production of every piece of information that might interest the corporate critics, regardless of the cost society would ultimately have to bear.

If we have learned anything from the professional corporate critics in the past, it is that their animus against the private sector is so intense that they cannot be trusted to address real problems sensibly. At one time, a staple of their proregulation rhetoric was flammable children's sleepwear. When government solved that problem in a fashion that ultimately resulted in expensive carcinogenic pajamas, the critics continued to attack the manufacturers. Gas-guzzling antipollution and safety devices were heaped upon cars at the behest of corporate critics without regard to fuel consumption, but when the energy crisis hit, car manufacturers and oil companies were said to be at fault. The critics' present remedy for that crisis is to keep gas prices low to prevent corporate price "gouging"—the most effective device known to human kind for encouraging consumption. The Corporate Democracy Act comes from the same crowd, and goes in the same unthinking direction. It is the Love Canal of the New Class.

CORPORATE GOVERNANCE AND
THE MARKET FOR CORPORATE CONTROL
Richard R. West

I. INTRODUCTION

When Henry Manne first suggested that the working title for my talk today might be, "Taming the Giant Corporation: The Role of The Stock Market," I was delighted. Like Professor Manne, I have long been a fervent supporter of market oriented approaches to directing and constraining corporate affairs, and I relished the idea of being able to praise the stock market's ability to influence corporate behavior more effectively than legions of Federal bureaucrats and Naderites.

As I went about preparing my remarks, however, I became increasingly concerned about recent attempts by incumbent managements to strip the stock market of much of its ability to influence them.* Indeed, by the time I was ready to put pen to paper, I sensed that a more appropriate title might be, "Taming the Stock Market: The Role of The Giant Corporation."

II. OWNERSHIP AND CONTROL

On the very first page of his well-known book, *The Economic Theory of "Managerial" Capitalism,* the British economist Robin Marris makes the following observations about the development of a class of professional managers in the modern corporation:

> In many sectors of economic activity the classical entrepreneur has virtually disappeared. His role was essentially active and unitary; once dismembered, no device of collective abstraction could put him together again. As a result, entrepreneurship in the modern corporation has been taken over by transcendent management, whose functions differ in kind from those of the traditional subordinate or "mere manager." These people, it is argued, can wield considerable power without

*Author's Note: This lecture was written prior to the 1980 election and delivered before the Reagan Administration took office. Clearly, the tone of comments from the new Chairman of the SEC is different from that of his predecessor. In addition, the tenor of the Congress is changing. Whether these developments will make for a more robust market for corporate control remains to be seen.

In recent months, of course, the so-called MEGA mergers have demonstrated that the tender offer market remains alive. All the same, events such as the aborted AMAX tender indicate that a management bent on resisting has many weapons at its disposal.

Richard R. West, "Corporate Governance and the Market for Corporate Control," in *Corporte Governance: Past and Future*, ITT Key Issues Lecture Series, ed. Henry G. Manne (New York: K.C.G. Productions, Inc., 1982), pp. 46–69. Reprinted with permission.

necessarily holding equity, sharing profits or carrying risks.[1]

Surely no one even vaguely familiar with what goes on in a large public corporation would take issue with Marris's characterization. Today's managers do wield enormous power. Their domains are frequently larger than entire nations, employing hundreds of thousands of workers on several continents. And while many high corporate officials participate in some form of profit sharing scheme and most have modest stockholdings in the companies they run, the vast majority own little more than a minuscule piece of the equity. Like the people whose destinies they so greatly influence, they are the employees of the corporation, not its owners.

The relevant question, however, is not whether modern corporations are operated by a class of professional managers; they obviously are. Rather, it is whether such managers have reason to feel that they are in a position to ignore the interests of those who put up the risk capital—the shareholders.

From the earliest days of corporate enterprise, of course, it was recognized that managers needed to have a good bit of operating latitude. Even before the civil war, in an era when the typical company's shareholders were few in number and well known to the management, the courts began ruling that a firm's owners could not hold the directors personally responsible for poor operating results, so long as they were acting in good faith and with due care.[2] In addition, boards were acknowledged to have the power to delegate considerable authority to corporate officers, who, in turn, were exempt from personal liability so long as they too operated in a prudent manner.

Over the years, the courts' practice of insulating officers and directors from liabilities resulting from their exercise of managerial discretion became generally known as the business judgement rule. Under this rule, judges have consistently demonstrated a reluctance to permit shareholders to sue directors or managers for making "honest mistakes." In more recent years, however, they have also used the rule to dismiss suits questioning whether corporate decision making actually reflected an abiding concern for the interests of the shareholders. Indeed, some critics of the courts now feel that the business judgment rule has been applied, as one recently put it, "ad absurdum."[3]

Nor surprisingly, the courts' reluctance to question the decisions of management has led some to argue that giving managers operating latitude must result, sooner or later, in having them lose sight of the interests of shareholders. This, however, is a non sequitur. If the courts were reasonably "hardnosed" in distinguishing between honest mistakes and clear breaches of faith with the

[1]Robin Marris, *The Economic Theory of "Managerial" Capitalism,* The MacMillan Company, London, 1967, p. 1.

[2]See James Willard Hurst, *The Legitimacy of the Business Corporation in the U.S.,* The University Press of Virginia, Charlottesville, Virginia, 1970, pp. 25-27 and 48-49.

[3]Paul Blustein, "Court Gives Firms More Power to Fight Takeovers," *The Wall Street Journal,* September 26, 1980, p. 33.

shareholders, officers and directors would not be encouraged to think that their freedom to make business decisions was a license to ignore the interests of the owners. It has been the reluctance of many judges to make this distinction, rather than the business judgment principle itself, that forms the basis for many of the questions about the degree to which some managers may currently feel a diminished sense of responsibility to shareholders.[4]

The growth of government regulation of business activity has also been put forward as a reason why corporate managements should feel less beholden to shareholders. But this, too, is a non sequitur. The concept of the primacy of the shareholders never created a basis for arguing that corporations could do anything they pleased in the name of profit-seeking. From their earlier days, corporations have been subject to various forms of regulation and control.[5] Hence, to suggest that the contemporary increase in the *scope* of regulation necessarily alters the fundamental relationship between owners and managers is both illogical and mischievous. By analogy, it's a bit like saying that when the National Collegiate Athletic Association tries to reduce football injuries by changing the definition of "clipping," players and coaches should conclude that scoring touchdowns is no longer relevant.

A much more compelling argument, one that was first introduced by Adolf A. Berle and Gardiner C. Means in the early 1930's, is that widespread shareholdership itself creates a separation between the ownership and control in the large modern corporation.[6] According to Berle and Means, shareholders are powerless, both individually and collectively. Each senses that his actions will have little effect on management, and that few of his fellows will be interested in taking the time and trouble to join in a collective action.[7] As a result, the logic goes, managements feel they are in a position to disregard flagrantly the interests of shareholders.

If it is correct, Berle and Means's thesis of an inevitable separation of ownership and control in the modern corporation has momentous implications for the governance of corporate behavior. By completely undercutting the notion that shareholders can influence the behavior of management, it fosters the idea that government has an obligation, not simply to define the ground rules within which the pursuit of shareholders' interests will take place, but to determine the ends to which corporate enterprise is directed.

What is more, it encourages attacks on fundamental property rights. Indeed, the major theme of Berle and Means's book was that owners who could

---

[4]Some argue that it would be a bad thing for the courts ever to question whether a management was really using its business judgment. Their argument is that this would tend toward having the courts end up running firms. But this is not a position with which I can concur. Why should managers be given the right to exercise judgment and the courts be told they should never exercise judgment? And more pointedly, what is there to suggest that courts would have any reason to question legitimate business judgments, as opposed to clear breaches of faith with the shareholders?

[5]See Hurst, op.cit.

[6]Adolf A. Berle and Gardiner C. Means, *The Modern Corporation and Private Property,* The McMillan Company, New York, 1933.

[7]Berle and Means maintain that institutional shareholders are similarly impotent.

not control the use to which their property was put should not enjoy all of the traditional rights associated therewith. As Berle asked in the preface to the most recent edition of their book:

> "Because an owner who also exercises control over his wealth is protected in the full receipt of the advantages derived from it, must it *necessarily* follow that an owner who has surrendered control of his wealth should likewise be protected to the full? May not this surrender have so essentially changed his relation to his wealth as to have changed the logic applicable to his interest in that wealth?"[8]

His answer, of course, was that it did not necessarily follow, because the "surrender" has been so complete as to create the presumption for an abrogation of private property rights in the corporate sector.

III THE MARKET FOR CORPORATE CONTROL

Over the years, Berle and Means' arguments have attracted wide support of private property rights in the corporate sector.

Over the years, Berle and Means' arguments have attracted wide support from those interested in injecting government more thoroughly into the affairs of corporations. But they have also been roundly criticized for failing to recognize adequately the role the stock market can play in harmonizing the interests of shareholders and managers.[9] Their critics point out that when a firm's shareholders become convinced that management is not trading for their good, they can be expected to start selling their shares, thereby putting downward pressure on share prices. The more disgruntled they become, the greater the downward pressure on share prices. As this process takes place, the management, of course, tends to feel less secure. It may even start taking the shareholders' interests more seriously, fearing that to do otherwise will encourage a struggle for corporate control. Alternately, it may choose to try to "tough it out," in which case the likelihood of a struggle increases. Either way, however, the final outcome is likely to be the same: the management learns that it cannot disregard the interests of the shareholders without running the risk that it will lose control of the corporation.

Please don't misunderstand what is being said. Critics of Berle and Means are realistic, not romantics. They do not believe that legions of individual shareholders will take up arms against an incumbent management that has been ignoring their interests. To the contrary, they too acknowledge that the small shareholder in a giant corporation typically feels relatively impotent; that he would rather switch than fight.

But if individual shareholders cannot be expected to engage an incumbent management, who can? The answer is the corporate raider, that often

---

[8]Berle and Means, note six.

[9]See in particular, Henry G. Manne, "Mergers and the Market for Corporate Control," *Journal of Political Economy,* April 1965, pp. 110–120.

vilified actor in the drama for corporate control. It is the raider who searches for mismanaged companies and takes on their managements in a struggle for control. Make no mistake, corporate raiders are not altruists or social workers. They seek primarily to enrich themselves, not to enhance the economy's allocation of capital and labor or to improve the lot of small shareholders. In the process of trading for their own good, however, they also provide powerful checks on managements that might otherwise operate with little or no regard for the interests of the shareholders.

Incumbent managements, of course, tend to see things in a rather different light. From their perspective, corporate raiders are little more than pirates in three piece suits bent on plundering well managed companies for their own gratification. Consider, for example, the following statement by an executive of a firm that specializes in soliciting proxies: "The better a corporation is run, the stronger its market position, the more advanced its product, the cleaner its balance sheet and financial controls, the more likely it is to be a target."[10]

Which position do the facts support? Are they consistent with the argument that raiders are useful scavengers who keep the corporate landscape from becoming littered with the carcasses of poorly managed companies, or do they support those who see raids as a vehicle for permitting highly efficient firms to become the victims of industrial piracy? The answer to this question is quite clear: the data indicate that raiders tend to seek out firms whose earnings and stock prices have been lagging—firms whose shareholders have ample grounds for being dissatisfied with the performance of management.

The following is an excerpt from the editor's summary of a paper entitled, "Do Tender Offers Damage Stockholders?" by Robert Smiley:

> Although takeover bids, or tender offers, are often criticized as the tools of corporate raiders, they benefit both consumers and shareholders. Takeover bids typically are aimed at unprofitable, sluggish companies. Everyone concerned, except the inefficient managers, benefits from a management change. Takeover bids facilitate the liquidation of assets and the shift of resources to other, more highly valued uses. Acquiring firms do not make abnormal profits through takeovers and stockholders in acquired firms tend to be better off after the takeovers. Takeover bids and tender offers promote the efficient operation of corporations.[11]

Putting matters somewhat more colorfully, Smiley himself stated that "it simply is not true that the targets of most takeover bids are well-managed, fine old firms; they are much more often poorly managed firms—firms in which everyone but the ousted managers would benefit from a management change."[12]

---

[10]Winthrop C. Neilson, "A Fairness Doctrine for Tender Offers," *Financial Executive,* February, 1979, p. 50.

[11]Robert Smiley, "Do Tender Offers Damage Stockholders?," *The Attack on Corporate America,* edited by M. Bruce Johnson, McGraw Hill, 1978 p. 97.

[12]Ibid., p. 98.

Perhaps the most relevant data concerning the operations of the market for corporate control are contained in a recent paper by Donald R. Kummer and J. Ronald Hoffmeister.[13] The authors studied cash tender offers made between January, 1956 and June, 1974 for firms on the New York Stock Exchange. Using methodology that is now a standard part of the tool kit of financial economists, they tested the following hypotheses: (1) that investors in the common stock of target firms generally experienced abnormally low returns in the period prior to a takeover attempt; (2) that the stockholders of firms which resisted a tender experienced especially low returns prior to a takeover attempt; and (3) that successful tenders lead to an improved wealth position for the shareholders of both firms involved. Overall, their results supported all three hypotheses, thereby leading them to conclude that takeover activities are "consistent with a competitive market for corporate control that leads to the efficient utilization of corporate resources."[14]

IV. THE ASSAULT ON THE MARKET FOR CORPORATE CONTROL

Having so much to lose from successful takeover bids, incumbent managements have become increasingly active in seeking protection from corporate raiders. Their activities have ranged from supporting federal and state regulation of tender offers to espousing charter and bylaw amendments designed to make raids more difficult. And with increasing frequency their efforts have met with success. Mounting an attack on an imcumbent management that is willing to resist has become an increasingly costly and risky venture—one that even the boldest raider must now approach with caution.

Prior to the 1950's, the market for corporate control was left largely to its own devices, presumably on the grounds that enlightened self interest, rather than government controls, would best serve investors and the public at large.[15] With the growth of unfriendly tender offers, however, incumbent managements began to press hard for government intervention. At the federal level, their efforts galvanized around a bill introduced by Senator Harrison Williams in 1965.[16] What made this legislation so unique was that it represented the first attempt by a member of Congress to propose a securities law for the benefit of issuers

---

[13]Donald R. Kummer and J. Ronald Hoffmeister, "Valuation Consequences of Cash Tender Offers," *Journal of Finance,* May 1978, pp. 505–516.

[14]Ibid., p. 516.

[15]Prior to the 1960's fights for control tended to resolves proxy contests. With growth in federal regulation of proxies, however, takeover bids became more popular. For more on this point, see Peter Dodd, *The Impact of the Market for Corporate Control on Stockholder Wealth,* University of Rochester Thesis, 1978.

[16]For an excellent discussion of the history of the legislation, see Edward R. Aranow and Herbert A. Einhorn, *Tender Offers for Corporate Control,* Columbia University Press, New York, 1973.

rather than investors. Senator Williams made absolutely no attempt to hide his blatantly pro-management/antiraider biases, consistently referring to target firms as "proud old companies," and corporate raiders as "pirates" engaged in "industrial espionage."[17] In the mid 1960's, however, relatively few members of Congress were ready to vote for legislation that was proposed explicitly for the purpose of aiding a special interest group. The vast majority still needed to be told that they were voting for a bill on the grounds that its enactment would further the public good.

Williams may have been somewhat ahead of his time, but he was also an "old hand" at getting legislation passed. Hence, he quickly changed his tune. Gone were all references to protecting incumbent managements and proud old companies. In their place were phrases like "investor protection through full disclosure." As one knowledgeable observer saw things, the revised versions of the bill were rationalized in terms of a need "to give shareholders and investors sufficient information to make intelligent decisions . . . and not to tip the balance in favor of incumbent management in the battle for control."[18]

With its rationale suitably altered, Senator Williams's basic proposal gained wide support and passed easily on July 29, 1968.[19] The Securities and Exchange Commission (SEC), that bastion of full disclosure, was solidly behind the legislation, as were the New York and American Stock Exchanges, the National Association of Securities Dealers, the Investment Bankers Association, and a myriad of corporate executives. Indeed, the only dissenters were a few academics like Professor Manne, who sought in vain to establish the need to protect the market for corporate control from regulatory intrusions.[20]

The final version of the Williams Act went a long way toward making tender offers more difficult, costly and, above all, risky. By requiring raiders to provide the SEC with information about their reasons for making a tender offer and their plans for a target firm, the bill greatly increased the likelihood of counter offers and bidding wars.[21] A provision that tenderers be given the right to withdraw their shares during a so-called cooling off period had a similar effect,[22] as did a requirement that all tenderers receive the highest price paid for any shares acquired during the offer period.[23] Of course the bill's numerous filing provisions increased the direct expenses of mounting a tender offer and

[17]III Congressional Record 28256-80, October 22, 1965.

[18]James D. Cox, "Acquisitions and Mergers," *Corporate Law Review,* Fall, 1978, pp. 339–340.

[19]Pub. L. No. 90-439, 82 State 454.

[20]For a discussion of the arguments against the Bill, see Robert Mundheim, "Why the Bill on Tender Offers Should Not Be Passed," *Institutional Investor,* May, 1967, p. 24; and Henry Manne, "Why Tender Offers Should Remain Unregulated," *Commercial and Financial Chronicle,* May 23, 1968, p. 12.

[21]This is provided for in Section 13d.

[22]This is provided for in Section 14d5.

[23]This is provided for in Section 14d6.

its many technical features provided incumbent managements with fertile grounds for waging long and costly lawsuits.

The Williams Act was amended in 1970.[24] Three major changes were made. The threshold ownership level for reporting was reduced from 10% to 5%. In addition, exchange offers, which had previously been exempt from regulation, were brought under the same requirements as offers for cash. Finally, the SEC was given increased power to promulgate rules to prohibit fraudulent practices associated with tenders.

Using the regulatory powers granted it by the original Act and the 1970 amendments, the SEC has consistently taken actions that have further increased the difficulty of mounting a tender. Early in 1980, for example, the Commission adopted a series of rules that increased both the minimum number of days a tender can be in effect and the time period during which shareholders can withdraw tendered shares.[25] Even more recently, it has proposed that Congress adopt major changes in the Williams Act, all of which would have the effect of increasing the ability of incumbent managements to fend off tenders.[26]

Within a few years of the Williams Act's passage, economists, interested in the operations of the market for corporate control, began to investigate its impact on the tender process. The first published study,[27] by Robert Smiley, reported that the Act had materially increased the transaction costs of tender offers in some cases by more than 25%. He recommended that this impact "should be considered the next time a legislative body begins consideration of a market mechanism which could (if left alone or encouraged) be instrumental in providing market-imposed discipline on managers of U.S. firms."[28] Smiley, apparently, was unaware that Senator Williams had considered it in some detail the first time around!

Of course, supporters of the Williams Act might argue that some increase in transactions costs of tenders has represented a reasonable price to pay for giving investors more information about an acquirer and more time to make a decision. Matters, however, have not stopped with increases in transactions costs. As Gregg A. Jarrell and Michael Bradley recently wrote:

A casual acquaintance with the financial press reveals that the Williams Act has had an important effect on the market for tender offers. The sudden takeovers of the 1960's are almost extinct. There seem to be more cases of besieged targets combining with less "hostile" suitors, called "white knights." Surrounding today's tender offers are impressive amounts of litigation, with legal recourse being used to stall and sometimes to prevent attempted takeovers. Competing bidders

[24]Pub. L. No. 91-567, 84 Stat. 1497.

[25]See SEC Release No. 16384, December 6, 1979 at 44 FR 70376.

[26]See Federal Securities Law Report, No. 847, February 27, 1980, pp. 2–3.

[27]Robert Smiley, "The Effect of the Williams Amendment and Other Factors on Transaction Costs in Tender Offers," *Industrial Organization Review,* Vol. 3, 1975, pp. 138–145.

[28]Ibid., p. 145.

often jump into the fray while the initial tender offer remains open. Most startling are the substantial premiums that are ultimately paid to target shareholders in the modern takeover.[29]

Jarrell and Bradley found that premiums increased from 32% before the Williams Act to nearly 53% after its passage and concluded that the Act's provisions have been highly successful in garnering higher returns for target shareholders. However, they did not view this outcome with favor. To the contrary, their judgment was that the Williams Act has generated substantial social costs in the form of forgone valuable corporate contributions. As they observed:

> [S]udden takeovers are a market solution to what would be a public good problem, with the public good being information concerning the precise sources of the economic gains from corporate combinations. Disclosure requirements and the delay of execution caused by minimum offer periods and legal actions freely provide potential competing bidders with time and information. The successful bidder, under the regulations, is forced to pay higher premiums to outbid this increased competition for the target. This regulation-induced "tax" on takeovers appears as a benefit to the shareholders of acquired firms. But the tax, which is in the form of higher premiums, is expected to discourage some investment in acquisition-oriented innovations and to deter some otherwise profitable corporate takeovers. Therefore, by our interpretation, the higher premiums to tendering shareholders cause losses to shareholders of firms not acquired because of the deterrent effect.[30]

Not being content to stop with federal legislation and the growing support of the SEC, incumbent managements also petitioned to state legislatures for assistance, and with few exceptions they found receptive audiences. Legislatures were particularly taken by the claim that tender offers should be regulated because they typically represented intrusions by "outlanders" seeking to control local firms. The rhetoric used to support state regulations included all the classic, protectionist arguments that have come to be associated with opposition to foreign ownership of U.S. companies, e.g., including a loss of local control, the possibility of plant closings, etc.

One of the earlier state statutes was the Ohio Takeover Act of 1969,[31] passed in the wake of a bitter fight between B.F. Goodrich Co., a firm incorporated in Ohio, and Northwest Industries, Inc., a Delaware incorporated firm, seeking control of Goodrich. In spite of being characterized as special interest legislation inspired by incumbent managements under the fiction of requiring full disclosure to shareholders, the Act was highly popular with members of the Ohio legislature and passed easily.

By the end of 1977, more than three-fourths of the states had enacted some

[29]Gregg A. Jarrell and Michael Bradley, "The Economic Effects of Federal and State Regulation of Cash Tender Offers," *Journal of Law and Economics,* October 1980, p. 372.
[30]Ibid., p. 373.
[31]For a listing of all the state statutes, see Ibid., p. 406–407.

form of antitender legislation. While varying somewhat from jurisdiction to jurisdiction, the various state statutes, like the Williams Act, typically have focused on substantive disclosure requirements and provisions for shareholders to withdraw tendered shares during some cooling off period. Their major impact, however, has come from requiring bidders to notify the state in advance of submitting a tender, thereby giving target companies and the state's commission of securities additional time to question its merits. Most statutes permit the state's commissioner and the management of a target company to request a formal hearing at which the bidder may be asked to defend not only the adequacy of his disclosures, but also the fairness and equity of his offer.

Over the past several years, corporate raiders have questioned the legality of various of the state tender offer statutes with increasing frequency. The courts have generally responded favorably to these challenges on the grounds that the statutes involve excessive extraterritoriality, making investors in all states subject to the terms and conditions deemed to be appropriate by a single jurisdiction.[32] Simply by creating the basis for burdensome and costly lawsuits, however, the statutes have assisted incumbent managements in the short run.

That the statutes have actually deterred some tenders is unquestioned. Robert Smiley has reported that state regulations stopped at least 41 tenders between 1972 and 1978.[33] His conclusion, not surprisingly, was that "the state statutes increased the likelihood that tender offers would fail and provided a measurable and statistically significant deterrent to tender offer activity."[34]

Jarrell and Bradley have also found that state statutes act as a deterrent to tender offer activity. More importantly, however, they have reported that these laws, like the Williams Act, tend to increase the level of premiums paid to the shareholders of a target firm. They conclude that, in some instances, raiders could not find "suitable substatutes" for the targets in regulated states, thereby requiring them to "bear the added cost of the higher takeover premiums."[35]

Whether state involvement in tender offers continues over the long run will depend not only on the actions of courts but also the fate of attempts to have federal regulation dominate the tender scene. Some of the SEC's recent actions have already negated certain features of the state statutes, but the most promising vehicle for eliminating all state involvement is the proposed Federal Securities Code, now before Congress.[36] Unfortunately, however, the Code's own language incorporates the most onerous features of state regulation. As

[32]For more on this subject see, Howard M. Friedman, "The Validity of State Tender Offer Statutes—An Update," *Mergers and Acquisitions,* Fall, 1978, pp. 18–20.

[33]See Robert Smiley, "The Effect of State Securities Statutes on Tender Offer Activity," mimeo, *Economic Inquiry,* July 1981.

[34]Ibid., p. 12.

[35]Jarrell and Bradley, *op.cit,* p. 402.

[36]*Federal Securities Code,* Adopted by the American Law Institute, May 19, 1978, American Law Institute, 1980.

currently written, it calls for all tenderers to comply with a ten-day advance filing requirement and a considerable extension in the minimum offer period. What makes these provisions particularly irksome is the fact that the codifiers alleged they were trying to maintain neutrality as between bidders and target firms.[37] One can't help but wonder how the Code might have read if they had deliberately tilted in favor of incumbent managements!

As the old adage goes, "The Lord helps those who help themselves." Hence it is not very surprising that incumbent managements have also attempted to reduce their vulnerability to raids by taking defensive measures available under the states' general corporate statutes. Chief among them has been a variety of charter and bylaw amendments known collectively as "shark repellent." Most forms of shark repellent have a common objective: to make it difficult for a raider who gains a majority ownership interest to obtain effective working control of a company. Amendments staggering the terms of board members, for example, hold out the possibility that a new owner won't be able to dominate the board for several years. Of course, because the ability to "pack" a board can nullify this particular feature, most amendments for staggered terms are coupled with proposals to limit the size of the board and permit cumulative share voting.

Among the various forms of shark repellent, the most effective, not to mention insidious, are amendments requiring super-majority votes to effect mergers. While differing in detail, all super-majority clauses have the effect of discriminating between shareholders on the basis of the size of their holdings, thereby making it possible for an incumbent management to have veto power over almost any business combination by owning a minority interest in the company. When an amendment is sufficiently discriminatory, a management may be able to thwart mergers by owning only a small percentage of the outstanding shares.

The most common form of super-majority amendment is known as an 80–10 provision, since it calls for an 80% favorable vote for a merger with a corporation owning more than 10% of any class of the company's equity securities. The typical 80–10 provision is drafted in very broad form, so that stock in the hands of so-called "affiliated persons" is included in the 10% calculation. Similarly, the term "merger" is defined to include virtually all forms of business combination.

Even more restrictive amendments have been proposed, including some that call for a favorable vote of as high a percentage of the minority shares as are owned by the majority shareholder. Thus, for example, a raider owning 70% of the shares of a firm would have to get 70% of the remaining votes in order to affect a merger. Or, to put it more pointedly, the holder of less than 10% of the shares would be able to block a merger!

---

[37]On this point see Richard R. West, "The Federal Securities Code: Some Comments on Process and Outcome," *University of Miami Law Review,* September, 1980, pp. 1445–1494.

Quite recently, some companies have begun resorting to charter and bylaw amendments designed to give their boards of directors explicit authorization to consider factors other than the welfare of shareholders when evaluating an unfriendly tender offer. In 1978, Control Data's directors proposed that the company's certificate of incorporation be modified to require the board "when reviewing any proposal by another corporation to acquire or combine with the company, to consider all relevant factors, including the expected social and economic effects of the transaction on the various constituents of the company."[38] In a similar vein, McDonald's directors recently recommended a charter amendment that charged the board, when reviewing any takeover bid, to consider "such factors as it determines to be relevant, including the social, legal, and economic effects on franchises, employees, suppliers, customers, and business."[39]

On the premise that all corporations should be more "socially responsible," it might be argued that charter amendments such as these represent nothing more than what any good board should be proposing. Certainly, this is what Control Data's directors wanted the firm's shareholders to believe. In the company's 1968 proxy statement, the directors said that their proposal would be incorporated in the firm's "Policy on Ethics," in a section on "the social justice considerations regarding uninvited attempts by outsiders to take control of the company."[40] They went on to say that although stockholders had a right to a "reasonable return on their investment," many other groups have "a stake in the corporation"—a stake that the directors should protect.

It would be wrong, of course, to conclude that protecting the interests of customers and employees is necessarily inconsistent with furthering the interests of shareholders, or vice versa. One must assume, however, that the directors of Control Data and McDonald's envisioned the possibility that a takeover attempt could have conflicting impacts on the firms' various constituents—impacts that might cause them to tilt counter to the best interests of the shareholders. Why else would they have deemed it appropriate to propose charter amendments? Directors, after all, hardly need to be told what to do when they are in a position to take actions that will redound to everyone's benefit.

That the two boards' proposals actually reflected a desire to meet their companies social responsibilities seems doubtful. A more plausible explanation is that they were stimulated principally by a desire to protect themselves and their incumbent managements from the threat of unfriendly takeovers. In an offhand fashion, Control Data's proxy statement acknowledged that the directors' proposal "might" have this effect. McDonald's proxy, being more can-

---

[38]Control Data Corporation, Notice of Annual Meeting of Shareholders to be held May 3, 1978, p. 1.

[39]McDonald's Corporation, Proxy Statement and Notice of 1979 Annual Meeting of Stockholders, p. 11.

[40]Control Data Corporation, Proxy Statement for 1978, p. 3–4.

did and expansive, went so far as to admit that "one effect of the proposed amendment might be to discourage, *in advance*, an acquisition proposal."[41]

Of course, the same could be said about all forms of shark repellent. Boards of directors are not simply interested in being able to retain control after a raider has purchased a majority position. Their ultimate objective is to discourage raiders from making a move in the first place.

A recent study by the National Association of Accountants of 177 of the nation's larger 1000 industrial corporations revealed that more than one third have proposed some form of charter amendment designed to disocurage unfriendly tenders.[42] Researchers at the University of Chicago's Business School report they have found over 300 companies that have done likewise, and DeAngelo and Rice have identified approximately 200 NYSE listed companies in this category.[43] Shark repellent, it would seem, is in strong demand these days.

In a recent speech, SEC Chairman Harold M. Williams argued against defensive charter and bylaw amendments, saying that "Tenders should be considered on their merits, on a case-by-case basis, and not warded off by building castles and moats."[44] Unfortunately, however, the Chairman also endorsed the concept of having directors evaluate tenders in terms of their impact on all of the firm's various stakeholders, not just the shareholders. After characterizing recent tender activity as "most disturbing" because of the degree to which it has made hostile offers "legitimate," Mr. Williams argued vigorously that the motive behind such offers was too often nothing more than the ego satisfaction and self aggrandizement of raiders. Finally, he warned that if outside directors don't do something to get matters under control, government may have to step in. To quote Mr. Williams, "It is, of course, important to bear in mind that a society which places as much reliance as does ours on government as an instrument to check the perceived excesses of business is unlikely to tolerate indefinitely business behavior which the public regards as contrary to its interests."[45]

With support like this from the Chairman of the SEC, incumbent managements may not have to be concerned about building castles and moats. Washington may decide to slay all of the corporate dragons for them.

[41]McDonald Proxy Statement, *Op.Cit.,* p. 12.

[42]"Takeovers: A Survey of Corporate Defense Strategies," *Merges and Acquisitions,* Spring, 1980, pp. 21–35.

[43]Harry DeAngelo and Edward M. Rice, "Anti-Takeover Charter Amendments and Stockholder Wealth," October, 1980 mimeo. The authors find that, on average, proposals to add anti-takeover provisions to a corporation's charter and by laws produce downward pressure on stock prices. This result is generally consistent with the hypothesis that these proposals are designed to protect incumbent managements rather than shareholders.

[44]Harold M. Williams, "Tender Offers and Corporate Directors," speech before 7th Annual Securities Regulation Institute, San Diego, California, January 17, 1980. Reprinted in *Federal Securities Law Reports,* February 6, 1980, pp. 82,875–82,882.

[45]Ibid., p. 82,877.

IV. SOME CONCLUDING COMMENTS

At this point three interrelated questions would seem to be in order: First, what have been the effects of actions of incumbent managements on the operations of the market for corporate control? Second, what do these effects imply for resource allocation and the governance of corporate behavior? Third, what might be done to preclude managements from taking further steps designed to insulate themselves from the stock market's discipline?

Those who are skeptical about the thrust of my arguments might approach the first question by arguing that the continuing popularity of tender offers amply testifies to the robustness of the market for corporate control. They might even suggest that federal and state regulation of tenders has improved the overall behavior of the market by giving shareholders more information and an enhanced opportunity to profit from bidding wars.[46]

While points such as these cannot be rejected outright, they need to be kept in perspective. To be sure, tender offers continue to be made, and some shareholders have clearly profited from competition between rival tenderers. But this is only part of the picture. It must also be recognized that tenders are being challenged and repulsed by incumbent managements with increasing frequency. And what about the tenders that have never taken place because of changes in the law and the effective use of shark repellent? Although the market may appear to be quite healthy, the changes in its vital signs are all in the wrong direction.

But who cares if the market for corporate control no longer operates efficiently? What difference does it really make? The answer, of course, is that it makes a great deal of difference. The arguments about the relationship between a healthy market for corporate control and an efficient allocation of resources have been well stated elsewhere, and I will not bother to detail them here. Suffice it to say that when the control market is not functioning effectively, the probability increases that large aggregations of resources can be mismanaged for some period of time.[47]

[46]For more on this point, see Jarrell and Bradley, *op. cit.,* pp. 379–382.

[47]All is not lost, however. To begin with, competitive markets have a way of protecting the public. A firm that is not responsive to the interests of shareholders tends to be a poor competitor, losing out to firms which are more concerned with operating in an efficient manner.

Fama has also suggested that the market for managerial talent acts to encourage managers to do what is in the interests of shareholders. His argument is that managers must be concerned about the value of their human capital, which tends to be higher when decisions that improve the lot of investors are made. On this point see Eugene F. Fama, ''Agency Problems and the Theory of the Firm,'' *Journal of Political Economy,* April, 1980, pp. 288–307.

Unfortunately, both competition and the market for managerial talent may take a long time to have an effect. The first does not take assets directly out of the hands of current managers, but rather assumes that additional resources will be harder to come by. The latter works only to the extent that managers are concerned about their next jobs. In the case of older managers, particularly those nearing retirement, its impact may be minimal.

And then there is the broader question of the legitimacy of corporate behavior. In his fascinating monograph on the history of the corporation in American society, the eminent legal scholar, James Willard Hurst, offers the following insights into the role of the shareholder in legitimizing corporate activity:

> Prime reliance . . . was upon a competitive market, the discipline of which would curb waste, excessive ambition, oppressive charges and disregard of productive service. But within the framework of market discipline, we relied on the self-interested care of those who put their capital at risk to police the fidelity and efficiency of the policy making and management of particular firms.[48]

In short, competition was to constrain the corporation from becoming too aggressive, while the shareholders were to ensure that it became aggressive enough!

When the market for corporate control isn't functioning effectively, however, there is less assurance that corporations will be aggressive enough. Managers are separated from shareholders in much the way that Berle and Means described, and all of the questions they raised about power and property rights become highly relevant. The legitimacy of corporate behavior itself becomes an open question.

Earlier this year, the American Enterprise Institute's journal on government and society, *Regulation,* presented a debate on the Corporate Democracy Act of 1980.[49] Arguing in favor of the Act's passage was Mark Green, an associate of Ralph Nader and the leader of "Big Business Day—1980." As expected, Mr. Green argued that corporate power is out of control, that shareholder democracy is a myth and that government must play a much more prominent role in the governance of large public companies. To quote Mr. Green:

> The issue is not big government versus freedom . . . nor is it capitalism versus socialism. Rather, it is autocracy versus democracy. The Corporate Democracy Act of 1980 aspires to reform the *internal* governance structure of our largest corporations so that—consistent with a market economy—companies would exercise their power and discretion more democratically and accountably.[50]

Writing in opposition to Mr. Green was Ralph K. Winter, the William K. Townsend Professor of Law at Yale University. After questioning whether the Corporate Democracy Act really has anything to do with democratizing corporations, Professor Winter turned to the role of the market for corporate control in directing and legitimizing corporate behavior. As Professor Winter put matters:

[48]Hurst, *op.cit.,* p. 82.
[49]"On the Corporate Democracy Act," *Regulation,* May/June, 1980, pp. 20–31.
[50]Ibid., p. 25.

> Existing voting rights in common stock play a critical function, because they blend the investment market with a market for control that permits takeovers. The provisions of the Corporate Democracy Act are irrelevant to this aspect of voting rights—the only aspect that significantly matters.[51]

Apparently neither Professor Winter nor Mr. Green was aware of the degree to which incumbent managements are waging an assault on the market for corporate control. Had they been, the former would likely have extolled the market's virtues more gingerly, while the latter would most certainly have discounted its relevance.

We come now to what Dr. I. Q. would have called the "$64 question"—namely, what can be done to keep the market for corporate control from becoming less effective in the future? The answer, I fear, is "not much." There have been no attempts to repeal the Williams Act or to make its various provisions less burdensome. To the contrary, as I noted earlier, the SEC is planning for even more restrictive measures. And then there is the Federal Securities Code, with its provisions for advance notification and longer offer periods.

At the individual firm level, the picture is not any more promising. Charter and bylaw amendments designed to discourage unfriendly tenders are quite popular these days and hordes of highly paid corporate lawyers are working overtime to develop new forms of shark repellent. In addition, some are doing their best to make the case that the activities of corporate raiders are not in the national interest. Martin Lipton, a well-known lawyer who specializes in representing incumbent managements, recently wrote that, "Even if there were no empirical evidence that refuted the argument that shareholders almost always benefit from a takeover . . . and even if there were no real evidence, but only suspicion, that proscribing the ability of companies to defend against takeovers would adversely affect long-term planning and thereby jeopardize the economy, the policy considerations in favor of not jeopardizing the economy are so strong that not even a remote risk is acceptable."[52] Mr. Lipton did not explain why an uninhibited market for corporate control would discourage firms from planning for the future, nor did he tell us why this would, to use his words, "jeopardize the economy." One suspects that if he could have invoked national securities issues, he would have done so. Waving the flag, after all, is an excellent way to shut off all rational discourse.

At one time I was somewhat hopeful that the growing trend toward boards with majorities of independent directors would truncate the efforts of incumbent managements to insulate themselves from takeover attempts. Alas, I was naive. As empirical data become more copious, it is clear that many companies

[51]Ibid., p. 28.

[52]Martin Lipton, "Takeover Bids in the Target's Boardroom," *The Business Lawyer,* November, 1979, pp. 104–105.

with so-called "outside boards" have already applied ample amounts of shark repellent. Independent directors, it would seem, often side with management when it comes to deciding whether to protect the firm from unfriendly take-over bids.

Where does all this leave us? The answer, I suspect, is that it leaves us with an economy in which growing numbers of managers may have good reason to feel that they can make decisions with little or no regard for what is in the best interests of their shareholders. It just may be that Berle and Means were on the right track after all; they simply were a little early.

DISCUSSION QUESTIONS

1. What are the economic, moral, and political justifications for private property rights?

2. Should the separation of ownership and direct management control invalidate stockholders' basic property rights if stockholders exercise effective *market* control over corporate decision making? Should stockholders' property rights be invalidated even if they have no significant control over the use of their assets? What basic property rights do stockholders (bond holders) have when they invest in large corporations?

3. Does the Corporate Democracy Act represent orderly evolution, or a revolution in the relationship of business to society?

4. Corporate governance proposals do not come primarily from stockholders, who should be the group most disadvantaged by any loss of effective control over corporate decision making. If investors are not dissatisfied with existing business-stockholder relationships, what groups are, and what are their corporate governance concerns?

5. Would corporations be operated more or less in the public interest if they were controlled by their stakeholders? What effect would stakeholder control have upon the firm's cost of raising capital?

6. What is the proper role of the board of directors in controlling the modern corporation? How could their control of the corporation be improved? Should all directors be representatives of the stockholders?

7. Does state chartering of corporations result in the "law for sale" or does competition among the states for business charters benefit stockholders, consumers, and the general public?

8. What are the limitations of external regulatory controls of business which corporate governance is designed to overcome? Would corporate governance reforms result in "self-regulation"?

9. Which groups benefit and which groups are disadvantaged by government regulation of the market for corporate control? Do these regulations reflect a strong political bias for the status quo?

10. The separation of ownership and control, and the implications for management behavior did not escape the attention of Adam Smith who criticized joint-stock companies (corporations) as negligent and profuse:

The directors of such companies, however, being the managers rather of other people's money than of their own, it cannot well be expected, that they should watch over it with the same anxious vigilance with which the partners in a private copartnery frequently watch over their own. Like the stewards of a rich man, they are apt to consider attention to small matters as not for their master's honour, and very easily give themselves a dispensation from having it. Negligence and profusion, therefore, must always prevail, more or less, in the management of the affairs of such a company. It is upon this account that joint stock companies for foreign trade have seldom been able to maintain the competition against private adventurers. They have, accordingly, very seldom succeeded without an exclusive privilege; and frequently have not succeeded with one. Without an exclusive privilege they have commonly mismanaged the trade. With an exclusive privilege they have both mismanaged and confined it. [*Wealth of Nations,* Random House, Modern Library Edition, p. 700.]

Would Adam Smith hold this same view of large corporations today? What factors might alter his opinion of corporations today?

ADDITIONAL READINGS

GOLDBERG, ARTHUR J., "Some Observations on the Effectiveness of Outside Directors," *Journal of Contemporary Business,* 8, no. 1 (1979), 33–41.

JONES, THOMAS M., and LEONARD D. GOLDBERG, "Governing the Large Corporation: More Arguments for Public Directors," *Academy of Management Review,* 7, no. 4 (1982), 603–11.

MANNE, HENRY G., "Controlling the Giant Corporation: Myths and Realities," in *Corporate Governance: Past and Future,* ITT Key Issues Lecture Series, 124–39, ed. Henry G. Manne. New York: K.C.G. Productions Incorporated, 1982.

NADER, RALPH, MARK GREEN, and JOEL SELIGMAN, "Who Rules the Giant Corporation?" *Business and Society Review,* 6 (Summer 1973), 37–43.

PURCELL, THEODORE V., "Management and the 'Ethical' Investor," *Harvard Business Review,* 57, no. 5 (September–October 1979), 24–44.

SECURITIES AND EXCHANGE COMMISSION, *Staff Report on Corporate Accountability.* Washington, D.C.: U.S. Government Printing Office, 1980.

STONE, CHRISTOPHER P., "Public Directors Merit a Try," *Harvard Business Review,* 54, no. 2 (March–April 1976), 20–28.

WOODWARD, HERBERT N., "Is Bigger Always Better? The Conflict Between Managers and Shareholders," *Journal of Contemporary Business,* 8, no. 1 (1979), 5–18.

CHAPTER 3
CONSUMER
RELATIONSHIPS

There are three fundamental business-consumer relationship issues which underlie the vast bulk of discussion and controversy in this area: consumer sovereignty, consumer protection, and freedom of choice. A thorough understanding of each of these issues and of the complex interdependencies among them is necessary to the formulation of rational private and public policy responses to perceived inequities in existing business-consumer relationships. Further, no business-society issue can be adequately addressed without an understanding of the fundamental economic relationship between business and consumers.

CONSUMER SOVEREIGNTY

The consumer is king in the classical market control model. As Otis Smith notes in the first reading, the most basic corporate governance issue is not stockholder control of management decision making, but consumer control. Consumers determine the types and quantities of goods and services produced by their dollar votes in the marketplace, and competition among suppliers ensures that these goods and services are produced at minimum cost. Thus, it is the consumer who exercises ultimate control over business decision making. Consumer control is consistent with stockholder interests since stockholders realize their goals (increased earnings and dividends) only to the degree the business is successful in meeting consumer demands. Thus, proposals in the prior chapter to strengthen stockholder control are consistent with the classical notion of consumer sovereignty. Other corporate governance reforms (e.g., the appointment of public interest directors), might undermine this fundamental relationship.

There are two basic consumer sovereignty issues which must be clearly differentiated to understand the various criticisms of business-consumer relationships and proposed reforms. Does the consumer effectively exercise control over business decision making in today's modern economy; and even more fundamentally, should consumers exercise ultimate control over the types of goods and services to be produced?

The production of goods and services may not be responsive to consumer demands if markets are not sufficiently competitive. Competition is the crucial issue here because consumer control of business decision making is exercised almost exclusively through market mechanisms. Like stockholders, dissatisfied consumers control business decisions by exiting, that is, by taking their patronage elsewhere. The biggest obstacle to effective consumer control of business decision making is thus monopoly. Monopoly eliminates effective consumer control of business by denying consumers the exit option through which this control is exercised. A viable exit option requires the availability of substitute goods, which, in the case of monopoly, are absent by definition. Monopoly, of course, has broad inefficiency (high cost) and inequity (redistribution of income from consumers to monopoly producers) implications for society.

The analysis of consumers' ability to make informed decisions in the marketplace raises a more complicated set of conceptual issues than monopoly. Monopoly reduces consumer control of business decisions by eliminating the exit option. However, if consumers do not possess sufficient information to make informed choices, their control over business decision making is also reduced. Consumers' ability to make informed decisions (i.e., to ensure the production of goods and services that are truly desired) may be impeded by inadequate market information, fraudulent or misleading advertising and marketing practices, or an inability to evaluate complex information. In these circumstances, consumer protection may be necessary.

An even more fundamental issue is whether consumers should control business decision making, that is whether the production of goods and services should be determined by consumer preferences effectively expressed in the marketplace. The legitimacy of consumer control of business decision making is questioned in two respects. While business may be responsive to consumer needs, such responses may not be in the broader public interest. This is most obviously the case when the satisfaction of individual consumer demands generates important "externalities"—harmful (less frequently, beneficial) third-party effects, such as pollution. In other circumstances, critics may simply find the goods and services produced in response to individual demands an affront to their own values and paternalistic instincts. Professor Richard Posner illustrates this vividly:

> And here I think lies the essential clue to the hostility of intellectuals to free markets. In free markets, preferences are weighted by willingness to pay rather than some

intrinsic nonpecuniary worth of the preference. The hard hat's taste for Mickey Spillane has the same status in the market as the intellectual's taste for Jean Genet. Intellectuals do not like this democratization of preference. They believe that their preferences are superior to ordinary people's being the product of superior education, intelligence, and sophistication. They want to impose their preferences on the society, which requires the displacement of a market system of resource allocation by some form of central planning in which people like themselves make the major allocative decisions. The market system stands in their way, so naturally they dislike it.[1]

CONSUMER PROTECTION

The public policy responses to monopoly and inadequate or fraudulent product information are straightforward and relatively noncontroversial. Public policy logically calls for the elimination of monopoly, prohibition of fraudulent practices, and provision of consumer information when market data are incomplete. These policies enhance the consumer's freedom of choice and effective control over business decision making. This is not the case, however, when it is questionable whether the consumer possesses sufficient technical expertise or psychological detachment ("it can't happen to me") to make an informed choice. When these limitations on informed choice are coupled with high cost of incorrect decision making, there is a strong rationale for the substitution of public for private choice since government provision of additional information would be obviously ineffective. This issue surfaces most poignantly in the discussion of cost-benefit analysis in life-threatening situations in Chapter 9. The government may have to eliminate free consumer choice by prohibiting the sale of high-risk products which are difficult for consumers to assess. This creates a severe dilemma for a democratic government committed to the preservation of both life and liberty. As Professor Thorelli notes in the third reading, the consumer's right to choose may conflict with his right to safety.

Consumer protection raises a second fundamental issue in addition to the substitution of collective choice for individual decision making. Should consumer protection be based on the relative costs and benefits of protection or, as suggested by Thorelli, do consumers have fundamental "rights" to safety. A Federal Trade Commission staff comment on proposed United Nations guidelines for consumer protection stated: "Consumer protection is fundamentally an economic proposition." It went on: "To base consumer protection guidelines on a series of 'rights' as the proposed U.N. guidelines do, obscures the real task that government faces in the area: how much of the various goods enumerated as 'rights' (physical safety, economic safety, information, consumer education, redress, and consumer organization) is justified by the cost?"[2]

[1]Richard A. Posner, "Intellectual Hostility to the Free Market System: One Analysis," in *At Issue: The Controversy Over Concentrated Industries* (Oakland, Cal.: Kaiser Aluminum and Chemical Corporation, 1978), p. 30.

[2]"FTC Official Calls Consumer Protection an Economic Proposition," *The Bureau of National Affairs*, no. 97 (May 18, 1983), A3–A4.

Michael Pertschuk, former chairman of the Federal Trade Commission and a staunch consumer advocate, expressed the opposite philosophy, and endorsed the U.N. guidelines as supporting "the fundamental premise that in a civilized society, government ensures some minimum consumer rights for its citizens."[3]

A "right" is something to which one has a just moral or legal claim and, as discussed in Chapters 5 and 7, something which cannot be traded for economic gain. But, unlike political or religious rights, economic rights (a moral or legal claim on society's assets) are subject to the basic scarcity or resources. Thus, rights for one group mean costs for others. The morality of assigning rights to one group and obligations to others is questioned in Chapter 6 (Moral Relationships) where it is concluded that such a relationship may be more political than ethical. Whether economic rights can be guaranteed to consumers, employees, or any other group in society without consideration of the inevitable social trade-offs (i.e., the costs) is the fundamental issue.

FREEDOM OF CHOICE

Government protection can conflict with individual free choice. The freedom of individual consumer choice is the basis for consumer control of business decision making. Indeed, monopoly, inadequate or misleading information, or an inability to assess technically complex information are, at root, all issues of free choice. Freedom of choice, however, is also a fundamental civil liberty in a political democracy. It acts as a control on excessive centralization of government power as well as business authority. The strong attachment to free individual choice is based on the belief that every individual knows what is best for himself. This philosophy can be found in Adam Smith who wrote: "Every man, as the stoics used to say is first and principally recommended to his own care; and every man is certainly, in every respect, fitter and abler to take care of himself than of any other person. Every man feels his own pleasures and his own pains more sensitively than those of other people."[4]

M.F. Cohen and George Stigler warn: "It is of regulation that the consumer must beware."[5] Or, as put more colorfully by Henry David Thoreau: "If I knew for a certainty that a man was coming to my house with the conscious design of doing me good, I should run for my life."[6] Government regulation may have a net negative effect on the overall level of consumer protection by atrophying the effectiveness of individual choice. Reliance upon individual self-interest and competition among producers to safeguard consumers may provide greater protection than regulatory agencies. Abandoning these natural self-

---

[3]"FTC Official Calls Consumer Protection an Economic Proposition," A4.

[4]Adam Smith, *The Theory of Moral Sentiments* (Indianapolis: Liberty Fund, Inc., 1976), p. 359. Quoted with permission of the Liberty Fund, Inc.

[5]M.F. Cohen and George J. Stigler, *Can Regulatory Agencies Protect Consumers?* (Washington, D.C.: American Enterprise institute, 1971), p. 17.

[6]*Walden and Other Writings*, Brooks Atkinson, Ed. (New York: Modern Library, 1950), p. 66.

defenses in the (mistaken) belief that one is adequately protected by an ever diligent regulatory agency may only expose the consumer to additional risk.

That market information for informed consumer decision making may be misleading is undeniable. The potential profitability of such opportunistic behavior convinces us of this. However, that the market is also an extremely efficient information-processing system which has numerous self-policing mechanisms against fraudulent behavior seems to be less appreciated than the economics of "fly-by-night" business.

The vast majority of firms do not provide misleading or fraudulent information to consumers because it is not in their self-interests to do so. Modern industries with large capital investments in specialized assets are profitable only if they retain consumers' patronage over the many years needed to amortize these investments. Such patronage would be severely jeopardized by fraudulent behavior. As Woodrow Eckard puts it: "In effect, manufacturers guarantee the quality of their products by offering the value of their assets as 'hostage' to consumers who can punish opportunistic behavior by simply withholding future purchases."[7] Thus, the large investments required to produce efficiently in today's economy enhance consumers' control of business by making exit even more costly to the firm.

The competitive market also responds to consumer information and safety needs in numerous ways. For example, department stores continuously monitor the quality of a broad range of products and assure customers of a certain level of product quality. Sears' reputation for quality tools, for example, efficiently provides consumers with a vast quantity of quality and performance information. That such companies would jeopardize their good will for short-run opportunistic gains is extremely doubtful: Not because of their social responsiveness nor concern for consumer welfare, but because of their concern for their own self-interest, a concern we can be assured will not be neglected. The important point is that private markets respond to consumer demands for accurate information and safe products the same as they respond to consumer demands for other goods and services because providing consumers with what they want is profitable, a point emphasized by Otis Smith in the first reading.

In this reading, Otis Smith integrates the corporate governance concerns in the previous chapter with fundamental business-consumer issues. This is essential because of the complementarity between stockholder and consumer controls over business decisions. He suggests that proponents of corporate governance do not really want to restore stockholder control, but rather want to make corporations accountable to their constituencies—consumers, employees, environmentalists, and the general public. Smith argues, however, that the corporation is already accountable to consumers, which is to say they are accountable to the general public except in those circumstances where con-

[7]E. Woodrow Eckard, Jr., "The Free Market Incentive: Self Interest vs. Greed," *Business Economics* (September 1980), p. 34.

sumer interests diverge from the public interest (e.g., in the case of harmful third-party effects).

Further, he explains that accountability to consumers ensures that management is acting in the best interests of stockholders whose wealth is maximized only by meeting consumer demands. Smith writes: "In general, to the degree that a company makes money, it is acting in accordance with the popular mandate; to the degree that a company loses money, its managers have failed in their perception of the popular will." He argues that the attempt to make a profit is really an attempt to secure a popular mandate—"the marketplace is an instrument of popular sovereignty."

Picking up on the criticisms of consumer sovereignty, Smith suggests: "The corporate critics' quarrel here is not really with managers' decisions, but with customers' choices." He goes on: "The real issue may not be whether corporate managers are 'unresponsive' to the public; it may be whether they are entirely too responsive to the public, which persists in wanting things that some social critics disapprove." Smith uses a plant-closing decision to illustrate. A plant-closing decision is criticized because of the adverse effects on the local community. But a socially responsive decision not to close the plant would impose costs on another community where the plant would be reopened, and on the general public to the extent that an inefficient plant continued producing products at higher than minimum costs. As Smith notes: "The imposition of these costs on society, through inaction, could be said to involve the exercise of 'power' too." Echoing Milton Friedman's arguments against social responsibility in Chapter 6, deciding whether to close a plant on the basis of social concerns would represent an exercise of uncontrolled, discretionary power far greater than any market-driven decision. Do we really want businessmen making such socially responsive (political) decisions? Again, as Friedman asks, on what criteria are businessmen to decide which city is to benefit and which is to bear the cost?

Robert Reich argues that consumer protection has engulfed business and government in endless controversy, distracting attention in the U.S. from the increasing encroachment of international competitors. As a result, imports are taking larger and larger shares of U.S. markets because of the superior quality of their products. Or, in the words of Otis Smith, imports are doing a better job of serving the popular will in the U.S.

Reich argues that other countries use consumer protection to improve product quality and international competitive position while we fight over consumer protection in the U.S. He believes that business and government should work together to provide consumers with the quality products they want. But, as Otis Smith suggests, do all corporate critics in the U.S. desire to give consumers what they want? For example, proposed plant-closing legislation is clearly not in response to consumers' demands. In fact, it is an attempt to rebuff completely consumers' demands.

One also has to wonder why business has to be regulated to make products which consumers want, unless government can read consumer demands more accurately than business. Reich illustrates government's positive contributions to meeting consumer demands with the motor vehicle fuel economy standards resisted by U.S. auto manufacturers while fuel-efficient imports captured larger shares of the U.S. market in 1980. But, if consumers wanted greater fuel economy, why would domestic auto manufacturers not provide such vehicles as quickly as possible? There is great uncertainty about just what consumers do want in the motor vehicle industry. The Iranian oil crisis in 1979 and subsequent tripling of gasoline prices created a large sudden shift in demand for small vehicles with good fuel economy. But, three years later, domestic auto manufacturers might fail to meet government fuel economy standards because of consumer demands for large cars following the stabilization of gas prices. If that occurred, the domestic auto makers would face substantial government fines, *for meeting consumer demands.* Clearly, the intent of the fuel economy legislation was never to help manufacturers meet consumer demands or to improve their international competitive position. The intent was just the opposite. The government was trying to prevent the auto manufacturers from meeting consumer demands for large vehicles stimulated by U.S. energy policies which artificially held U.S. gasoline prices below world levels. The Iranian oil crisis only temporarily made government fuel economy regulations consistent with market demands.

Professor Thorelli analyzes consumers' four basic "rights": right to choose; right to be informed; right to be heard; and right to be safe. Of these, the right to choose freely is the most fundamental. As Thorelli illustrates with automobile seat belt usage, there are conflicts and necessary trade-offs among these rights. Thorelli also stresses that consumers have responsibilities as well as rights.

Thorelli believes that consumer protection policies should rely primarily on education and information, rather than protection, allowing consumers to choose the trade-offs among their four rights. He concludes: "Informed consumers are the protected consumers. Not only that: they are the liberated consumers." However, he notes that the Consumer Product Safety Commission exhibits a strong bias against the fundamental right of free choice which he attributes to the agency's political biases for collective over individual choice.

Thorelli argues that consumers need higher-quality information rather than simply greater quantities of information since information overload can be as much a problem for informed decision making as inadequate information. In this regard, the market's information—processing economies are a considerable aid to rational consumer choice.

THE CONSUMER'S ROLE
IN CORPORATE GOVERNANCE
Otis M. Smith

It is with a great deal of pleasure and anticipation that I join you in discussing corporate governance within the context of the larger subject, the ethics of corporate conduct. This is not only a topic for our time; it is a topic, I believe, for all times.

I hope to make some small contribution to these sessions by expressing a somewhat unconventional view of corporate governance. Of the last 21 years of my professional life, about half was spent in government and the other half in a business setting and, therefore, I have learned to look at business from a government viewpoint and then to see government from the business point of view. These tend to be very different views, indeed, but I hope that public assemblies like this one will help bring them closer together.

I think we must recognize at the outset that just as the issue of corporate governance is only a part of the overall subject of the ethics of corporate conduct, so matters of business ethics are only a part of the things we have to talk about when we consider the subject of corporate governance. Undoubtedly, much of the current interest in corporate governance has been stimulated by recently reported business scandals, involving ethical transgressions like bribes and political slush funds. But the issues run much deeper than that, and, in my opinion, corporate governance would be a lively subject of debate today even if all business managers were models of probity.

This didn't used to be so. I think it is fair to say that up to now the main thrust of the law relating to the governance of corporations has been directed toward the matter of keeping corporate managers honest in their dealings with investors. Various reports are required so that investors can find out how their companies are using their money and how the enterprise is faring. Disclosure requirements are imposed on those who seek to attract new investors. Managers are forbidden to manipulate stock prices or use their corporate position to further their own advantage at the expense of investors.

Otis M. Smith, "The Consumer's Role in Corporate Governance." Address before the National Capital Assembly at The Catholic University of America, Washington, D.C., November 10, 1977. Reprinted with permission.

A GROWING PUBLIC CONCERN

This body of law, however, has had an impact far beyond the investment community. Because so much of it involves open disclosure, it has not only produced businessmen who are more sensitive to public opinion, but it has also produced a public that is better informed and more concerned about business conduct. And we are beginning to see legal rules that seem to have been prompted more by the perceived concerns of the general public than by the more narrow interests of investors. One familiar example is the recent expansion of the materiality rule by the SEC to require disclosure of such things as questionable payments abroad. The test of materiality here is not directly related to the bottom line on the balance sheet. Materiality reporting is now designed to give outside directors, stockholders and, presumably, the general public a better view of the quality of corporate management.

It is significant that the impetus for such changes does not appear to come from the stockholders who have, after all, the most to lose, but from others who purport to act for them. I do not detect any widespread feeling that investors want additional protection from corporate managers. I will go further and say that there does not seem to be any widespread demand for investors to participate personally on a broader scale in the management of corporations. (Indeed, most dissident stockholder proposals garner a very small percentage of votes, something less than five percent.) One view is that the basic reason why stockholders invest in public enterprises, rather than in businesses of their own, is because they want other people to manage their savings for them while they occupy themselves in other activities.

THE REAL ISSUE IS POWER

I submit that the real corporate governance issue today is not so much one of honesty or of ethics, but of *power*. A lot of people seem to believe that even scrupulously honest corporate managers have too much of it. A. A. Sommer, Jr., an SEC Commissioner, summarized this viewpoint well at a recent conference on Federal and state laws regulating corporate management:

> . . . the real name for what has been feared has been power: the power of certain people to do certain undesirable things to other people . . . Corporations as such have no power; the people who control them—whatever that means—have the power to decide whether a plant will be closed, thus impoverishing a community; to decide to curtail production, thereby adding massively, in some instances, to the rolls of the unemployed, thus creating a problem for the political bodies; to blunder and thereby harm the interests of those depending upon the prosperity of the enterprise for jobs, dividends, security . . .

The debate over governance, accordingly, is no longer confined to lawyers practicing in the corporate and securities area. It has engaged the attention of environmentalists, consumerists, and also people interested in the enforcement of the antitrust laws. For example, a leading government official recently stated publicly that the antitrust laws are concerned with "centralization of wealth and economic and political power in the hands of an unelected and an unaccountable few," by which he means corporate managers. This, interestingly enough, is how many business people would describe some of the appointed government regulators.

As you all know, this broader attention to the issues of corporate governance has led to a variety of proposals designed to circumscribe further the actions of corporate managers. There are proposals for the Federal chartering of corporations which would not only regulate the internal governance of corporations, but also limit severely the permissible areas of corporate endeavor in the outside world. There are proposals for so-called "public interest directors" or for directors who, whether nominally stockholders or not, are openly designated as representatives of political constituencies other than stockholders, such as employees and customers. There are proposals to break up large corporations into smaller ones so that individual corporate actions will have a narrower impact. The implicit objective of all these proposals is not the enforcement of management's fidelity to investors' interests, but rather the control of management in aid of other interests which are believed to be conflicting.

THE DEMAND FOR ACCOUNTABILITY

Let me try to focus the issue even more narrowly. The perceived problem is not that a relatively small group of people actually make and execute big decisions. Nobody really proposes that corporations be run like town meetings. A smaller group has to make the actual determination whether to bring a new product to market or whether to locate a new plant in Jackson, Michigan, or Jackson, Mississippi. The issue is the extent to which the decisionmakers are accountable and the constituency to which they are properly accountable. In political terms, whose votes should they be counting and by what mechanism should these votes be cast and tallied?

To narrow the issue still further, it is important to remember that the discretion of corporate managers is limited, in constantly increasing measure, by public regulation. On many issues, managers cannot begin to count "votes" at all. The kinds of products which a company sells may be regulated in close detail by safety or environmental rules; the sources or prices of its supplies may be strongly affected by labor laws or by government licenses; its communications to consumers must satisfy various disclosure requirements; and its production processes must be in accord with environmental safety and health regulations. These specific rules, established at both the national and the local level, are continually being expanded. It is accurate to say that the business entity is the most regulated entity in our society.

The demonstrated capability of public regulators to make rules that deal directly and indirectly with a wide range of issues should at least raise a question about the necessity for further broad changes in the way that corporations are governed internally. Moreover, I submit that the "public" influence over corporate decisions extends far beyond those areas that are regulated by government.

THE CONSUMER AS REGULATOR

The basic thought that I would like to leave with you today is that we simply haven't paid enough attention to our natural "regulator," the consumer of the products and services that corporations produce—and reference to consumers is just another way of talking about the public at large. Most people seem willing to concede that consumers ultimately determine whether a given enterprise will live or die, but they tend to discount the day-to-day control that consumers exercise over the conduct of business affairs. They forget that the overriding consideration in the corporate boardroom must be what the public wants and needs, and how best to supply it.

We frequently hear, for example, that corportions ignore the "real" consumer preference for simple and utilitarian products, and obstinately persist in making more expensive products, with unnecessary frills, simply because they are "more profitable." By whose standards are the added-cost features unnecessary? If consumers didn't consider the more expensive products relatively more valuable than simpler ones that are cheaper to produce, they would choose the cheaper ones. The corporate critic's quarrel here is not really with managers' decisions, but with customers' choices.

The same thing is true on the supply side. Just as product decisions are determined by what consumers demand, so procurement decisions are determined by what the suppliers of goods and services (including labor) can demand for their contribution. Again, a critic who disagrees with a management decision to shift a source of supply may really be quarreling with the value that the marketplace has determined for the things the corporation buys.

Management's challenge is to maximize the difference in the value of a corporation's inputs and its outputs. *The profit which a company makes represents nothing more than the difference between the value which the public places on the products that company sells and the value which the public places on the resources which are consumed in bringing those products to market.* Think about that.

The public may be deceived about the value of products, of course, if management misrepresents them—but there are specific laws to deal with that problem and, even in the absence of laws, no company can prosper for long by deceiving its customers. The price which management pays for the resources consumed may be distorted. But, these also are problems which can be addressed specifically—for example, by repealing laws which protect local monopoly over supplies or by passing laws which recognize that some supposedly "free" resources (like clean air and water) are not really free at all.

PEOPLE "VOTE" IN THE MARKETPLACE

But these possible distortions, which can be dealt with as necessary, do not alter the fact that the marketplace is an instrument of popular sovereignty. The public exercises its sovereignty by casting ballots in the form of dollars and its votes are tallied in the financial results of an enterprise. In general, *to the degree that a company makes money, it is acting in accordance with the popular mandate;* to the degree that a company loses money, its managers have failed in their perception of the popular will.

People who argue for the inclusion of supposedly more "democratic" procedures in the corporate decision-making process forget that the attempt to make a profit is really an attempt to secure a popular mandate. In fact, the market mandate is more directly attuned to popular will than the formal political process. The chairman of my company recently expressed the idea as follows:

> "The free-market system is the most responsive and finely tuned instrument of popular sovereignty that has ever been devised. Government is inherently clumsier and less flexible. In the political system a citizen must delegate his sovereignty first to elected officials and these officials in turn delegate it to the actual administrators or 'planners.' A citizen can express his displeasure with their decisions, from which he is at least twice removed, only periodically in elections and then his particular disagreement may be obscured in a host of other issues embodied in the broad platforms on which candidates run.
>
> "In the market, however, the citizen in effect participates directly in a continuing referendum on every single item in a finely detailed platform. Moreover, unlike the political system, 'voters' with different ideas can each win. The market will therefore respond to individual desires far more accurately and promptly than government planners can ever do . . . ."

The attempt of corporate management to succeed in the continuing referendum of the marketplace is, of course, entirely consistent with the interests of the corporation's stockholders, because success or failure is measured in terms of profitability. And, incidentally, the ability of stockholders to hold management directly accountable for success or failure has been much underrated. Just because proxy contests or public ousters of executives are relatively rare does not mean that executives can afford to be inattentive to stockholders' concerns. In fact, as indicated earlier, the responsiveness of management to stockholders or investors is not the real issue anyway. The issue that has been raised is whether managers, under the present method of corporate governance, are responsive to a larger public—and I submit that they are.

THE BASIS OF OUR SYSTEM

The idea that the pursuit of private profit is in the larger public interest, once taken for granted, seems shocking to some today. But, that idea happens to be the first principle of a free-market system. If we believe in a free-market system (and very few people are willing to stand up and say otherwise), we must recognize that it will only function if corporate managers are basically motivated by the desire to maximize gain, through the efficient production of the things most desired by consumers. The idea may seem less upsetting if we remember that this basic profit motivation is shared by all of us in differing forms. You too are a profit-maximizer when you seek out the best bargains for your purchasing dollar or when you seek out the best employment opportunity in which to utilize your skills.

It might be helpful to examine this concept of popular sovereignty in the context of a hard case: one that is frequently used as an example. Company managers must decide whether or not to transfer production from existing facilities to facilities in another area where costs are lower, because of different wage rates, transportation costs, or some other factor. People tend to concentrate on the distress which will be felt if a transfer is made and existing employees lose their jobs. They argue that it is wrong for corporate managers to have such "power" over the lives of others. For some reason, people don't focus on the lost opportunities for potential employees in the lower-cost area and the broad "tax" which will ultimately be borne by consumers if enterprises are not free, indeed compelled, to seek out lower-cost alternatives. The imposition of these costs on society, through inaction, could be said to involve the exercise of "power" too.

But someone has to make a decision on whether to move or not to move, or whether to build a new plant or not, or whether to bring out a new product or not. Our entire free-market economy is premised on the idea that these decisions are best made on the basis of market forces, which are the ultimate reflection of the public's choices. Corporate managers may appear to make the decisions, but their mandate comes from the public which makes the market.

POLITICS IS ALSO A MARKET FACT

Public policy, of course, may dictate that measures be imposed through the external political process which are designed to mitigate the shock of sudden adjustments in the free-market system. Moreover, a prudent corporate management may well anticipate possible political consequences and itself take steps internally to alleviate hardships caused by the iron discipline of the market. Some might call this "corporate social responsibility"; but you can also think of it as profit-maximizing over a long time-frame. The costs imposed through political action by an aroused public are real costs, and managers are derelict in their responsibilities if they do not take these possibilities into account. General public opinion, which can be translated into specific laws and regulations, is a most important market fact too.

Since political regulation is now more pervasive than ever before, it is essential that corporate management be alert to the larger movements in society. What is really needed is an early-warning system, and different companies try to meet this need in different ways. In many companies, for example, the majority of the directors are "outsiders," men and women not currently a part of corporate management. They may be deliberately selected from diverse backgrounds and occupations. Committees with particular responsibility for public policy issues or internal audits of the management often are composed entirely of outside directors.

NO "SPECIAL-INTEREST" DIRECTORS

The important thing to remember, however, is that these outside directors are there to bring a broader vision to the decision-making process—a more accurate prediction of the election returns, if you will. They are not representatives of particular constituencies, specially licensed to ignore the ballots which will ultimately be cast in the marketplace and tallied in the financial results. Indeed, the inclusion of special-interest representatives on boards would not make them more responsive to the public at large; it would make them less so.

Even the inclusion of directors designated as "public representatives" by a government agency would tend to make boards less responsive to the general public, because these representatives would also presumably not be bound by the results of the market referendum. This observation may come as a surprise to some, but I don't think it will really surprise those who are actively seeking to restructure corporate boards. There are many social critics who believe that, left to their own devices, people will make choices that are wasteful, shortsighted, and dangerous, and that it is a legitimate function of government to limit their freedom to choose unwisely.

My purpose here is not to argue whether people should or should not be protected against themselves. My purpose is to ask for greater candor in the corporate governance debate. The real issue may not be whether corporate managers are "unresponsive" to the public; it may be whether they are entirely too responsive to the public, which persists in wanting things that some social critics disapprove.

THE IMPORTANCE OF ETHICS

How, you might ask, does this discussion of the marketplace as a sovereign instrument involve the subject of corporate ethics with which the talk began? The answer is that we have been talking about ethics all along. The "invisible hand" of Adam Smith does not thrive in a moral vacuum; the market functions best to the extent that people are ethical and can trust one another. The point can perhaps be best illustrated by the operation of securities or commodity exchanges, where commitments for millions are made on the basis of a word or a signal. If general trust, reinforced by a rigid code of ethics, did not exist and if parties had to draw up and sign formal legal contracts every time they made a trade, these markets simply could not function. Other examples may not be quite so obvious, but the principle is universal.

The importance of business ethics to a free-market system was recently well summarized by Professor Harold Johnson in an excerpt published by *The Wall Street Journal*. Commenting on Adam Smith's view of business ethics, Professor Johnson wrote:

> "Smith would have found very congenial the modern proposition that a viable market system requires a vital ethical-moral context in which to thrive. In contemporary language, fraud, bribery, deceit and dishonesty so increase already high levels of uncertainty in the economic world that many participants opt out of trade and commerce. The benefits gained from exchange are swamped out by excessive policing and transaction costs—if it really is a dog-eat-dog world.
>
> "If fear exists that other participants by deception know more than you do about the situation and will cheat you at every turn, then you don't play the game. A retrenchment to bare-bones levels of trade and exchange takes place—or perhaps more realistically given the tenor of 20th-Century politics—radical changes in the system are sought.
>
> "For Smith, participants in the market game who seek to maximize gains are policed and directed *both* by the social forces of competition and of ethics to a general advance in human welfare."

There are, of course, some who have prospered in the "market game" by cheating, but dishonesty in the "government game" is not unknown either. The bad judgments of businessmen in misreading the market have bankrupted many companies; the bad judgments of governments who can ignore the market entirely have bankrupted entire industries and nations.

There are imperfections in all systems of governance because they depend upon human beings, who are sometimes frail and always fallible. We cannot perfect human beings by laws or by institutions, but we can try to contain the harm which human weaknesses will cause. We therefore look for the means of insuring accountability of individuals to the larger society; we seek to devise workable instruments of popular sovereignty. The marketplace is nothing to be ashamed of and we should not forget that it is a powerful instrument for the implementation of popular control over corporations.,

BUSINESS CAN PROFIT
FROM CONSUMER PROTECTION
Robert B. Reich

We stand on the brink of a fundamental change in the relationship of business and government for consumer protection. The last dozen years have been punctuated by acrimony and confrontation. Government agencies born or reborn in the flush of consumerism found enough flagrant examples of deceptive advertising, unscrupulous marketing, unsafe or defective products, unfulfilled warranties, and inadequate servicing to justify zealous regulation and litigation. Businesses whose autonomy was suddenly threatened found enough evidence of regulatory incompetence or naiveté to fuel their self-righteous resistance.

The battle lines were drawn. There was trench warfare, with regulations fought out for years within highly formal proceedings, before hearing officers, commissioners, administrators, and appeals courts; in rehearings, remands, subpoena challenges, enforcement proceedings, recall orders, endless consent negotiations; in congressional lobbying, log rolling, grassroots organizing, quiet threats to withhold campaign contributions, heated debates within committees, eleventh-hour compromises, and at least two days when one regulatory agency had to close itself down.

We have created a billion-dollar industry comprised of lawyers, lobbyists, and Washington representatives, who feed off the battle. The longer, more arduous, and more dramatic the confrontation, the richer this industry becomes. Hostility breeds hostility, until the combat industry provides the sole means through which business and government communicate with each other.

All this would be merely sad rather than tragic had it not taken our attention away from a far more serious battle that we are losing. I speak of our battle for competitive survival in the world economy. In industry after industry, consumers in America and elsewhere are turning their backs on U.S. manufactured products in favor of foreign competitors: 27 percent of our automobiles are now manufactured abroad by non-U.S. companies, 30 percent of our sporting and athletic goods, 30 percent of microwave ovens, almost 100 percent of video cassettes. The list goes on and gets longer year by year: radial tires, home calculators, televisions, food processors, premium beer, stereo components, digital watches, pianos, outboard motors. And these particular consumer markets are among our fastest growing.

Why are we losing this battle? Some lay blame on cheap foreign labor or on "dumping" at prices below those prevailing in home markets. But foreign

Robert B. Reich, "Business Can Profit from Consumer Protection." Reprinted by permission from the *Business and Society Review*, Fall 1980, number 35, 60–63. Copyright © 1980, Warren, Gorham & Lamont Inc., 210 South Street, Boston, Massachusetts. All rights reserved.

wage rates are rapidly catching up with our own; Japan's labor costs are now on par with ours. And many of these imports sell here at prices comparable to or in excess of American-made counterparts. By the mid-1970s Japanese and West German autos had lost any price advantage over their American-made competitors. French-made radial tires are as expensive as those produced here.

WHAT TO BLAME?

Some lay blame on regulation. But imports must meet the same standards as American products in order to be sold here. And in any event, health, safety, and environmental regulation are as strict—if not stricter—in Japan and West Europe as they are in the United States.

Some blame foreign trade barriers for allegedly making it more difficult for U.S. manufacturers to gain access to world markets. But foreign trade barriers have been reduced rapidly since the late 1960s.

Part of the problem is our failure to invest in future productivity. Japan's personal savings rate has been averaging about 20 percent a year while our own has fallen to less than 4 percent. Last year, Japan's per capita investment in new plant and equipment was twice our own. Moreover, the proportion of gross national product going into research and development has been rising rapidly in Japan but falling in the United States.

But another part of our problem, perhaps more serious over the long term, doesn't show up in national accounts and can't be measured in terms of savings and investment. That problem is increasing consumer dissatisfaction with our products. We are losing the battle for competitive survival, in part, because too many of our products are less reliable, less durable, and less efficient than the imports. Too many of our products are poorly designed, badly assembled, carelessly shipped. Too many of our products provide inadequate instructions, warnings, or disclaimers. Too many of our products fall apart too soon, need inordinate repair, are too expensive to use and maintain.

While American business has been worried about price competition from abroad, the real battle has become one of competitive quality. While American business and government have been fighting tooth and nail over consumer protection, other nations have been using consumer protection to improve industry performance and to enhance national reputation for commercial quality.

"Made in Japan" used to mean "cheap imitation." Then the Japanese Government established a program of rigorous quality standards and inspection, awarding a Japanese Industrial Seal only to products that made the grade. By the mid-1970s, "Made in Japan" had become a symbol of painstaking quality. The failure rates of Japanese products are now a fraction of the rates of their American competitors. Some advertisers now boast that their products are imported from Japan.

Similarly, Sweden's Board for Consumer Policies has established rigorous standards for product grading, along with detailed product information for prospective purchasers—features that have earned Sweden a reputation for quality automobiles, vacuum cleaners, and hand tools. The French regulatory system ensures consumers the world over that when they purchase a French wine they will receive the quality they expect, and this assurance has increased world demand for the product. And West Germany has pioneered exacting standards for product performance and consumer information, thereby boosting its world sales of cameras, furniture, and household appliances.

Consumer protection in each of these countries has improved competitive position because consumer protection is part of a national marketing strategy. Government and business, working together, have identified markets in which they have a competitive advantage and devised strategies to penetrate and capture those markets by giving consumers what they want. Government and business, working together, have ensured product quality and provided reliable product information.

ECONOMIC WAR

While American business and government have been at war with one another over consumer protection, foreign businesses and governments have been quietly waging economic war on us, and they are winning. We have deluded ourselves into playing a zero-sum game, refereed by federal judges, when the real game is in the marketplace, refereed by millions of consumers.

Of course, there are unscrupulous sellers whose antics harm the reputations of all others. Government should come down hard on them. Responsible businesses have a strong interest in working with government to identify these bad apples before the rot spreads. And there will continue to be product hazards and defects that are difficult for consumers to learn about or evaluate until it's too late. Responsible businesses have a duty to alert consumers and the government to such problems, as soon as there is reason to believe that they exist, and to develop quick means of remedying them. Failure to sound the alarm in these circumstances will be among the most serious regulatory offenses of the future.

No matter what happens in litigation, American business cannot stall the inexorable march of consumers away from products that disappoint them. Products that are unsafe, defective, or shoddy, that fail to live up to their advertising claims, or that neglect to disclose important information to their purchasers, often will lose the battle of the marketplace regardless of the outcome of protracted government litigation.

A few months ago the U.S. Government levied a fine—the largest ever

assessed under the Motor Vehicle Safety Act—against a major U.S. tire manufacturer for its failure to voluntarily recall tires that it knew did not meet federal
safety standards. Is it mere coincidence that while that manufacturer was failing to correct the problem, before the government even knew that the problem
existed, a foreign tire manufacturer captured a one-half-billion-dollar share of
the U.S. tire market?

Or consider the endless battle waged by American auto makers over the
government's auto fuel economy standards—only to have fuel-efficient imports
claim the allegiance of more and more cost-conscious consumers.

Or ponder a recent FTC order against a major auto maker in connection
with a particular design defect. The order requires the manufacturer to tell car
owners and dealers of the availability of plain-language technical service bul-
letins and to point out defects costing more than $125 to repair. The company's
executive vice-president predicts that the scheme will actually help sales, since
consumers will appreciate the information they're getting, and that the "repair
information service," as he calls it, will become an industry practice. How sad
that it required an FTC complaint and more than a year of pretrial litigation
to devise the scheme.

Or, finally, consider a recent study sponsored by the American Association of Advertising Agencies, showing that 80 percent of television viewers misunderstand commercials they see. Instead of worrying about the implications
of such data for effectively communicating product information to consumers,
the Association is touting the study as an important argument against correc-
tive advertising and similar regulatory orders.

In ways such as these, and in countless others, American business has engaged in regulatory battles while losing the competitive war. Equally self-de-
feating is the tendency of many businesses to regard consumer complaints as
a nuisance that wastes valuable corporate time. They leave to public relations
specialists in consumer service departments the job of placating the complain-
ers, hoping that the government doesn't get involved.

VALUABLE COMPLAINTS

The fact is that consumer complaints are one of the most important marketing
assets available. They can serve as early warning devices—signaling that brand
loyalty may be in jeopardy unless certain changes are made. Business should
actively solicit complaints, using them as part of marketing strategy, putting
toll-free telephone numbers on packages and labels, and instructing consumers
to call in immediately with any problems they have. There is no excuse for waiting until consumers go to the government to complain. The fact that the government receives complaints means that business isn't receiving valuable information, or isn't acting on it.

Both business and government must work together to identify consumer problems and their remedies before they become scandals. We must share information and ideas early on, before issues are defined and proposals take shape. Unrealistic regulatory goals, demanding product perfection without any risk, create uncertainty and promote endless litigation; goals that are inflexible, that rely on narrow legal precedent or unalterable formulae, make it difficult for business to react to rapidly changing market conditions.

Of course, the danger exists that a close, cooperative working relationship between business and government will lead to—or at least create the appearance of—regulatory "capture" by business. Not so many years ago public confidence in the ability of our regulatory agencies to protect the public interest was undermined by disclosures of secret deals, holiday weekends financed by regulated businesses, and seductive promises of future employment for regulatory commissioners. Indeed, much of the formal and legalistic apparatus with which we are now saddled is in direct response to these sorts of abuse.

However, the notion of a unitary, nonpartisan public good to which regulators aspire, as distinct from that which motivates the best managers and most enlightened marketers in American business, has only limited relevance to the realities of international competition. Surely the government must guard the public welfare to ensure that consumers are getting truthful and adequate product information, safe and efficient products, and the warranties they are promised. Yet if American business is to survive in an increasingly competitive world economy, these are precisely the goals that business must strive to attain.

What is good for business may or may not be good for consumers. But as our foreign competitors have learned all too well, what is good for consumers is bound to be good for business. Consumers are more concerned about product reliability and safety than ever before. Marketing strategies that focus on quality and performance, that elicit feedback from consumers and make fine-tuned corrections in products, that provide consumers with clear and useful information about product attributes, are much more likely to succeed in the 1980s.

Business and government are not inevitable adversaries over consumer protection. Our broad goals are the same. The public to which we are accountable—consumers, shareholders, taxpayers—is the same. Our national interest is the same. There will be tensions and conflicts over means toward these ends, and government would not be doing its job if it didn't maintain a firm check on isolated instances of business abuse. But we have neither the time nor the national resources to go on sniping at one another.

CONSUMER RIGHTS AND CONSUMER POLICY: SETTING THE STAGE

Hans B. Thorelli

Consumer policy is an integral part of economic policy; it is not just another social welfare policy. It is more private than public, much as the contrary impression remains prevalent. It includes any measure taken to implement consumer interests. Its delivery system comprises consumer education, consumer information and consumer protection.

Consumer interests are perhaps most readily identified with established or at least articulated consumer rights. Paradoxically, the most important consumer right is hardly ever mentioned. This is the "freedom to consume," a right that is greater than and antecedent to the four consumer rights enunciated almost two decades ago. Like any "special" interest, the consumer interest is a subset of the public interest. What is good for the consumer may not always be good for the country. Nevertheless, as it concerns everyone, the consumer interest is clearly a subset of grand importance. And to those of us who believe that inextricable links exist between political democracy and free markets, the consumer interest is a matter of paramount concern.

To define "the consumer interest" in specific situations tends to be a task fraught with ambiguity. The fractionalization of the consumer interest begins right in the marketplace. Preferences with regard to style, quality and price, as well as the total bundle of products desired, vary greatly among consumers of different income, age and educational groups, and frequently even within these groups. The open market is the equilibrating mechanism among all these consumer "interests." Beyond the marketplace, some consumers are ecologically oriented in the process of consumption and the disposal of refuse while others are not. Indeed, it is precisely because our role as consumers is such an all-pervasive aspect of life that consumer interests are so differentiated. Consumerism as an ongoing social and political force may well grow in importance as the phenomena in which it originated are likely to manifest themselves even more dramatically. The complexity of the marketplace due to the proliferation, rapidity of change and technical intricacy of market offerings increases in parallel with a widening functional distance between producer and consumer, coupled with a revolution in consumer aspirations.

Consumer policy is in part a subset of public policy and in part a subset of private policy. Individual citizens have their own "consumer policies" as they pursue their interests in the marketplace. Of greater interest here, however, are the policies affecting collective consumer interests. Makers of con-

Hans B. Thorelli, "Consumer Rights and Consumer Policy: Setting the Stage," *Journal of Contemporary Business*, 7, no. 4 (1979), 3–15. Reprinted with permission (excluding pp. 8–13).

sumer policy in this broader sense include consumer organizations, other citizen groups, business, educational institutions, the mass media, and, of course, governments.

CONSUMER POLICY: INFORMATION, EDUCATION AND PROTECTION

In a general sense, consumer information comprises all data about individual markets and offerings. It is oriented to specific buying decisions. By contrast, consumer education may be thought of as "consumer civics." It provides the knowledge foundation necessary to develop citizens into intelligent consumers, or at least to make their self-development into intelligent consumers possible. Thus consumer education extends all the way from conveying an understanding of how the market economy operates in the consumer decision making process to such pragmatic matters as the properties of different textile fibers and dietary concerns. Consumer protection includes measures taken by consumer groups, government agencies, and businesses to safeguard consumer rights. Consumer protection ranges from antitrust policy to control restrictive or deceptive practices and the handling of consumer complaints to standards and other rules and regulations to maintain consumer health and safety.

Clearly, the distinctions between consumer information, education and protection are not hard and fast. For instance, the same information may have multiple uses. Americans will find the phrase "The Surgeon General has determined that cigarette smoking is dangerous to your health" on every cigarette package. That the message is intended for consumer protection is evident. But it could also be viewed as educational. And it could also be regarded as consumer information about any single brand you might happen to select. About the border area between consumer education and information, we may say that the more "generic" the data in terms of product or consumer characteristics, the more likely it is that consumer education is the appropriate term. The more specifically data are related to individual offerings (brands) or to the needs of individual consumers, the more appropriate it is to speak of consumer information.

RIGHTS, RESPONSIBILITIES, POLICIES AND POLICYMAKERS

The nature and scope of consumer policy can be understood most readily by viewing it in the context of consumer rights and responsibilities. The graphic representation in the diagram will serve as a point of reference. (See Figure 3-1.) The matrix array aspects of policy are in the left-hand columns. Private and

CONSUMER POLICY	CONSUMER RIGHTS			
	1. CHOOSE FREELY	2. BE INFORMED	3. BE HEARD	4. BE SAFE
A. EDUCATION	decision-making budgeting; nature of market economy, rights and responsibilities	generic product and materials data, information sources	how to assert consumer rights	importance of health and safety, user manuals and training
B. INFORMATION	buying criteria buying advice	models and brands data, independent consumer info programs	market research, two-way market dialogue	safety certification, care and maintenance data
C. PROTECTION	maintain open markets, antitrust; stop hi-pressure and deceptive tactics	truly informative advertising, product claims substantiation	complaints handling machinery	minimize health and accident risks
	CHOOSE WISELY	KEEP INFORMED	SOUND OFF	SAFETY RISK
	CONSUMER RESPONSIBILITIES			

A third dimension of the matrix would show the makers of consumer policy. These policy-makers include consumer organizations, other citizen groups, government, educational institutions and the mass media.

FIGURE 3–1   Consumer Policy and Consumer Rights and Responsibilities

public policymakers would be another logical dimension if three dimensional diagrams were possible. In our typology of consumer policy we noted that the distinctions between education, information and protection are not hard and fast. The matrix makes two vital points:

> the enforcement of literally every consumer right logically depends on all three types of consumer policy: education, information and protection.
> for every consumer right there is a corresponding consumer responsibility.

The lesson here is simple and crucial: no matter how aggressively we may use consumer policy, it will not in itself suffice to enforce consumer rights. In the end consumer rights will exist only if at least some consumers really exercise some of their rights and responsibilities at least some of the time.

Positive and Negative Rights and Responsibilities

Rights and responsibilities are inherently two-faced. To the positive right to choose between alternatives (including having access to suppliers of the brands in question) corresponds the negative right not to have choice imposed. This could occur through some central planning authority, or by overly well-meaning consumer "protectionists." To the right to be informed corresponds the right not to be deceived. To the right to be heard corresponds the right to privacy. To the right to safety corresponds the right to take some safety risks. Some example of such risks would be smoking cigarettes or driving without a safety belt. This should be a right at least as long as we are aware of the risks and are respecting the rights of other consumers.

Consumer responsibilities present us with an analogous situation. The positive imperative to choose wisely is negated by our freedom to choose what we know is wrong for us, or to spend our money foolishly. To the positive duty to keep informed corresponds the "negative" phenomenon of impulse buying, or of taking a deliberate chance at an auction. At least as yet no voice has been raised to prohibit these types of behavior. To the duty of sounding off corresponds the urge to keep quiet, to avoid the unpleasantness and the waste of time involved in asserting our rights. And instead of battling for safety first at all times, some of us at least occasionally will put performance or, indeed, even fun above safety. Or we may simply neglect maintenance, which in and of itself may be enough to bring safety hazards. The point is, we cannot expect most consumers to be vigilantes of the marketplace most of the time.

It may be observed that most of us have quite positive—often adamant— feelings about what here is loosely termed the negative rights and responsibilities of consumers. Indeed, they all seem to represent widely embraced Western ideals. For the enforcement of positive consumer responsibilities society relies almost exclusively on voluntarism among consumers themselves. On the other hand, the positive consumer rights, while perhaps evident in theory, seemingly need to be constantly reasserted to stay alive. Even though the reassertion of these consumer rights is logically the prime responsibility of consumers, governments and other groups are having to add their weight. The market economy may create the potential for the realization of positive consumer rights, but in a complex society there is no automatic way for them to be realized.

Consumer Policy Measures

The cells in the diagram give some examples of consumer policy measures. There is nothing sacred about the arrangement; in several instances it is a matter of taste and emphasis rather than principle. This is almost inevitable, given the overlaps between education, information and protection, as well as between the several consumer rights. The right half of the matrix is self-explanatory. We shall comment on some of the rights and responsibilities in the left half.

The effective implementation of the right to choose freely assumes a mature consumer. This is a consumer who through a process of formal or informal education has acquired some degree of understanding of personal and household decision making and budgeting and who has developed a sense of judgment in making buying decisions. As indicated by cell (A) they will also have some insight into the nature of the market economy and an attendant awareness of consumer rights and responsibilities. Their chances of making use of freedom to choose wisely will be enhanced if they are also aware of how needs will change over the life cycle and of such basic notions as cost-benefit analysis, discounted cash flow, the economics of information and the value of time.

To make a choice on any basis other than pure whim or impulse, consumers have to articulate (at least to themselves) what major criteria in buying the product really are. They need information inputs (B1) to help define what their requirements in the product should be, given their own set of values and circumstances.

Proceeding to the right to be informed, we observe the need for generic product and materials information as a logical prelude to the choice among models and brands. This type of information in our conceptual scheme falls under the heading of education (A2). Some examples of this type of information would be (what will a tape recorder do that a record player will not; what is the difference between nylon and cotton in shirts?) The furnishing of data about models and brands is the purpose of information policies implementing the right to be informed, as indicated by cell B2.

There is a broadly felt need in Western countries to safeguard the integrity of product information. In several countries there is mounting pressure—within industry as well as without—toward more informative advertising (C2). We note that the Federal Trade Commission is a pioneer exponent of the view that advertisers should be prepared to substantiate specific claims made for their products, or to retract false or misleading claims.

Policymakers

The third dimension of the diagram was left to the imagination of the reader. In a basic and pervasive sense individual buyers making the myriad day-to-day decisions in the marketplace are the crucial makers of consumer policy. As long as we wish to retain a high degree of consumer sovereignty this must be so. As suggested earlier, however, our focus here is on organized efforts by the private and public policy making agencies indicated.

• • •

RALPH NADER AND THE CPSC:
COLLEAGUES IN SIN?

Consumer information as a policy is not popular with Ralph Nader or with the Consumer Product Safety Commission. During the first few years of the Commission the emphasis on outright regulatory measures and procedures has been striking. This was probably natural. In the interest of agency survival and growth the Commission had to make headlines. As Ralph Nader had already discovered, headlines call for heroics rather than education and information programs. At this time, however, one may well argue that the duty of CPSC to inform and educate consumers in the safe use of products is in some respects more important than the development of physical standards of product safety. One might say that its sins of omission are the sins of the Commission!

Neither Nader nor the CPSC appear to root their actions on a belief in the idea of the autonomous, self-reliant, self-actualizing individual, surely the very core of Western civilization. Their seeming interest in publicity for themselves rather than publicity in the interest of consumers raises serious questions concerning credibility. Credibility is hard to come by once lost, as the FDA discovered in the recent furor over saccharin. That episode might well have been avoided if the agency had relied on a strategy involving a mix of education, information and regulation rather than an outright ban.

In the safety regulation area, again illustrating the tradeoff possibilities, at a certain average level of consumer education and/or information-consciousness it should be reasonable in some instances to restore to consumers the right to decide what level of safety they prefer relative to economy and performance of product. In such cases some safety devices could simply be made optional. Given a comprehensive education-information program, the current controversy over elaborate lawnmower safety standards, for example, might be resolved in this manner.

CONSUMERS' LIBERATION

The prime object of consumer policy is to foster self-reliance and to implement consumer rights in an open market. The principal vehicles of consumers' liberation are education and information. There is also a role for protective measures of various kinds. But new protective measures should not be adopted lightly or without serious reflection on undersirable side effects that typically attend them. While some protective measures aim at keeping markets open, most constrict the area of consumer choice.

Consumers' lib calls for equality of opportunity in decision making—decision making in meeting individual and family needs that develop spontaneously or in pluralist interaction, and are satisfied in the same manner. The rationale of CI programs in simple. CI is an instrument to enrich the quality of life. It helps to free time and resources for other concerns than purely material ones. It helps save on material resources for society as a whole.

Informed consumers are the protected consumers. Not only that: they are the liberated consumers.

DISCUSSION QUESTIONS

1. Is the consumer king in modern society? Should the consumer be king in a political democracy?
2. Are criticisms of business decision making really criticisms of consumer choice?

3. Would the corporate governance proposals in the prior chapter make business more or less responsive to consumer demands?

4. What rights do consumers have? How do economic rights differ from political rights? Do consumer rights create costs and obligations for other social constituencies?

5. Does the individual consumer have the right to purchase risky products or engage in risky activities? What are the economic, moral, and political bases for government prohibition of risky products or activities?

6. In a recent discussion of the saccharin controversy, one author pondered: "We might now ask what it is about saccharin that distinguishes it from other, greater risk we leave to individual choice. Why, for example, do we find ourselves serenely contemplating a person's plan to climb a dangerous Himalayan peak at the same time that we propose making it illegal for her to buy a can of Tab?" (W. R. Havender, "Ruminations on a Rat—Saccharin and Human Risks," *Regulation* (March–April 1979), p. 23.)

   Is government consumer-protection policy rational, consistent, and reliable?

7. Justice Brandeis wrote: "Experience should teach us to be most on our guard to protect liberty when the government's purposes are beneficial. Men born to freedom are naturally alert to repel invasion of their liberty by evil-minded rulers. The greater dangers to liberty lurk in insidious encroachment by men of zeal, well-meaning but without understanding." [*Olmstead vs. United States*, 277 U.S. 479 (1928).]

   Why should consumers be wary of government protection? How could greater reliance upon government protection result in greater risks for consumers?

8. Robert Reich wrote in his reading: "Business and government are not inevitable adversaries over consumer protection. Our broad goals are the same. The public to which we are accountable—consumers, shareholders, taxpayers—is the same. Our national interest is the same."

   Are the consumer-protection goals of business and government the same? Are business and government accountable to the same public?

9. Does the market effectively respond to consumer demands for greater product quality, reliability, and safety the same as it responds to all other consumer demands?

10. Under what circumstances might the consumer's interest be inconsistent with the public interest?

ADDITIONAL READINGS

ANDERSEN, ALLEN, R., AND ARTHUR BEST, "Consumers Complain—Does Business Respond?" *Harvard Business Review* (July–August 1977), pp. 93–101.

BARKSDALE, HIRAM C., AND WILLIAM D. PERREAULT, JR., "Can Consumers Be Satisfied?" *MSU Business Topics* (Spring 1980), pp. 19–30.

BLOOM, PAUL N., AND STEVEN A. GREYSER, "The Maturing of Consumerism," *Harvard Business Review* (November–December 1981), pp. 130–39.

KEATING-EDH, BARBARA, "Consumer Legislation vs. Liberty," *Credit World*, 70, no. 5 (April–May 1982), 11–14.

McGUIRE, PATRICK E.,   "Consumerism Lives! . . .and Grows," *Across the Board* (January 1980), pp. 57–62.

MOLITOR, GRAHAM T. T.,   "Consumer Policy Issues: Global Trends for the 1980's," in *Advances in Consumer Research*, 8, 458–66, ed. Kent Monroe. Ann Arbor, Michigan: Association for Consumer Research, 1981.

WILDAVSKY, AARON,   "Richer Is Safer," *The Public Interest*, no. 60 (Summer 1980), 23–39.

CHAPTER 4
EMPLOYEE RELATIONSHIPS

Business-employee relationships are being critically reexamined at three funda-mental decision-making levels: on the plant floor (participatory management); in the corporate board room (industrial democracy); and at the national macro policy level (industrial policy). At the plant floor level, business-labor relations are changing in recognition of the need for greater worker participation in plant management decisions. Much of the impetus for greater employee involvement in workplace decisions comes from observations of Japan's success with worker involvement. These observations have led to a serious rethinking of "scientific management" which has provided the traditional foundations for business-labor relationships on the plant floor. The principles of scientific management treat labor as an extension of the machine. Like costly capital equipment, labor must be organized and operated efficiently in accordance with time and motion studies and sound engineering principles. There has been almost total neglect of labor's ability to contribute to the design, organization, and productivity of the work-place, and of the effects of the quality of worklife on employee productivity. It is now widely recognized that American labor is a very under utilized resource capable of making important contributions to improved productivity and prod-uct quality. The key to more productive business-labor relationships at the plant floor level is a greater sharing of business information and decision-making con-trol with labor.

At the macro policy level, new business-labor relationships are an essen-tial part of most industrial policy proposals which include a variety of joint, business-labor-government efforts to formulate coordinated national industrial policies for improving the allocation of the nation's resources. These proposals find more support among labor and academic groups than among business which fears the encroachment of greater political control over business decision making.

This chapter is concerned with business-labor relationships in the board room—with the fundamental issue of industrial democracy. The traditional market relationship between business and labor is institutionalized in the employment contract. The standard sales contract is recognized by the absence of authority relationships. The buyer and seller agree to exchange a specific product or service for a specified price determined by the market. The buyer (employer) exercises no decision-making authority over the seller (employee) as to how the good is to be produced or the service performed. In sharp contrast, the employment contract represents a purchase by the buyer (employer) of a future stream of loosely defined services from the seller (employee) in return for a periodic wage payment. The distinguishing feature of the employment contract is the employee's acceptance of the employer's authority to direct his efforts within an agreed-upon range of activities. Thus, the legitimacy of business' authority to allocate labor resources resides in labor's voluntary acceptance of this authority in return for the wage payment. This decision-making authority is granted from the bottom, not imposed from the top.

Employment contracts are more efficient than sales contracts when the specific services which must be performed are uncertain, and when coordination of individual effort is essential. The authority relationship in the employment contract greatly reduces the cost of negotiating for the performance of each task which becomes necessary over the life of the contract.

Challenges to existing business-labor relationships are being generated by a questioning of the legitimacy of the authority granted in the employment contract. Is this authority consistent with fundamental principles of political democracy? The employment contract is a market control instrument. It is neither political nor democratic. And, at first blush, it is somewhat ironic that the idea of industrial democracy meets with so much opposition in a country which supports political democracy, democratic school boards, and labor union democracy. It is hard to oppose democracy in any form (shareholder democracy, consumer democracy, or industrial democracy) in the U.S. For example, Halal and Brown write: "There is something particularly ironic in the fact that the American Revolution once led the world in creating democratic forms of governance, yet the United States now lags behind most other industrialized nations in extending the principles of democracy to include the work place."[1]

Professor Simon (the 1978 Nobel Laureate in Economics) made a penetrating analysis of political democracy that provides some bases for reconciling the apparent contradictions in our eclectic support of democracy in the U.S. According to Simon, the basic goal of political democracy is to protect individual civil liberties by controlling the exercise of power. Political democracy is

[1]William E. Halal and Bob S. Brown, "Participative Management: Myth and Reality," *California Management Review*, 23, no. 4 (Summer 1981), 31.

not simply a mechanism for recording and imposing the majority's will on society. Indeed, in addition to making government accountable to the people through popular elections, civil liberties must also be protected from the power of the elected majority through an elaborate system of checks and balances which disperse power throughout the government.

The basic goal of business organization is efficiency. As noted above, this requires an authoritative decision-making relationship with labor when cooperative effort under conditions of uncertainty is necessary. Day-to-day business decisions cannot be made on the basis of majority voting in the workplace anymore than day-to-day political decisions can be made at town hall meetings. Nevertheless, just as with political power, business must be held accountable for the exercise of the power granted in the employment contract to protect the civil liberties of employees. Industrial democracy, like political democracy, must therefore be viewed primarily as a means of controlling management decision-making authority in the workplace in order to protect the civil liberties of individual workers, rather than as a means for implementing majority preferences.

Control of management authority is provided by both market mechanisms and government regulations. Market controls work through the classic exit option. Workers (customers, stockholders, or suppliers) dissatisfied with the exercise of management decision-making authority quit, that is, they terminate the voluntary employment contract and the authority granted to management in that contract. Competition among firms for the best workers makes this an effective control over business decision making. This control mechanism has been greatly strengthened by union representation, which essentially confronts management with a collective exit option.

The exit option is effective as long as alternative employment opportunities exist. However, senior workers who have developed skills that are specific to their particular employer may not be readily employable elsewhere at a comparable wage. Massive employment relocations due to rapid decline of industrial sectors exposed to severe international competition may require workers to relocate to distant communities which are not viewed as close substitutes by workers who increasingly value stable, long-term community relationships. Finally, when unemployment is high, alternative employment opportunities are scarce for all. As the availability of close substitutes declines, exit becomes a less-effective control mechanism, and less palpable to labor which then seeks greater political control of management decision making.

Government regulation of plant safety and health, minimum wages, and hiring and firing practices are a second means of controlling the exercise of management decision-making authority in the employment contract. Simon argues that decentralized market controls of business authority are superior to regulatory controls because the latter centralize power in regulatory agencies which may represent an even greater threat to individual civil liberties. When these market and regulatory control mechanisms are deemed inadequate, proposals come forth for industrial democracy—for greater political control of management authority through more effective labor voice in the business decision-making process. Such a proposal was an essential part of Mark Green's Corporate Democracy Act (Chapter 2).

Simon, however, is concerned that greater political control of business decision making by labor would not protect the public's civil liberties because labor's interest is not the same as the public's interest. It does not follow therefore that because we rely upon the general population to control the political power of elected representatives, that we can similarly rely upon employees to control the power of business decision makers.

Thus, the issue is whether industrial democracy is democracy at all (Professor Winter did not find much democracy in the Corporate Democracy Act). Business decision-making authority would perhaps be subjected to greater majority rule, but that majority would not represent the public interest, and would not be subject to adequate checks and balances.

The German experience with codetermination (joint business-labor decision making) provides an additional perspective for assessing industrial democracy reforms in the U.S. There are two distinct aspects to German codetermination: One involves individual worker participation in business decision making through works councils; the other, employee representation on corporate supervisory boards.

Under the "Works Council Law of 1952" both hourly and salaried workers participate through elected works councils in business decisions affecting employment, promotion, working conditions, safety, and social issues. The works councils do not engage in wage negotiations. "The Codetermination Law of 1951," which applies only to the coal and steel industries, provides for selection of five stockholder representatives, and trade union appointment of three union officials and two company employees to the supervisory board. These ten members elect an eleventh, neutral member to avoid tie votes.

This law reflects the union's concept of industrial democracy in Germany wherein the unions represent the workers and appoint representatives to the supervisory boards. The unions also want to participate in macroeconomic policy decision making at the national level. Union critics, however, argue that this represents union political control, not industrial democracy. Industrial democracy, these critics contend, requires participation in business decisions by individual employees as is provided by the works councils.

The "Codetermination Reform Law of 1976" represents a compromise between these contrasting views of industrial democracy. This law gives employees and the national unions combined representation equal to that of stockholders on the supervisory board. But all employee representatives are elected by the work force rather than appointed by the unions. The board chairman represents stockholders, and has a tie-breaking vote.

The German experience with industrial democracy thus seems to raise similar concerns for the control of power and the protection of the basic rights of the individual. There are, of course, important institutional differences between the U.S. and Germany which affect the relationships among business, labor, and society. One of the most fundamental is the much greater historical dependence of German manufacturers upon export business which, unlike in the U.S., has been essential to success. This large dependence upon export markets provides a significant global market constraint on potential business-labor coalitions which could run contrary to the public interest; for example, the necessity of exporting limits business-labor attempts to raise wages and prices. As indicated in Chapter 1, the increasing global integration of the U.S. economy may create conditions favorable to new business-labor relationships.

Douglas Fraser was the first labor representative elected to the corporate board of a major U.S. corporation. Fraser was elected to the Chrysler board as a *quid pro quo* for labor concessions in the face of Chrysler's imminent bankruptcy.[2] Fraser's appointment, as well as numerous other changes in business-labor relationships at the plant floor level in the motor vehicle industry, are clearly responses to the serious international competitive threats confronting the industry. As suggested above, global integration is fostering new business-labor relationships. Fraser notes that his appointment is not founded on any theoretical concept. Arguably, the appointment of a labor director to the corporate board represents a fundamental change in business-labor relationships that should be based on sound principles and a thoughtful, articulated vision of the role of business in society. The appointment of labor representatives to corporate boards as a *quid pro quo* for labor concessions is not a promising way to bring about fundamental improvements in business-labor realtionships.

Fraser believes that labor representation on corporate boards is a good idea because it allows labor to participate in the decision-making process before decisions are set in stone. This illustrates a basic difference between exit and voice controls. Exit is an *ex post* control mechanism, while voice is an *ex ante* procedure for influencing decisions as they are being debated. Voice thus has advantages over exit in circumstances where decisions have important consequences which are hard to undo. Labor also brings a new perspective to the board. Fraser established a plant-closing committee on the Chrysler board to broaden its awareness of the effects of plant closings on employees and local communities. In the second chapter, Otis Smith acknowledged that such broader perspectives represent valuable contributions to the board, but maintained that all directors should still represent the stockholders.

Efforts to increase labor's voice in corporate decision making need not be limited to the appointment of labor representatives to the boards of directors, as Fraser notes. Alternatives include periodic addresses to corporate boards by labor representatives, and the appointment of labor representatives to high-level operating committees.

---

[2]Fraser was also elected to the AMC board, but did not accept because of Justice Department concerns for possible antitrust problems if a UAW representative was on the boards of competing companies.

Fraser argues that there is a need for more labor-management coopera-tion and less confrontation. He cites labor-management cooperation on the trig-ger-price mechanism (tariffs on imported steel): "Labor and management were working together for a common goal." This, however, is an illustration of Professor Simon's concern for business-labor goals which do not represent the public (consumer's) interest. Similarly, the Chrysler board committee on plant closings could coalesce into a labor–management–community effort to protect the status quo from the dynamic, economic changes necessary to promote the public's long-term interest and welfare.

Fraser also notes that management decision making is autocratic, where-as unions are democratic, political institutions. Union officials are elected by members who must ratify agreements with management. The union's political decision-making machinery sometimes clashes with management's hierarchical decision-making process. The political control of union decision making makes it especially difficult to convince workers of needed sacrifices to restore inter-national competitiveness.

Professor Thorelli, who was concerned with consumer protection in Chap-ter 3, is again concerned with the consumer's interests in the industrial democracy debate. He asks, if labor is on corporate boards, why not consumers? Thorelli also is concerned that labor and management might form a coalition against consumers' interests by, for example, increasing wages and prices, resisting in-novation, or by seeking protective tariffs. The analysis of business and labor political activities in Chapter 8 provides a basis for assessing the potential politi-cal influence of such a coalition.

Thorelli believes the market's ability to control corporate decision mak-ing is limited. He views the modern corporation as a "political community of internal and external interest groups." Management's role is to achieve a work-ing balance among these special interest groups. This is essentially the business statesman role advocated by The Business Roundtable and other proponents of corporate social responsibility (Chapter 6). In this context, it might be neces-sary to have all special interest groups (employees, consumers, local com-munities, environmentalists, etc.) represented on the corporate board, though Thorelli recognizes the difficulty of consumer representation, in particular, be-cause of their numbers and varying interests. To whom would a consumer direc-tor be accountable? In Otis Smith's opinion, the company is already accountable to consumers.

WHAT IS INDUSTRIAL DEMOCRACY?
Herbert A. Simon

To understand what might be meant by industrial democracy, and what its consequences might be, we must first understand the general principles that underlie the design of political democracies. Our feelings and attitudes about democracy within organizations—that is to say, industrial democracy—derive very much from our attitudes toward and experiences with the democratic political institutions that govern our country. The prestige of the label "industrial democracy" is determined very much by the value we attach to our democratic rights and privileges in our society as a whole.

The United States has had a long history of experience with a democratic political and social system. Just a few years ago, we celebrated the two hundredth anniversary of our democratic institutions. Since those institutions have survived and prospered for such a long time, we may gain some valuable lessons from their history, and from the thinking of those who were responsible for their design and construction—the Founding Fathers, men like Jefferson, Franklin, Madison, Adams, and Washington. For them, democracy was a very complex sort of institution. Now it is not necessary that the meaning of democracy to the men who wrote the American Constitution be the same as the meaning of democracy to us today. Human institutions change in response to human conditions and human experience. Perhaps human beings sometimes even learn from human history, although that is a more debatable proposition. It is certain that human institutions adjust as time goes on. In spite of the passage of time, and in the light of the 200 years of more or less successful experience of American political institutions, we would do well to take very seriously the practical judgment, the knowledge and experience, that went into their construction, and the political sophistication of the men who put those institutions together.

What was the conception that the Founding Fathers held of democracy? It was woven out of at least four separable and distinguishable ideas:

1. The first is the idea of *political democracy*—the idea that those who hold the power of the state should be elected by the general population, and should thereby be made accountable to them. Of course, in the beginning, "general population" did not mean all adults, or even all adult males, but only those adult males whose ownership of property gave them a substantial stake in the "success" of the society. That definition was gradually broadened over a century of experience until it did come to include all persons over the age of eighteen. But the central idea was not an arithmetic idea, an idea of exact mathematical equality. Rather it was the idea

Herbert A. Simon, "What Is Industrial Democracy?" *Statsvetenskaplig Tidskrift, (The Swedish Journal of Political Science),* 2 (1979), 77–86. Reprinted with permission.

that political democracy rested upon broad participation in the society's deci-sion-making process, primarily through participation in the election of the repre-sentatives who would make the laws and the executives who would administer them.

2.   The second strand in the democratic tradition is the idea of personal and *civil liber-ties*, and foremost among those liberties, the rights of free speech, free conscience, freedom to conduct one's life with a minimum of interference from others or from the government. This idea was even more central in the thinking of the Founding Fathers than the idea of political democracy.

3.   Another strand in the democratic tradition was not completely shared by all the Founding Fathers, and, indeed, was considered a rather radical idea at the time of the American Revolution. Its most prominent exponent was Thomas Jeffer-son. This was the idea of *equality of opportunity*—the idea that life is some kind of race, and that everyone should have a chance to win the race, to realize his basic potential as a human being. This notion of fair handicapping was the idea of equality of opportunity.

4.   The fourth strand in the tradition, the idea that people should not merely have equality of opportunity, but *equality of reward*—that the race should not only be fairly handicapped, but that there should be equal prizes for all—was not wide-ly held in the early years of the American republic. Among prominent patriots, Thomas Paine comes closest to being an advocate of equality, but he was regarded as a dangerous radical by most of his contemporaries.

Of course the third and fourth strands of the democratic tradition, equality of opportunity and equality of reward, are very different ideas. The latter be-came only very slowly a part of the American conception of democracy, and still has a much weaker acceptance as a genuine part of the tradition than do the other three strands. Logically, all four strands are quite distinct, but we can understand how, psychologically, a demand for equality of political participation and equality of civil rights could broaden itself gradually into de-mands also for equality of opportunity or even equality of rewards.

The central idea of the American Revolution, with its emphasis upon politi-cal democracy and civil liberties, was very different from the slogan of *liberté, egalité, fraternité,* put forward by the French Revolution a few years later. One reason it was different is that the framers of the American constitution and government were very pragmatic men who had had a good deal of experience of democratic government under the English Constitution. What they were primarily seeking, through their newly designed institutions, was a wide measure of personal freedom, of civil liberty; and they looked to political democracy primarily as a means rather than an end. They looked to it as a means—the only means they knew—of safeguarding their personal freedom.

DEMOCRACY AND HUMAN NATURE

The people who framed the American Constitution were pragmatists in another way. Constructing a constitution for a nation or an organization for a business firm, a government agency, or a university is a task of design. When you design anything, you have to know the properties of the materials you are going to employ in its construction.

The materials for the construction of governments, of course, are men and women, are human beings. In order to design a government, we have to understand what we can expect from human beings. One way to go about the design is to imagine that you have available a new material, that is to say, to fashion a dogma about the New Man who is going to be your building material. Such a hope or dream of a New Man revives itself periodically. It reappeared in the experiment of the Russian Revolution, and in our own time, it appeared again in China's Maoist Revolution.

It is a seductive idea, the idea of not only designing a new constitution for a society, but of having as building material for that society a new and better form of humanity. I think many of us are skeptical whether the social and political revolutions of the past two hundred years have succeeded in molding this new man or—if they have molded one—whether it was the one they had in mind.

Moreover, it is not clear that if we could have the New Man, we would really want him. In human mythology, in the stories we tell about ourselves, in our vision of the human present and future, we sometimes imagine human beings who always behave properly, who always do what is expected of them, who are always unselfish in their support of society and its goals. On the other hand, we attach an immense value to human freedom, which includes the right of every human being to try to realize his own potential, to make his own choices. But of course when people have freedom to choose, they sometimes exercise that freedom in ways that society finds unpleasant and undesirable.

There are many literary works that celebrate the unruliness of man, the unpredictability of his choices, and his difficulty as a raw material of a social system. They underline the potential, and often realized, contradiction between human freedom and social requirements. One example of such a work is Orwell's *1984* (a date that is not far away), which calls strongly into question whether we want a New Man who will conform entirely to the demands of society, or whether we want to preserve a kind of residual unruliness in the human species that breaks out of the laws of society. Clearly Orwell (and, I suspect, most of his readers) is on the side of personal freedom at the expense of social order.

The same theme is illustrated even more poignantly in *Liliom*, the work of the Hungarian playwright Molnar. Liliom, who is more an anti-hero than a hero, is a very imperfect man who acts upon his impulses, and in acting, hurts the people he wants to love and help. Nevertheless, we empathize with Liliom because he is very human in his weakness. Whatever damage he does, he acts as a free human spirit. We can be angry with him, but we forgive him.

Our preference for freedom versus order is tested even more severely by a motion picture like *The Clockwork Orange*. Here, some completely vicious human beings, sadistic and destructive, can be tamed to live acceptably in society only by destroying their power of initiative and choice, by reducing them to robots. The movie traps us between two equal repulsions—at their bestiality, and at their dehumanization.

The Clockwork Orange simply presents in intensified form a dilemma that every society faces. We wish people were always well behaved, but we don't want to destroy the sense of person, the root of unruliness in the human species.

The architects of the American Constitution took a particular position with respect to this dilemma. They didn't ask for a New Man. They didn't set out to design a set of social institutions whose effectiveness would depend on human beings' behaving nicely, instead of their behaving humanly. They took man as they saw him, as they had experienced him and knew him; an imperfect being, who was at best a very unsatisfactory material with which to fashion a social organization. And they tried to design that constitution of government with the knowledge that it had to be operated by those imperfect men.

Let me provide just one example of the awareness of the Founding Fathers of the nature of their building material. At the time the Constitution was drafted and proposed, there were bitter political campaigns in the thirteen states to determine whether those states would accept this new charter. In the course of the adoption campaigns, in 1787, a number of statesmen who favored the new constitution wrote articles supporting it for the newspapers. Among the most famous of these articles were the so-called *Federalist Papers* that appeared in the State of New York while the constitutional convention was meeting there. Some of these papers were written by James Madison, some by Alexander Hamilton, and some by John Jay. I quote from one of these (*Federalist*, Number 51), in which Madison, later a President of the United States, discusses some of the fundamental issues in the architecture of the proposed constitution. He is writing here about the dangers of the concentration of power in any society.

> But the great security against a gradual concentration of the several powers in the same department consists in giving to those who administer each department the necessary constitutional means and personal motives to resist encroachments of the others. The provision for defense must in this, as in all other cases, be made commensurate to the danger of attack. Ambition must be made to counteract ambition. The interest of man must be connected with the constitutional rights of the place. It may be a reflection on human nature that such devices should be necessary to control the abuses of government. But what is government itself, but the greatest of all reflections on human nature? If men were angels, no government would be necessary. In framing a government which is to be administered by men over men, the great difficulty lies in this: you must first enable the government to control the governed; and in the next place oblige it to control itself. A dependence on the people is, no doubt, the primary control on the government; but experience has taught mankind the necessity of auxiliary precautions.

Here Madison is saying very clearly, "Yes, we need political democracy because it is really the best device we have found for preventing power from being seized in a few hands; but even political democracy may be used to gather power on behalf of the majority, and to suppress the rights of those who are not part of the group that holds the power."

This is a very different rationale for democratic institutions from the one so often repeated today, where democracy is treated as a matter of arithmetic—as a matter simply of counting up opinions and seeing where the majority opinion lies. In the latter simpleminded view there is very little difference between conducting a democratic government and conducting a well-designed public opinion poll. According to that view, if you are careful in sampling, you get an almost exact result.

What Madison, and the other designers of the American Constitution, saw is that democracy is not simply a set of institutions for measuring and reflecting preferences. Democracy is a system for *controlling* power, including the power of majorities. One pays a price for its checks and balances. In the American system, for example, we sometimes stumble about a good deal because power in our system does tend to be broadly distributed over the different organs of government, and sometimes we are unable to organize that power and use it in ways in which it needs to be used. A good contemporary example of this is the difficulty the United States has been experiencing in the past years in formulating and agreeing to a national energy policy.

With a simpler form of government, with a government designed primarily to exercise power rather than to control it, these problems of reaching agreement on an energy policy could be solved in a day. We could have an energy policy—somebody's energy policy, at any rate. In a governmental structure designed to control power, it may often be a much more complex and difficult matter to get positive action. That's one of the prices to be paid for controlling power.

In any task of complex design, there is a balancing of advantages and disadvantages of each proposed feature. In the design of the American Constitution, the primary objective set by the designers was to secure personal freedom. To achieve this, governmental power must be subject to control (hence, political democracy), but it must also be protected against concentration, even in the hands of political majorities. The arithmetic of political equality was at no time a central theme of the designers of that constitution, concerned as they were to fabricate durable institutions from imperfect human materials.

THE DESIGN OF INDUSTRIAL ORGANIZATIONS

Let me turn now from American constitutional history to the specific question of industrial democracy. We descend from the level of organization of the state to the level of organization of the corporation or government department, and of the offices within it. Our concern is with the design of the work place, of the factories and offices where we do our everyday work. Again we must specify what the criteria are to be for judging the design. What are we trying to accomplish when we set up a new organization or change an existing one? I will talk mainly about business organizations, but what I will say applies to government departments and universities as well.

Our first goal in the design of organizations is to achieve a high level of productivity and efficiency, because the primary reason for having business and industrial organizations is to produce the goods and services we need and want. Most of us like to eat, we like to sleep in warm places—I don't need to go down the whole list of things that we either want or imagine we need. It is the industrial structure on which we depend to produce these things. And so of course productivity, efficiency in the use of resources, has to be a major and central goal of this system.

Second, in order to determine who will have claims on these goods and services after they are produced, the structure has to arrange for a system of rewards for those who have participated in the production process: wages for the employees, profits for those who provided the invested capital, payments for raw materials, and so on. Hence, a second goal of the system must be to provide an appropriate system for the distribution of rewards.

Third, since we spend an important part of our lives in these factories and offices, we are concerned with the quality of working life in them. We have to balance our goals of productivity and efficiency against the safety of these environments for the people who are working in them, and against the pleasantness of the work itself and of social interactions in the work place.

Fourth, we have to be concerned, in the design of organizations, with the structure of authority relations. One of the conditions for getting productive work done in an organization is to set up relations that permit some people to give orders to other people—subject, of course, to limits and constraints. To bring about the efficient coordination of the efforts of many people we must erect some kind of structure of authority.

Even in a university, which we don't usually consider a very authoritarian kind of organization, authority relations are needed. In my university, someone—a clerk, I suppose, in the Registrar's office—decides that my class is going to meet at a certain hour in a certain room. If I don't like the hour or the room, I can try to negotiate a change; I can sometimes persuade the scheduling authorities to assign me another room that is open at that hour. Nevertheless, most of the time I accept those decisions; I accept that authority. And so do we all in many arrangements of our lives, and particularly in our working relations. Of course in the university there are more important authority relations than those that assign classrooms. There are authoritative procedures for approving the list of courses and curricula, there are procedures for setting salaries, and for determining whether faculty appointments will be renewed. Thus, that broad range of professional discretion that we call academic freedom, and which is so essential to the life of the university, exists within an orderly structure of authority relations.

In some organizations, the authority relations take very strong forms. An army is an obvious example. A less obvious one is a symphony orchestra. It is essential for the "productivity" of a symphony orchestra that the director—at least during concerts and rehearsals—have very strict authority over the smallest movements of the hands and mouths of the players in that orchestra. We take this for granted, and don't even think about it, unless, of course, we play in an orchestra. The relation of a director to his orchestra is not only an authority relation; it is an authoritarian relation.

It would be an interesting experiment to try to run a symphony orchestra in such a way that all decisions were reached by some sort of participative process. I, at least, am not optimistic about the result of such an experiment. In any event, all of the organizations we know make extensive use of authority, and we must clearly understand the reasons for this if we are to understand the prospects and problems of industrial democracy.

In summary, the design of an effective organization must take into account at least four kinds of criteria: productivity and efficiency; the distribution of rewards; the quality of the work place; and the nature of the authority relations. Since not all people respond to these four criteria in the same way, we must pause for a moment to consider how organizational design is affected by the diversity of human needs and wants.

INDIVIDUAL DIFFERENCES

All people have the same number of arms, legs, ears, eyes, and noses. Nevertheless, there are tremendously important differences among human beings, and organizations will be more humane places for people to live and work in if we take those differences into account.

There is a famous story of the meeting of a revolutionary organization in which the speaker is telling his audience of the delights of life after the revolution. At the climax of his speech, he says, "Comes the revolution, we will all eat strawberries, even in January." Then someone in the very back of the room speaks up and protests, "But Sir, I don't like strawberries; they give me hives." To which the speaker replies: "Comes the revolution, you'll *eat* strawberries." It isn't a very humane revolution that forces us all to eat strawberries, indifferent to our liking for them or our tolerance of them.

All of our social institutions do, to a certain extent, model themselves on some sort of picture of the average human being, and force us into some kind of mold shaped on that average. But as we learn to design more effective, more humane, institutions, we have to take into account individual diversity in needs and in abilities—in what people want out of life, and in what they can do.

Individual differences in needs and wants have been studied by social psychologists. The work of David McClelland and John Atkinson is, I think, especially instructive. They talk, first of all, about the need some people have for *achievement*. For some people it is extremely important that they work in a situation where they feel they can use their abilities and powers.

There are other people who have a strong need for warm social relations with other human beings, who have a need for *affiliation* with other people. It is important for them to work in a situation where they can have meaningful relations with others.

There are still other people who have a great need for *power*. They want a work situation that they feel they control, where they feel they have some mastery. It is important to them to have power over the behavior of the other people in their environment. The need for power isn't a human motive we find very pleasant or admirable, most of us, but it is very important to some people (even some who don't approve of it).

And finally, everyone has some needs for *external rewards* from his work, because we depend on what we earn in the work place to satisfy our needs outside the work place.

This classification of human needs, based on the work of McClelland and Atkinson, is just one of several possible ways of approaching the topic. There are other classifications that may be equally perceptive and useful. But what is important for our purposes is the human diversity they imply.

As we design organizations to meet the needs of the people working in them, we must remember that although all persons probably experience all of these needs to some degree, different people attach very different weights and priorities to them. If, for example, we find someone who is strongly interested in political affairs or in management, it would be a good first guess (although it might turn out to be wrong) that that person has a relatively strong need for power. If he participated in designing an organization, it would probably be very important to him as to how power was allocated in it. Such a person might mistakenly suppose that the allocation of power mattered as much to everyone else as it mattered to him.

On the other hand, looking over the range of human values and desires, it is not hard to find other people who have very little concern with the exercise of power. In fact many people have a strong need for freedom from heavy responsibility.

I am not trying to make any evaluative judgments here, or to persuade you that a particular combination and balance of needs is the most desirable one. In our culture, when we are designing heroes for our books, we generally endow them with a high need for achievement, a more or less average need for affiliation, and very modest needs for power. Of course, not very many of our books have genuine heroes any more, and we have considerable freedom to design tragic heroes or anti-heroes whose fate is determined by a conflict between achievement and affiliation, or between power and achievement. But we certainly do not expect everyone to be a hero, and we would not want everyone to be an anti-hero.

The fact, however, that some people have a strong need for power has important consequences for organizations. For such people, authority relations are not simply neutral mechanisms for achieving organizational goals. They become ends in themselves. It becomes essential to such people that the authority structure be such that they can exercise authority and can avoid its exercise over them. They become preoccupied with the authority relations themselves, and if sufficiently preoccupied, lose sight of the productivity goals of the organization.

AUTHORITY AND THE EMPLOYMENT RELATION

What is the nature of authority in the work place—in industry, in business offices, and in government agencies? When we go to work for an organization, we sell our services to that organization. But there are several ways of selling one's services.

One way is through a sales contract. If the roof on my house leaks and I need a new roof, I go to several people and ask them to make a bid of the price they would require to fix it according to certain specifications. I choose one of the bidders, and we sign a contract. Then the contractor goes to work within the limits of the terms written in the contract. He does the work at his own discretion, and I am not welcome if I come around to supervise the job. For he has not contracted to accept my authority; he has contracted to do a specified piece of work of specified quality for a specified price. Much of the work of society is done by sales contracts which exchange goods or services for money on this basis.

Another important kind of contract in our society is the employment contract. It is specifically a contract in which the employee agrees to sell his services to the employer in such a way that he will accept the authority of the employer—accept his direction of the work within limits that are sometimes spelled out and sometimes understood implicitly between the parties. At the very core of the employment contract is the agreement of the employee to do those things, within reason, that the employer instructs him to do.

When will an employment contract be preferred to a sales contract? It will be preferred when it cannot be predicted easily in advance just what things need to be done, just what activities the employee should engage in. The employment contract is advantageous whenever there is a good deal of uncertainty, either about events in the world that determine what actions will be appropriate, or uncertainty arising from the fact that the effectiveness of the behavior of any one participant in the organization depends on the coordination of that behavior with the behaviors of other participants.

I have a secretary, and I know that I am going to have to ask her to write many letters for me. But at the time I employed her, I didn't know what letters would need to be written over the ensuing weeks and months. We couldn't write that specification into the contract between us. Instead, she agreed (implicitly) to write whatever letters I would later instruct her to write. It didn't make much difference to her which letters she would write—whether to Mr. Smith or Mr. Jones—but it made a great deal of difference to me. Hence it was advantageous to both of us to agree to an employment contract that defined her duties in general terms and that gave me authority to instruct her just when certain things, consistent with the general definition, were to be done.

We have authority in organizations, based on the employment relation between employee and employer, because it provides a very effective way of organizing human efforts under conditions of uncertainty—under conditions where coordinated action is needed, but where it isn't known today in detail what actions will be needed tomorrow. The employment relation permits effective, coordinated action to be carried out by organizations under such conditions of uncertainty. And the employment relation is the primary source of authority in organizations in our society.

THE CONTROL OF AUTHORITY

If we feel, as the Founding Fathers did, that authority relations of human beings over other human beings are potentially dangerous because they limit the human rights and freedoms of those over whom the authority is exercised; and if authority relations are at the very core of the operation of our organizations; then we must consider how those authority relations are going to be controlled so that they will not lead to abuse and violation of basic human rights. This is the basis, I think, for our concern with industrial democracy. The term democracy refers to the methods we have devised for controlling authority in our society as a whole. We coin the term "industrial democracy" to designate the mechanisms to be used for controlling authority in the work place.

How far shall we pursue the analogy between political democracy in the society and industrial democracy in the work place? In our society as a whole, we control authority by instituting voting arrangements, so that the persons who exercise top authority are themselves elected officials. If enough of us don't like what they do, then at the next election we can exchange one group of them for another. But I must remind you that it is essential to construct these voting institutions so that there is some protection of minorities against majorities. As James Madison pointed out in the statement quoted earlier, authority vested in a majority may also constitute a threat to freedom unless it is checked in some way.

But what about authority in the work place? We are not concerned with a whole society now, but with a business organization, say, that operates within the framework of a society—within a set of political and legal institutions which are already subject to democratic controls. What are the controls over authority in the work place itself? First of all, there is the control mechanism that economists like to speak of, the control exercised by market forces. A company has to sell its products, and can only raise the revenues it needs for its operations if the products are acceptable in the market at the prices it charges. Labor is exchanged in markets, and can only be hired at the going wage rates and by offering conditions of employment that are competitive with those offered by other employers. Companies need capital, which they can only obtain by offering attractive terms to potential investors. One of the really remarkable, even radical, institutions of modern industrial society are markets, and the control that is exercised over the power of business enterprises by their need to satisfy market conditions.

I don't want to stand here as a latter-day resurrection of Adam Smith. Almost all of us recognize that there are severe limits to the perfection with which markets operate in our society—just as there are severe limits to the perfection with which most of our other institutions operate. But for the moment, I would like to stress the power of markets, rather than their limitations, and particularly their power to check and curb power. The manager of an industrial concern can do anything (legal) that he wants to, provided that he doesn't drive his customers away, provided that his workers don't quit, and provided that he can obtain the investment capital he needs for his operation. Anyone who has experience of modern management will know that these requirements place severe constraints on his action, severe constraints on the arbitrary exercise of power.

Since, of course, we don't believe in the complete efficacy of markets as controls over private authority, every modern society supplements market controls with a wide spectrum of public governmental controls over the operations of business: safety regulations; minimum wage regulations; laws governing working conditions; regulations protecting the environment.

Hence, if we ask in our modern industrial societies what methods we use to control the tremendous concentrations of authority we find in large business organizations, we see that this authority is controlled by market mechanisms conjoined with government regulation. These are extremely powerful controls that greatly reduce the measure of discretion that remains to the businessman.

It is often argued that business should be controlled also by its sense of social responsibility. I am suspicious of social responsibility as a major source of control over business, for social responsibility is self-control, and smacks a little bit of the New Man, who does what is good for society rather than what his interest dictates.

The primary responsibility of a business to society is to operate efficiently—that is, to make profits while staying well within the law. If a business has so much discretion and leeway that it can decide, on important matters, what is the socially responsible thing to do, then one would do well to begin worrying about the amount of power that is concentrated in the hands of the management of that business, and to wonder whether there should not be some additional control on that discretion. Social responsibility needs to be defined primarily by the society, and not by particular private organizations within the society.

I worry also when I hear universities talking about *their* collective social responsibility. Universities cannot be trusted any more than other organizations to define "social responsibility" in a way that is consistent with the interests of the whole society. Using power in a socially responsible way too easily becomes a rationalization for looking out for one's own interests.

CONTROL OF AUTHORITY BY PARTICIPATION

The call for industrial democracy rests, implicitly or explicitly, on the assumption that the controls over administrative authority in organizations maintained by markets and by governmental regulation are insufficient, and that, in particular, additional controls are needed to safeguard the basic human freedom of employees. The idea of industrial democracy is that employees (in analogy with the others in the state) should be able to participate directly in the decision-making process in the organization, as a way of safeguarding their interests.

Employees are only one of the groups whose interests are affected by organizational decisions. There are also the managers and the owners—who often represent quite different interests. And there are the customers of the organization and its suppliers. We might raise the question of "industrial democracy" for any or all of these groups. But it is most appropriate to raise it with respect to employees, for it is they who stand in an authority relation with the organization.

When we talk about the participation of a group in decision-making, one of the questions we have to ask is: Whom does the group represent? Who is represented by management? Who is represented by the owners? And who is represented by the workers? In particular, can any of these groups be considered to represent the society as distinguished from a special interest within the society?

It is clear who the owners of the typical modern industrial concern represent: they represent the interest of the invested capital, and they are primarily concerned with profits and with the dividends that are paid from the profits. That is one of the reasons, of course, why moderen industrialized states have paid considerable attention to the control of monopoly. For if we have monopoly, or anything approaching monopoly, then the owners of the corporation can exercise substantial power, and can use the monopoly power to gain additional profits.

Matters are not so simple when, as is often the case under modern conditions, business organizations are controlled by professional managers and not by the owners. Where ownership is widely dispersed, the shareholders are often in no position to check the power of the managers, and it is the latter who can decide how any surplus is to be distributed. And what is the interest of management? If we are cynical about human nature, or pragmatic about it as James Madison was, we will assume that managers are interested both in the power they exercise, and in the incomes they obtain from their positions, and that these interests may not coincide with those of the investors.

Let us come back, now, to the matter of worker participation. We can ignore the customers, because they exercise their power over the firm by deciding to buy or not to buy, and not by participating in internal decisions. (Cooperatives are exceptional in this respect.) But what is the interest of the people who work in the organization? Can they be said to represent the public interest? Like any other group we have considered, the employees have a conflict of interest: a conflict between their interest as workers in a particular concern and their interests as members of the broader society and as consumers in that society.

As workers, employees have a strong interest in maintaining pleasant conditions on the job. I won't say that they have an interest in inactivity—most of us are only moderately lazy, and prefer to put in a good day's work. But an employee's view of what is a good day's work is not always the same as his employer's. Hence, there is a conflict of interest about productivity, about how hard employees should work. It is in the interest of society and in the interest of a firm's customers that employees work very hard, be very efficient and very productive.

Next, in considering industrial democracy, we must define the precise group of workers who are to participate in decisions. Are we talking about the employees of a particular business concern? Are we talking about these employees as individuals, or as workers organized in a union that participates in decisions as an organized entity? Are we talking about a union of the employees of one concern, or a union that represents all the employees in an industry? For of course the significance of worker participation in the decision-making process is very different in these different kinds of situations.

In none of the situations I have mentioned is there any reason to suppose that the interest of the workers in a particular firm or industry is synonymous with the interest of society as a whole. Given a chance to exercise oligopoly or monopoly power, most of us are fully able—perhaps more unconsciously than consciously—to confuse the public interest with our private interest.

We need to design the relations of authority and control in our society under the assumption that each of the participants, most of the time, is going to be concerned with protecting and advancing its own interests, and that none of these special interests will coincide with the public interest. For this reason, I am skeptical that introducing a wider measure of worker participation is a particularly effective means for controlling power in industrial organizations.

If there are reasons for encouraging participation, then, they must derive from other considerations than the crude analogy between political democracy and industrial democracy. That analogy does not hold up under examination. Such other considerations do exist. The social psychological evidence is fairly convincing that bringing people "into the act," informing them about what is going on, consulting them, drawing upon their knowledge in the decision-making process is advantageous in almost any organization. Employees who are informed and consulted can usually be expected to work more effectively and with more enthusiasm than those who are not, and to contribute important elements of expertness to the decision-making process. I suppose that even the conductor of the symphony orchestra asks the concertmaster for suggestions during rehearsals—or if he doesn't, might improve the orchestra's quality by doing so. But that is a very different matter from organizing the orchestra as a voting body with the members holding formal rights to participate in most of the management decisions.

DEMOCRACY AND POLITICS

Let me try now to draw my discussion to a conclusion. In society as a whole, we attach fundamental importance to maintaining democratic political controls over that society, primarily through the mechanisms of voting. We do this without any illusion that democratic institutions provide a magic way of identifying and responding to some public or general interest. We do it primarily as a way of preventing the concentration of power in the hands of a few people, who would almost certainly subvert that power in the service of their own interests.

In the United States, and perhaps in Sweden also, when we want to talk about our political institutions, we have a choice between two words. We have the word "democracy," which sums up all the things we like about our institutions—everything we think good in them. We also have the word "politics," which we use when we want to talk about the imperfections of our governmental institutions.

In the United States, most people are not proud to be called politicians. And yet "politician" should be the noblest occupation in a democracy, the occupation concerned with and responsible for making our democratic institutions work. But the working of democratic institutions calls for bargaining and compromise, which seems sordid to us. We try to avoid the dilemma by saying, "These are our good democratic institutions, but these are our bad political processes."

We must learn that democracy and politics are all part of the same package of imperfect human institutions, constructed of imperfect human beings. We want to have democratic institutions, and the price we pay for them is to put up with the political process. There seems to be no institutional design that gives us the benefits of the one without the costs of the other.

Even though we place supreme importance on having democratic control (that is, employee control) of political institutions, it does not follow as a matter of logic that we want similar democratic control of the authority in business organizations—as contrasted with controls through markets, through bargaining, and through governmental regulation, or some combination of these. It does not follow as a matter of logic that, simply because voting is the primary mechanism of control at the societal level, it has to be the primary mechanism of control of the level of individual institutions within the society. There are many alternative control mechanisms we can consider at the level of business, governmental, and educational organizations.

Nor should we suppose that any particular group or organizational participants, even as numerous a group as the employees, represents an interest that is synonymous with or closely parallel with the public interest. Democracy is not an exercise in arithmetic, a counting of heads. It is a design for a social organization, composed of imperfect human beings, having a diversity of wants and needs. It is a design aimed not at translating those wants and needs into a general will, but at safeguarding human freedoms by avoiding any concentration of power, even its concentration in the hands of majorities.

LABOR ON CORPORATE BOARDS
Douglas A. Fraser

Q. You are President of the United States Automobile Workers and at the same time you sit on the Board of Directors of the Chrysler Corporation. What does this mean for the relationship between labor and business? Could it be called the wave of the future?

A. Well, I'm uncertain as to whether it's the wave of the future. I would argue that it should be. In time, labor leaders are going to reach the conclusion that it's not enough to protest management decisions that are already made, that are irreversible, and have an adverse impact upon the members you represent. I'm not saying that labor should have the controlling voice, but certainly labor should have some input before final decisions are made. The labor representatives sitting on the boards do not have to be high-level union officials like myself. There are many options, such as adding workers with current jobs in the corporation to the board.

Let me tell you just one story about my Chrysler experience: I got elected at my first meeting, which was in June 1980. In July, at the second meeting I attended, I suggested we should have a Board committee on plant closings and economic dislocation. The Board should look not only at the economics of such decisions but how they affect the workers, and the communities in which the workers live. The idea wasn't exactly embraced. When I introduced the

Douglas A. Fraser, "Labor on Corporate Boards," *Challenge,* 24, no. 3 (July–August 1981), 30–33. This article is reprinted with permission of publisher, M.E. Sharpe, Inc., Armonk, New York, 10504. Mr. Fraser was interviewed by Richard D. Bartell, executive editor of *Challenge.*

amendment, it met at first with an awful silence. One member of the Chrysler Board described the usual situation when a couple of plants were shut down; they had counselors there to tell the people how to get unemployment compensation. I said, I'm not talking about that, I'm talking about basic matters—how you arrive at a decision to close a plant and move to some other location.

Q.   Wouldn't management just view that as labor's attempt to dig in its heels and prevent any change at all?
A.   Oh yes, they could view it that way. But that's not the way it works in Germany. I can tell you how it works there because of the practical experience I had at Volkswagen, where management had to convince the works councils in Germany before the company could come to America to produce cars. The United States was an important piece of the market for them, and they could build the cars more economically here. Management persuaded the works council—a very powerful minority—that if Volkswagen didn't produce in America, their share in the U.S. market would decline, decline, decline.

Q.   In effect you drew from your Volkswagen experience a model for the Chrysler proposal?
A.   Yes. At Chrysler we eventually established the Board committee on plant closings and economic dislocation. I got them to adopt finally, maybe not on the first attempt, a policy that prior notice was absolutely crucial. Maybe by notifying the union, and just talking through the problem, you could find ways to change things sufficiently to alter the basic economics of the situation. It might change the Board's decision and change the impact in a particular community. But there is another point I want to make. At a recent meeting, I casually talked with a couple of Chrysler board members. One of them said to me: "I'll never forget that speech you gave in July. You know, I've been talking to other board members and we just never thought of the problem of economic dislocation in that way before—the impact upon individuals and communities." Well, I thought to myself, why is that? Not because businessmen are mean-spirited or that they lack compassion. They never thought of it because they come from a different background and have a different perspective. And that's what is important about labor participation with management. Labor participation can be beneficial to management, if it is organized right—and I think it can be. The worker representative could come from the plant and would understand the workers from their own perspective.

Q.   Do you think that this Chrysler experiment will be a new model and will make Chrysler a leader in labor-management relations?
A.   I think there are people in Chrysler who believe so. I think Iacocca feels strongly about it. We also negotiated board representation subsequently with American Motors, but we had a bit of a hang-up there. The Labor Department and the Federal Trade Commission did not find legal problems—anti-trust problems—with a worker representative on the AMC board. But the Justice

Department, when it responded to us in February, was unable to give a definitive answer on the same question—whether two members of our union can serve on two different corporate boards. The courts haven't said no, but the question is there. At first that's disturbing, because obviously it would complicate winning a labor representative on the Ford and GM boards. It would be outrageous for the courts to bar our representation absolutely, when you look at the fact that historically a bank has had different individuals sitting on boards even of competing corporations. But if the courts do bar it, then we'd probably want to sit on the operating committee, and we would simply work out a new structure for this alternative. I haven't even sprung this idea yet. You wouldn't necessarily lose what I think is valuable input at the board level.

Another fallback if the courts block us would be to say to the company, okay, we won't need union members on the board but let us pick two or three workers who would have an opportunity to come to the board—maybe not to every meeting, but perhaps every other one, or perhaps upon request any time. Previously designated workers would be able to come to the board meeting at the appropriate spot on the agenda. It seems to me that if the courts bar us from having regular members on the board at Ford and GM from the same labor organization, we could figure out an alternative mechanism.

Q. Does labor now have an effective input into all the discussions with bankers and company boards about the revitalization of the auto industry in the Midwest?
A.   No.

Q.   How can it move in that direction?
A.   It may well be that these are the most difficult times in the history of our union, and perhaps in the history of the auto industry, since the great depression. Adversity causes people to think about different structures and alternative ways of doing things. It's very interesting now that GM President Roger Smith and Board Chairman Philip Caldwell embrace profit-sharing; they had resisted it since 1955. We have asked for it every time we've gone to the bargaining table. What caused them to change their minds? Somebody suggested it was because they were in a loss situation. So what? As long as you adopt the principle for the long run, if the corporation keeps losing money, there won't be a corporation for long. Management is beginning to think about a lot of different things—about the way corporations are accustomed to doing business and their relationships with labor unions. I think that's exactly right.

Financial disclosure by the company to the union is another issue the union will have to pursue in the future. Financial disclosure was something that came out of our last Chrysler negotiations. Along these lines, the companies are going to have to give away some cherished managerial prerogatives that they've so jealously guarded over many years. They have come to realize that it's a different ball game. This is a development that was forced upon them by adversity; it didn't come out of a theoretical concept. They were in a desperate situation and they were looking for new ways to handle it. This may be a beneficial aspect of the adversary relationship.

Q.   How long do you think it's going to take the nation as a whole to get a cooperative process going?
A.   Many, many years. Unfortunately, the American labor movement isn't even there yet, let alone the companies. With many corporations hiring union-busting experts and attacking labor's right to organize, it's hard to see the right kind of climate developing soon.

Q.   Do you think American industry is going to survive long enough to develop that kind of arrangement?
A.   I think if more industries get into difficulties, you're going to see more models for cooperative action. For example, the steel industry has had a joint labor-management committee to tackle the problem of the trigger price mechanism. Labor and management were working together for a common goal. And why? Once again economic adversity was threatening jobs and they had to act together to form a unified policy. No abstract thinking would have brought them together; they were forced by circumstances to that conclusion.

Q.   What about labor participation directly in the formulation of macroeconomic policy—like monetary and fiscal policy—as is done in some European countries, particularly Germany?
A.   I think that's absolutely essential, although we really don't have adequate mechanisms for labor input into these areas of the government decision-making process. And, under the Reagan administration, I doubt they'll develop. With labor participation, for example, in decision-making on monetary policy, we probably would not have ruinous interest rates of 20 plus percent. You can't have it both ways. You can't tell the labor movement to restrain its demands and criticize the contracts they negotiate as being irresponsible and inflationary, and then expect them to respond positively to policy discussions. Labor has to participate first in corporate decision-making processes. You're absolutely right, that's why they are successful in Germany.
    One thing I keep telling GM and Ford is that a great gulf separates management and labor. Management is accustomed to operating in an autocratic setting, really a dictatorial one. In our union, the membership makes decisions in a democratic setting. Labor leaders from UAW can't just go into a room and meet officials from Ford, five against five, to decide what economic facts force us to do at the moment. It is the membership that decides. We don't rule our members autocratically. In Chrysler negotiations, to cite a case, three times we had to convince the membership of the company's terrible economic situation that we union leaders were portraying. The choice we posed was to make enormous economic sacrifices—absolute wage reduction of $46 a week—or else lose their jobs. We had to go out on the hustings to convince them that this

was the situation. That's how we reached decisions through the democratic process and it's very, very difficult for company officials to understand. It's tough to get our members to know the truth. We have to do some educating of our members. Adversity is teaching hard lessons. Our members are much more conscious and sensitive to the quality of our products than they were two or three years ago. We are all learning a hell of a lot about Japanese competition these days.

Q.   And union leaders have to face elections just like congressmen.
A.   Yes, and we'll be going through our triannual local elections this May and June. We have to face what a congressman never faces. Did you ever hear a candidate for Congress, a candidate for President of the United States, run on the theme, if you vote for me, I will guarantee you I'll reduce your standard of living, I'll reduce your purchasing power? That's the position our local union people are in.

Q.   But you could pose it as a choice—either lower your standard of living and keep your jobs or lose your jobs altogether?
A.   Well, this is precisely the choice we gave the Chrysler workers. But it's important to note that this cannot be a one-way street. In return for concessions, we achieved a number of significant breakthroughs. We've talked already about the seat on the board. We also won the right to have a say in how our pension funds are invested. In addition, we forced Chrysler to agree to the principle of "equality of sacrifice," which means that management must share an equitable portion of the hardship which results from the corporation's restructuring. Unprecedented restrictions on the corporation's ability to close plants and "outsource" were also implemented, as was an employee stock ownership plan under which up to one-sixth of Chrysler could be owned by our members by 1984. In addition, we won profit-sharing—the details of which we're still negotiating.

You also have to remember the situation at Chrysler really was not free collective bargaining. The company was rescued from the brink of bankruptcy only by extraordinary action, a key component of which was federal legislation that required worker concessions if the company was to receive government loan guarantees. General Motors, which returned to profitability in the first quarter, certainly is not in the shape Chrysler was in. You can't make the case at Ford at this point, either. And that is precisely the point I made to Phil Caldwell. We, in our union, believe with fervor in the democratic process and it's very difficult to get sufficient momentum to do something in our country unless there is a crisis. That's unfortunate, but that's the way the democratic process is now working because everybody's cynical. In this town-hall democracy, you really have to prove your case if you want to get momentum and movement. There are always people out there who criticize your position. That's what democratic debate is all about. Even in the Chrysler thing, on the second go-around, some people said well, management really hasn't told you the whole story. They're really not that bad off. A ridiculous argument, but people were accepting it because that's what they wanted to believe.

Q.   Apart from collective bargaining, what national policies would help auto workers and their industry?
A.   There are many. The auto industry will be depressed as long as the Fed keeps interest rates sky-high. We need relief there, as well as a program of targeted economic stimulus, rather than the trickle-down approach the administration has proposed. We need a trade policy that will limit the savaging of the domestic market in this period of rapid restructuring and conversion to smaller, more fuel-efficient vehicles. Ultimately, I think we'll need "content" legislation that would require companies that sell large numbers of vehicles in this country to produce a certain percentage of the domestic content and assembling with labor here, where their market is. During this traumatic period, auto workers should have the protection of unemployment insurance, trade adjustment assistance, retraining and relocation allowances, and the other programs that the budget-cutters mistakenly are slashing. But in the current climate, I frankly see little hope that all these initiatives will be achieved.

CODETERMINATION FOR CONSUMERS?
Hans B. Thorelli

Mr. Douglas A. Fraser, president of the United Auto Workers union, has been elected by Chrysler Corporation to the board of that company in return for moderation in union demands prompted by Chrysler's current financial plight. The election of Mr. Fraser raises a number of important questions. Is this a precedent for widespread union (or employee) representation on boards or other types of formal codetermination? What are some of the issues in such codetermination? Even more importantly, if labor is thus represented in company decision making, why should consumers be left out?

Germany, France, Scandinavia, and other European countries have introduced various forms of employee participation in decision making. Employee representation on the board of directors, at least in larger companies, is typical, but there may also be formal representation in managements, as in the case

Hans B. Thorelli, "Codetermination for Consumers?" *Business Horizons,* 23, no. 4 (August 1980), 3–6. Reprinted with permission.

of the German Arbeitsdirektor. Sweden passed a law in 1976 which set aside
the section of the bylaws of the Employers' Confederation concerning management prerogatives ("the right to lead and divide the work"), and declared any
and all matters of company decision making bargainable items. Among other
things, executive appointments, new investments in plant and machinery, new
product decisions, and other matters of crucial managerial significance may well
become subject to more or less formalized labor-management codetermination
procedures. Should the Social Democrats on a return to power enact the so-
called wage-earner fund proposals in a form at all close to that suggested by
the trade union economists with whom the idea originated, employees might
in fifteen or twenty years own a majority interest in most of Swedish industry.
In effect, this interest would be managed by the unions, suggesting that Sweden
gradually might be transformed into some kind of postindustrial Yugoslavia.

Other nations are not likely to proceed nearly as far as might the Swedes.
Americans, for example, tend to be pragmatic about their institutions, and thus
far a formal increase in the degree of codetermination has not been high on
the agenda of the individual employee. Perhaps this is a reflection of the traditional open and direct relationship between factories and offices. Unions have
shied away from becoming actively involved in managerial responsibility, pre-
ferring an armslength relationship. Indeed, the prospect of Mr. Fraser's election to the Chrysler board apparently is not viewed with much favor by many
members or officials of his union. Nevertheless, the participative management
trend in the Western world is there for all to see.

CONSUMER REACTION

The trend towards increased employee participation is likely to have an impact
on consumers. In the ideal case, increased participation will work a revolution
in employee motivation, constantly spurring labor and management to produce
better products at lower prices and in other ways to improve service to consumers. The possibility of such an outcome should not be excluded, and I do
not claim the expertise in industrial relations and psychology necessary to gauge
its probability. Government would perhaps be able to play the role of a countervailing power in some countries, though not in nations dominated by Social
Democrat or Labor Parties, which are more or less captive of local trade unions.
However, in the absence of a countervailing power such as government, a risk
that labor and management will conspire at the cost of third parties is ever present. The third party closest in view would be consumers, who constitute the
sole source of income of the corporation and who are poorly organized, if at all.

It is easy to give possible examples. Merchants and their sales personnel
might get together to limit store hours. Employers in many countries might agree
to higher wages—and prices—in a tempting cartel system comprising both labor
and product markets, though in the U.S. the antitrust laws might offer some

resistance. In several countries such arrangements already exist in trades involving a high professional-labor cost component, such as barbers, painters, and plumbers. With the instinct to resist change characteristic of most human beings, the collective power also might be used to resist innovation in products and in manufacturing and marketing processes. Traditional labor concern with employment security added to the corporation's interest in staying in business might result in pressures on government to bail out inefficient firms by subsidies, loan guarantees, tariff increases, and the like, with the cost of such arrangements ultimately shifted to tax-paying consumers.

How will consumers react if this is the kind of impact to be expected from employee codetermination? One obvious possibility is that such a development would bring about consumers unions of a type much stronger and more aggressive than we have seen thus far in any country. Even in the absence of such organizations, it is quite likely that the consumer viewpoint would manifest itself in demands for increased participation by consumers in corporate decision making. To some extent, of course, such demands already constitute an aspect of modern consumerism. What we are talking about is a drastic escalation in the range and intensity of such claims.

CHANGING VIEW OF THE CORPORATION

The traditional view of the company in corporation law as well as in the theory of the firm is that it is an instrument serving the interests of its owners. The interests of management are assumed to be identical with those of the owners. Thanks to the invisible hand, the firm serves the interests of consumers while pursuing those of the owners.

It is an understatement to say that these postulates are no longer fully valid (if ever they were). We are taking fumbling steps to replace the image of the past with a new image based on new theories. Thus, the modern corporation might be viewed as a "political community of internal and external interest groups."* In this pluralist view of the firm, the principal member interests of that community are consumers, management, other employees, stockholders and other creditors, suppliers, distributors and dealers, competitors, the plant community and increasingly, the public at large—plus, of course, government. Each interest group is at once a contributor (time, money, component parts, and the like) and a claimant (of money, goods, ego-gratification, and the like) in the corporate nexus. The role of management is to achieve a working balance, through time, of claims and contributions, thereby insuring the survival and growth of the firm as a venture.

The degree and forms of direct and indirect representation of the interest

*Hans B. Thorelli, "The Political Economy of the Firm: Basis for a New Theory of Competition?" *Schweizerische Zeitschrift für* Volkswirtschaft und Statistik, 101 (1965:3): 248–62.

groups differ widely, both within and across cultures. It may be helpful to compare labor's position at the turn of the century with that of the consumer's since World War II vis-a-vis the corporation. Around 1900 it was becoming widely recognized that the individual worker was nearly powerless in relation to management. Unions were organized and gradually became recognized by society as well as by employers. The power struggle shifted from the micro (worker) to the macro (union, industry) level. It was assumed that union functionaries could adequately represent all the interests of individual members. Labor markets were no longer open, and traditional market forces were set aside (just how much is, of course, a bone of contention). The Clayton Act of 1914, explicitly exempting American labor unions from the antitrust laws, declared that "the labor of a human being is not a commodity or article of commerce," and in most industrial countries laws have been passed protecting union shop, closed shop, collective bargaining rights, and other union perquisites. There can be no doubt that the vast increase in the power of labor at the macro level has greatly improved the situation of the worker at the micro level in human dignity and interpersonal relations, if not necessarily in long-range economic terms. The only trouble is that unions in several nations have gained such positions of strength that at least in the short term there is hardly any countervailing power other than their own voluntary restraint. And it is at this very juncture that codetermination is being introduced in the form of board representation or even farther-reaching measures.

Contrast with this the situation of consumers. It is probably true that with the growth of discretionary income, the intensification of cross-product competition, and so on, consumer power has been rapidly increasing at the macro level in the last thirty years. But consumers are poorly organized. Though sporadic consumer boycotts have met with some success in Europe, Japan, and the U.S., collective bargaining by consumers is not within the field of vision. Their individual interests are markedly different, and probably more diverse than those of employees—at least the employee interests recognized thus far. Their individual interest in any given product market is often trivial and transitory. Further, people do not often look upon themselves as "consumers." At the micro level, in the last few decades we have detected a helplessness of the individual consumer somewhat analogous to that of the individual worker of yesteryear. One solution has been to reach for antitrust laws and consumer information programs (comparative testing, for example) to reinforce open product-markets. Another has been for governments to take on the role of St. George, building a wall of protective measures around the consumer. In this area, of course, we are setting aside the free play of market forces by a different route from that followed by labor.

In the aggregate, deciding whether consumer interests are, or are not, well taken care of depends on our evaluation of the effectiveness of the open market system. Certainly, the superstructure of consumer organizations, legislations, and formal representation is a good deal less impressive than that of employees. My view happens to be that open markets by and large have served consumers well indeed, at least when modified by such private and public institutional arrangements as those present in the United States. Certainly consumer standards of living are far higher, and consumer freedom of choice is exponentially greater in the advanced open economies than anywhere else in the world. Therefore, we may envisage the impact of employee codetermination on both open markets and consumers with some trepidation.

In the triangular drama which might emerge there is, of course, the possibility that management will seek the support of consumers against excessive labor demands. However, this is not very likely—at least as long as consumers are not organized. Or, labor and consumers may discover a close affinity. Of course, it is true that a majority of workers are consumers and vice versa. However, on detailed examination, it turns out that labor nowhere has played a truly pioneering or heavily supportive role in consumer matters, with the largely historical exception of the cooperative societies. Furthermore, even if the affinity were strong in some respects, this would not prevent a *particular* union (or group of employees) from having producer-oriented interests in relation to consumers in general.

In principle, it would seem that consumers are fully as much entitled to be represented on corporate boards and decision-making councils as are employees or any other interest group in addition to the stockholders. But both conceptual and practical obstacles stand in the way of consumer codetermination on a formal representation basis. The tremendous range of consumer interests precludes their easy representation. The question of from what organization or what constituency the consumer representatives should be (s)elected and to whom they would be accountable must be answered. A "professional" consumerist would surely be valuable as a sounding board and idea person on nearly any corporate board, but the question of representativeness would remain. Government-appointed consumer representatives certainly would not meet the need. They would merely add another layer between grassroots consumers and the corporation.

As long as consumers are largely unorganized, it seems inadvisable to recommend formal representation on corporate boards *merely* because employees—or other interest groups—might be given such representation. The issue may rapidly become a live one, however, in case our fears turn out to be justified that an emerging labor-management power block succumbs to the temptation of exploiting third parties.

DISCUSSION QUESTIONS

1. Some argue that now that democracy has been industrialized, industry must be democratized. Is this logical, or is it a non sequitur?
2. What are the basic differences between political democracy and industrial democracy? Would industrial democracy serve the same purposes as political

democracy? How would industrial democracy control business decision making in the public interest?

3. Are labor-management relationships in western European countries such as Germany, France, and Sweden more democratic than they are in the U.S.?
4. Should labor be represented on corporate boards? Would labor representatives make the company more or less responsive to consumers and the public?
5. If labor is represented on corporate boards, should consumers (local communities, etc.) also be represented? Would this eventually lead to the corporate governance model of business control proposed in Chapter 2?
6. Douglas Fraser said that UAW decisions are made "through the democratic process and it's very, very difficult for company officials to understand. It's tough to get our members to know the truth." Why is it hard for unions members to accept the truth? Would having labor representatives on corporate boards make it easier or more difficult to get union members to accept the truth?
7. What are the basic differences between sales and employment contracts? Under what conditions is one more effective than the other?
8. What are the economic, moral, and political justifications for authority in business-labor relationships?
9. Samuel Gompers wrote: "The worst crime against the working people is a company that fails to make a profit." Was Gompers concerned primarily with corporate stockholders or employees?
10. What are the fundamental economic, social, and political advantages and disadvantages of greater labor participation in management decision making at the plant floor level?

ADDITIONAL READINGS

HALAL, WILLIAM E., and BOB S. BROWN, "Participative Management: Myth and Reality," *California Management Review,* 23, no. 4 (Summer 1981), 20–32.
KATZ, HARRY C., "SMR Forum: Assessing the New Auto Labor Agreements," *Sloan Management Review,* 23, no. 4 (Summer 1982), 57–63.
NEHRBASS, RICHARD G., "The Myths of Industrial Democracy," *Personnel Journal,* 61, no. 7 (July 1982), 486–87.
ROSOW, JEROME N., "Changing Attitudes to Work and Life Style," *Journal of Contemporary Business,* 8, no. 4 (1979), 27–32.
STAFFORD, FRANK P., "Firm Size, Workplace, Public Goods and Worker Welfare," in *The Economics of Firm Size, Market Structure and Social Performance,* pp. 326–47, ed. John J. Siegfried. Proceedings of a Conference sponsored by the Federal Trade Commission. Washington, DC: U.S. Government Printing Office, 1980.
SWEENY, KEVIN M., and others, "Can Workplace Democracy Boost Productivity?" *Business and Society Review,* no. 43 (Fall 1982), 10–15.
THIMM, ALFRED L., "How Far Should German Codetermiantion Go?" *Challenge* (July–August 1981), pp. 13–22.

CHAPTER 5
COMMUNITY RELATIONSHIPS

The fundamental relationships between business and its host communities have attracted much greater attention in recent years because of the dynamic transitions occuring in the economy. The acceleration of the movement of industry from the Frostbelt to the Sunbelt; the emergence of service and information industries; and the industrial restructuring forced in autos, steel, and other major industries by the increasing global integration of product markets all have very severe community impacts. Employment in the community, local taxes, social services and educational facilities, and the community's entire sociopolitical infrastructure are affected by these transitions. These community effects, or social transition costs, have not been adequately addressed in the classical market control model.

Every society attempts to protect itself from wrenching, short-run adjustments as it pursues the long-run gains from dynamic economic growth. Every society tries to temper the speed and direction of the flow of economic resources to minimize these transition costs, and to ensure an equitable social sharing of these costs. Thus, the fundamental issue, as in the prior chapters, is the control over the allocation of the nation's resources, and the social legitimacy of that control. Therefore, the foundations of business-community relationships can also be analyzed within the basic business policy decision-making framework. This approach surfaces two fundamental business-community issues: business responsibilities for the effects of its decisions on the community as distinct from its responsibilities to individual stockholders, employees, and consumers; and the balance of market and political control over these decisions—the issue of community democracy (like stockholder, consumer, and industrial democracy).

The resolution of both of these issues turns on whether the relationship between business and the community should be primarily economic or political. There are also some unique ethical issues involved in the discussion of business-community relationships because of the state's responsibilities for the protection of civil liberties.

The most fundamental business-community issue is whether the relationship of business to the community is adequately defined as simply the sum of individual market transactions between firms, employees, and consumers, or if primary, or at least distinct, importance is to be attached to the community and the contributions of business to that community. This issue is raised squarely in Milton Friedman's discussion of corporate social responsibilities in the following chapter. In the market view, "Society is a collection of individuals and of the various groups they voluntarily form." But in the political view, Friedman states: "It is appropriate for some to require others to contribute to a general social purpose whether they wish to or not."

Mark Green, who proposed the Corporate Democracy Act in Chapter 2, clearly believes that large firms have important impacts on local communities which transcend in significance the sum of individual market transactions. In one of the suggested additional readings for this chapter, Green cites the adverse effects of big business on civic welfare, political sway, environmental quality, local taxes and investment and racial discrimination.[1] Large firms can either dominate local politics and public services, or create a local leadership vacuum with equally adverse results on the community's welfare, self-rule and sociopolitical infrastructure: "Like sleeping with an elephant, every thrashing, grunt, or inaction cannot but have major consequence on its bedmate."[2]

Other analyses of the effects of business decision making on community welfare have focused on plant-closing decisions. A plant-closing decision by a large firm can have a dramatic effect on local community welfare. It is the most visible and consequential use of the market exit control mechanism. Mark Green's Corporate Democracy Act (Chapter 2) contained provisions for reviewing these decisions, Douglas Fraser created a plant-closing committee on the Chrysler board of directors (Chapter 4), and several plant-closing bills have been introduced at the state and national levels.

It is through plant closings, openings, and relocations that business responds to dynamic competitive pressures, and it is through this "voting with their feet" that business limits the concentration of undue political power over economic decisions.[3] However, do local communities, like stockholders, employees, and consumers, also have market controls over undue business power.

---

[1]Mark J. Green, "The Corporation and the Community," in *Corporate Power in America,* Eds. R. Nader and M. J. Green, (New York: Grossman Publishers, 1973).

[2]*Ibid.,* p. 61.

[3]It is difficult for the state to violate civil liberties when its citizens can freely exit. Totalitarian states are quick to close their borders. Thus, any proposal to restrict the freedom to vote with your feet at any level in society must be approached with great caution.

The exit option is not readily apparent for local communities which cannot simply quit when dissatisfied with business performance. However the effectiveness of market controls depends upon the availability of reasonable substitutes, and there is no shortage of alternative business firms which the community can attract by offering competitive (with other communities) development assistance, tax and regulatory incentives. The community's ability to utilize market controls, however, is limited by its greater concern for social stability, equity, and the less advantaged, and by the greater mobility of capital relative to labor, especially unskilled low-income labor, for which the community has a special responsibility.

In addition to competitive market controls, communities exercise considerable regulatory control over business decision making at the federal, state, and local levels. Proposals for plant-closing legislation, however, represent more than just additional regulation. These proposals would largely eliminate the market relationship between business and the community by denying business its exit option over excessive community regulation, imposition of taxes, or other public requirements. It would eliminate competition among communities as local-content proposals would essentially eliminate competition among countries by denying firms an exit visa. This would change the traditional economic basis of business-community relationships in a political democracy with far-reaching implications for the role of business in society. The economic, political, and moral implications of such fundamental changes in traditional business-community relationship are the subjects of the McKenzie and Kelman readings.

It is argued that business should not have the unilateral authority to close plants because of the severe social impact on the community. Professor McKenzie, who opposes plant closing legislation, immediately notes that plant-closing restrictions are also plant-opening restrictions. Those who argue that management has a social responsibility to the community (Otis Smith would ask, which one?) may only be expressing a political bias for the status quo and entrenched interest groups—a political bias for communities which would lose plants over communities which would gain plants. Displaced workers are not likely to vote for incumbent representatives who allowed their plant to close, while those who find new employment opportunities will not know whom to thank in the next election.[4]

McKenzie makes two other critical points commonly overlooked by plant-closing proponents: Plant-closing costs cannot be magically eliminated by legislation, only redistributed among different groups in society; and attempts to redistribute these costs legislatively would result in higher total cost.

The risks of a plant becoming noncompetitive cannot be eliminated by legislation. If a plant becomes noncompetitive because of higher cost or inferior

---

[4]This bias actually results from a political "externality," since the incumbent representatives are not compensated (with votes) for their efforts. The result is the same as would occur in the market, uncompensated functions are not adequately performed regardless of their total social value.

product quality, someone will have to bear these costs whether the plant is closed, operated temporarily at a loss, or subsidized. Legislation can only redistribute these costs. Legislation transfers a greater burden of the risks of plant closings to business by making it liable to workers and local communities (perhaps even the U.S. government) for lost wages and taxes resulting from the closing. However, this then leads to higher consumer prices and reduced employee wages as firms build the necessary reserves or purchase plant-closing insurance to cover these additional penalties if they do become noncompetitive.

Workers are currently compensated through higher wages for accepting employment in plants with high closing risks (e.g., in the automobile industry) just as they are compensated for all other occupational risks and disagreeable job characteristics.[5] Thus, a legislative transfer of these risks to employers would result in reduced employee wages (reduced wage risk premiums).

Further, since most plant-closing legislation makes business responsible for workers' wages for an extended period following the closing, this legislation would amount to an excise tax on labor which would reduce the demand for labor as employers substituted capital for labor to reduce their exposure to potential plant-closing penalities.

The trade-off of lower wages for lower risks, however, would result in a net welfare loss for employees and society. Plant-closing legislation is essentially a social insurance device which, because of its inefficiencies, would result in higher total costs than would be incurred if these risks were compensated through upward wage adjustments reflective of specific plant risks and individual worker preferences. The employees best prepared to cope with high plant-closing risks would prefer higher wages and be attracted to such plants, while risk-averse employees would seek more secure employment. With plant-closing legislation, all workers will be forced to accept lower wages and lower risks (be forced to purchase plant-closing insurance). Thus, there will be a net increase in total social cost and a subsidy from mobile to risk-averse workers. Some increase in the total social cost of plant closings might be justified if the redistribution of risk, cost, and benefits were specifically designed to achieve fundamental social equity goals. It would not be justified if the legislation merely reflected political biases for the status quo and special-interest pleadings.

McKenzie also raises intriguing questions about workers' responsibilities to local communities when they move, or consumers' responsibilities when they purchase goods or services produced in other communities. Do they also have obligations to compensate the local community for the adverse effects of their decisions on the community? While the adverse effects of individual worker or consumer decisions on local communities are obviously too small to moni-

[5]See the article discussing cost benefit analysis by T. Marx in Chapter 9 for a further discussion of compensation for occupational risks.

tor, in the spirit of community responsibilities, one might realistically inquire about labor's obligation to the community if it strikes a plant.

McKenzie finally criticizes plant closing restrictions as protectionist policies designed to avoid competition for business among communities. Like all protectionist policies, they result in a net reduction in social welfare. Professor Kelman also notes that the elimination of competition among the states—the substitution of political for economic business-community relationships—would reduce total social welfare. He argues however, that competition among communities (states) raises a different set of ethical questions than competition among firms or labor since the state is charged with the protection of individual civil liberties.

States may compete for business by offering lower tax rates, less-restrictive environmental regulations, or relaxed safety standards. Economists generally favor such competition because it allows local communities to make the unavoidable trade-offs between economic and social goals rather than have uniform standards imposed on all states by the federal government despite substantial differences in individual community preferences for alternative goals. Kelman, however, argues that business has no ethical right to seek lax regulation or lower taxes in return for locating a plant within a community. Communities should not compete with each other to meet the immoral demands of business.

Kelman illustrates his position by asking if states should allow business to murder infants if that were what they demanded in exchange for locating a plant in the community. Kelman's, point, of course, is that society must respect people's basic rights—rights to clean air and safe work places—and that these basic rights cannot be traded for economic gains. Kelman opposes competition among the states on this moral basis. In Chapter 7 (Moral Relationships) John Rawls also argues that fundamental social and political rights cannot be traded for economic gains. Whether cleaner air and safer workplaces are economic goods or fundamental rights, however, might be debated, as well as how these rights are to be reconciled with consumer rights to choose goods freely, and with stockholders' basic property rights.

THE CASE FOR PLANT CLOSURES
Richard B. McKenzie

When he introduced the National Employment Priorities Act of 1977,[1] Rep. William Ford (D.-Mich.) was concerned mainly with restricting the movement of business from the "frostbelt" to the "sunbelt." He called the industrial shift "the runaway plant phenomenon." This year he has expanded his vision and introduced legislation (a substantial revision of the earlier bill but under the same title)[2] that will severely penalize firms that want to cease operations for *any* reason. And the legislation is not limited to the "corporate giants," the favorite whipping boy of the new left; it applies to any firm that has as little as $250,000 in annual sales.

In 1977 Rep. Ford was content to penalize firms that moved "without adequte justification" by denying them tax benefits associated with moves and requiring them to give a two-year notice of their intention to relocate. This year he proposes that any firm that shuts down must (1) effectively give its employees fifty-two weeks of severance pay; (2) pay the community an amount equal to 85 percent of one year's taxes; (3) offer the affected employees jobs at other plant locations with no cut in either wages or fringe benefits and pay moving expenses for a period of three years; and (4) if it decides to move abroad, pay the federal government an amount equal to 300 percent of one year's total lost taxes. As in earlier proposed legislation, the new Ford bill requires an advance notice of plant closings (up to two years) and provides for a variety of governmental aid to affected workers and communities and, if closings can be prevented, to firms.

Once concerned primarily with the economic harm caused by the movement of firms, Rep. Ford and his followers have now broadened their case, and the political appeal of their legislation, by stressing the economic *and* social costs of all plant closings. In introducing this year's bill, Rep. Ford notes that workers displaced by plant closings have a suicide rate thirty times the national average and "suffer a far higher incidence of heart disease and hypertension,

"The Case for Plant Closures," by Richard B. McKenzie, is reprinted from *Policy Review,* 15 (Winter 1981), 119–33. *Policy Review* is a publication of the Heritage Foundation, 214 Massachusetts Avenue, N.E., Washington, D.C. 20002.

[1]U.S. Congress, *National Employment Priorities Act of 1977* (H.R. 76). For a summary of the major provisions of the Act, *see* Richard B. McKenzie, *Restrictions on Business Mobility: A Study in Political Rhetoric and Economic Reality,* Washington, D.C.: American Enterprise Institute for Public Policy Research, 1979, pp. 1–6.

[2]U.S. Congress, *National Employment Priorities Act of 1979* (H.R. 5040 and S. 2400).

diabetes, peptic ulcers, gout, and joint swelling than the general population. They also incur serious psychological problems, including extreme depression, insecurity, anxiety, and the loss of self-esteem.''[3] Barry Bluestone and Bennett Harrison, in their study for the Progressive Alliance, echo Rep. Ford's sentiments and conclude: ''Unplanned, uncoordinated growth without adequate attention to national development leads to many of the same problems that we see in the emerging ghost towns—growing inequality in income and wealth, loss of local control over resources, congestion and pollution, and skyrocketing crime.''[4]

Arguments offered three years ago in favor of restrictions on business movements had only flimsy and misleading empirical support. Proponents apparently found that arguments pitting the North against the South had (120 years after the Civil War) little emotional and political appeal. Virtually anyone could see that restrictions designed to retard the economic development of the South would work to the detriment of the North. This year, by tugging on the heartstrings of all workers and communities that have experienced plant closings, the movement has veered sharply into new political waters, and the empirical support has become somewhat more sophisticated. However, the statistical claims still grossly distort economic reality, and the arguments offered in support of the restrictions remain inane, thin veils for the socialist's dream of strong central control of the economy.[5]

UNEMPLOYMENT AND CORPORATE "SOCIAL DUTIES"

In the past, proponents of restrictons on business movements focused attention on the loss of more than a million northern manufacturing jobs in the previous ten years or so. Now that those job losses have evaporated with the resurgence of manufacturing employment, especially in the North, their attention has switched to the total number of jobs *destroyed* by plant closings nationwide. Hearing the proponents' claim that over 15 million jobs have been lost

[3]Rep. William Ford, "National Employment Priorities Act of 1979," *Congressional Record—House,* August 2, 1979, p. H-7240.

[4]Barry Bluestone and Bennett Harrison, *Capital and Communities: The Causes and Consequences of Private Disinvestment,* Washington: The Progressive Alliance, 1980, p. 103.

[5]For a detailed statement of the type of ideology that underpins the movement for restrictions, *see* Bluestone and Harrison, *op. cit.* For additional views of the supporters of restrictive legislation, *see* Edward Kelly, "The Industrial Exodus: Public Strategies for Control of Runaway Plants," Washington: Conference/Alternative State and Local Public Policies and the Ohio Public Interest Campaign, 1977; U.S. House Subcommittee on Labor Standards of the Committee on Education and Labor, (95th Congress, 2d Session), *"National Employment Priorities Act of 1977"* (H.R. 76), 1978; and U.S. Senate Committee on Labor and Human Resources, (96th Congress, 1st Session), Hearings on "Employee Protection and Community Stabilization Act of 1979" (S. 1609), October 19, 1979, and on "Plant Closings and Relocations," January 22, 1979.

from plant closings during the last decade,[6] one gets the impression that employment is actually falling nationwide—*which it is not*. Indeed, between 1969 and 1979 total employment rose by about 20 million, or by 25 percent, meaning that the number of jobs *created* during this period was in the neighborhood of 35 million (or about 44 percent of the total number of jobs in existence in 1969).[7] The point is simple: the free market economy that advocates of restrictive legislation disparage as destructive of the social good and harmful to the interests of workers has done reasonably well in providing people with the working opportunities they need. The proponents' myopic concentration on job losses is on par with an evaluation of the banking industry by focussing solely on withdrawals. Such an evaluation leads inextricably to the conclusion that all banks will eventually close.

Backers of this new restrictive legislation fervently contend that firms have a social responsibility to their workers and to the communities in which they exist, a responsibility that extends beyond the labor contract and the shutting of a plant's doors. They point to the social disruption caused by plant closings (and ignore the good that is done): the loss of tax base, idle workers and plants, impairment of community services because of lower tax revenues, and higher taxes imposed on others because of higher unemployment and social welfare expenditures. Dayton—a moderate-sized manufacturing city in western Ohio—is, to the proponents, a grand example of what plant closings can mean. In a relatively short period during early 1980, three medium-sized employers, including Dayton Tire Company, a subsidiary of Firestone, announced their intentions to close. Eighteen hundred jobs were lost at the Dayton Tire plant alone. Workers and town officials, interviewed for television, recounted the personal hardships the closings had imposed on themselves, their families, and the communities; and several denounced the company for giving them little notice of the intended closings and for being socially irresponsible.[8] No one seriously contends that firms do not have a responsibility to their communities, but it is hard to accept the assumption that entrepreneurs and their management teams are any less socially responsible than their workers. If nothing else, the development of good community relationships is sensible strictly from a profit perspective. Rather than enlightening listeners and readers, such public stances only camouflage basic underlying issues; Where does a firm's social responsibility end, who is at fault in plant closings, and what are the alternatives open to workers and communities for dealing with the problems encountered when a

---

[6]Bluestone and Harrison, *op. cit.,* especially chapter 2.

[7]Bluestone and Harrison stress that their estimate of 15 million jobs loss is very "conservative." That simply implies that the number of jobs created during the 1970s is greater than 35 million.

[8]A program on plant closings was broadcast on "The McNeil/Lehrer Report," Public Broadcasting System, June 19, 1980. During the week of June 18, 1980, the "Today" program, National Broadcasting System, ran a series of programs on plant closings, focusing on the closing of Ford Motor Company's plant in Mawah, N.J. Not all workers interviewed appraised the closings in the same manner; a few viewed the closings as an opportunity to take other jobs.

plant shuts down? Admittedly, plant closings create hardships for some people. The important question to ask, however, is whether the remedy—Rep. Ford's proposed restrictions—is more damaging to social and economic progress than the disease. Further, should a firm's social responsibility remain a moral obligation or be made a legal liability? For any society that wishes to retain the remnants of individual freedom, a sharp but important distinction must be recognized between voluntary acceptance of social responsibility and forced compliance with a government edict.

Through wages and an array of taxes—from property to sales to income taxes—businesses contribute directly to the welfare of a community.[9] Through personal savings, workers can secure their own individual futures against job displacement. Indeed, wages tend to reflect the risk of plant closings: the greater the risk—everything else equal—the higher the wages. The proposed restrictive legislation will, if proponents are correct, reduce the risks of job displacement for some (but by no means all or even most) workers. The reduced risk will lead to a reduction in their wages. These workers will, in effect, be forced to buy a social insurance policy that, because of its national coverage, will not be suitable to many of their individual needs—but may be suitable to the limited number of people orchestrating the legislative drive.

Proponents of the plant closing legislation seem to imagine that in the absence of government restrictions workers will be exploited and, as a consequence, would be unable to prepare in a precautionary way for their own futures. They also imagine that the risk of job displacement will somehow disappear with government restrictions and that the costs of the restrictions, which are either overlooked or presumed to be trivial, will be borne fully by the "firm." However, for a firm like Dayton Tire, employing 1,800 workers and paying the average wage in Dayton in 1979, the costs of the two-year notice, plus the one-year severance pay (at 85 percent of the previous year's pay), plus the fringe benefits, plus the community payments, are anything but trivial; they can easily exceed $110 million! If the National Employment Priorities had recently been enacted and Firestone had been prevented from closing the Dayton plant (along with four others scattered around the country) the company would have possibly had to incur more than a half a billion dollars in production costs over the next three years, for which it would have been unprepared. Very likely, the financial solvency of the entire company and the jobs of the tens of thousands of other Firestone workers would have been placed in jeopardy.

To operate in a financially sound manner under such a law over the long run, a company must prepare for the eventual expenditure associated with closing: it can establish its own contingency fund or buy insurance against the risk that it must assume. Either way, the cost will be recovered from wages that

---

[9]It is not all clear that businesses use more community resources than they pay for. In the intense competition, many communities effectively "pay" plants to locate in their areas through below-cost sewage and wage facilities and interest rates. Whether or not the competition that now exists among communities is socially beneficial is a question that needs careful attention.

would otherwise have been paid, or from higher prices charged consumers, in which case the purchasing power of workers' incomes is reduced. Owners of companies will be hurt by the legislaton—no question about it—but that is not the point that needs emphasis. Workers will not escape paying for the benefits received under the restrictions.[10]

Instead of restricting business rights, communities could set aside funds from their taxes, and these funds could be used to alleviate social problems created by plant closings. In the absence of national legislation, communities could set up their contingency fund to meet local needs and to account for the trade-offs that people in the community are willing and able to make. If taxes are not sufficient to set up a contingency fund, then tax rates could be raised. Of course, such an increase would discourage firms from setting up or expanding their operations. But the proposed restrictions have the same effect. They are a subtle form of business taxation that, like all taxes, would deter investment and, thereby, further erode growth in productivity and worker wages. Contrary, perhaps, to the good intentions of its advocates, the new restrictive legislation increases the "social cost" associated with business operations.

MOBILITY: A KEY ECONOMIC LIBERTY

Still, proponents of restrictions insist that firms draw on the resources of the communities and have an obligation to recompensate the community for all the benefits they received over the years. Proponents are particularly concerned when companies use their profits made in one place to expand elsewhere. Does not the company owe the community a "fair share" of any future expansion? Messrs. Bluestone and Harrison describe with some eloquence how northern firms are "disinvesting" themselves of their plants in the North by earning a profit and then expanding their operations in the South and West.[11] A principal problem with such a line of argument is that it is perfectly applicable to employees: they also draw on a community's services and the resources of their plant. When they decide to resign their employment and move elsewhere, do they not owe a social debt to their community, and should they not compensate their employers (as restrictive legislation proposes that firms repay their

---

[10]In the narrow case in which a plant is prevented from moving by government restrictions, the workers in the plant may be "better off." However, if all firms are prevented from moving to locations where costs of production are lower, then the workers at any given plant must pay higher prices for the many goods they buy. Further, they will not then have the opportunity of having higher paying plants moving into their areas. On balance and over time, the real incomes of most workers should be reduced by the restrictions.

[11]As indicated in the text above, proponents of restrictions were originally interested in retarding the movement of businesses from the North to the South and only incidentally concerned with the more general problem of plant closings. Now that plant closings have become the focus of the legislation, the movement shows every sign of shifting its attention to controlling and directing the *expansion* plans of companies. The Bluestone-Harrison study, *op. cit.,* seriously questions the right of firm to make a profit in our community and expand in another community.

employees and communities)? Through wages received and purchases made on household goods, employees send their incomes out of the community. To be consistent, shouldn't proponents propose that the "public interest" dictates that employees spend a "fair share" of their incomes in the community? Shouldn't employees (and their unions) be told how much of their incomes must be invested back in their companies?

These questions are not intended to make the case for restrictions on employee earnings and expenditures. Rather, the point is that we allow individuals the freedom to do what they wish with their incomes and to move when and where they please for very good reasons. First, a worker's income is only one half of a *quid pro quo,* a contractual agreement between the employer and employee that is freely struck and presumably mutually beneficial. Second, freedom gives workers the opportunity to seek out the lowest-priced and highest-quality goods compatible with their preferences; that very same freedom forces sellers to compete for the purchases of the workers and provides workers with the security of having alternate places to work and buy the goods they want. Third, but foremost, there is the firm belief—call it faith—that people are indeed created with certain "unalienable rights." Individuals know, within tolerable limits, what is best for them in their individual circumstances, and they are the ones best qualified to say what they should do and where they should live—how and where they should invest their resources, labor *and* financial capital. The right of entrepreneurs to use their capital assets is part and parcel of a truly free society; the centralization of authority to determine where and under what circumstances firms should invest leads to the concentration of economic power in the hands of the people who run government. Private rights to move, to invest, to buy, to sell are social devices for the dispersion of economic power.

There are those who think that the case made against this restrictive legislation is obviously an apology for the "corporate giants." Not so. Embedded in the proposed legislation are provisions that effectively institutionalize the Chrysler bailout of 1979 and 1980. The government is given broad discretionary authority to provide unspecified forms of aid to companies that get into financial straits.[12] Effectively, the bill could swing the doors of the federal treasury wide open to any firm sufficiently large and with sufficient political muscle to enlist the attention and sympathies of the Secretary of Labor. The bill destroys, in part, the incentive firms now have to watch their costs and avoid going broke. Because votes are what count in politics, under the proposed law the incentive firms have to avoid losses diminishes as the size of the firm (meaning number of employees) grows.

Large rather than small companies will be most likely to secure access to the discretionary authority of government. Chrysler was "bailed-out" in 1979, not because it was the only firm that went broke that year (there were hundreds

[12]U.S. House, *National Employment Priorities Act of 1979* (H.R. 5040), pp. 34–36.

of thousands of others), but because it was large and had—through its employees, stockholders, and suppliers—the necessary political clout. We can only imagine what this bill portends for the future.

VISIBLE AND INVISIBLE EFFECTS OF RESTRICTION

Supporters of the legislation frequently point to the emotional and physical difficulties of those who suffer job displacement. These problems can be serious; there is no debate on that point. However, the political attractiveness of restrictive legislation can be appraised by the *visibility* of the harm done by plant closings and the *invisibility* of the harm done by restrictions on closings. The hardship associated with closings is easily observed. The media can take pictures of idle plants and interview unemployed workers; researchers can identify and study the psychological effects of job displacement. *On the other hand, restrictions on plant closings are also restrictions on plant openings.* They reduce the competitive drive of business, deter investment, and reduce the growth in truly productive employment—in general, retard the efficiency of the economy. However, it is impossible for the media to photograph plants not opened because of the restrictions on plant closings, or to interview workers not able to find employment (who, as a consequence, develop hypertension, peptic ulcers, and severe depression) because of the inability (or lack of incentive) of firms to open or expand plants.

Proponents contend that they support the "little person," the low-income, uneducated worker, as well as the relatively highly paid, skilled worker, who may otherwise be exploited by the "system." The fact of the matter is that the proposed protective legislation will work to the detriment of some of the lower-income, uneducated, and "trapped" workers in our midst. The legislation imposes a severe penalty on entrepreneurs who seek to establish production facilities where the chance of success is just above the risk of failure. Plants that would otherwise be built, will, with this law, not be constructed. The law would, therefor, work to the detriment of workers in low-income neighborhoods in the inner cities, because that is where the chance of success is often lowest. Furthermore, if the law were ever put on the books, it would freeze in place for a period of at least three years the production facilities of the country. Relatively depressed areas like Dayton, Ohio, would lose one of their best opportunities for recovering from the recent loss of jobs: the recruitment of plants from other parts of the country.

With tunnel vision, limited by the size of the TV screen and fostered by the need to make news accounts "hard-hitting" and "dramatic," television coverage often fails to consider the widespread economic growth occurring over time in a particular area. Dayton Tire shut down in 1980; manufacturing employment in the Dayton area was down slightly from what it was in 1970. These are the stories we hear repeatedly. What we do not hear is that total employment in Dayton and in Ohio rose during the 1970s by 10 and 16 percent, respectively; that the average weekly wage in Dayton is 50 percent higher than what it is in Greenville, South Carolina[13]; and that earnings during the 1970s, after adjusting for inflation, rose modestly but several times faster than the earnings in the rest of the country. These are the good things brought about, to a significant extent, by the ability of firms to adjust—by closings and openings— to changing economic circumstances.

It is difficult to measure the value of goods that are never produced because of the greater (government imposed) cost of capital. Nonetheless, if the legislation is passed, goods will go unproduced and many of the goods produced will be things consumers do not want. Firestone closed Dayton Tire because it produced bias-ply tires. The tire market had only months prior to the announced closing of Dayton Tire, gone sour; domestic car sales plummeted with the general downturn in the economy due to higher automobile prices (brought on partially by safety and environmental regulations), higher fuel prices, and the shift in consumer tastes to smaller imported cars. In addition, consumers revealed through their purchases that they wanted safer, more fuel-efficient, and more reliable radial tires. If Firestone had been required to keep the Dayton plant open, along with five others scheduled for closing, Firestone would have been forced to produce tires that consumers did not buy, or consumers would have been forced to purchase bias tires that they did not want.

If either Rep. Ford's bill or the Senate version of Senator Donald Riegle (D-Mich.) is ever passed, its victims will be largely invisible. Disenchanted consumers and unemployed workers may very well not realize they have been victimized; and if they do realize it, they will probably be unable to determine who is at fault. Therein lies the political appeal of restrictive legislation; Rep. Ford and others can champion this cause of the political left without ever confronting those harmed by it.

Rep. Ford, Mr. Bluestone, Mr. Harrison, and others dislike the fact that in the American economic system, businesses strive for profit. They fear that without government rules and regulations, employees and communities will be left without "protection." They seem to imagine businesses as giant, voracious octopuses, totally unconcerned about their community and workers, willing to do anything for a buck. To Rep. Ford and his supporters profit is a "four-letter word." Although it is hard to argue that businesses are any less socially concerned than the government bureaucrats who run control programs, we must acknowledge that profit is the basic driving force behind the business system— *and it should be.* It is the motivating force that gives rise to competition, to new and better products for consumers, and to cost savings. And the drive for profits provides workers and communities with the primary means of keeping the businesses they have, and expanding their business tax base. By holding taxes

---

[13]Greenville, South Carolina, is a city near a plant opened by one of the firms that left Dayton.

and wages in line with the competition, workers and communities can induce firms to stay and expand—to buy out and to put back in operation those plants that are closed. Contrary to what is so often written and heard, profit, provides protection.[14] Unfortunately, many of the advocates of the restrictive legislation—including unions—don't want to meet the competition. Proponents Bluestone and Harrison say as much:

> Trade unionists are especially concerned with how firms use capital mobility to keep labor off guard, to play off workers in one region against those in another, and how the threat of capital relocation is used to weaken labor's ability to resist corporate attacks on the social wage itself.[15]

What advocates of restrictions seem to want is protection from competition and from threat of pricing themselves out of the market. Consumers and taxpayers should be gravely concerned about plant closing restrictions. As the bill is now written, it hands over to unions the power to price labor out of the market—to turn a profitable concern into a losing proposition—and then gives them access to the coffers of the federal government for a "bailout" or "buyout."

LIMITATIONS ON REINVESTMENT

Proponents point out that many plants are closed not because they are losing money, but because they can make more money elsewhere. The defect in the argument is obvious. No profit-making firm will intentionally shut down a plant that is truly profitable—one that is actually more than covering the risks of doing business and what Peter Drucker calls the costs of staying in business.[16] It is a blatant contradiction to suggest that "money grubbing capitalists" will deny themselves profits by shutting down profitable plants. Of course, firms must always keep an eye on their competition, and must constantly look to the future. At times, a firm may close a plant because of cost savings and greater

---

[14]On "The McNeil/Lehrer Report" (*see* footnote 8) workers expressed dismay that Firestone was asking $20 million for a plant it felt compelled to close. Actually, the workers should have been elated with the "high" price tag. A high asking price tends to indicate that the plant has a market value, an alternative use to some other firm willing to pay the price for the facility. A selling price approximating zero would tend to indicate that the plant has no alternative use and that the plant and workers will tend to remain idle.

[15]Bluestone and Harrison, *op. cit.,* p. 7.

[16]Peter Drucker, *Managing in Turbulent Times* (New York: 1979). Modern inflation tends to mislead people into thinking that businesses are more profitable than they actually are. Because costs of plants and equipment used on profit and loss statements tend to be based on their historical purchase prices, and not on their higher replacement prices, and because revenues are computed from current sales at current prices, profits of businesses tend to be substantially over-stated, perhaps by as much as 30 or 40 percent. Some businesses reporting profits during these inflationary times are actually losing money. *See* Richard B. McKenzie, "What We Have Learned from Inflation: Ten Short Lessons" (Clemson, S.C.: Economics Department, Clemson University, 1980).

profits at another location. It knows that if it does not take advantage of lower production costs elsewhere, someone else surely will; and this someone else will be able to undersell and out-compete other producers.

Dayton Tire was, at the time of its closing, making a paper profit. Using an accounting system common in large companies, Firestone on paper "bought" tires from the Dayton plant at a price above plant costs. However, after adding in warehousing and marketing costs, the total cost of the tires produced exceeded the price that could be charged in the market. In short, the production of this tire was really not profitable.

Granted, as proponents of restrictions contend, there are companies that use plants as "cash flows"—a means of securing a flow of funds through the depreciation of buildings and equipment. Again, however, no plant will be intentionally "depreciated away" if, in the long run, its operation is expected to be profitable. Plants are allowed to depreciate to oblivion for one overriding reason: replacement of buildings and equipment at current prices and continued operations will mean future company losses. From this perspective, a company that operates a "cash cow" is, if anything, extending the life of the plant, *not* cutting it short. The company is using the buildings and equipment (both of which are scarce resources) to their fullest—the economical thing to do. (From a social perspective, is it better to have equipment that is no longer economical to replace sit idle, or be used until it is no longer productive?)

Proponents of restrictions are especially concerned about the foreign investments of domestic firms. As Messrs. Bluestone and Harrison have written, "dollars invested abroad are unavailable for economic development at home."[17] The deduction all too readily (and incorrectly) drawn is that foreign investment denies American jobs. On the contrary, foreign investments and production actually allow Americans to take higher-paying jobs created by trade. And what is the probable effect of Rep. Ford's bill on foreign investment? It seems clear that American companies will have one more reason to set up production facilities in countries that do not have similar restrictions. Foreign firms will have less of an incentive to invest in our domestic economy. Finally, when firms do invest in this country, they will, because of the severance pay requirements, be inclined to substitute capital for labor, to establish more automated plants than would otherwise be economically desirable. We must never forget that restrictions on plant closings in the U.S. are equivalent to an excise tax businesses must pay on their use of labor in the domestic economy. Such a tax can only reduce the demand for labor.

Finally, the proposed law authorizes the Secretary of Labor to provide financial aid to displaced employees who would like to buy a closed plant and continue its operations. This provision is based on the presumption that many profitable plants are closed. If that is true, then the employees really don't need the aid; private investors should be willing to provide the necessary financial

[17]Bluestone and Harrison, *op. cit.,* p. 27.

capital. Indeed, employees and their unions should be able to raise the money among themselves. After all, working people do save and invest. Private pension funds have hundreds of billions of dollars in assets, and a profitable plant should be a good investment.[18] If funds cannot be raised privately, this would indicate that the plant is not potentially profitable and taxpayers, who then must foot the bill for the purchase, will be taken for another welfare ride.

Furthermore, without government aid, the proposed restrictions on firms very likely will reduce the chance that employee-owned and managed businesses might be financially successful. If this bill is enacted, the employees—as the owners—will then be the ones who have to assume the risks and costs that the proposed restrictions impose on the firm. *They* will be the ones who will be responsible for giving the two-year notice, fifty-two weeks of severance pay, and restitution to the community. *They* will be the ones who might see their savings go up in the smoke of a lost cause and the extended period of time they must wait before they could close their doors. The chances, for example, of the Dayton Tire workers making their plant a going and profitable concern are very slim at best, especially without the management skills, the licenses and patents, the warehousing and distribution capabilities, and marketing talents that would probably not be sold with the plant but would be retained by Firestone. The workers, if they own the plant, would have to look squarely and soberly at the stark facts of the bias tire market faced by Firestone and ask whether they are willing to take the implied market- and government-imposed risks. With the proposed restrictions on the books, it appears that, without government aid, the employees will be less willing to put their money where their hearts are. Certainly, if they take time to reflect on their other job opportunity, they will have second thoughts about investing in their own firm.

Regardless of how inane the proponents' arguments are, they are blessed with tremendous emotional appeal. Still, the expanded scope of the proposed restrictive laws guarantees that, if they are enacted, domestic plants and equipment will become economic hostages of the state. Opponents of the legislation must keep that basic fact before the public and the Congress and must assert over and over the beneficial effects of the free flow of domestic resources. They must also stress the one constructive means by which employees and communities can prevent and overcome problems created by plant closings: meet the competition. Those communities, especially in the North, that are having difficulties keeping and expanding their industrial base should search for ways to attract industries and induce them to stay. There are many areas of the country, like Spartanburg and Anderson, South Carolina, that are having tremendous success in building a solid industrial base. Other communities should take a look

---

[18]Many of the proponents of restrictions seem to think that businesses are almost totally owned by higher-income groups, not people of the working class, and that the costs of the restrictions borne by businesses will inevitably be imposed on higher-income groups. However, through the investments of their pension funds, workers and their unions have a substantial stake in the profitability of businesses. Restrictions on plant closings can seriously affect the retirement incomes of present and future members of all income classes.

at what they are doing, and duplicate (and expand upon) their efforts. Through appropriate, competitive positioning of wages and taxes, workers and communities can ensure that firms can cover their costs of doing and staying in business. This is not intended to be a pro-business position. Rather, it is a pro-people and pro-freedom argument. Appeals to the private interests of entrepreneurs *and* workers (and not to the restrictive, coercive powers of government) will remain the hallmark of a free society.

THE ETHICS OF REGULATORY COMPETITION
Steven Kelman

The political air is now filled with proposals, of which President Reagan's "New Federalism" is only the most dramatic, to turn various activities of the federal government over, or back, to the states. Among those activities is regulation: environmental regulation in particular, but other sorts as well.

Critics of these proposals often object that the states, in order to keep or attract business, would compete with each other to offer firms the lowest tax rates or the laxest regulations. Many fear that, especially in a time of low growth and plant closings, such competition among states would set in motion a dynamic that would "gut" environmental protection, spending to aid the poor, and so forth. They also note that after this competitive process reached a resting point, no state would actually turn out to have gained an advantage in attracting industry: all (or most) states would end up at the same level of lax regulations, large tax incentives, and low spending for the poor. The suggestion, often unarticulated, is that it would be "unseemly" for states to compete for business in such ways, and that these environmental and social issues should be decided "on their own merits," not subjected to an auction among states anxious to attract new jobs.

Many of those who favor devolution of federal responsibilities to the states agree that it will bring about such a competition. But they contend that there is nothing wrong with that happening—indeed, that such competition will produce optimal public policies. Part of this group, of course, favors the competition simply because it wishes to bring about less regulation and less social spending. But others, including some economists, raise two theoretical arguments that seemingly do not depend on whether one in general favors stricter or laxer regulation. The first is that devolution allows the citizens of the state to make the kinds of trade-offs between, say, environmental quality and jobs

Steven Kelman, "The Ethics of Regulatory Competition," *Regulation,* 6, no. 3 (May–June 1982), 39–44. Copyright 1982 American Enterprise Institute. Reprinted with permission.

that they most prefer, rather than having to accept a grosser and less differentiated trade-off made at the federal level for the population as a whole. The second argument suggests that, even if the states (and their citizens) can make themselves better off by reaching an agreement not to compete with each other—in short, by federal preemption—such an agreement constitutes an undesirable "cartel" of states that, as cartels always do, reduces total social welfare.

The latter two arguments are the ones I wish to address in this paper. I will be assuming throughout that states accurately represent the preferences of their citizens. This need not, of course, be the case. If they do not, however, this creates problems different from the problem of competition among the states. Also, it should be noted, I will consider businesses not as citizens participating in the development of the preferences to which states give expression, but rather as "outsiders" with preferences of their own, bargaining with states and their citizens. This is obviously an oversimplification, but it is an analytically useful one.

The first argument for the devolution of federal programs is essentially an antipaternalist one: when goals conflict with each other, why not trust people to make their own trade-offs rather than impose a trade-off on them? To criticize states for lowering environmental standards to attract industry is to impose our preferences (for greater environmental quality instead of jobs) on them. If people place any value at all on environmental protection, they will presumably not permit their states to become simple dumping grounds for garbage.

According to this argument, a variety of trade-offs based on local preferences would lead to higher welfare than a single trade-off based on the aggregated preferences of U.S. citizens as a whole. Both voting behavior and opinion surveys suggest that people think differently in different parts of the country. If decisions were made at the state level, it might seem, there would be a better match between the preferences of each group of citizens and the policies they live under.

The problem with this argument is that competition among the states may itself dramatically worsen the trade-off between jobs and environmental protection, forcing states, at the extreme, to accept a trade-off that none would have chosen without such competition. In effect, the states may face the situation familiar to game theorists as the "prisoner's dilemma." In the classic dilemma, two confederates in crime have been arrested by the police and are being interrogated separately. If neither confesses, the warden will be unable to prove the crime and both will go free. If one confesses and the other does not, the first will not only go free but be rewarded for his cooperation with a token sum of money, while the other will get an unusually harsh sentence. If both confess, however, both get relatively harsh sentences, although not so harsh as that of the prisoner who refuses to confess while his confederate is doing so.

If the prisoners could bind each other to an agreement to both remain silent, they would both go free. But they cannot. Each knows that if he remains silent while his confederate confesses, it will lead to the worst possible outcome for him. This puts pressure on each to confess. But if both prisoners succumb to the pressure, both will get a relatively harsh sentence. Cooperation would produce an outcome preferable to competition for both prisoners. States competing for industry, then, may resemble the prisoners in the dilemma.

Like the warden, businesses would be in a very good negotiating position. In any negotiation, if one party cannot secure a minimally acceptable set of terms, he will prefer not to make a deal at all. How much (if anything) a party gets over and above this minimum acceptable set of terms depends in large measure on how anxious the other party is to make the deal. A person standing alone with a buoy on a dock might get a drowning man to promise to hand over most, perhaps all, of his wealth in exchange for throwing him the buoy, although the buoy holder's *minimum* acceptable terms might be extremely modest. Similarly, businesses making location or expansion decisions may be more than happy to take the benefits of reduced regulations, but might be willing to invest anyway even if nobody offered them.

To the extent that competition among states leads states to offer all companies greater inducements than they would be willing to settle for, federal preemption allows states (and their citizens) to have their cake and eat it too: they can attain strict environmental standards without sacrificing industrial investment. Since the failure to offer businesses lax regulations does bring some of them under the minimum terms they require to make the investment in question, there is still a trade-off, and some jobs are still sacrificed for improved environmental quality. But it is a more favorable trade-off for the states, because their bargaining position with respect to businesses is strengthened. They need to make less of a sacrifice in environmental quality to achieve a given level of investment and jobs.

How much the environment/investment trade-off will improve depends on how much competition there is among the *sellers* of business investment, the businesses that make location decisions. In economic terms, the buoy holder received monopoly profits because the drowning man had no alternative source of buoys. But what if there were many sources? Then competition among buoy purveyors would cause the price of rescue to decline dramatically toward the level minimally acceptable to the buoy holder who was willing to sell for the lowest price. In a competitive world of many sellers, as opposed to a bargaining world of few sellers, firms at the margin do not attain terms in excess of their minimum acceptable ones. If the "market" for business investment is competitive, federal preemption therefore reduces, to some extent at least, the total quantity of business investment.

Even in a competitive world, however, benefits that indeed "make the difference" for decisions on projects at the margin also end up being granted to projects that would be profitable even without these benefits. Such projects receive benefits that are not required in order to call forth the projects. (The only way for governments to avoid paying such benefits would be to discriminate among firms or investment projects in fixing tax levels or regulations, which is difficult.) These investments will still go forward. Economic theory can demonstrate that states, by not competing, can, even given a competitive market for business investment, attain a better mix of jobs and environmental protection than if they competed.

And, furthermore, considering the relatively small number of major plant expansion decisions pending at any given moment, the market seems very imperfectly competitive. (Certainly there appears to be a fair amount of lengthy, face-to-face bargaining that would hardly typify a competitive market.) This suggests that many firms may be receiving more than their minimum acceptable terms, which would allow some leeway for states to strengthen environmental regulation without sacrificing a lot of investment.

In sum, the view that "if states prefer more jobs to more environmental protection, we should accept that choice" seems much too simplistic. If they agree not to compete, states can attain a greater sum total of jobs and environmental protection.

A REGULATORS' CARTEL?

But, someone might ask, why are we looking at the results of an agreement not to compete only from the point of view of the states themselves? It is, one might continue, hardly surprising to learn that economic actors can improve their situation by reaching a cartel agreement. That story is as venerable as conspiracies in restraint of trade and as modern as OPEC. Cartels may benefit those who agree not to compete, but they hurt those with whom they deal—in this case, companies considering investments.

Scholars working in the area of "public choice theory," applying economics to the analysis of political institutions, sometimes treat governments as service-producing "firms" and citizens (or businesses) as "consumers." As Milton and Rose Friedman state with characteristic pithiness in *Free to Choose:*

> You may decide to live in one community rather than another partly on the basis of the kind of services its government offers. If it engages in activities you object to or are unwilling to pay for, and these more than balance the activities you favor and are willing to pay for, you can vote with your feet by moving elsewhere. There is competition, limited but real, so long as there are available alternatives.

Under federal preemption, businesses will not be able to "switch brands"—to "vote with their feet"—by moving to a state with policies more attractive to them, because the different "sellers" will all be offering the same "product."

The proponents of this argument take on the advocates of federal preemption at the most fundamental possible level. They accept the empirical prediction that turning programs over to the states will produce a competition for business investment that will tend to lower taxes and regulatory standards. But they regard such competition as desirable rather than pernicious. And not, it is important to note, because competition leads to certain substantive results (low taxes or lax regulations) that they might regard as desirable, but rather because competition is better than cartelization at maximizing the sum total of economic welfare in society. Economic theory demonstrates that while cartels or monopolies can increase the welfare of those who undertake them, those benefits are smaller than the losses consumers suffer. Similarly, these critics even agree that all states will end up providing similar inducements and thus that no state, at the end of the process, will gain any locational advantage over other states. But they interpret this outcome differently, as the normal way the competitive process works to promote the welfare of consumers. In any competitive market, producers will constantly undercut each other's prices to attract more business, but all producers will end up charging similar prices and none will gain any advantage, compared with his competitors. The only gainers are consumers.

The argument comparing federal preemption with a cartel among "producing" governments in an arresting one. It is also, I believe, mistaken. But I am glad it has been made, because it forces us to think about issues that are better treated from the perspective of philosophical than of economic theory and that otherwise tend to be obscured in discussions of devolution of federal programs.

TAKING PREFERENCES AS THEY ARE

Up until now, the various arguments I have discussed have all involved simply the interests or preferences of states and their citizens on the one hand and of businesses on the other. States and their citizens wanted environmental protection and businesses did not (or at least did not want to pay for it). In the prisoner's dilemma analysis, the states and their citizens were simply trying to maximize their welfare, given their preferences for both job-producing business investments and environmental protection. In the public choice analysis, the assumption was also that "all preferences are created equal," and that the welfare of businesses ought to be taken into account in calculating the sum total of overall welfare. The notion that we simply take preferences as they are—that we not judge among them for purposes of deciding what social arrangements are right—grows naturally out of the tradition of economic analysis. It has a tolerant, democratic ring to it as well.

But what if it should turn out that, for purposes of judging what social arrangements are right, the preferences of various actors should not simply be accepted? What if the desire of states for strict environmental regulation or welfare measures for the poor should not simply be thrown in together with the desire of businesses to avoid regulations or taxes? This is the argument I wish to develop in the remainder of this essay.

Let's start by examining the interactions between producers and consumers in an ordinary market for goods, say, oranges. Assuming away for the purposes of the discussion external effects on third parties, producers are doing nothing ethically wrong in growing and offering oranges for sale, and consumers are doing nothing ethically wrong in wishing to buy them. Producers have a right to produce, and consumers have a right to buy. It is within such a context of rights enjoyed by both parties that producer cartels are criticized. A producer cartel raises prices and restricts output for consumers. Adam Smith himself said in *The Wealth of Nations* that "the interest of the producer should be attended to only so far as it may be necessary for promoting that of the consumer"; and even if we look at the combined welfare of consumers and producers, we can demonstrate that cartels reduce the welfare of consumers more than they increase that of producers.

DOES BUSINESS HAVE A RIGHT TO BUY LAX RULES?

Like any analogy, the analogy between federal preemption and a producer cartel gains its force from the assumption that there are not relevant differences between the two situations. There may, however, be an important difference: those who want to "buy" regulatory laxity may not be acting within their rights in the way those who buy oranges are. If not, then we have grounds for condemning the producer cartel but not the "federal cartel."

Imagine a situation where the people who possessed some skill that others valued extremely highly—say, that of inventing useful products—also had the desire, perhaps through some genetic linkage, to murder and devour small infants at periodic intervals. In deciding where to locate their businesses, one thing these inventors would take into consideration was whether the jurisdiction in question allowed them to satisfy this want by granting them an exemption from laws against murder and cannibalism. If states were competing among each other for the services of these inventors, one can surely imagine a situation where one state might decide, reluctantly, to allow the inventors to indulge their desires. And once that one state did so, that state might attract all the inventors, which in turn might force other states to allow the practice as well or else lose the services of these valuable people (alternatively, other states might compete by offering other advantages that the inventors might value at least as much as the freedom to engage in their vice.)

Perhaps, a reader might suggest, no state would ever agree to such a thing. No valued skills are *that* valuable; no state would permit a practice like *that*. But that is not the point. The point is that the inventors want to do something unethical, something they have no right to do; whether they succeed in getting away with their brazen effort does not affect how we evaluate their attempt. If just any old citizen requested permission of his state government to kill and consume small infants, the request would not be given a moment's consideration. Surely the morality of a practice is not contingent on whether people who may want to behave that way happen to possess certain other skills. Yet a process of competition that sets no limits on the wants that the parties may satisfy would, by its dynamics, make morality exactly that. There is thus no presumption at all in favor of competition taking place in such cases. Indeed, there is the opposite. Any arrangement that prevented people from using the skills they have to wrest permission to kill and consume small infants, thus defeating such grossly unethical plans, would garner our hearty endorsement. Agreements among states not to compete constitute such an arrangement, and they are therefore to be applauded. It is thus impossible to decide whether an instance of competition among the states is justified until one has ethically examined the specific policy at issue. If businesses are asking permission to behave unethically in exchange for deciding to invest or locate in a particular place, there is no ethical need to give their desires weight.

Economic theory may demonstrate that a competitive regime would maximize net benefits, but philosophers have argued that other concepts—which they call duties—often outweigh such considerations. One such duty is the duty to respect people's rights, either by not interfering with something they do (negative rights) or by taking some action they are entitled to have you take (positive rights). Another is the duty to do justice, that is, to treat people as they deserve. This in turn implies treating people alike unless there is a relevant difference, under their control, between them. Within this framework, one may then debate questions such as: Do people especially sensitive to air pollution (the elderly or asthmatics, for example) have a right to air clean enough to protect their health? Do the poor have a right to a certain minimum standard of living? Do workers have a right to a safe and healthy workplace? Is it unjust that old people receive a lower level of services because they live in one area, where there are lots of old people and providing the service costs more, rather than another area, where there are few old people and providing the service costs less?

In any of these cases, if the determination is made that considerations of rights or justice require a certain public policy, then all citizens, including businesses, have a corresponding duty to act to achieve these policies. The desires of businesses to save money by spewing poisons into the environment or to avoid spending money to aid the poor then become analytically similar to the desire to kill and consume small infants. There is no moral obligation to take these desires into consideration—indeed, it is right to try to frustrate them—because the individuals concerned are asking to behave in ways they have no right to behave. (Which does not, of course, mean they have no right to *argue* that they have the right to behave that way.)

Clearly, to state questions of this nature is not to answer them. They will be subject to debate, and the political system is a proper arbiter of that debate. But I suspect that it is intuitive reactions somewhat along the lines I have been developing here that underlie much of the gut hostility to devolution of federal responsibilities that people express and much of the "unseemliness" that they perceive in competition among the states.

It was noted earlier that while the states could make themselves better off on balance by agreeing not to compete, there would likely be some costs in investment and jobs. That people with certain skills do desire to behave in unethical ways is a fact whose effects can unfortunately only be obviated, not eliminated, by a decision to do one's best (through an agreement not to compete) to get around the fact of their desires. We could eliminate the effects of those desires only if there were a duty by firms to invest, with a corresponding government right to require investment. Such a duty would be very difficult to justify. Even then, it probably would not eliminate the effects of these desires completely, because forced investment would doubtless not be as productive, and therefore as job- or welfare-enhancing, as investment undertaken voluntarily.

The key question, then, is whether businesses have a right in any particular instance to behave as they like. If they do not, the simple fact that they happen to possess certain skills that might lead others reluctantly to let them realize their desires is irrelevant; it does not make the desires any more ethically acceptable. The proper method for determining what acts are right is debate and argument. It is not negotiation. To resolve these arguments—and thus to determine when competition among the states is desirable or reprehensible—the tools of ethical theory that philosophers use are the most appropriate ones. Economic theory is not enough.

DISCUSSION QUESTIONS

1. Is the community simply the sum of the individuals which comprise it, or is the community greater than the sum of its parts? Are business-community relationships adequately addressed through individual market transactions?
2. What duties and responsibilities do large corporations have to their host communities? What are the economic, ethical, and political bases for these responsibilities?
3. If business has social responsibilities to local communities, do labor, consumers, and other constituencies also have social responsibilities to the community? Do labor and consumers receive community benefits comparable to business.
4. Do basic property rights in a political democracy include the right to move your assets across political boundries, that is does business have the right to vote with its feet?
5. How can the resource mobility necessary for dynamic economic efficiency be reconciled with social stability goals?
6. Can large corporations have "monopoly power" in their host communities even if they face substantial competition in their product markets?
7. In the *Federalist Papers, No. 51,* James Madison wrote the following in support of government competition:

> In a single republic, all the power surrendered by the people is submitted to the administration of a single government; and the usurpations are guarded

against by a division of the government into distinct and separate departments. In the *compound* republic of America, the power surrendered by the people is first divided between two distinct governments, and then the portion allotted to each subdivided among distinct and separate departments. Hence a double security arises to the rights of people. The different governments will control each other, at the same time each will be controlled by itself.

What are the economic, moral and political arguments for and against competition among community (state) governments?

8. Would plant-closing prohibitions yield net social benefits for society or just benefit some groups at the expense of others? Is plant-closing legislation a "beggar thy neighbor" protectionist policy, or a reasonable exercise of political control of business decisions affecting individuals and communities which have made large investments in the firm?

9. Steven Kelman argues that states should not compete to satisfy the immoral demands of business; for example, states should not reduce regulations or lower taxes to attract business. The individual has certain inalienable rights in a political democracy which the state (the elected majority) cannot negotiate away.

    Are regulatory relief and lower taxes immoral business demands? Would political attempts (e.g., lobbying and voting) to obtain regulatory relief or lower taxes also be unethical, or is it only unethical to pursue these goals through market processes?

10. How do the arguments for and against federal preemption of safety, health, and environmental regulation compare with the pro and con arguments for federal chartering of large corporations proposed in Chapter 2?

ADDITIONAL READINGS

BLUESTONE, BARRY, and BENNETT HARRISON,   *The Deindustrialization of America.* New York: Basic Books, 1982.

DUNN, L. F.,   "Measuring the Value of Community," *Journal of Urban Economics,* 6 (1979), 371–82.

GREEN, M. J.,   "The Corporation and the Community," in *Corporate Power in America,* Eds. R. Nader and M. J. Green. New York: Grossman Publishers, 1973.

JACOBS, JERRY,   "Corporate Subsidies from the Fifty States," *Business and Society Review,* 33 (Spring 1980), 47–50.

KELLY, EDWARD,   *Industrial Exodus, Public Strategies for Control of Corporate Relocation.* Washington, D.C.: Conference for Alternative State and Local Policies, 1977.

MCKENZIE, RICHARD B.,   ed., *Plant Closing: Public or Private Choices.* Washington D.C.: Cato Institute, 1982.

OLSON, WALTER,   "Competition among the States: A Response," *Regulation* (May–June 1982), pp. 44–47.

STERN, ROBERT N., and HOWARD ALDRICH,   "The Effect of Absentee Firm Control on Local Community Welfare: A Survey," in *The Economics of Firm Size, Market Structure and Social Performance,* pp. 162–81, ed., John J. Siegfried. Proceedings of a Conference sponsored by the Federal Trade Commission. Washington, D.C.: U.S. Government Printing Office, 1980.

"The Second War Between the States," *Business Week,* May 17, 1976, pp. 92–112.

CHAPTER **6**
GOALS AND RESPONSIBILITIES

Having surveyed the foundations of basic constituency relationships in Part I, the initial set of readings in Part II immediately surfaces the most fundamental institutional issue—the legitimate goals and responsibilities of the business firm in modern society. The traditional role of the private business firm as a specialized institution for the production of goods and services demanded by consumers in the marketplace is now challenged on several scores. The sheer size and broad economic and political influence of the business firm raises doubts about the capacity of competitive markets to turn the pursuit of self-interest to the maximization of social welfare. Uncontrolled exercises of economic and political power are the primary concern of those who challenge the traditional, private-production-for-profit role of the business firm.

The efficacy of the private business system is also questioned for an increasingly interdependent society in which private market transactions often generate harmful third-party effects such as the pollution of the atmosphere or community exposure to toxic wastes. The effects of business decisions on workers' welfare, local communities, the social infrastructure, and broader social interests are important consequences of private economic decision making which many feel have too long been ignored. In short, the ability of the private market system to reconcile private and public interests is seriously challenged. As suggested in Chapter 1, these challenges arise from perceived control loss and goal adherence problems at the societal level.

While the traditional role of the business firm as a private institution for the organization of production and distribution is inadequate for those concerned with broader societal goals, no single alternative commands a broad consensus. Some argue that the social failures of the private market system are grossly exaggerated and that market control deficiencies can be corrected through the judicious application of antitrust laws and eclectic government regulations. Others believe that the growing tensions between business and society can best be alleviated by enthusiastic business acceptance of greater social responsibility. Harsher critics insist on more fundamental reforms which would substitute political controls for the mythical controls of the market.

In the first reading, Professor Galbraith questions the traditional and most fundamental institutional relationship between business and society: "Are they [2,000 largest corporations] to be assimilated to the public sector of the economy? Or do they remain a part of what has always been called the private or market sector of the economy? Is one to have a public or a traditional view of the modern corporation?" In Professor Galbraith's view, large firms are no longer subject to market controls. Private businesses exercise substantial public power (the power to affect the health and well-being of broad elements of society) and therefore must be treated as public institutions and subjected to appropriate public controls, perhaps even public ownership. He rejects arguments for imposing effective market controls on the modern corporation as naive. He sees the myths of market competition and antitrust enforcement as convenient masquerades shielding private business decision making from legitimate public control.

Galbraith, lacking faith in businesses' ability to behave in a socially responsive manner, would proceed directly to public control of private business decision making. Milton Friedman, the 1976 Nobel Laureate in Economics, also lacks confidence in businesses' ability to accept greater social responsibility, but not for the same reasons as Galbraith. Galbraith argues that business will not act with social responsibility because of inadequate market controls; Friedman argues that it can not do so because of market controls. Businesses' inability to engage in socially responsive behavior is probably all that Friedman and Galbraith would agree upon. Not surprisingly, diametrically opposite prescriptions follow from these varying diagnoses of the market's health.

Galbraith is anxious to administer the last rites to the traditional market system while Friedman would like to do likewise for the government agencies which regulate the market. Friedman's unabashed position is that the social responsibility of business is to maximize its profits: ". . . there is one and only one social responsibility of business—to use its resources and engage in activities designed to increase its profits so long as it stays within the rules of the game, which is to say, engages in open and free competition without deception or fraud." Compliance with the market and the law, however, may be a necessary but not sufficient condition for a legitimate business-society relationship in an integrated society where the distinction between economic and social goals is increasingly blurred.

In stark contrast to the manager trustee role advocated by many proponents of greater business social responsibility, Friedman maintains that businessmen are agents of the company's owners and thus responsible only for pursuing their goals, which is generally to make as much money as possible. Friedman argues that only individuals, acting as principals and not as agents, can exercise social responsibilities. Requiring businessmen, as agents of stockholders, to engage in socially responsive activities is to require them to use stockholder assets in ways stockholders do not wish. In Friedman's view, this is tantamount to "taxation without representation"—to creating politically the uncontrolled exercise of decision-making authority which Galbraith and other business critics find so objectionable.

Friedman is also deeply concerned that the acceptance of social responsibilities by business would politicize the private business system, making managers civil servants and jeopardizing productive efficiency by confounding economic efficiency with political welfare goals. He argues that social responsibility is based on the socialist doctrine that resources should be allocated through political rather than market decisions. Galbraith argues that large private corporations already have confounded private and public goals, and, therefore, should be treated as public institutions. As noted in Chapter 1, at the polar extreme the debate over market and political, or private and public, controls over business decision making and the allocation of the nation's resources is a debate between capitalism and socialism.

Professor Friedman also makes the critical distinction between socially responsive behavior and conduct which, while serving some social purpose, is nevertheless in the firm's long-run self-interests; for example, improving living conditions in the local community to attract more highly skilled employees. Friedman contends that many of the social responsibility programs proclaimed by business leaders are simply actions undertaken in their own best, long-run interests. He argues that such claims are counterproductive to business interests because they legitimize the social claims made upon business, and encourage expectations of still greater socially responsive behavior.

The critical distinction between socially responsible behavior and the firm's long-run self-interests is frequently muddled. The Business Roundtable *Statement on Corporate Responsibility* concludes: "We think that's [social responsibility] good business." Presumably, if it's good business, no compulsion is necessary and, it's not social responsibility, at least not as proposed by active proponents of corporate social responsibility. The distinction between good business and social responsibility reaches the level of sophistry when, faced with an ominous threat of government intervention, business suddenly gets religion.

The Business Roundtable *Statement on Corporate Responsibility* has found its harshest critics among staunch supporters of the private market system. To Friedman, this is precisely the type of statement which undermines the private business systems by endorsing the social responsibility doctrine. The Business Roundtable recognizes the legitimacy of customer, employee, supplier, community and broad societal claims on business resources in addition to those of the stockholders. The Business Roundtable concludes that business ". . . must be a thoughtful institution which rises above the bottom line to consider the impact of its actions on all, from shareholders to the society at large.'' The business executive must attempt to balance these competing claims in a manager trustee role.

The Business Roundtable also recognizes that business must be profitable before it can accept social responsibilities: ''If the bottom line is minus, there is no plus for society.'' This, however, misses the basic social responsibility issue which is what business does in the course of making profits, not what it does with profits after they have been earned.

Paul MacAvoy's criticisms of The Business Roundtable's position reflect many of the basic Friedman critiques of social responsibility. Like Friedman, MacAvoy argues that business should attempt to maximize its profits, noting the many social benefits which follow from profit maximization. MacAvoy argues that by accepting the legitimacy of external constituencies' claims on business assets, The Business Roundtable is promoting the politization of business decision making. He is particulary critical of The Roundtable's treatment of stockholders as just one of businesses' many social constituencies—it is their assets everyone is claiming.

In their reply to MacAvoy, The Roundtable noted that the changing role of stockholders, also discussed in Chapter 2, suggests that they no longer have exclusive property right claims to the corporation's assets. The Business Roundtable also concluded that ''. . . a corporation best serves its shareholders by carefully balancing the legitimate interests of all constituents.'' They argue that social responsibilities are compatible with traditional economic responsibilities. MacAvoy and Friedman (and Galbraith) conclude just the opposite. Does The Roundtable only mean that a failure to accept social responsibilities will lead to more restrictive government controls? If this is the case, is The Business Roundtable advocating social responsibility or maximization of stockholders' long-run interests?

ON THE ECONOMIC IMAGE OF CORPORATE ENTERPRISE

John Kenneth Galbraith

Any discussion of the modern corporation—of the two thousand largest firms that contribute around half of total product in the United States—requires, if it is to be useful, a remarkably basic decision. How, in relation to the state, are these firms to be regarded? Are they to be assimilated to the public sector of the economy? Or do they remain a part of what has always been called the private or market sector of the economy? Is one to have a public or a traditional view of the modern corporation?

In the traditional image of the corporation, a conceptually sharp, even immutable line divides the corporation from the state. There is government; there is private enterprise; the two do not meet. The distinction is deeply cherished by all whose careers and livelihoods are identified with the firms in question. No matter how intricately the firm is involved with the government, it is still private enterprise. This image of the corporation as something separate and wholly distinct from the state is not normally assumed to require any theoretical justification. It is the way things are—the way they were ordained to be. Only someone with an instinct for inconvenience suggests that firms such as Lockheed or General Dynamics, which do most of their business with the government, make extensive use of plants owned by the government, have their working capital supplied by the government, have their cost overruns socialized by the government, and (as in the case of Lockheed) are rescued from misfortune on their nongovernmental business by the government, are anything but the purest manifestation of private enterprise. And this being so of Lockheed, the question certainly does not arise with American Telephone & Telegraph, General Motors, or General Electric.

But there is, of course, a theoretical justification. The corporation can be private because its operations are subject to the regulation—to the presumptively comprehensive discipline—of the market. The market allows of private purpose because it keeps it aligned with public purpose. The market is an expression of public preference and desire. The firm responds to the market. The firm is thus under public control and the public cannot be in conflict with itself. There are, admittedly, exceptions. Thus, no scholar of independent mind who

John Kenneth Galbraith, "On the Economic Image of Corporate Enterprise," in *Corporate Power in America*, eds. Ralph Nader and Mark J. Green (New York: Grossman Publishers, 1973) pp. 3–9. Copyright © 1973 by Ralph Nader. Reprinted with permission of Viking Penguin Incorporated.

was unpaid for his opinion would argue that Lockheed or General Dynamics was subordinate to the market. Or (the counterpart case) would it be suggested by many that these firms are subordinate to the political process—that the demand for their products is an expression of public need in which they themselves play a passive role. It is recognized that the Department of Defense persuades the modern weapons firm to produce what it needs. And it is recognized that these firms persuade the Department of Defense to need what they produce. Such firms retain their rationale as private enterprise not because of any conceivable theoretical justification but as a consequence of political inertia and caution. It is politically convenient so to regard them, and also for many politicians a great deal safer.

It is also recognized that the market rationale fails in respect of other large firms. They become large and powerful in their markets. Monopoly or oligopoly replaces competition. So great is their power that the state may be in some measure suborned. But the market in theory remains, though imperfectly, a decisive force. The monopoly pursues profits; what it can make is ultimately subject to the decisions of consumers as to what to by or not to buy. Though he pays more than he should to the monopolist, the consumer is still presumably sovereign.

And there is a remedy for excessive power by the corporation both in markets and over the government, which is to decentralize the firm, to break it up. Then the original competitive power of the market is restored; the power to suborn the state is reduced or eliminated. The conditions under which private business can be private are thus re-established. But this alternative means recourse to the antitrust laws—laws, it is agreed even by their friends, which have not been effective over the past eighty years of their existence. Big business has indubitably become bigger, more powerful, more monopolistic; still, the antitrust laws are absolutely indispensable to the traditional imagery of the private corporation. Many cannot accept the modern corporation at it is, but they can accept it as it might be if the antitrust laws were enforced. And they can always imagine that some day these laws might be enforced. So with the aid of the antitrust laws they can remain, with no appreciable damage to conscience, with the traditional and essentially conservative position.

The public view of the corporation involves a basic break with the foregoing dialectic. It holds that not only Lockheed and General Dynamics but also A.T.&T., General Motors, Jersey Standard, United States Steel Corporation, and the other great corporations involve a clear break from the economy and polity of the classical market. As they grow and become more powerful, such firms acquire, increasingly, a public character. They become public institutions. The clichés of private enterprise survive but serve primarily to disguise the essentially public character of the great corporation, including its private exercise of what is, in fact, a public power. Such a corporation fixes its prices; it controls its costs; it persuades its consumers; it organizes its supply of raw materials;

it has powerful leverage in the community; its needs are, *pro tanto*, sound public policy; it has, on frequent occasion, a hammerlock on the Pentagon.

In this view the large specialized weapons firm is only the extreme case. The line here between public and private enterprise is so exotic as to be impalpable. One can accept it only as a device for diverting the eyes of Congressional committees, the Comptroller General, and the general public away from things like executive compensation, lobbying, political activity by executives and employees, profits, and bureaucratic error or nonfeasance; in the case of an admitted public bureaucracy or a full-fledged public corporation, these items would invite highly unwelcome attention. It is a formula for hiding public business behind the cloak of corporate privacy.

Again, the specialized weapons firm only begins the analysis. General Motors sets the prices for its cars (and, in conjunction with the other automobile companies, for all cars) with public effect. And it negotiates wage contracts with public effect. And it designs cars and incorporates or rejects safety features with public effect. And it decides on engine design and emissions with public effect. And it persuades the public to its designs with public effect. And it powerfully influences highway construction with public effect. The public decisions of General Motors in the course of any year are far more consequential than those of any state legislature. So with other large firms.

The public view of the corporation not only accepts the tendency for it to assimilate itself to the state but regards this tendency as irreversible. It follows that there is no longer a presumption that the corporation has private affairs that are protected from public scrutiny. Nor is there any presumption that it must be free of public regulation or, for that matter, public ownership. On the contrary, the presumption is favorable to public intervention. The great corporation exercises public power, power that affects the health, well-being, and general happiness of those who are subject to it. This power is exercised—as even its possessors concede—in pursuit of the interests of the corporation. Since this power is no longer subject to the discipline of the market—is no longer *aligned* with public purposes by the market—there is no reason to believe that, except by accident, the exercise of public power by the corporation coincides with the public interest. There is, accordingly, a presumption in favor of action that aligns it with the public interest. So it comes about that on matters as diverse as design of products, acceptance or rejection of technical innovation (such as the SST), prohibition of adverse environmental effects both of the production and consumption of products, military policy, control of wages and prices, and control (as in the case of cigarettes) of public persuasion, one finds the legislature intervening to align corporate power with public purpose. In all this effort there must be an acute perception of the danger that the corporation will regulate its regulators. But it is to such regulation and other recognition of the public character of the firm, and not to the rehabilitation of market constraints, that one looks for protection and advance of the public interest.

It will not come to everyone as a shock that I think the public view of the corporation is the right one. The market will not be restored. Great currents of history cannot be reversed by small laws. The technological, capital, and planning requirements of modern economic activity are inconsistent with the classical market. As to the antitrust laws, they are eighty years old and the last really important dissolution occurred sixty years ago. Each new generation of reformers has held that only the feckless ineptitude and cowardice of their predecessors had kept the market from being restored. Then, their bravery notwithstanding, they too have failed. It is sensible to conclude that if these laws were going to work wonders for anyone but the lawyers, they would have worked their wonder by now.

They have become, in fact, a basic support to irresponsible corporate power. For they sustain the hope, and thus perpetuate the myth, of the all-powerful market. Consequently, they keep alive the illusion that business is private. They keep the burden of proof on those who propose regulation, or even disclosure. And they totally suppress the possibility (or specter) of public ownership. No one could do more for General Motors than this.

To recognize that the great corporation is essentially a public entity is to accept that its acts have a profoundly public effect. And that is to accept, as noted, the legitimacy of regulation that aligns its actions with public goals. Autonomy may still be accorded to the corporation. This is necessary for effective administration—for efficiency. But this is a pragmatic decision, and no principle is involved. Where the public interest—in safety of products, effect on environment, effect of price and wage settlements on the economy, the equity of profits and executive compensation—is at issue, there is no natural right to be left alone. Nor is there any natural right to secrecy. Nor is there any barrier in the case of the specialized weapons firms like Lockheed or incompetent ones like Penn Central to stripping away the purely artificial facade of private enterprise and converting the corporation into a fully public enterprise. In recent years church groups and other people of conscience have been agonizing over whether they should invest funds for good works in makers of weapons. It is a ridiculous question. They should be asking whether these firms should exist as private profit-making entities in a civilized state.

Some will say that the public view of the corporation reacts far too lightly to the problem of bureaucracy. At a time when we are learning to appreciate the power of the Pentagon, can we accept the continued existence of industrial bureaucracy? And, in this case of the weapons firms, can we think of adding the industrial to the public bureaucracy? The concern is well grounded. But we have the corporate bureaucracy now, and we have it now in a worse form. For the one thing more inimical than a bureaucracy that we see is a bureaucracy that we pretend not to see. The one thing worse than a General Motors whose public character is recognized is a General Motors whose public character is denied—and whose immunity to public regulation is defended on such grounds.

The one thing worse than a General Dynamics or Lockheed that is publicly owned and publicly controlled is a General Dynamics or Lockheed that is publicly owned but privately controlled. There is no magic in stripping away the myth that the market controls the modern corporation or could be made to do so. But it is the first essential for any reform.

It will be suggested that I have not been exactly evenhanded in my judgments between the traditional and the public view of the corporation. And more is involved in the choice than the wholly explicable self-interest of economists in what they teach and write and lawyers in what they believe and practice. The defense of the market and the antitrust laws has never been a strictly secular phenomenon. Profoundly religious attitudes are involved. Neoclassical doctrine which lies back of these attitudes is more than a mere science; it is a highly developed theology. Added to the sense of unfairness will be the sense of outrage that, inevitably, focuses on anyone who appears to ride roughshod over established faith. Yet both truth and great questions are involved. One can sympathize with religious feeling when he cannot bow to it. As to evenhandedness, there is no natural obligation to be neutral between truth and error—between the right path in economic development and the wrong. Economics is not a branch of the television business.

The great issue that is involved is the future structure of the economic system in the most profound sense. Although it is accepted doctrine in Detroit, not many scholars would insist that the modern great corporation is the ultimate achievement of man. The public view of the coporation portends a public development, foreseeing that the great corporations eventually become public enterprises. It invites the use of a word long banned from reputable discussion in the United States, or whispered only among minority cults, which is socialism. The traditional view, as its proponents will be the first to concede, holds up no such prospect—or specter. And that, indeed, is another way of describing its service to the *status quo*. For as long as there is a serious effort to turn back to the eighteenth century, there will assuredly be no advance to the twenty-first or even the twentieth.

SOCIAL RESPONSIBILITY OF BUSINESS
Milton Friedman

When I hear businessmen speak eloquently about the "social responsibilities of business in a free enterprise system," I am reminded of the wonderful line about the Frenchman who discovered at the age of 70 that he had been speaking prose all his life.

The businessmen believe that they are defending free enterprise when they declaim that business is not concerned "merely" with profit but also with promoting desirable "social" ends; that business has a "social conscience" and takes seriously its responsibilities for providing employment, eliminating discrimination, avoiding pollution and whatever else may be the catchwords of the contemporary crop of reformers.

In fact they are—or would be if they or anyone else took them seriously—preaching pure and unadulterated socialism. Businessmen who talk this way are unwitting puppets of the intellectual forces that have been undermining the basis of a free society these past decades.

The discussions of the "social responsibilities of business" are notable for their analytical looseness and lack of rigor. What does it mean to say that "business" has responsibilities? Only people can have responsibilities. A corporation is an artificial person and in this sense may have artificial responsibilities, but "business" as a whole cannot be said to have responsibilities, even in this vague sense. The first step toward clarity in examining the doctrine of the social responsibility of business is to ask precisely what it implies for whom.

Presumably, the individuals who are to be responsible are businessmen, which means individual proprietors or corporate executives. Most of the discussion of social responsibility is directed at corporations, so in what follows I shall mostly neglect the individual proprietor and speak of corporate executives.

In a free-enterprise, private-property system, a corporate executive is an employee of the owners of the business. He has direct responsibility to his employers. That responsibility is to conduct the business in accordance with their desires, which generally will be to make as much money as possible while conforming to the basic rules of the society, both those embodied in law and those embodied in ethical custom. Of course, in some cases his employers may have a different objective. A group of persons might establish a corporation for an eleemosynary purpose—for example, a hospital or a school. The manager of such a corporation will not have money profit as his objective but the rendering of certain services.

In either case, the key point is that, in his capacity as a corporate executive, the manager is the agent of the individuals who own the corporation or establish the eleemosynary institution, and his primary responsibility is to them.

Needless to say, this does not mean that it is easy to judge how well he is performing his task. But at least the criterion of performance is straightforward and the persons among whom a voluntary contractual arrangement exists are clearly defined.

Of course, the corporate executive is also a person in his own right. As a person, he may have other responsibilities that he recognizes or assumes voluntarily—to his family, his conscience, his feelings of charity, his church, his clubs, his city, his country. He may feel impelled by these responsibilities to devote part of his income to causes he regards as worthy, to refuse to work for particular corporations, even to leave his job, for example, to join his country's armed forces. If we wish, we may refer to some of these responsibilities as "social responsibilities." But in these respects he is acting as a principal, not an agent; he is spending his own money or time or energy, not the money of his employers or the time or energy he has contracted to devote to their purposes. If these are "social responsibilities," they are the social responsibilities of individuals, not of business.

What does it mean to say that the corporate executive has a "social responsibility" in his capacity as businessman? If this statement is not pure rhetoric, it must mean that he is to act in some way that is not in the interest of his employers. For example, that he is to refrain from increasing the price of the product in order to contribute to the social objective of preventing inflation, even though a price increase would be in the best interests of the corporation. Or that he is to make expenditures on reducing pollution beyond the amount that is in the best interests of the corporation or that is required by law in order to contribute to the social objective of improving the environment. Or that, at the expense of corporate profits, he is to hire "hard-core" unemployed instead of better-qualified available workmen to contribute to the social objective of reducing poverty.

In each of these cases, the corporate executive would be spending someone else's money for a general social interest. Insofar as his actions in accord with his "social responsibility" reduce returns to stockholders, he is spending their money. Insofar as his actions raise the price to customers, he is spending the customers' money. Insofar as his actions lower the wages of some employees, he is spending their money.

The stockholders or the customers or the employees could separately spend their own money on the particular action if they wished to do so. The executive is exercising a distinct "social responsibility," rather than serving as an agent of the stockholders or the customers or the employees, only if he spends the money in a different way than they would have spent it.

But if he does this, he is in effect imposing taxes, on the one hand, and deciding how the tax proceeds shall be spent, on the other.

This process raises political questions on two levels: principle and consequences. On the level of political principle, the imposition of taxes and the expenditure of tax proceeds are governmental functions. We have established elaborate constitutional, parliamentary, and judicial provisions to control these functions, to assure that taxes are imposed so far as possible in accordance with the preferences and desires of the public—after all, "taxation without representation" was one of the battle cries of the American revolution. We have a system of checks and balances to separate the legislative function of imposing taxes and enacting expenditures from the executive function of collecting taxes and administering expenditure programs and from the judicial function of mediating disputes and interpreting the law.

Here the businessman—self-selected or appointed directly or indirectly by stockholders—is to be simultaneously legislator, executive, and jurist. He is to decide whom to tax by how much and for what purpose, and he is to spend the proceeds—all this guided only by general exhortations from on high to restrain inflation, improve the environment, fight poverty and so on and on.

The whole justification for permitting the corporate executive to be selected by the stockholders is that the executive is an agent serving the interests of his principal. This justification disappears when the corporate executive imposes taxes and spends the proceeds for "social" purposes. He becomes in effect a public employee, a civil servant, even though he remains in name an employee of a private enterpise. On grounds of political principle, it is intolerable that such civil servants—insofar as their actions in the name of social responsibility are real and not just window dressing—should be selected as they are now. If they are to be civil servants, then they must be selected through a political process. If they are to impose taxes and make expenditures to foster "social" objectives, then political machinery must be set up to guide the assessment of taxes and to determine through a political process the objectives to be served.

This is the basic reason why the doctrine of "social responsibility" involves the acceptance of the socialist view that political mechanisms, not market mechanisms, are the appropriate way to determine the allocation of scarce resources to alternative uses.

On the grounds of consequences, can the corporate executive in fact discharge his alleged "social responsibilities"? On the other hand, suppose he could get away with spending the stockholders' or customers' or employees' money. How is he to know how to spend it? He is told that he must contribute to fighting inflation. How is he to know what action of his will contribute to that end? He is presumably an expert in running his company—in producing a product or selling it or financing it. But nothing about his selection makes him an expert on inflation. Will his holding down the price of his product reduce inflationary pressure? Or, by leaving more spending power in the hands of his customers, simply divert it elsewhere? Or, by forcing him to produce less because of the lower price, will it simply contribute to shortages? Even if he could answer these questions, how much cost is he justified in imposing on his stockholders, customers and employees for this social purpose? What is his appropriate share and what is the appropriate share of others?

And, whether he wants to or not can he get away with spending his stockholders', customers', or employees' money? Will not the stockholders fire him? (Either the present ones or those who take over when his actions in the name of social responsibility have reduced the corporation's profits and the price of his stock). His customers and his employees can desert him for other producers and employers less scrupulous in exercising their social responsibilities.

This facet of "social responsibility" doctrine is brought into sharp relief when the doctrine is used to justify wage restraint by trade unions. The conflict of interest is naked and clear when union officials are asked to subordinate the interest of their members to some more general social purpose. If the union officials try to enforce wage restraint, the consequence is likely to be wildcat strikes, rank-and-file revolts and the emergences of strong competitors for their jobs. We thus have the ironic phenomenon that union leaders—at least in the United States—have objected to government interference with the market far more consistently and courageously than have business leaders.

The difficulty of exercising "social responsibility" illustrates, of course, the great virtue of private competitive enterprise—it forces people to be responsible for their own actions and makes it difficult for them to "exploit" other people for either selfish or unselfish purposes. They can do good—but only at their own expense.

Many a reader who has followed the argument this far may be tempted to remonstrate that it is all well and good to speak of government's having the responsibility to impose taxes and determine expenditures for such "social" purposes as controlling pollution or training the hard-core unemployed, but that the problems are too urgent to wait on the slow course of political processes, that the exercise of social responsibility by businessmen is a quicker and surer way to solve pressing current problems.

Aside from the question of fact—I share Adam Smith's skepticism about the benefits that can be expected from "those who affected to trade for the public good"—this argument must be rejected on grounds of principle. What it amounts to is an assertion that those who favor the taxes and expenditures in question have failed to persuade a majority of their fellow citizens to be of like mind and that they are seeking to attain by undemocratic procedures what they cannot attain by democratic procedures. In a free society, it is hard for "good" people to do "good," but that is a small price to pay for making it hard for "evil" people to do "evil," especially since one man's good is another's evil.

I have, for simplicity, concentrated on the special case of the corporate executive, except only for the brief digression on trade unions. But precisely the same argument applies to the newer phenomenon of calling upon stockholders to require corporations to exercise social responsibility [the recent G. M. crusade, for example]. In most of these cases, what is in effect involved is some stockholders trying to get other stockholders [or customers or employees] to contribute against their will to "social" causes favored by the activists. Insofar as they succeed, they are again imposing taxes and spending the proceeds. The situation of the individual proprietor is somewhat different. If he acts to reduce the returns of his enterprise in order to exercise his "social responsibility," he is spending his own money, not someone else's. If he wishes to spend his money on such purposes, that is his right, and I cannot see that there is any objection to his doing so. In the process, he, too, may impose costs on employees and customers. However, because he is far less likely than a large corporation or union to have monopolistic power, any such side effects will tend to be minor.

Of course, in practice the doctrine of social responsibility is frequently a cloak for actions that are justified on other grounds rather than a reason for those actions.

To illustrate, it may well be in the long-run interest of a corporation that is a major employer in a small community to devote resources to providing amenities to that community or to improving its government. That may make it easier to attract desirable employees, it may reduce the wage bill or lesson losses from pilferage and sabotage or have other worthwhile effects. Or it may be that, given the laws about the deductibility of corporate charitable contributions, the stockholders can contribute more to charities they favor by having the corporation make the gift than by doing it themselves, since they can in that way contribute an amount that would otherwise have been paid as corporate taxes.

In each of these—and many similar—cases, there is a strong temptation to rationalize these actions as an exercise of "social responsibility." In the present climate of opinion, with its widespread aversion to "capitalism," "profits," the "soulless corporation" and so on, this is one way for a corporation to generate goodwill as a by-product of expenditures that are entirely justified in its own self-interest.

It would be inconsistent of me to call on corporate executives to refrain from this hypocritical window-dressing because it harms the foundations of a free society. That would be to call on them to exercise a "social responsibility"! If our institutions, and the attitudes of the public make it in their self-interest to cloak their actions in this way, I cannot summon much indignation to denounce them. At the same time, I can express admiration for those individual proprietors or owners of closely held corporations or stockholders of more broadly held corporations who disdain such tactics as approaching fraud.

Whether blameworthy or not, the use of the cloak of social responsibility, and the nonsense spoken in its name by influential and prestigious businessmen, does clearly harm the foundations of a free society. I have been impressed time and again by the schizophrenic character of many businessmen. They are capable of being extremely farsighted and clear-headed in matters that are internal to their businesses. They are incredibly shortsighted and muddle headed in matters that are outside their businesses but affect the possible survival of business in general. This short sightedness is strikingly exemplified in the calls from many businessmen for wage and price guidelines or controls or incomes policies. There is nothing that could do more in a brief period to destroy a market system and replace it by a centrally controlled system than effective governmental control of prices and wages.

The shortsightedness is also exemplified in speeches by businessmen on social responsibility. This may gain them kudos in the short run. But it helps to strengthen the already too prevalent view that the pursuit of profits is wicked and immoral and must be curbed and controlled by external forces. Once this view is adopted, the external forces that curb the market will not be the social consciences, however highly developed, of the pontificating executives; it will be the iron fist of government bureaucrats. Here, as with price and wage controls, businessmen seem to me to reveal a suicidal impulse.

The political principle that underlies the market mechanism is unanimity. In an ideal free market resting on private property, no individual can coerce any other, all cooperation is voluntary, all parties to such cooperation benefit or they need not participate. There are no "social" values, no "social" responsibilities in any sense other than the shared values and responsibilities of individuals. Society is a collection of individuals and of the various groups they voluntarily form.

The political principle that underlies the political mechanism is conformity. The individual must serve a more general social interest—whether that be determined by a church or a dictator or a majority. The individual may have a vote and a say in what is to be done, but if he is overruled, he must conform. It is appropriate for some to require others to contribute to a general social purpose whether they wish to or not.

Unfortunately, unanimity is not always feasible. There are some respects in which conformity appears unavoidable, so I do not see how one can avoid the use of the political mechanism altogether.

But the doctrine of "social responsibility" taken seriously would extend the scope of the political mechanism to every human activity. It does not differ in philosophy from the most explicitly collectivist doctrine. It differs only by professing to believe that collectivist ends can be attained without collectivist means. That is why, in my book *Capitalism and Freedom,* I have called it a "fundamentally subversive doctrine" in a free society, and have said that in such a society, "there is one and only one social responsibility of business—to use its resources and engage in activities designed to increase its profits so long as it stays within the rules of the game, which is to say, engages in open and free competition without deception or fraud."

STATEMENT ON CORPORATE RESPONSIBILITY
The Business Roundtable

INTRODUCTION

The Business Roundtable issues this statement out of a strong conviction that the future of this nation depends upon the existence of strong and responsive business enterprises and that, in turn, the long-term viability of the business sector is linked to its responsibility to the society of which it is a part.

As our colleague Reginald Jones, former chairman and chief executive officer of General Electric, has put it:

> Public policy and social issues are no longer adjuncts to business planning and management. They are in the mainstream of it. The concern must be pervasive in companies today, from boardroom to factory floor. Management must be measured for performance in noneconomic and economic areas alike. And top management must lead.*

Over the past century, large organizations have emerged as central elements in the social, economic and political life of the United States, including big government, big universities, big trade unions, big foundations, and big business organizations. These institutions have evolved in response to felt needs. As corporations have evolved and developed through the years, society's expectations of them have changed greatly. Their importance to the well-being and quality of life of the average person has created perceptions and expectations that go far beyond what many considered their historic purpose, which was the creation of goods and services at a profit.

In his 1980 book, *The Revolutionary Corporations,* John Desmond Glover, professor emeritus of the Harvard University Graduate School of Business Administration, wrote that the extraordinary levels of American production and consumption would simply not be possible without an industrial organization of the sort represented by corporations. He called corporations the "principal engines" creating plenty, pushing growth, and leading change in the United States. And yet, he granted that the corporation "is also one of the least understood of our institutions, and one of the most controversial."

There is a widespread idea that corporations have relatively unlimited

The Business Roundtable, *Statement on Corporate Responsibility,* October, 1981. Reprinted with permission.

Business and Society: Strategies for the 1980's, published by U.S. Department of Commerce, December 1980.

power, and there is unmistakable evidence of much mistrust and resentment of corporations and their perceived effects on society. To some degree, that set of attitudes is based on reality—mistakes, failures, and aberrant performance by people who manage and work for corporations. To a considerable extent, the antipathy toward corporations is rooted in misconceptions of what corporations are and what their role is in the economic system. Corporations' record of efficiency in the production of goods and services has led to unrealistic expectations that they can do the same in solving social problems. The most challenging aspect of these attitudes lies in the fact that public expectations with regard to corporate performance have changed materially and are continuing to change. At the same time, corporations have been progressively surrounded by limitations imposed by economics, law, government regulation, and taxation.

The public debate about the proper role of corporations in the society has been underway for years and can be expected to continue well into the future. Earlier, the discussion turned largely around issues of corporate governance. In 1978, The Business Roundtable issued a position paper dealing with some fundamental aspects of that subject.*

Today the discussion centers more directly on the substantive side, although some structural issues are still quite current. It is clear that the corporate community must deal effectively with the issues in this debate, either by explaining the corporate role satisfactorily (and thereby changing public expectations) or by meeting new expectations—or both. If public expectations and perceived corporate performance are at odds, corporations will be attacked more and more on social and political as well as economic grounds. The result would be adverse public opinion leading to further government involvement in their operations.

PUBLIC EXPECTATIONS

Many people believe that corporations are generally concerned only about profits and not about the impact their operations may have on society. At the same time, it is clear that a large percentage of the public now measures corporations by a yardstick beyond strictly economic objectives.

People are concerned about how the actions of corporations and managers affect them not only as employees and customers but also as members of the society in which corporations operate. While the range of these concerns is broad, some of the most prominent relate to:

product pricing, quality and advertising
fair treatment of employees

---

*The Role and Composition of the Board of Directors of the Large Publicly Owned Corporation, January 1978.

health and safety in the workplace
plant openings and closing
effects on the environment
role in the community
philanthropy

At a time when the Federal Government has set a policy of less rather than more regulation and aims to reduce the rates of increase in government spending, public expectations of corporate performance in these areas of concern are even higher. As a result, the responsibility problem for corporations is even greater. More than ever, managers of corporations are expected to serve the public interest as well as private profit. While the business sector must deal with this new challenge, it should not be expected to substitute corporate dollars for a large proportion of the Federal funds that are being reduced or eliminated.

As the corporate community addresses growing public expectations with regard to corporate performance, there must be recognition of the fundamental importance of profits and their contributions to the long-term economic viability of the enterprise. If a corporation is not profitable in the long run, there is no way that it can fulfill any responsibilities to society. If the bottom line is a minus, there is no plus for society. Thus corporate long-term viability and corporate responsibility to society are interrelated.

THE EXPECTATIONS OF CONSTITUENCIES

Corporations operate within a web of complex, often competing relationships which demand the attention of corporate managers. The decision-making process requires an understanding of the corporation's many constituencies and their various expectations. Key among these are the following:

Customers.   Customers have a primary claim for corporate attention. Without them, the enterprise will fail. They expect reliable products and services, fair value, good service and accurate advertising. If customer expectations are not satisfied, the corporation suffers long-term as well as short-term damage. The public attitude toward business is substantially conditioned by the marketplace.

Employees.   Management's relationship with employees once was expressed simply as a fair day's pay for a fair day's work. Now the relationship is more complicated. Employees expect not only fair pay but also such conditions as equal opportunity, workplaces that protect health and safety, financial security, personal privacy, freedom of expression, and concern for their quality of life.

Experience has shown that employees will perform well for corporations which have earned their loyalty, rewarded their performance, and involved them in the decision-making process. At the same time, corporations need to weigh employee benefits in the light of competition around the world and the fundamental necessity to produce profits to support the continuing existence of the enterprise.

Communities.   While much of the public discussion about the impact of corporations on the lives of people is cast in general terms, corporations most closely touch people's lives in the individual communities where they operate. Here they are expected to be concerned with local needs and problems—schools, traffic, pollution, health, recreation—and to explain their activities to the people of the community.

Society at large.   Operating in national and multinational spheres, corporations affect the lives of people around the world. Their performance is subject to scrutiny by a diverse public which includes academia, government, and the media. They are expected to respond to concerns and issues of national and international significance. At the same time, the corporations' first responsibility to society is to maintain its economic viability as a producer of goods and services, as an employer, and as a creator of jobs.

Suppliers.   Most suppliers to corporations are smaller businesses, which expect and need fair purchasing practices and prompt payment. The relationship between the large corporations and the supplier is a vital element in the economic system, for the very existence of many suppliers is dependent on fair treatment by corporations.

Shareholders.   Shareholders have a special relationship to the corporation. As providers of risk capital, shareholders make the corporation possible. They supply funds for corporate birth, development, and growth. Any approach to corporate responsibility must begin with the practical recognition that the corporation must be profitable enough to provide shareholders a return that will encourage continuation of investment. The interest of shareholders must be considered in all important activities of the corporation.

At one time most shareholders were long-term, personally-involved individual investors. Now a high proportion of them is made up of institutionally-grouped and often unidentified shorter-term buyers most interested in near-term gain. This has affected their role among business constituencies. The expectation of near-term gain can exert pressure to subordinate long-range objectives to more immediate profit considerations. Despite such expectations, management needs to maintain long-range perspective.

BALANCING THE INTERESTS OF CONSTITUENCIES

Carefully weighing the impacts of decisions and balancing different constituent interests—in the context of both near-term and long-term effects—must be an integral part of the corporation's decision-making and management process.

Resolving the differences involves compromises and trade-offs. It is important that all sides be heard but impossible to assure that all will be satisfied because competing claims may be mutually exclusive.

A classic example of the varying interests of constituencies arises when management must consider whether to establish, expand, or close a plant. For shareholders, customers, and society at large, closing a plant could bring positive results by paving the way for production of better products more economically in a new plant at a new location. It may be only in that way that the company is able to meet domestic and foreign competition. Employees and the community, however, may object to the plant closing because of the impact on jobs and other local economic factors. Sensitive community issues also arise in connection with decisions on the location of new plants and expansion of existing ones.

Balancing the shareholder's expectations of maximum return against other priorities is one of the fundamental problems confronting corporate management. The shareholder must receive a good return but the legitimate concerns of other constituencies also must have the appropriate attention.

Striving to reach the appropriate balance, some leading managers have come to believe that the primary role of corporations is to help meet society's legitimate need for goods and services and to earn a reasonable return for the shareholders in the process. They are aware that this must be done in a socially acceptable manner. They believe that by giving enlightened consideration to balancing the legitimate claims of all its constituents, a corporation will best serve the interest of its shareholders.

CORPORATE RESPONSE

How can companies best react to the various new demands being made on them? How should their response be organized? Leading managers have been at work on answers to those questions.

Many companies now include the whole spectrum of corporate social objectives in strategic planning. This requires planners to consider not only economic and technological trends and events but also the social and political; to study not only the expectations of shareholders, employees, customers, and suppliers, but also those of the community and the public. Such an approach encourages a broad, systematic corporate overview and an evaluation of a wide range of performance expectations.

Some companies have established committees of the board of directors to deal with corporate responsibility issues. Such committees provide guidance to management in defining the company's role, assessing the effectiveness of performance, and recommending changes. These committees of the board can serve as independent auditors of issues affecting the company and of how those issues are being addressed.

In companies which have developed a structured approach to matters of responsibility, staff groups (often including an officer of the company) examine and raise questions related to these issues. They seek to encourage employees in all sections of the business to recognize public policy as part of their regular work and call on them for analysis of the particular issues in their area. Such companies have a process for checking what is being done by employees throughout the company with regard to total performance objectives. That performance then becomes part of the evaluation of employees.

Companies have also found it useful to have such policy instruments as:

a written code of conduct

a written policy on corporate disclosure

well-defined corporate policies with regard to such matters as executive compensation, fair pay, equal employment opportunity, personal privacy, freedom of expression

a continuing focus on corporate impact on the environment, health and safety in the workplace, and the impact of plant openings and closings on communities and employees

continuing concern about product quality, acceptable pricing policies, and ethics in advertising

a high priority for and high level attention to the size and direction of corporate philanthropy*

a program designed to inform, sensitize, and train present and future management to deal with public policy and corporate responsibility issues

It is in the day-to-day—even hour-to-hour—management of the business at all levels that corporate objectives for total performance must be carried out. Top managers regard the selection, training, and motivation of people as essential to success in dealing with these issues. They also stress that it is not enough that top management and headquarters organizations have well-defined goals of responsibility. To assure that these objectives will be effective in field operations and factories, specific programs should be developed and implemented throughout the organization.

---

*In March 1981 The Business Roundtable issued a position paper on corporate philanthropy urging corporations to increase contributions for educational, health, welfare, and cultural activities and to give philanthropic efforts greater importance.

RECOMMENDATIONS AND CONCLUSIONS

Corporations have a responsibility, first of all, to make available to the public quality goods and services at fair prices, thereby earning a profit that attracts investment to continue and enhance the enterprise, provide jobs, and build the economy. In carrying out this mission, corporations have made an impressive contribution to the well-being and standard of living of people in the United States and many other countries.

That economic responsibility is by no means incompatible with other corporate responsibilities in society. In contemporary society all corporate responsibilities are so interrelated that they should not and cannot be separated.

The issue is one of defining, and achieving, responsible corporate management which fully integrates into the entire corporate planning, management, and decision-making process consideration of the impacts of all operating and policy decisions on each of the corporation's constituents. Responsibility to all these constituents *in toto* constitutes responsibility to society, making the corporation both an economically and socially viable entity. Business and society have a symbiotic relationship: The long-term viability of the corporation depends upon its responsibility to the society of which it is a part. And the well-being of society depends upon profitable and responsible business enterprises.

Just how a corporation focuses on these interrelated responsibilities will vary from one company to another. Each corporation has an individual character, related to its products, markets, facilities, manufacturing processes, and other aspects of its business.

Amidst that diversity, it is possible to set out some fundamental approaches. The Business Roundtable recommends that the directors, officers, and managers of corporations consider:

1. Which issues of responsibility have particular relevance to their business.
2. Whether the company has effective policies, the right personnel, and adequate structure to deal with both the economic and social expectations of constituencies and the general public.
3. What changes, if any, should be made in company structure, staffing policies, operations, attitudes, and behavior in order to deal effectively with public policy and social issues.
4. What steps can be taken to assure that responsibilities to all corporate constituents are given adequate consideration in the selection, assignment, evaluation, and compensation of employees.
5. How the company can inform, sensitize, and train present and future management to deal with these matters.
6. What can be done to assure that the company's larger role in society is understood by management, employees and other constituencies.
7. What are the most effective ways for the company to communicate its concern for all its responsibilities to the general public.

While it would be neither sensible nor possible to direct the full thrust of the corporate community's efforts to curing all the nation's social ills, it is important that each corporation give attention to all the consequences of its activities. Business enterprises are not designed to be either political or cultural institutions, but the business community will be well served by a habit of mind that stays alert to social currents.

In considerable part, increased public confidence in business as a positive force in society will depend upon the way corporations respond to the public's new and expanded expectations regarding business.

Corporations are surrounded by a complicated pattern of economic, social, ethical, and political ideas and expectations. They have a responsibility to themselves, to each other, and to their constituencies—including society at large—to make a reasonable and effective response.

A corporation's responsibilities include how the whole business is conducted every day. It must be a thoughtful institution which rises above the bottom line to consider the impact of its actions on all, from shareholders to the society at large. Its business activities must make social sense just as its social activities must make business sense.

THE BUSINESS LOBBY'S WRONG BUSINESS
Paul W. MacAvoy

"More than ever, managers of corporations are expected to serve the public interest as well as private profit." So begins the new pronouncement on corporate responsibility of the Business Roundtable. That this message was agreed to by the leading lobby for the country's largest corporations is important in and of itself. The question is just how, and how much, public service should be provided by the corporation.

In tackling that question, the Roundtable divides the world into constituencies consisting of customers, employees, communities and society at large, and shareholders—all of whom lay claim to a share of corporate resources.

The Roundtable is an organization worth listening to. By far the most successful lobby in Washington on economic policy these days, the group backs

Paul W. MacAvoy, "The Business Lobby's Wrong Business," *The New York Times,* December 20, 1981, copyright 1981 by *The New York Times Company.* Reprinted by permission.

up its views on Federal policies with the jobs and votes of the country's largest corporations. It knows quite a bit about trade-offs of economic for social or political results.

But in a statement long on rhetoric and short on operational strategy, the Roundtable provides us only with an indication as to how hard it is to make these trade-offs. Worse than that, its counsel, while failing to be specific, still seems to lead in the wrong direction.

The Roundtable concerns itself with the "expectations of constituencies" of the corporation. This implies that the large corporation is a political entity subject to the votes of interest groups, rather than an economic organization subject to the market test for efficient use of resources.

In fact, the corporation should be using its resources to maximize investment returns, so as to stimulate the investment required to produce the largest amount of goods and services for which consumers are willing to pay. Prices should be equal to the long-run marginal costs, including investment costs, of production and distribution. Unless social and charitable activities reduce long-run marginal costs or increase consumer demand then they divert resources from the social goals inherent in maximum production.

But the Roundtable, by treating with equal concern the constituencies involved, invites every faction to share investment returns. The vague notion of "expectations" misleads us into believing that each interest group should have an equal share. Consider the Roundtable's description of the constituencies' demands.

Customers "expect reliable products and services, fair value, good service and accurate advertising." Most of these reduce long-run marginal costs and add to demand, and therefore should be met. Moreover, these demands are by and large now actually being met. The largest corporations cannot make long-run profits on fraud, or on faulty products, in present-day highly competitive markets. They can make bad mistakes, of the Pinto, Firestone 500, or DC-10 variety, but these are disasters quite incompatible with both social and their own profit interests.

But what is fair value? Economists since Thomas Aquinas have attempted to provide a definition. The Roundtable's definition is never explicit, but by implication, since fair value is the demand of a constituency for lower prices than now prudent, it must be prices lower than long-run marginal costs. Such constituency-determined low prices are a mistake, since they lead to poor service and unreliable products.

Employees, according to the Roundtable, expect not only "fair pay, but also such conditions as financial security, personal privacy, freedom of expression, and concern for the quality of life." These are legitimate because responding to them leads to greater productivity and lower long-run costs. But when pushed further, they lead to even higher costs and competitive disadvantage.

These days, the disastrous earnings record of employee pension plans has put enormous pressure on the corporation to increase benefits. Long-term employment, in the Japanese model, is of special urgency as the 1981–82 recession increases layoffs. Plant safety is a matter of increasing concern, because accident rates do not seem to have improved from all the government regulations that were adopted in the early 1970's.

The Roundtable does not tell us how far to go. *Communities* expect the corporation "to be concerned with local needs and problems—schools, traffic, pollution, health, recreation." Added to this is the interest of society at large in expecting the corporation to respond to concerns and issues of national and international significance.

These interests clearly go beyond those in keeping with the long-term economic viability of the corporation. By giving them every consideration in its statement, the Business Roundtable is paying lip service to resource waste. Political interests should not be served from corporate investment returns. If the stockholder wishes to support the local schools, or solutions to international problems, then he or she should do so with his or her own dividends.

Shareholders are treated last. They have "a special relationship to the corporation," which is the most remarkably misleading understatement in this whole misleading document.

The Roundtable fails to understand that the corporation is the agent for the shareholder, who is the source of all corporate resources the various constituencies are laying claim to. To use the shareholder's risk capital to do all the things that are called "socially responsible" is actually responsible only if the shareholder agrees.

Even worse, the Roundtable states that "the corporation must be profitable enough to provide shareholders a return that will encourage continuation of investment." In present-day competitive markets, profitable enough is all the profits that are available from production of goods and services. There is nothing left over with which to make the payments to these other hypothetical constituencies that the Roundtable elevates in its statement.

In short, the Roundtable statement says that "competing claims may be mutually exclusive," but does not tell us how to resolve the conflict. By giving space to every group trying to politicize the corporation so as to make it the source of a gift or grant, the Roundtable contributes to the decline in efficiency of the enterprise system in this country.

That must be the result of corporate executives not managing their companies, but rather becoming politicians on the Roundtable.

ROUNDTABLE REPLY
Andrew C. Sigler

"The Business Roundtable issues this statement out of a strong conviction that the future of this nation depends upon the existence of strong and responsive business enterprises and that, in turn, the long-term viability of the business sector is linked to its responsibility to the society of which it is a part."

That's how we began the Roundtable's recent paper on Corporate Responsibility, contrary to what Paul MacAvoy stated in "The Business Lobby's Wrong Business" (Dec. 20).

His article took our statement to task in ways that suggest an almost deliberate misunderstanding of our position. Let me try to summarize what we said so it can be judged on its merits, for we believe it was a clear statement of where we came from and where we mean to go.

The 16 chief executive officers of major companies who participated in developing the paper agreed that the corporate community must deal effectively with the issues in the public debate about the role of the corporation in society. This must be done by either explaining the corporate role satisfactorily or by meeting new expectations—or both. Failure to do so might mean no corporations as we now know them.

We recognized that corporations have a responsibility, first of all, to make available to the public quality goods and services at fair prices, thereby earning a profit that attracts investment to continue and enhance the enterprise, provide jobs and build the economy. And we said that all sides must recognize the fundamental importance of profits and their contribution to the long-term viability of the enterprise: "If the bottom line is a minus, there is no plus for society."

Perhaps Samuel Gompers, father of the American labor movement, put it better when he said, "The worst crime against the working people is a company that fails to make a profit."

As shareholders make the corporation possible by providing funds for corporate birth, growth and development, we said that the interest of shareholders must be considered in all important corporate activities.

But the character of shareholders has changed. At one time most of them were long-term, personally involved individual investors. Now large numbers of them are grouped in institutions as unidentified short-term buyers most interested in maximum near-term gain. Such intererst must be balanced with a long-term perspective. The simple theory that management can get along by considering only the shareholder has been left behind in old economic dissertations.

Chief executive officers who have been out there facing reality know that corporations are surrounded by a complicated pattern of economic, social, ethical, and political ideas and expectations. They know that they have to be concerned not only about shareholders but about such constituent groups as customers, employees, communities, suppliers and society at large. And they believe a corporation best serves its shareholders by carefully balancing the legitimate interests of all constituents.

Reginald H. Jones, former chairman of the General Electric Company, put it well: "Public policy and social issues are no longer adjuncts to business planning and management. They are in the mainstream of it. The concern must be pervasive in companies today, from boardroom to factory floor."

Carefully weighing the effects of decisions and balancing different constituent interests must be an integral part of the corporation's decision-making and management process. A corporation's economic responsibility is by no means incompatible with other corporate responsibilities.

The specifics of how a corporation addresses these responsibilities will vary from one company to another. Each corporation has an individual character, related to its products, markets, facilities, manufacturing process and other aspects of its business. Some theorists may long for a total operational strategy or even a statute to dictate corporate responsibility, but only the naive or contentious would seek to fashion such a document.

It is true that business enterprises are not designed to be either political or cultural institutions, but the business community will be well-served by habit of mind that stays alert to social currents. That fundamental point carried through to the conclusion of our statement: "A corporation's responsibilities include how the whole business is conducted every day. It must be a thoughtful institution which rises above the bottom line to consider the impact of its action on all, from shareholders to the society at large. Its business activities must make social sense just as its social activities must make business sense."

We think that's good business.

DISCUSSION QUESTIONS

1. Is the modern business firm a private, semipublic, or public institution? How do these different interpretations of the basic social character of the business firm affect business policy decision making?
2. Does the separation of ownership and control alter the traditional management responsibility for profit maximization?
3. How does the business firm promote social welfare by maximizing profits?
4. Is social responsibility consistent with businesses' best long-run interests?
5. How does the competitive market system conflict with the goals of business social responsibility?

6. Are business firms effective institutions for solving a broad array of social problems?
7. What will increasing politization of private business firms mean for business policy decision making? Why do Milton Friedman and Paul MacAvoy see this as a serious threat to the efficacy of the private market system?
8. Why does Milton Friedman say that the greatest enemies of the free market system are businessmen and intellectuals?
9. Is business acceptance of greater social responsibility inevitable?
10. Is social responsibility an operational concept to which business can respond, or simply a general criticism of business conduct? How could the concept of social responsibility be made more operational?

ADDITIONAL READINGS

BYRON, WILLIAM J., "In Defense of Social Responsibility," *Journal of Economics and Business,* 34, no. 2 (1982), 187–92.
DAVIS, K., "Social Responsibility is Inevitable," *California Management Review,* 19, no. 1 (1976), pp. 14–20.
FREDERICK, WILLIAM C., "Free Market vs. Social Responsibility, Decision Time at the CED," *California Management Review* (Spring 1981), pp. 20–28.
JONES, THOMAS M., "Corporate Social Responsibility Revisited, Redefined," *California Management Review,* 22, no. 3 (Spring 1980), 59–67.
MANNE, HENRY G., "Should Corporations Assume More Social Responsibilities," in *The Attack on Corporate America,* pp. 3–8, ed. M. Bruce Johnson. New York: McGraw-Hill, 1978.
PRESTON, LEE E., and JAMES E. POST, "Private Management and Public Purpose," *California Management Review* (Spring 1981), pp. 56–62.
TUZZOLINO, FRANK, and BARRY R. ARMANDI, "A Need-Hierarchy Framework for Assessing Corporate Social Responsibility," *Academy of Management Review,* 6, no. 1 (January 1981), 21–28.
WEIDENBAUM, M.L., "What is True Corporate Responsibility?," *Regulation,* 4, no. 3 (May-June 1980), 30–31.

CHAPTER 7
MORAL RELATIONSHIPS

Max Weber argued that a successful business system must be compatible with the society's moral ethos.[1] An incongruence between society's moral and economic institutions creates intolerable strains on business-society relationships. Moral issues permeate the analysis of rights and responsibilities in the relationship of business to its stockholders, employees, consumers, and host communities. Corporate social responsibilities are justified by their proponents on the moral grounds that business has the knowledge, skills, and resources to bring about constructive social change and thus the ethical responsibility to do so. If knowledge is power, it too must be subject to socially legitimate controls, and used for the public good. Others argue that business contributes to society's ills (e.g., pollution) and benefits from the use of society's resources, and therefore has a moral responsibility to help solve problems it helped create. It is essential to understanding the role of business in society, and to assessing the possibilities for constructive change to distinguish between business-society relationships which have their foundations in morality as opposed to political or market relationships. These critical distinctions are not always clear, and are often intentionally blurred by zealous advocates of one persuasion or the other.

[1]Max Weber, *The Protestant Ethic and the Spirit of Capitalism* (New York: Scribner's, 1958). Karl Marx, however, believed just the opposite, that ethics merely reflected economic conditions.

BUSINESS ETHICS

The two main themes of the readings are the ethics of individual business behavior, and the morality of the private business system which motivates and
controls that behavior. Ethics is the study of right behavior. The basic ethical
prescription is: "Do unto others as you would have them do unto you." But
what is business ethics, what is right business behavior? Peter Drucker concludes
that business ethics is not ethics at all. Like Friedman's and MacAvoy's insis-
tences in Chapter 6 that only individuals can be socially responsible, Drucker
argues that only individuals can be ethical, and that there is only one code of
ethical behavior for all individuals whether they are in the board room, the Congress, the classroom, or church. There is no separate code of ethical behavior
for businessmen.

If business ethics is not ethics, what is it? Drucker answers that it is
casuistry—a disdained branch of ethics which calls upon those whose actions
affect society to subordinate their individual conscience to their social responsibilities. But, as Drucker notes, this is politics, not ethics. Social responsibilities
are determined politically, they are not an ethical imperative. Ethical business
behavior thus becomes any behavior which yields the desired political goal. The
fatal flaw is that any business behavior can be called ethical by reference to
a particular set of political goals—the ends justify the means.

In one of the suggested additional readings, Albert Carr takes the opposite view that there is a special ethics for business—the ethics of a poker game.
The ethics of poker and business are less demanding than the ethics which govern
the rest of our lives. Business, like poker, calls for bluffing, distrust, cunning,
deception, and concealment. However, Carr states, "No one thinks any worse
of poker on that account. and no one should think any the worse of the game
of business because its standards of right and wrong differ from the prevailing
traditions of morality in our society."[2] Carr, however, cautions businessmen,
perhaps to avoid schizophrenia, to understand these different standards and
to subordinate their personal feelings to the rules of the game. For Drucker,
this would only be casuistry with ethics subordinated to personal rather than
political ends.

In the context of the analysis of goals and responsibilities (Chapter 6),
business ethics becomes the politics of social responsibility. Business is obliged
to meet the politically determined "rights" of stockholders, employees, consumers, local communities, and society. A relationship in which one side has
rights and the other obligations is not an ethical relationship. It is a political

[2]Albert Z. Carr, "Is Business Bluffing Ethical?", *Harvard Business Review* (January–February
1968), p. 145. Copyright © 1968 by the President and Fellows of Harvard College; all rights reserved. Quoted with permission of the *Harvard Business Review.*

relationship in which one side possesses sufficient power to impose its will on the other. Drucker offers as a substitute for "business ethics" the ancient Confucian ethics of interdependence which is based upon mutual obligations between interdependent parties (father and child, superior and subordinate, etc.). The introduction of power (the assignment of "rights") into such a relationship is unethical. Each party in an ethical relationship is obligated to provide what the other needs. Business ethics denies both the interdependence and mutual obligation necessary for an ethical relationship by imposing obligations on one party and granting entitlements to the other. In Part I, a long list of stockholder rights, consumer rights, employee rights, and the rights of local communities were repeatedly encountered. In the context of the Confucian ethics of interdependence, market relationships where buyer and seller voluntarily provide what the other needs may be more ethical than business-society relationships defined by the political assignment of rights and duties.

The next three readings address the morality of the market system rather than the morality of the decision makers in that system. The two severest moral criticisms of the market system are criticisms of the pursuit of self-interest, and the unequal distribution of wealth and income.

SELF-INTEREST

Moral critics interpret self-interest as greed, selfishness, and opportunism, and charge that the pursuit of self-interest required by the market system has a corrupting influence on human morality. Businessmen have traditionally acceded the moral superiority of their critics and responded to their charges with efficiency arguments; for example, self-interest motivates people to work hard. Moral criticisms, however, demand moral responses (is an efficient capitalist more ethical than an inefficient one?).

Self-interest is, indeed, the driving force behind the private enterprise system as originally observed by Adam Smith: "It is not from the benevolence of the butcher, the brewer or the baker, that we expect our dinner, but from their regard to their own interests. We address ourselves, not to their humanity but to their self-love, and never talk to them of our necessities but of their advantages."[3] However, Smith also observed that the pursuit of self-interest is turned to the promotion of the social welfare by the invisible hand of competition:

> Every individual necessarily labors to render the annual revenue of the society as great as he can. He generally, indeed, neither intends to promote the public interest nor knows how much he is promoting it. . . . By directing that industry in such a manner as its produce may be of the greatest value, he intends only his own gain, and he is in this, as in many other cases, led by an invisible hand to

[3]Adam Smith, *The Wealth of Nations* (New York: Random House, 1937), p. 14.

promote an end which was no part of his intention. Nor is it always the worse for the society that it was no part of it. By pursuing his own interests, he frequently promotes that of the society more effectually than when he really intends to promote it. I have never known much good done by those who affected to trade for the public good. It is an affectation, indeed, not very common among merchants, and very few words need to be employed in dissuading them from it.[4]

This, of course, is a powerful efficiency rationale for self-interest pursuit, but not an ethical justification.

The self-interest, profit-maximizing role is a very uncomfortable one for many businessmen who are often as critical of self-interest as their staunchest opponents, as indicated by The Business Roundtable in Chapter 6 (and severely criticized by Paul MacAvoy). Perhaps businessmen's uneasiness with their assigned social role reflects their own dissatisfaction with efficiency responses to moral criticisms. That competition turns self-interest toward the maximization of social welfare is not very morally satisfying. The pursuit of self-interest must itself be ethical. In moral philosophy terms, a utilitarian justification alone is insufficient to determine if self-interest is "right" behavior. It is also necessary that moral duties and obligations be satisfied.

Adam Smith did not consider self-interest unethical. Self-interest (prudence) was one of three virtues in Smith's moral philosophy, along with benevolence and justice. Prudence is necessary to advance ". . . the two great purposes in nature, the support of the individual and the propagation of the species."[5] Smith continues: "The habits of economy, industry, discretion, attention and application of thought, are generally supposed to be cultivated by self-interest motives, and at the same time are apprehended to be very praiseworthy qualities, which deserve the esteem and approbation of everybody."[6]

Self-interest is the only one of Smith's virtues capable of organizing economic activity. Because of the extensive division of labor needed for efficient production, every individual is dependent upon innumerable others for his daily sustenance. Appeals to the benevolence of these unknown multitudes is futile, not because man is not benevolent and just as well as self-interested, but because man's capacity for benevolence is not without limit. In a revealing, introspective look at man, Smith surveys these limits:

Let us suppose that the great empire of China, with all its myriads of inhabitants, was suddenly swallowed up by an earthquake, and let us consider how a man of humanity in Europe, who had no sort of connection with that part of the world would be affected upon receiving intelligence of this dreadful calamity. He would, I imagine, first of all express very strongly his sorrow for the misfortune of that unhappy people, he would make many melancholy reflections upon the precarious-

[4]*Ibid.*, p. 423.

[5]Adam Smith, *The Theory of Moral Sentiments* (Indianapolis: Liberty Fund, Inc., 1976), p. 168. Quoted with permission of Liberty Fund, Inc.

[6]*Ibid.*, p. 481. Quoted with permission of Liberty Fund, Inc.

ness of human life, and the vanity of all the labors of man, which could thus be annihilated in a moment. He would too, perhaps, if he was a man of speculation, enter into many reasonings concerning the effects which this disaster might produce upon the commerce of Europe, and the trade and business of the world in general. And when this fine philosophy was over, when all these humane sentiments had been once fairly expressed, he would pursue his business or his pleasure, take his repose or his diversion, with the same ease and tranquility as if no such accident had happened. The most frivolous disaster which could befall himself would occasion a more real disturbance. If he was to lose his little finger tomorrow, he would not sleep to-night; but provided he never saw them, he will snore with the most profound security over the ruin of a hundred millions of his brethren, and the destruction of that immense multitude seems plainly an object less interesting to him than this paltry misfortune of his own.[7]

Confucian ethics, which Peter Drucker introduces us to in the first reading, also considers benevolence (*jen*) to be one of the most important virtues. The perfection of human nature lies in extending the natural affection which exists among family members to complete strangers. Smith, being an astute observer of the world in which he lived, simply noted that in the middle eighteenth century man had not yet achieved that perfection of human nature, and it does not appear that much progress has been made since then.

Japanese business leaders, however, are also motivated by self-interest, and special interest groups in Japan are as well organized and active as anywhere else in the world. While Japanese Confucianism looks with distrust upon self-sacrifice, Drucker tells us that Japanese businessmen nevertheless have a long history of putting the national interest first: "Each group is, however, expected to fit its self-interest into a framework of national needs, national goals, national aspirations, and national values."[8] This tradition may reflect the importance of loyalty as well as benevolence in Japanese Confucianism. The result is that the Japanese appear to have achieved a very productive balance of self-interest, benevolence, and loyalty which fulfills their needs for a morally acceptable integration of economic and social interests.

Professor Schumpeter, however, believes that capitalism will not survive because "nobody loves it." His basic message, and the message of corporate social responsibility discussed in Chapter 6, is that business can no longer simply be stuck to society with pins from Adam Smith's factory, no matter how efficiently produced. The business system must be securely woven into the moral fabric which binds society together. Society is increasingly demanding a better integration of ethical, social and economic values, but Professor Kenneth Boulding tells us:

[7]*Ibid.*, pp. 233–34. Quoted with permission of Liberty Fund, Inc.

[8]Peter F. Drucker, "Behind Japan's Success," *Harvard Business Review* (January–February 1981), p. 86. Copyright © 1981 by the President and Fellows of Harvard College; all rights reserved. Quoted with permission of the *Harvard Business Review*.

The integrative system has to come out of religion, or nationalism, [as may be the case in Japan] or education, or the family or something of that kind. Exchange in itself is such an abstract and stripped kind of relationship that it will not develop a very strong integrative system. Suppose you say, "ask not what General Motors can do for you; ask what you can do for General Motors." This may be all right for General Motors, but it sounds a little silly.[9]

Exchange, itself, may be an abstract concept incapable of integrating complex social values in modern society. Business, however, need not be so. It may not have sounded quite so silly if Professor Boulding had said: "Ask not what Toyota can do for you; ask what you can do for Toyota"!

Socialists argue that the demise of the market system would eliminate selfishness and harness man's higher morality for social performance rather than private profit. Professor Hirshleifer thinks not. Capitalism takes human beings as it finds them. "It is not capitalism which makes people selfish—people other than saints simply are more interested in their own health, comfort and safety than in other people's and will continue to be until the establishment of the Kingdom of God on earth." Hirshleifer contends that any economic system must confront human self-interest, and it is naive to think otherwise. The case for the private market system rests on its ability to direct self-interests towards social goals more effectively than any other economic system. Hirshleifer states: "What is sentimental [about socialism] here is the belief that a change in social organization is all that is required to abolish human selfishness. As Mr. Dooley said, 'A man that'd expect to train lobsters to fly in a year is called a lunatic; but a man that thinks men can be turned into angels by an election is called a reformer and remains at large.' "

Professor Simon stated that: "If men were angels, no government would be necessary." But, he also tells us in Chapter 4 that the design of our political democracy was based on the acceptance of human beings as the architects of the Constitution found them. They did not design a system requiring people to be more virtuous than they are: "They didn't ask for a New Man. They didn't set out to design a set of social institutions whose effectiveness would depend on human beings' behaving nicely, instead of their behaving humanly." The theory of justice developed by John Rawls in the third reading in this chapter is also derived from the ambitions of self-interested individuals, for otherwise such a theory would not be necessary:

> Justice is the virtue of practices where there are assumed to be competing interests and conflicting claims, and where it is supposed that persons will press their rights on each other. That persons are mutually self-interested in certain situations and for certain purposes is what gives rise to the question of justice in practices covering those circumstances. Amongst an association of saints, if such a

[9]Kenneth E. Boulding, *Beyond Economics* (Ann Arbor: University of Michigan Press, 1968), p. 50.

community could really exist, the disputes about justice could hardly occur; for they would all work selflessly together for one end, the glory of God as defined by their common religion, and references to this end would settle every question of right.[10]

Thus, the market system, political democracy, and at least one major system of distributive justice are all constructed upon the acceptance of human self-interest, and are all designed to harness that self-interest for the social good. The voluntary acceptance of social responsibility by business, however, may require a "New Man" in whom economists, political scientists, and ethicists have scant faith.

INEQUALITY

The unequal distribution of income and wealth generated by the private market system is also morally criticized. Christoffel, Finkelhor, and Gilbarg argue that ours is a class society where ". . . the major portion of the wealth and nearly all the power in the society are concentrated in the hands of a few giant institutions and the people that run them," and that "A good society requires economic equality, not just absence of poverty."[11]

The most reasoned ethical criticism of the unequal reward structure of the private market system originates with Professor John Rawls. Rawls' theory of justice is essentially a formula for making the difficult trade-offs between economic efficiency and equity or justice. A competitive market economy will produce an efficient allocation of resources because voluntary exchange will continue until there are no possibilities for further exchange which would benefit both individuals involved, or at least benefit one individual without imposing losses on the other.[12] This, however, can lead to many different distributions of income, all of which are efficient, but not equally just. Rawls' theory provides a basis for selecting the just distribution. Rawls develops a theory of distributive justice by asking what principles for dividing the gains from social cooperation would individuals in an original position of equality voluntarily accept. Rawls argues that such individuals would not subscribe to a utilitarian ethic that sought the "greatest good for the greatest number." He argues that

[10]John Rawls, "Justice as Fairness," in *Philosophy, Politics and Society,* 2nd series, eds. P. Laslett and W. G. Runciman (New York: Barnes & Noble, 1962), p. 142.

[11]T. Christoffel, D. Finkelhor, and D. Gilbarg, *Up Against the American Myth* (New York: Holt Paperback, 1979), p. 11.

[12]Economists measure economic efficiency by the criterion of Pareto Optimality. The distribution of resources is efficient—Pareto Optimal—when there is no alternative distribution which would make at least one individual better off without making another worse off. Clearly if we could redistribute income so as to make at least one individual better off without making another worse off we should do so for this would be a pure welfare gain to society. Failure to do so would represent an inefficient use of society's resources. However, nothing objective can be said about a redistribution which makes some individuals better off while making others worse off because of the need to make interpersonal comparisons of utility gains and losses.

rational, self-interested individuals in an original position of equality would not agree to sacrifice their individual liberty, income, or wealth for the greater good of society:

> Offhand it hardly seems likely that persons who view themselves as equals, entitled to press their claims upon one another, would agree to a principle which may require lesser life prospects for some simply for the sake of a greater sum of advantages enjoyed by others. Since each desires to protect his interests, his capacity to advance his conception of the good, no one has a reason to acquiesce in an enduring loss for himself in order to bring about a greater net balance of satisfaction. In the absence of strong and lasting benevolent impulses, [which seems likely] a rational man would not accept a basic structure merely because it maximized the algebraic sum of advantages irrespective of its permanent effects on his own basic rights and interests. Thus it seems that the principal of utility is incompatible with the conception of social cooperation among equals for mutual advantage.[13]

The basic point is that rational, self-interested individuals would not agree to inequalities in the distribution of liberties, income, or wealth which could make them worse off than they would be in an egalitarian society. Thus the only inequalities which would be acceptable to all individuals are those which make everyone better off than they would be under a system of equality. From this reasoning Rawls derives his two principles of distributive justice:

> Each person is to have an equal right to the most extensive basic liberty compatible with a similar liberty for others;
> Social and economic inequalities are to be arranged so that they are to everyone's advantage, and are attached to positions and offices open to all.

The first principle of distributive justice requires that basic liberties (the right to vote, freedom of speech, freedom from arbitrary arrest and seizure, etc.) be equal for all since citizens of a just society are all to have the same basic rights. The second part of the second principle requires that all members of society enjoy an equal opportunity for better positions and higher rewards. The first part of the second principle is Rawls' famous "difference principle." This principle is interpreted to mean that inequalities in the distribution of income are just only if they are to the advantage of the least-advantaged members of society. Thus, inequalities in income must provide incentives for production, investment, technological innovation, and the like, which benefit the least-advantaged groups in society. These two principles can be incorporated into a general statement of Rawls' theory of distributive justice: "All social primary goods—liberty and opportunity, income and wealth, and the bases of self-respect—are to be distributed equally unless an unequal distribution of any or all of these goods is to the advantage of the least favored."[14] Inequalities

[13]John Rawls, *A Theory of Justice* (Cambridge: Harvard University Press, 1971), p. 14.
[14]*Ibid*, p. 303.

which do not improve the position of the least-advantaged groups in society are unjust.

In the zero-sum society, Lester Thurow advocates a distribution of income for the entire population that is no more unequal than that now existing for fully employed white males.[15] This group has not been handicapped by discrimination, lack of skills, or unemployment. Their average income is much higher than the average for society, and the difference in income between the top and bottom quintiles is much less than in the rest of society. Thurow thus argues that a similar distribution for all of society would not decrease incentives to work since the lesser inequalities among white males provide adequate incentives for them to work. The greater income inequalities found for the rest of society are thus unnecessary (unjust).

Rawls also does not allow any trade-offs between basic liberties and income, that is, basic liberties cannot be sacrificed for higher earnings in a just society. This philosophy has been encountered throughout the text. Consumer, labor, and community rights are treated as moral absolutes which cannot be balanced against competing economic goals. But the fulfillment of economic rights (as opposed to fundamental political liberties) which require some use of society's resources must confront the inevitable scarcity of resources relative to competing social goals or competing economic rights. The trade-offs can be denied, but not avoided. As discussed in Chapter 9, even the preservation of life (which requires the use of society's scarce resources) involves complex social trade-offs among competing private and public goals.

Rawls and other egalitarians also support greater income equality by arguing that the higher incomes received by some members of society are not morally deserved. These individuals have no moral claim to the superior ability or greater effort which produced their higher incomes. Superior ability is simply inherited, the individual has been lucky in the genetic lottery, not morally deserving. While somewhat more intractable, extra effort also does not provide a moral basis for higher income. Effort is highly correlated with natural ability (the greater prospects of success for those with greater natural ability encourages extra effort), or may also be simply inherited ("lazy genes"). In either case, income realized through greater effort, like income realized through greater ability, is morally undeserved.

Egalitarian ethics completely contradict the theory of private property rights underlying the market system which holds that the individual is entitled to the fruits of his own labor and that a wise government "shall not take from the mouth of labor the bread it has earned."[16] In his article, Marc Plattner totally disagrees with the egalitarian thesis that the individual's income is not morally deserved because ability and effort are arbitrary natural facts. He writes: "To deny that individuals deserve the fruits of their efforts and natural abilities is to deny that powerful principal of human justice which hold that each is en-

[15]Lester C. Thurow, *The Zero-Sum Society* (New York: Basic Books, 1980), pp. 200–11.
[16]Thomas Jefferson, *First Inaugural Address,* Capitol Building, Washington, D.C. (March 4, 1801).

titled to what is his own." He goes on, ". . . it entails the most extreme sort of invasion of the private sphere and the rights of the individual in the name of the public and communal good." Egalitarian moral philosophy denies the Lockean theory of private property that ". . . every man has a property in his own person; [presumably including his inherited genes and natural talents] this nobody has any right to but himself. The labor of his body and the work of his hands, we may say, are properly his." According to Plattner, egalitarianism undermines the moral foundations of political democracy.

Adam Smith distinguished between the intrinsic worth of the individual and moral desert. For Smith, rewards had to be deserved on the basis of service to mankind:

> The man who has performed no single action of importance, but whose whole conversation and deportment express the justest, the noblest, and most generous sentiments, can be entitled to demand no very high reward. . . . We can still ask him, what have you done? What actual service can you produce, to entitle you to so great a recompense? We esteem you and love you; but we owe you nothing.[17]

Plattner also notes that egalitarian moral philosophy has never been an accepted part of American moral or political thinking. As Professor Simon stated in Chapter 4, the founding fathers believed in equality of opportunity, not equal property.[18] A substantial amount of income redistribution occurs through progressive taxes and welfare programs, but the intent of these programs is to provide minimum living standards for the "least advantaged" and to distribute the tax burden fairly on the basis of ability to pay. With the exception of George McGovern, there has never been a platform for redistributing income in the U.S. with the explicit goal of reducing inequality.

Finally, Rawls concludes that a constitutional democracy can satisfy the two principles of distributive justice if the government maintains a competitive market system, provides for full employment and a wide dispersion of property, maintains minimum living standards, and guarantees equality of opportunity for all. Socialists, however, could equally argue that the inequalities in income produced by the market system do not benefit the least advantaged members of society. They could defend redistribution on the grounds that it is needed to eliminate unjust inequalities produced by the market system.

Rawls is concerned with ethical institutional relationships for a just society. Drucker, noting that ours is a society of institutions, suggests we need a system of organizational ethics to supplement individual ethics. This would require defining the fundamental economic, moral, and sociopolitical relationships and mutual obligations among society's institutions, and developing universal ethical codes which maximized the social benefits of these relationships.

---

[17]Smith, *Theory of Moral Sentiments,* p. 196. Quoted with permission of Liberty Fund, Inc.

[18]In *Federalist Papers #10,* James Madison makes this clear in an indirect reference to egalitarianism: "A rage for paper money, for an abolition of debts, for an equal division of property, or for any other improper or wicked project. . ."

WHAT IS "BUSINESS ETHICS"?
Peter F. Drucker

"Business ethics" is rapidly becoming the "in" subject, replacing yesterday's "social responsibilities." "Business ethics" is now being taught in departments of philosophy, business schools, and theological seminaries. There are countless seminars on it, speeches, articles, conferences and books, not to mention the many earnest attempts to write "business ethics" into the law. But what precisely is "business ethics"? And what could, or should, it be? Is it just another fad, and only the latest round in the hoary American blood sport of business baiting? Is there more to "business ethics" than the revivalist preacher's call to the sinner to repent? And if there is indeed something that one could call "business ethics" and could take seriously, what could it be?

Ethics is, after all, not a recent discovery. Over the centuries philosophers in their struggle with human behavior have developed different approaches to ethics, each leading to different conclusions, indeed to conflicting rules of behavior. Where does "business ethics" fit in—or does it fit in anywhere at all?

The confusion is so great—and the noise level even greater—that perhaps an attempt might be in order to sort out what "business ethics" might be, and what it might not be, in the light of the major approaches which philosophers have taken throughout the ages (though my only qualification for making this attempt is that I once, many years before anybody even thought of "business ethics," taught philosophy and religion, and then worked arduously on the tangled questions of "political ethics.")

BUSINESS ETHICS AND THE WESTERN TRADITION

To the moralist of the Western tradition "business ethics" would make no sense. Indeed, the very term would to him be most objectionable, and reeking of moral laxity. The authorities on ethics disagreed, of course, on what constitutes the grounds of morality—whether they be divine, human nature, or the needs of society. They equally disagreed on the specific rules of ethical behavior; that sternest of moral rules, the Ten Commandments, for instance, thunders "Thou shalt not covet thy neighbor's . . . maidservant." But it says nothing about "sex-

Peter F. Drucker, "What Is 'Business Ethics'?" *The Public Interest,* no. 63 (Spring 1981), 18–36. Reprinted with permission.

ual harassment" of "one's own" women employees, though it was surely just as common then as now.

All authorities of the Western tradition—from the Old Testament prophets all the way to Spinoza in the 17th century, to Kant in the 18th century, Kierkegaard in the 19th century and, in this century, the Englishman F.H. Bradley (*Ethical Studies*) or the American Edmond Cahn (*The Moral Decision*)—are, however, in complete agreement on one point: There is only one ethics, one set of rules of morality, one code, that of *individual* behavior in which the same rules apply to everyone alike.

A pagan could say, "Quod licet Jovi non licet bovi." He could thus hold that different rules of behavior apply to Jupiter from those that apply to the ox. A Jew or a Christian would have to reject such differentiation in ethics—and precisely because all experience shows that it always leads to exempting the "Jupiters," the great, powerful, and rich, from the rules which "the ox," the humble and poor, has to abide by.

The moralist of the Western tradition accepts "extenuating" and "aggravating" circumstances. He accepts that the poor widow who steals bread to feed her starving children deserves clemency and that it is a more heinous offense for the bishop to have a concubine than for the poor curate in the village. But before there can be "extenuating" or "aggravating" circumstances, there has to be an offense. And the offense is the same for rich and poor, for high and low alike—theft is theft, concubinage is concubinage. The reason for this insistence on a code that considers only the individual, and not his status in life or society, is precisely that otherwise the mighty, the powerful, the successful will gain exemption from the laws of ethics and morality.

The only differences between what is ethically right and ethically wrong behavior which traditional moralists, almost without exception, would accept—would indeed insist on—are differences grounded in social or cultural mores, and then only in respect to "venial" offences. That is, the way things are done rather than the substance of behavior. Even in the most licentious society, fidelity to the marriage vow is meritorious, all moralists would agree; but the sexual license of an extremely "permissive" society, say 17th century Restoration England or late 20th century America, might be considered an "extenuating circumstance" for the sexual transgressor. And even the sternest moralist has always insisted that, excepting only true "matters of conscience," practices that are of questionable morality in one place and culture, might be perfectly acceptable—and indeed might be quite ethical—in another cultural surrounding. Nepotism may be considered of dubious morality in one culture, in today's United States, for instance. In other cultures, a traditional Chinese one, for example, it may be the very essence of ethical behavior, both by satisfying the moral obligation to one's family and by making disinterested service to the public a little more likely.

But—and this is the crucial point—these are qualifications to the fundamental axiom on which the Western tradition of ethics has always been based:

There is only one code of ethics, that of individual behavior, for prince and pauper, for rich and poor, for the mighty and the meek alike. Ethics, in the Judaeo-Christian tradition, is the affirmation that all men and women are alike creatures—whether the Creator be called God, Nature, or Society.

And this fundamental axiom "business ethics" denies. Viewed from the mainstream of traditional ethics, "business ethics" is not ethics at all, whatever else it may be. For it asserts that acts that are not immoral or illegal if done by ordinary folk become immoral or illegal if done by "business."

One blatant example is the treatment of extortion in the current discussions of "business ethics." No one ever has had a good word to say for extortion, or has advocated paying it. But if you and I are found to have paid extortion money under threat of physical or material harm, we are not considered to have behaved immorally or illegally. The extortioner is both immoral and a criminal. If a business submits to extortion, however, current "business ethics" considers it to have acted unethically. There is no speech, article, book, or conference on "business ethics," for instance, which does not point an accusing finger in great indignation at Lockheed for giving in to a Japanese airline company, which extorted money as a prerequisite to considering the purchase of Lockheed's faltering L-1011 jet plane. There was very little difference between Lockheed's paying the Japanese and the pedestrian in New York's Central Park handing his wallet over to a mugger. Yet no one would consider the pedestrian to have acted "unethically."

Similarly, in Senate confirmation hearings, one of President Reagan's cabinet appointees was accused of "unethical practices" and investigated for weeks because his New Jersey construction company was alleged to have paid money to union goons under the threat of their beating up the employees, sabotaging the trucks, and vandalizing the building sites. The accusers were self-confessed labor racketeers; no one seemed to have worried about their "ethics."

One can argue that both Lockheed and the New Jersey builder were stupid to pay the holdup men. But as the old saying has it: "Stupidity is not a court martial offense." Under the new "business ethics," it does become exactly that, however. And this is not compatible with what "ethics" always were supposed to be.

The new "business ethics" also denies to business the adaptation to cultural mores which has always been considered a moral duty in the traditional approach to ethics. It is now considered "grossly unethical"—indeed it may even be a "questionable practice" if not criminal offense—for an American business operating in Japan to retain as a "counsellor" the distinguished civil servant who retires from his official position in the Japanese government. Yet the business that does not do this is considered in Japan to behave antisocially and to violate its clear ethical duties. Business taking care of retired senior civil servants, the Japanese hold, makes possible two practices they consider essential to the public interest: that a civil servant past age 45 must retire as soon as he is out-ranked by anyone younger than he; and that governmental salaries and retirement pensions—and with them the burden of the bureaucracy on the tax-payer—be kept low, with the difference between what a first-rate man gets in government service and what he might earn in private employment made up after his retirement through his "counsellor's fees." The Japanese maintain that the expectation of later on being a "counsellor" encourages a civil servant to remain incorruptible, impartial, and objective, and thus to serve only the public good; his counsellorships are obtained for him by his former ministry and its recommendation depends on his rating by his colleagues as a public servant. The Germans, who follow a somewhat similar practice—with senior civil servants expected to be "taken care of" through appointment as industry-association executives—share this conviction. Yet, despite the fact that both the Japanese and the German systems seem to serve their respective societies well and indeed honorably, and even despite the fact that it is considered perfectly "ethical" for American civil servants of equal rank and caliber to move into well-paid executive jobs in business and foundations and into even more lucrative law practices, the American company in Japan that abides by a practice the Japanese consider the very essence of "social responsibility," is pilloried in the present discussion of "business ethics" as a horrible example of "unethical practices."

Surely "business ethics" assumes that for some reason the ordinary rules of ethics do not apply to business. "Business ethics," in other words, is not "ethics" at all, as the term has commonly been used by Western philosophers and Western theologians. What is it then?

CASUISTRY: THE ETHICS OF SOCIAL RESPONSIBILITY

"It's casuistry," the historian of Western philosophy would answer. Casuistry asserted that rulers, because of their responsibility, have to strike a balance between the ordinary demands of ethics which apply to them as individuals and their "social responsibility" to their subjects, their kingdom—or their company.

"Casuistry" was first propounded in Calvin's *Institutes,* then taken over by the Catholic theologians of the Counter-Reformation (Bellarmin, for instance, or St. Charles Borromeus) and developed into a "political ethics" by their Jesuit disciples in the 17th century.

"Casuistry" was the first attempt to think through "social responsibility" and to embed it in a set of special ethics for those in power. In this respect, "business ethics" tries to do exactly what the casuists did 300 years ago. And it must end the same way. If "business ethics" continues to be "casuistry" its speedy demise in a cloud of illrepute can be confidently predicted.

To the Casuist the "social responsibility" inherent in being a "ruler"—that is, someone whose actions have impact on others—is by itself an ethical imperative. As such, the ruler has a duty, as Calvin first laid down, to subordinate his individual behavior and his individual conscience to the demands of his social responsibility.

The *locus classicus* of casuistry is Henry VIII and his first marriage to Catherine of Aragon. A consummated marriage—and Catherine of Aragon had a daughter by Henry, the future "Bloody Mary"—could not be dissolved except by death, both Catholic and Protestant theologians agreed. In casuistry, however, as both Catholics and Protestants agreed, Henry VIII had an ethical duty to seek annulment of the marriage. Until his father, well within living memory, had snatched the Crown by force of arms, England had suffered a century of bloody and destructive civil war because of the lack of a legitimate male heir. Without annulment of his marriage, Henry VIII, in other words, exposed his country and its people to mortal danger, well beyond anything he could in conscience justify. The one point on which Protestants and Catholics disagreed was whether the Pope also had a social, and thereby an ethical, responsibility to grant Henry's request. By not granting it, he drove the King and his English subjects out of the Catholic Church. But had he granted the annulment, the Catholic Casuists argued, the Pope would have driven Catherine's uncle, the Holy Roman Emperor, out of the Church and into the waiting arms of an emerging Protestantism; and that would have meant that instead of assigning a few million Englishmen to heresy, perdition, and hellfire, many times more souls—all the people in all the lands controlled by the Emperor, that is, in most of Europe—could have been consigned to everlasting perdition.

This may be considered a quaint example—but only because our time measures behavior in economic rather than theological absolutes. The example illustrates what is wrong with casuistry and indeed why it must fail as an approach to ethics. In the first place casuistry must end up becoming politicized, precisely because it considers social responsibility an ethical absolute. In giving primacy to political values and goals it subordinates ethics to politics. Clearly this is the approach "business ethics" today is taking. Its very origin is in politics rather than in ethics. It expresses a belief that the responsibility which business and the business executive have, precisely because they have social impact, must determine ethics—and this is a political rather than an ethical imperative.

Equally important, the Casuist inevitably becomes the apologist for the ruler, the powerful. Casuistry starts out with the insight that the behavior of "rulers" affects more than themselves and their families. It thus starts out by making demands on the ruler—the starting point for both Calvin and his Catholic disciples in the Counter-Reformation 50 years later. It then concludes that "rulers" must, therefore, in conscience and ethics, subordinate their interests, including their individual morality, to their social responsibility. But this implies that the rules which decide what is ethical for ordinary people do not apply equally, if at all, to those with social responsibility. Ethics for them is instead a cost-benefit calculation involving the demands of individual conscience and the demands of position—and that means that the "rulers" are exempt from the demands of ethics, if only their behavior can be argued to confer benefits on other people. And this is precisely how "business ethics" is going.

Indeed, under Casuist's analysis the ethical violations which to most present proponents of "business ethics" appear the most heinous crimes turn out to have been practically saintly.

Take Lockheed's bribe story for instance. Lockheed was led into paying extortion money to a Japanese airline by the collapse of the supplier of the engines for its wide-bodied L-1011 passenger jet, the English Rolls Royce Company. At that time Lockheed employed some 25,000 people making L-1011's, most of them in southern California which then, 1972–73, was suffering substantial unemployment from sharp cutbacks in defense orders in the aerospace industry. To safeguard the 25,000 jobs, Lockheed got a large government subsidy. But to be able to maintain these jobs, Lockheed needed at least one large L-1011 order from one major airline. The only one among the major airlines not then committed to a competitor's plane was All-Nippon Airways in Japan. The self-interest of Lockheed Corporation and of its stockholders would clearly have demanded speedy abandonment of the L-1011. It was certain that it would never make money—and it has not made a penny yet. Jettisoning the L-1011 would immediately have boosted Lockheed's earnings, maybe doubled them. It would have immediately boosted Lockheed's share price; stock market analysts and investment bankers pleaded with the firm to get rid of the albatross. If Lockheed had abandoned the L-1011, instead of paying extortion money to the Japanese for ordering a few planes and thus keeping the project alive, the company's earnings, its stock price, and the bonuses and stock options of top management, would immediately have risen sharply. Not to have paid extortion money to the Japanese would to a Casuist, have been self-serving. To a Casuist, paying the extortion money was a duty and social responsibility to which the self-interest of the company, its shareholders and its executives had to be subordinated. It was the discharge of social responsibility of the "ruler" to keep alive the jobs of 25,000 people at a time when jobs in the aircraft industry in southern California were scarce indeed.

Similarly, the other great "horror story" of "business ethics" would, to the Casuist, appear as an example of "business virtue" if not of unselfish "business martyrdom." In the "electrical apparatus conspiracy" of the late 1950's, several high-ranking General Electric executives were sent to jail. They were found guilty of a criminal conspiracy in violation of antitrust because orders for heavy generating equipment, such as turbines, were parcelled out among the three electrical apparatus manufacturers in the U.S.–General Electric, Westinghouse, and Allis Chalmers. But this "criminal conspiracy" only served to reduce General Electric's sales, its profits, and the bonuses and stock options of the General Electric executives who took part in the conspiracy. Since the electric apparatus cartel was destroyed by the criminal prosecution of the General Electric executives, General Electric sales and profits in the heavy apparatus field have sharply increased, as has market penetration by the company, which now has what amounts to a near-monopoly. The purpose of the cartel—

which incidentally was started under federal government pressure in the Depression years to fight unemployment—was the protection of the weakest and most dependent of the companies, Allis Chalmers (which is located in Milwaukee, a depressed and declining old industrial area). As soon as government action destroyed the cartel, Allis Chalmers had to go out of the turbine business and had to lay off several thousand people. And while there is still abundant competition in the world market for heavy electric apparatus, General Electric now enjoys such market dominance in the home market that the United States, in case of war, would not have major alternative suppliers of so critical a product as turbines.

The Casuist would agree that cartels are both illegal and considered immoral in the U.S.—although not necessarily anyplace else in the world. But he would also argue that the General Electric executive who violated U.S. law had an ethical duty to do so under the "higher law" of social responsibility to safeguard both employment in the Milwaukee area and the defense-production base of the United States.

The only thing that is surprising about these examples is that business has not yet used them to climb on the Casuist bandwagon of "business ethics." For just as almost any behavior indulged in by the 17th century ruler could be shown to be an ethical duty by the 17th century disciples of Calvin, of Bellarmin, and of Borromeus, so almost any behavior of the executive in organizations today—whether in a business, a hospital, a university, or a government agency—could be shown to be his ethical duty under the casuistic cost-benefit analysis between individual ethics and the demands of social responsibility. There are indeed signs aplenty that the most apolitical of "rulers," the American business executive, is waking up to the political potential of "business ethics." Some of the advertisements which large companies—Mobil Oil, for example—are now running to counter the attacks made on them in the name of "social responsibility" and "business ethics," clearly use the casuist approach to defend business, and indeed to counterattack. But if "business ethics" becomes a tool to defend as "ethical" acts on the part of executives that would be condemned if committed by anyone else, the present proponents of "business ethics," like their casuist predecessors 400 years ago, will have no one to blame but themselves.

Casuistry started out as high morality. In the end, its ethics came to be summed up in two well-known pieces of cynicism: "An ambassador is an honest man, lying abroad for the good of his country," went a well-known 18th century pun. And a hundred years later, Bismarck said, "What a scoundrel a minister would be if, in his own private life, he did half the things he has a duty to do to be true to his oath of office."

Long before that, however, casuistry had been killed off by moral revulsion. Its most lasting memory perhaps are the reactions to it which re-established ethics in the West as a universal system, binding the individual regardless of station, function, or "social responsibility": Spinoza's *Ethics,* and the *Pro-*

vincial Letters of his contemporary, Blaise Pascal. But also—and this is a lesson that might be pondered by today's proponents of "business ethics," so many of whom are clergymen—it was their embracing casuistry that made the Jesuits hated and despised, made "Jesuitical" a synonym of "immoral," and led to the Jesuit order being suppressed by the Pope in the 18th century. And it is casuistry, more than anything else, that has caused the anticlericalism of the intellectuals in Catholic Europe.

"Business ethics" undoubtedly is a close parallel to casuistry. Its origin is political, as was that of casuistry. Its basic thesis, that ethics for the ruler, and especially for the business executive, has to express "social responsibility" is exactly the starting point of the Casuist. But if "business ethics" is casuistry, then it will not last long—and long before it dies, it will have become a tool of the business executive to justify what for other people would be unethical behavior, rather than a tool to restrain the business executive and to impose tight ethical limits on business.

THE ETHICS OF PRUDENCE AND SELF-DEVELOPMENT

There is one other major tradition of ethics in the West, the Ethics of Prudence. It goes all the way back to Aristotle and his enthronement of Prudence as a cardinal virtue. It continued for almost 2,000 years in the popular literary tradition of the "Education of the Christian Prince," which reached its ultimate triumph and its reduction to absurdity in Machiavelli's *Prince*. Its spirit can best be summed up by the advice which then-Senator Harry Truman gave to an Army witness before his committee in the early years of World War II: "Generals should never do anything that needs to be explained to a Senate Committee—there is nothing one can explain to a Senate Committee."

"Generals," whether the organization is an army, a corporation, or a university, are highly visible. They must expect their behavior to be seen, scrutinized, analyzed, discussed, and questioned. Prudence thus demands that they shun actions that cannot easily be understood, explained, or justified. But "Generals," being visible, are also examples. They are "leaders" by their very position and visibility. Their only choice is whether their example leads others to right action or to wrong action. Their only choice is between direction and misdirection, between leadership and misleadership. They thus have an ethical obligation to give the example of right behavior and to avoid giving the example of wrong behavior.

The Ethics of Prudence do not spell out what "right" behavior is. They assume that what is wrong behavior is clear enough—and if there is any doubt, it is "questionable" and to be avoided. Prudence makes it an ethical duty for the leader to exemplify the precepts of ethics in his own behavior.

And by following Prudence, everyone regardless of status becomes a "leader," a "superior man" and will "fulfill himself," to use the contemporary idiom. One becomes the "superior man" by avoiding any act which would make one the kind of person one does not want to be, does not respect, does not accept as superior. "If you don't want to see a pimp when you look in the shaving mirror in the morning, don't hire call girls the night before to entertain congressmen, customers, or salesmen." On any other basis, hiring call girls may be condemned as vulgar and tasteless, and may be shunned as something fastidious people do not do. It may be frowned upon as uncouth. It may even be illegal. But only in Prudence is it ethically relevant. This is what Kierkegaard, the sternest moralist of the 19th century, meant when he said that aesthetics is the true ethics.

The Ethics of Prudence can easily degenerate. Concern with what one can justify becomes, only too easily, concern with appearances—Machiavelli was by no means the first to point out that in a "Prince," that is, in someone in authority and high visibility, appearances may matter more than substance. The Ethics of Prudence thus easily decay into the hypocrisy of "public relations." Leadership through right example easily degenerates into the sham of "charisma" and into a cloak for misdirection and misleadership—it is always the Hitlers and the Stalins who are the "great charismatic leaders." And fulfillment through self-development into a "superior person"—what Kierkegaard called "becoming a Christian"—may turn either into the smugness of the Pharisee who thanks God that he is not like other people, or into self-indulgence instead of self-discipline, moral sloth instead of self-respect, and into saying "I like," rather than "I know."

Yet, despite these degenerative tendencies, the Ethics of Prudence is surely appropriate to a society of organizations. Of course, it will not be "business ethics"—it makes absolutely no difference in the Ethics of Prudence whether the executive is a general in the Army, a bureau chief in the Treasury Department in Washington, a senator, a judge, a senior vice president in a bank, or a hospital administrator. But a "society of organizations" is a society in which an extraordinarily large number of people are in positions of high visibility, if only within one organization. They enjoy this visibility not, like the "Christian Prince," by virtue of birth, nor by virtue of wealth—that is, not because they are "personages." They are "functionaries" and important only through their responsibility to take right action. But this is exactly what the Ethics of Prudence are all about.

Similarly, executives set examples, whatever the organization. They "set the tone," "create the spirit," "decide the values" for an organization and for the people in it. They lead or mislead, in other words. And they have no choice but to do one or the other. Above all, the ethics or aesthetics of self-development would seem to be tailor-made for the specific dilemma of the executive in the modern organization. By himself he is a nobody and indeed anonymous. A week after he has retired and has left that big corner office on the twenty-sixth floor of his company's skyscraper or the Secretary's six-room corner suite on Constitution Avenue, no one in the building even recognizes him anymore. And his neighbors in the pleasant suburb in which he lives in a comfortable middle-class house—very different from anything one might call a "palace"—only know that "Joe works someplace on Park Avenue" or "does something in the government." Yet collectively these anonymous executives are the "leaders" in a modern society. Their function demands the self-discipline and the self-respect of the "superior man." To live up to the performance expectations society makes upon them, they have to strive for self-fulfillment rather than be content with lackadaisical mediocrity. Yet at the pinnacle of their career and success, they are still cogs in an organization and easily replaceable. And this is exactly what self-fulfillment in ethics, the Kierkegaardian "becoming a Christian," concerns itself with: how to become the "superior man," important and autonomous, without being a "big shot" let alone a "Prince".

One would therefore expect the discussion of "business ethics" to focus on the Ethics of Prudence. Some of the words, such as to "fulfill oneself," indeed sound the same, though they mean something quite different. But by and large, the discussion of "business ethics," even if more sensibly concerning itself with the "ethics of organization," will have nothing to do with prudence.

The reason is clearly that the Ethics of Prudence are the ethics of authority. And while today's discussion of "business ethics" (or of the ethics of university administration, of hospital administration, or of government) clamors for responsibility, it rejects out of hand any "authority" and, of course, particularly any authority of the business executive. Authority is not "legitimate"; it is "elitism." But there can be no responsibility where authority is denied. To deny it is not "anarchism" nor "radicalism," let alone "socialism". In a child, it is called a temper tantrum.

THE ETHICS OF INTERDEPENDENCE

Casuistry was so thoroughly discredited that the only mention of it to be found in most textbooks on the history of philosophy is in connection with its ultimate adversaries—Spinoza and Pascal. Indeed, only 10 or 15 years ago, few if any philosophers would have thought it possible for anything like "business ethics" to emerge. "Particularist ethics," a set of ethics that postulates that this or that group is different in its ethical responsibilities from everyone else, would have been considered doomed forever by the failure of casuistry. Ethics, almost anyone in the West would have considered axiomatic, would surely always be ethics of the individual and independent of rank and station.

But there is another, non-Western ethics that is situational. It is the most successful and most durable ethics of them all: the Confucian ethics of interdependence.

Confucian ethics elegantly sidesteps the trap into which the Casuists fell;

it is a universal ethics, in which the same rules and imperatives of behavior hold for every individual. There is no "social responsibility" overriding individual conscience, no cost-benefit calculation, no greater good or higher measure than the individual and his behavior, and altogether no casuistry. In the Confucian ethics, the rules are the same for all. But there are different general rules, according to the five basic relationships of interdependence, which for the Confucian embrace the totality of individual interactions in civil society: superior and subordinate (or master and servant); father and child; husband and wife; oldest brother and sibling; friend and friend. Right behavior—what in the English translation of Confucian ethics is usually called "sincerity"*—is that individual behavior which is truly appropriate to the specific relationship of mutual dependence because it optimizes benefits for both parties. Other behavior is "insincere" and therefore wrong behavior and unethical. It creates dissonance instead of harmony, exploitation instead of benefits, manipulation instead of trust.

An example of the Confucian approach to the ethical problems discussed under the heading of "business ethics" would be "sexual harrassment." To the Confucian it is clearly unethical behavior because it injects power into a relationship that is based on function. This makes it exploitation. That this "insincere,"—that is, grossly unethical—behavior on the part of a superior takes place within a business or any other kind of organization, is basically irrelevant. The master/servant or superior/subordinate relationship is one between individuals. Hence, the Confucian would make no distinction between a general manager forcing his secretary into sexual intercourse and Mr. Samuel Pepys, England's famous 17th century diarist, forcing his wife's maids to submit to his amorous advances. It would not even make much difference to the Confucian that today's secretary can, as a rule, quit without suffering more than inconvenience if she does not want to submit, whereas the poor wretches in Mrs. Pepys' employ ended up as prostitutes, either because they did not submit and were fired and out on the street, or because they did submit and were fired when they got pregnant. Nor would the Confucian see much difference between a corporation vice-president engaging in "sexual harrassment" and a college professor seducing coeds with implied promises to raise their grades.

And finally, it would be immaterial to the Confucian that the particular "insincerity" involves sexual relations. The superior would be equally guilty of grossly unethical behavior and violation of fundamental rules of conduct if, as a good many of the proponents of "business ethics" ardently advocate, he were to set himself up as a mental therapist for his subordinates and help them to "adjust." No matter how benevolent his intentions, this is equally in-

*No word has caused more misunderstanding in East/West relations than "sincerity." To a Westerner, "sincerity" means "words that are true to conviction and feelings"; to an Easterner, "sincerity" means "actions that are appropriate to a specific relationship and make it harmonious and of optimum mutual benefit." For the Westerner, "sincerity" has to do with intentions, that is, with morality; to the Easterner, "sincerity" has to do with behavior, that is, with ethics.

compatible with the integrity of the superior/subordinate relationship. It equally abuses rank based on function and imposes power. It is therefore exploitation whether done because of lust for power or manipulation or done out of bene-volence—either way it is unethical and destructive. Both sexual relations and the healer/patient relationship must be free of rank to be effective, harmon-ious, and ethically correct. They are constructive only as "friend to friend" or as "husband to wife" relations, in which differences in function confer no rank whatever.

This example makes it clear, I would say, that virtually all the concerns of "business ethics," indeed almost everything "business ethics" considers a problem, have to do with relationships of interdependence, whether that be-tween the organization and the employee, the manufacturer and the customer, the hospital and the patient, the university and the student, and so on.

Looking at the ethics of interdependence immediately resolves the con-undrum which confounds the present discussion of "business ethics": What difference does it make whether a certain act or behavior takes place in a "busi-ness," in a "non-profit organization," or outside any organization at all? The answer is clear: None at all. Indeed the questions that are so hotly debated in today's discussion of "business ethics," such as whether changing a hospital from "nonprofit" to "proprietary and for profit" will affect either its behavior or the ethics pertaining to it, the most cursory exposure to the ethics of inter-dependence reveals as sophistry and as nonquestions.

The ethics of interdependence thus does address itself to the question which "business ethics" tries to tackle. But today's discussion, explicit or implicity, denies the basic insight from which the ethics of interdependence starts and to which it owes its strength and durability: It denies *interdependence.*

The ethics of interdependence, as Confucian philosophers first codified it shortly after their Master's death in 479 B.C., considers illegitimate and un-ethical the injection of power into human relationships. It asserts that interde-pendence demands equality of obligations. Children owe obedience and respect to their parents. Parents, in turn, owe affection, sustenance and, yes, respect, to their children. For every paragon of filial piety in Confucian hagiology, such as the dutiful daughter, there is a paragon of parental sacrifice, such as the loving father who sacrificed his brilliant career at the court to the care of his five children and their demands on his time and attention. For every minister who risks his job, if not his life, by fearlessly correcting an Emperor guilty of violating harmony, there is an Emperor laying down his life rather than throw a loyal minister to the political wolves.

In the ethics of interdependence there are only "obligations," and all obligations are mutual obligations. Harmony and trust—that is, interdepend-ence—require that each side be obligated to provide what the other side needs to achieve its goals and to fulfill itself.

But in today's American—and European—discussion of "business ethics," ethics means that one side has obligations and the other side has rights, if not "entitlements." This is not compatible with the ethics of interdependence and indeed with any ethics at all. It is the politics of power, and indeed the politics of naked exploitation and repression. And within the context of interdependence the "exploiters" and the "oppressors" are not the "bosses," but the ones who assert their "rights" rather than accept mutual obligation, and with it, equality. To "redress the balance" in a relationship of interdependence—or at least so the ethics of interdependence would insist—demands not pitting power against power or right against right, but matching obligation to obligation.

To illustrate: Today's "ethics of organization" debate pays great attention to the duty to be a "whistle-blower" and to the protection of the "whistle-blower" against retaliation or suppression by his boss or by his organization. This sounds high-minded. Surely, the subordinate has a right, if not indeed a duty, to bring to public attention and remedial action his superior's misdeeds, let alone violation of the law on the part of a superior or of his employing organization. But in the context of the ethics of interdependence, "whistle-blowing" is ethically quite ambiguous. To be sure, there are misdeeds of the superior or of the employing organization which so grossly violate propriety and laws that the subordinate (or the friend, or the child, or even the wife) cannot remain silent. This is, after all, what the word "felony" implies; one becomes a partner to a felony and criminally liable by not reporting, and thus "compounding" it. But otherwise? It is not primarily that to encourage "whistle-blowing" corrodes the bond of trust that ties the superior to the subordinate. Encouraging the "whistle-blower" must make the subordinate lose his trust in the superior's willingness and ability to "protect his people." They simply are no longer "his people" and become potential enemies or political pawns. And in the end, encouraging and indeed even permitting "whistle-blowers" always makes the weaker one—that is, the subordinate—powerless against the unscrupulous superior, simply because the superior no longer can recognize or meet his obligation to the subordinate.

"Whistle-blowing," after all, is simply another word for "informing." And perhaps it is not quite irrelevant that the only societies in Western history that encouraged informers were bloody and infamous tyrannies—Tiberius and Nero in Rome, the Inquisition in the Spain of Philip II, the French Terror, and Stalin. It may also be no accident that Mao, when he tried to establish dictatorship in China, organized "whistle-blowing" on a massive scale. For under "whistle-blowing," under the regime of the "informer," no mutual trust, no interdependencies, and no ethics are possible. And Mao only followed history's first "totalitarians," the "legalists" of the Third Century B.C., who suppressed Confucius and burned his books because he had taught ethics and had rejected the absolutism of political power.

The limits of mutual obligation are indeed a central and difficult issue in the ethics of interdependencies. But to start out, as the advocates of "whistle-blowing" do, with the assumption that there are only rights on one side, makes any ethics impossible. And if the fundamental problem of ethics is the behavior in relations of interdependence, then obligations have to be mutual and have to be equal for both sides. Indeed, in a relationship of interdependence it is the mutuality of obligation that creates true equality, regardless of differences in rank, wealth, or power.

Today's discussion of "business ethics" stridently denies this. It tends to assert that in relations of interdependence one side has all the duties and the other one all the rights. But this is the assertion of the Legalist, the assertion of the totalitarians who shortly end up by denying all ethics. It must also mean that ethics becomes the tool of the powerful. If a set of ethics is one-sided, then the rules are written by those that have the position, the power, the wealth. If interdependence is not equality of obligations, it becomes domination.

Looking at "business ethics" as an ethics of interdependence reveals an additional and equally serious problem—indeed a *more* serious problem.

Can an ethics of interdependence be anything more than ethics for individuals? The Confucians said "no"—a main reason why Mao outlawed them. For the Confucian—but also for the philosopher of the Western tradition—only *law* can handle the rights and objections of collectives. *Ethics* is always a matter of the person.

But is this adequate for a "society of organizations" such as ours? This may be the central question for the philosopher of modern society, in which access to livelihood, career and achievement exist primarily in and through organizations—and especially for the highly-educated person for whom opportunities outside of organization are very scarce indeed. In such a society, both the society and the individual increasingly depend on the performance, as well as the "sincereity," of organizations.

But in today's discussion of "business ethics" it is not even seen that there is a problem.

"ETHICAL CHIC" OR ETHICS

"Business ethics," this discussion should have made clear, is to ethics what soft porn is to the Platonic Eros; soft porn too talks of something it calls "love." And insofar as "business ethics" comes even close to ethics, it comes close to casuistry and will, predictably, end up as a fig leaf for the shameless and as special pleading for the powerful and the wealthy.

Clearly, one major element of the peculiar stew that goes by the name of "business ethics" is plain old-fashioned hostility to business and to economic activity altogether—one of the oldest of American traditions and perhaps the only still-potent ingredient in the Puritan heritage. Otherwise, we would not even talk of "business ethics." There is no warrant in any ethics to consider one major sphere of activity as having its own ethical problems, let alone its own "ethics." "Business" or "economic activity" may have special political or legal dimensions as in "business and government," to cite the title of a once-popular college course, or as in the antitrust laws. And "business ethics" may be good politics or good electioneering. But that is all. For ethics deals with the right actions of individuals. And then it surely makes no difference whether the setting is a community hospital, with the actors a nursing supervisor and the "consumer" a patient, or whether the setting is National Universal General Corporation, the actors a quality control manager, and the consumer the buyer of a bicycle.

But one explanation for the popularity of "business ethics" is surely also the human frailty of which Pascal accused the Casuists of his day: the lust for power and prominence of a clerisy sworn to humility. "Business ethics" is fashionable, and provides speeches at conferences, lecture fees, consulting assignments, and lots of publicity. And surely "business ethics," with its tales of wrongdoing in high places, caters also to the age-old enjoyment of "society" gossip and to the prurience which—it was, I believe, Rabelais who said it—makes it fornication when a peasant has a toss in the hay and romance when the prince does it.

Altogether, "business ethics" might well be called "ethical chic" rather than ethics—and indeed might be considered more a media event than philosophy or morals.

But this discussion of the major approaches to ethics and of their concerns surely also shows that ethics has as much to say to the individual in our society of organizations as they ever had to say to the individual in earlier societies. They are just as important and just as needed nowadays. And they surely require hard and serious work.

A society of organizations is a society of interdependence. The specific relationship which the Confucian philosopher postulated as universal and basic may not be adequate, or even appropriate, to modern society and to the ethical problems within the modern organization and between the modern organization and its clients, customers, and constituents. But the fundamental concepts surely are. Indeed, if there ever is a viable "ethics of organization," it will almost certainly have to adopt the key concepts which have made Confucian ethics both durable and effective:

> clear definition of the fundamental relationships;
> universal and general rules of conduct—that is, rules that are binding on any one person or organization, according to its rules, function, and relationships;
> focus on right behavior rather than on avoiding wrongdoing, and on behavior rather than on motives or intentions; and finally
> an effective organization ethic, indeed an organization ethic that deserves to be seriously considered as "ethics," will have to define right behavior as the behavior which optimizes each party's benefits and thus makes the relationship harmonious, constructive, and mutually beneficial.

But a society of organizations is also a society in which a great many people are unimportant and indeed anonymous by themselves, yet are highly visible, and matter as "leaders" in society. And thus it is a society that must stress the Ethics of Prudence and self-development. It must expect its managers, executives, and professionals to demand of themselves that they shun behavior they would not respect in others, and instead practice behavior appropriate to the sort of person they would want to see "in the mirror in the morning."

CAPITALIST ETHICS—TOUGH OR SOFT?
Jack Hirshleifer

I have never known much good done by those who affected to trade for the public good. It is an affectation, indeed, not very common among merchants, and very few words need be employed in dissuading them from it.

Sometimes it is said that man cannot be trusted with the government of himself. Can he, then, be trusted with the government of others?

Few world outlooks have been responsible for greater social mischief than the ideology or social philosophy which might be called "sentimental socialism"— the cluster of ideas centering upon a contrast between the evil capitalist ethic and its supposedly superior socialist counterpart. Sentimental socialists maintain, for one thing, that, since the system of private enterprise for profit rewards pursuit of self-interest, it cannot serve the general interest. Consequently, a system banning selfish private enterprise for profit is bound to encourage economic activity in the public interest in the place of the proscribed private interest.

What is sentimental here is the belief that a change in social organization is all that is required to abolish human selfishness. As Mr. Dooley said, "A man that'd expect to train lobsters to fly in a year is called a lunatic; but a man that thinks men can be turned into angels by an election is called a reformer and remains at large." Among sentimental socialists are such disparate modern thinkers as Albert Einstein, Jawaharlal Nehru, and R. H. Tawney. Sentimental or "soft" socialism has an extraordinary appeal to gentle physicists, non-materialistic statesmen, Unitarian ministers, and social workers—to mention just a few vulnerable categories. The appalling experience of this century with an actual socialist system in Russia has shaken this set of beliefs, to the limited extent by which mere evidence can sway opinion, but even so the world-wide influence of the ideology of soft socialism is an incalculable asset to the system of organized terror now ruling most of the Eurasian continent.

By way of contrast, it is worth mentioning that Karl Marx was primarily

Jack Hirshleifer, "Capitalist Ethics—Tough or Soft?". Reprinted from *The Journal of Law and Economics*, 2 (October 1959), 114–19. Copyright 1959 by The University of Chicago Press.

a realistic or "tough" socialist. He despised the Utopians with their proposed ethical reconstitutions of society. Basically, Marx understood both capitalism and socialism as systems of power relations developing out of an ineluctable historical process. Marx did not deny that the system of bourgeois capitalism had made enormous productive contributions to social advancement. Rather, his view was that, having served this purpose and also having performed its historical function of crushing feudal remnants and developing an aroused proletariat, capitalism had evolved within itself the seeds of its successor—socialism. It is true that Marx's thought was infected by certain ethical considerations; his dictatorship of the proletariat was not utopia, but it was supposed to lead to a utopia in which the state would wither away with the disappearance of the economic disparities responsible for human conflict. For this reason, the true exemplar of socialist reality is not the inconsistent theoretician Marx but the practitioners Lenin, Stalin, and Mao, a group more consistently free of the taint of softness.

This, however, is an aside. Our concern here is with sentimental socialism in the realm of ideology, not with experienced socialism in the world of affairs. Now soft socialism as an ideology has two outlooks—one upon the capitalist system as seen or imagined, and one upon the socialist system. Proponents of capitalism have often, on varying grounds, attacked the beautiful image of beneficent socialism as a false picture. Alternatively, there have been attempts to construct an ideology of capitalism which will be less vulnerable to socialist criticism.

Such an attempt appears in a recent article by James C. Worthy, a vice-president of a leading American corporation, entitled "Religion and Its Role in the World of Business."[1] "Soft socialism" regards the business system as convicted of encouraging selfishness and, consequently, of failing to serve humanity. Speaking before a religious conference, an audience which he may (perhaps wrongly) have suspected of being especially likely to hold a soft view of human nature, Worthy propounded an ideology which might be called "sentimental capitalism" as the answer to sentimental socialism. Admitting that selfishness is socially harmful, Worthy declares that businessmen, despite appearances, are really unselfish. Modern management is faithfully responsive to the interests of employees and of the public. But, strangely, businessmen perform their good acts while avowing only that they pursue self-interest. The businessman's bark is worse than his bite; his harsh talk only masks his generous motives. He is like a doting father whose gruffness hides genuine affection for his son.

In Worthy's view, the reason for the businessman's odd behavior is the outmoded theory of laissez faire economics, which justifies and condones "rational" conduct based exclusively on self-interest. Businessmen, influenced by this ideology, feel constrained to explain their behavior in these terms. But this

[1] 31 J. Business 293 (1958).

explanation constitutes a grave liability for the business system: in the first place, society is unlikely to turn for leadership to a group which avows its merely selfish interest, and in the second place the actions of businessmen are less generous than they would be because they themselves cannot help but be influenced somewhat by their ethically barren ideology. In short, businessmen need to see themselves not as selfish agents, which they really are not, but as stewards for the welfare of others, which is their true role and one which they have essentially played in the past, though no doubt with lapses and imperfections.

There are several interesting things about this defense of capitalism—that capitalists are really not selfish after all. The first is that, as a defense, it is a hopeless failure. There are many reasons why this argument must fail, but perhaps the most conspicuous reason is that it is untrue. Instances of "generous" practice whether or not masked by "selfish" talk may exist, but they are not the characteristic examples that come immediately to mind as representative of business behavior. One doubts, for example, that the cigarette companies are giving serious consideration these days to stopping sales of their product merely because there is a strong suspicion that cigarette smoking causes lung cancer. Industries often ask to be relieved of tax burdens and only rarely that their taxes be increased. It is no revelation to note that "unselfish" talk or rationalization more typically accompanies "selfish" practices than the reverse. When firms raise prices, they rarely declare that they wish to increase their profits but rather that they must unavoidably meet an increase in costs. Firms seeking tariffs declare not that their objective is greater profits but rather that it is necessary to protect the jobs and living standard of American labor from foreign competition.

Of course, selfishness is not limited to capitalists, in our society or in any other. A gentle physicist may rise to wrath when someone steals his ideas or perhaps only disagrees with them; a non-materialistic statesman may call on the troops when the populace of a province prefers another government. Even socialist writers are rarely unconcerned with their royalties—unless, indeed, as is likely in a socialist society, this concern becomes trivial because of the more pressing need to keep head and neck firmly attached. The coalminer does not engage in his unpleasant job because he feels his responsibility to prevent people from freezing in the winter. The Chicago city councilman, whatever he may say, is rarely credited with a single-minded urge to serve the community, and so it goes.

What does all this prove? Simply that all the world is largely governed by self-interest, and all the world knows it. Consequently, the assertion that capitalists are exempt from this failing is unlikely to win many converts to capitalism.

The second interesting—even amazing—thing about Mr. Worthy's argument is that he, as defender of the capitalist system, completely misunderstands the fundamental nature of that system as viewed by the laissez faire ideology he attacks. Worthy's basic ideas are expressed in the following sentences:

> The ideas of fair play and self-restraint are essentially religious. They help keep dog-eat-dog practices in check and enable the economy to operate without strict governmental supervision and control: self-restraint rather than legal restraint is the rule. . . .
>
> The great weakness of laissez faire economics (both the earlier and the later variety) is not so much the reliance on individual freedom and the distrust of government controls but rather the absence—indeed, the explicit denial in official business theory—of any responsibility of the businessman to anyone but himself. . . .
>
> The principle that self-interest is a sufficient guide for personal and public policy (that private vices make for public good) makes the demand for greater public control inevitable. . . .

In other words, the alternatives Worthy recognizes are self-restraint or legal restraint. But the essence of the laissez faire idea is that there is a third form of "restraint" against antisocial practices—not so frail a reed as the hope of self-restraint, nor such a threat to individual freedom as legal restraint. I refer, of course, to the *market* restraint of competition. Under laissez faire, if a business charges high prices, either because of inefficiency or because it is attempting to exploit its position, competitors rush in to serve the public in the place of the firm which is failing to do so. It is competition, not self-interest or the lack of it, which forces businessmen (if they wish to succeed) to give the public what it wants at the lowest attainable price.

The third interesting point in Mr. Worthy's presentation is his implicit acceptance of the ideas of the "new managerialism"[2]—that the corporate manager (the typical "capitalist" of today) should serve the interest of all affected groups (owners, employees, customers, suppliers, and the community) rather than seek profits (i.e., serve stockholders) alone. Now, a corporate manager pursuing profits exclusively would at least be loyal to one master—the stockholder—and not be attempting to represent conflicting interests. No one can represent conflicting interests; he can at best mediate among them. Where there are conflicting masters, the servant is responsible to none. In this case the temptation is for the managers to serve neither their employers (the stockholders), other employees, customers, *nor* the public—but rather the interest of the managerial group itself. In this interpretation "unselfishness" of managers who deal with corporate funds (other people's money) may not be much of a virtue.

On all these grounds, a sentimental defense of capitalism cannot be accepted. Is it possible to give a tough-minded defense of capitalism—that is, to show that, taking people as they really are, capitalism can convert their energies to useful social results more effectively than other systems? The answer to this question, I believe, is "Yes." It is not capitalism which makes people selfish—

[2]Mason, The Apologetics of "Managerialism," 31 J. Business 1 (1958).

people other than saints simply are more interested in their own health, comfort, and safety than in other people's and will continue to be until the establishment of the Kingdom of God on earth. All *actual* social systems, though not all social philosophies, must recognize and cope with this fact.

Under the system of private enterprise for profit, men enjoy the opportunity to receive high returns if they provide people with goods and services that people are willing to pay for. The disciplining rod is competition; if some producers do not fill an existing public need or do not fill it well, others can begin to do so. In this system everyone can be selfish—consumers buy what they like, businessmen produce what they can sell, laborers work for whoever pays most—but the market forces them to serve one another's interests, the laborer by working, the employer by paying labor and organizing production, and the consumer by paying for the final product. (Of course, it is not true that everyone *must* be selfish under this system—all who choose to serve others without reward may do so, but the choice is their own.) In the laissez faire ideology, the major role for government is to insure the preservation of competition, as well as to provide for certain communal needs like national defense. To be sure, the system has more or less serious failings: among those usually cited are the arbitrariness of the distribution of inherited wealth, and possible divergences between what the public wants and what it ought to have. These and other real objections to the capitalist system can be raised, but it remains to be shown how alternative systems will perform better. Capitalism has the decisive merit, at least, of being based on human motives as they actually are.

If we ask how an actual socialist system would have to cope with the same motives, we see that the consumers, managers, workers, and government officials of a socialist system can on no reasonable ground be assumed to be less selfish than their equivalents in a capitalist society. The distinctive characteristic of the socialist system is that it encourages and gratifies a rather different aspect of human self-interest. The main rewards in capitalism go to those who serve others through providing services and products for which others are willing to pay. In a socialist system, the monopolization of the economic (together with the political) sphere by government eliminates the check of competition. The great rewards will then go not to those who serve the public but to those who control government and thereby *rule* the public. If a system of democratic socialism were really possible, rewards under it would be shared between a hypertrophied government bureaucracy and political parties. In dictatorial socialism, the rewards go, as they have gone in Russia, to "the fittest" in seizing power. In either variant, the unsentimental case for socialism is a much harder one to defend than that for the system of private enterprise.

Corresponding to the alternative "soft" and "tough" defenses which have been given for the private enterprise system in the economic sphere, it is of interest to note that there are both sentimental and realistic defenses for democracy in the political realm. The sentimental argument runs that the people are "good" (unselfish) and so deserve to rule. The unsentimental argument, in contrast, says that all are humanly selfish—rulers and ruled alike. Democracy is a good system because it sets up a regularized procedure whereby those in the seats of power are held in check by the necessity for election by the people they govern. As in the economic sphere, the test of a desirable social system is not whether the group to whom it grants power constitutes an unselfish class but whether the holders of power are effectively checked in their exercise of it.

In the economic sphere, the crucial check on private enterprise is market competition. In the political sphere, the crucial check on democratic rulers is the requirement that they be chosen over alternative groups who also seek to become the leaders—we might say that competition here also is the check—the competition for political leadership.

Men are selfish, so who can trust self-restraint? Since rulers are selfish and terrifyingly powerful as well, to put all trust in their guardianship is folly twice over. The true principle is to associate self-interest with public interest—by offering rewards for service to the public, and by insuring that all may compete for these rewards. Competition for reward is thus the key feature of those twin liberating social inventions—capitalism in the economic sphere and democracy in the political realm.

DISTRIBUTIVE JUSTICE[1]
John Rawls

I

We may think of a human society as a more or less self-sufficient association regulated by a common conception of justice and aimed at advancing the good of its members. As a co-operative venture for mutual advantage, it is characterized by a conflict as well as an identity of interests. There is an identity of interests since social co-operation makes possible a better life for all than any would have if everyone were to try to live by his own efforts; yet at the same

John Rawls, "Distributive Justice," in *Philosophy, Politics and Society*, third series, eds. Peter Laslett and W. G. Runciman (New York: Barnes and Noble, 1967), pp. 58–82. Reprinted with permission (excluding pp. 73–82 of original article.)

[1]In this essay I try to work out some of the implications of the two principles of justice discussed in "Justice as Fairness" which first appeared in the *Philosophical Review*, 1958, and which is reprinted in *Philosophy, Politics and Society*, Series II, pp. 132–57.

time men are not indifferent as to how the greater benefits produced by their joint labours are distributed, for in order to further their own aims each prefers a larger to a lesser share. A conception of justice is a set of principles for choosing between the social arrangements which determine this division and for underwriting a consensus as to the proper distributive shares.

Now at first sight the most rational conception of justice would seem to be utilitarian. For consider: each man in realizing his own good can certainly balance his own losses against his own gains. We can impose a sacrifice on ourselves now for the sake of a greater advantage later. A man quite properly acts, as long as others are not affected, to achieve his own greatest good, to advance his ends as far as possible. Now, why should not a society act on precisely the same principle? Why is not that which is rational in the case of one man right in the case of a group of men? Surely the simplest and most direct conception of the right, and so of justice, is that of maximizing the good. This assumes a prior understanding of what is good, but we can think of the good as already given by the interests of rational individuals. Thus just as the principle of individual choice is to achieve one's greatest good, to advance so far as possible one's own system of rational desires, so the principle of social choice is to realize the greatest good (similarly defined) summed over all the members of society. We arrive at the principle of utility in a natural way: by this principle a society is rightly ordered and hence just, when its institutions are arranged so as to realize the greatest sum of satisfactions.

The striking feature of the principle of utility is that it does not matter, except indirectly, how this sum of satisfactions is distributed among individuals, any more than it matters, except indirectly, how one man distributes his satisfactions over time. Since certain ways of distributing things affect the total sum of satisfactions, this fact must be taken into account in arranging social institutions; but according to this principle the explanation of common-sense precepts of justice and their seemingly stringent character is that they are those rules which experience shows must be strictly respected and departed from only under exceptional circumstances if the sum of advantages is to be maximized. The precepts of justice are derivative from the one end of attaining the greatest net balance of satisfactions. There is no reason in principle why the greater gains of some should not compensate for the lesser losses of others; or why the violation of the liberty of a few might not be made right by a greater good shared by many. It simply happens, at least under most conditions, that the greatest sum of advantages is not generally achieved in this way. From the standpoint of utility the strictness of common-sense notions of justice has a certain usefulness, but as a philosophical doctrine it is irrational.

If, then, we believe that as a matter of principle each member of society has an inviolability founded on justice which even the welfare of everyone else cannot over-ride, and that a loss of freedom for some is not made right by a greater sum of satisfactions enjoyed by many, we shall have to look for another account of the principles of justice. The principle of utility is incapable of explaining the fact that in a just society the liberties of equal citizenship are taken for granted, and the rights secured by justice are not subject to political bargaining nor to the calculus of social interests. Now, the most natural alternative to the principle of utility is its traditional rival, the theory of the social contract. The aim of the contract doctrine is precisely to account for the strictness of justice by supposing that its principles arise from an agreement among free and independent persons in an original position of equality and hence reflect the integrity and equal sovereignty of the rational persons who are the contractees. Instead of supposing that a conception of right, and so a conception of justice, is simply an extension of the principle of choice for one man to society as a whole, the contract doctrine assumes that the rational individuals who belong to society must choose together, in one joint act, what is to count among them as just and unjust. They are to decide among themselves once and for all what is to be their conception of justice. This decision is thought of as being made in a suitably defined initial situation one of the significant features of which is that no one knows his position in society, nor even his place in the distribution of natural talents and abilities. The principles of justice to which all are forever bound are chosen in the absence of this sort of specific information. A veil of ignorance prevents anyone from being advantaged or disadvantaged by the contingencies of social class and fortune; and hence the bargaining problems which arise in everyday life from the possession of this knowledge do not affect the choice of principles. On the contract doctrine, then, the theory of justice, and indeed ethics itself, is part of the general theory of rational choice, a fact perfectly clear in its Kantian formulation.

Once justice is thought of as arising from an original agreement of this kind, it is evident that the principle of utility is problematical. For why should rational individuals who have a system of ends they wish to advance agree to a violation of their liberty for the sake of a greater balance of satisfactions enjoyed by others? It seems more plausible to suppose that, when situated in an original position of equal right, they would insist upon institutions which returned compensating advantages for any sacrifices required. A rational man would not accept an institution merely because it maximized the sum of advantages irrespective of its effect on his own interests. It appears, then, that the principle of utility would be rejected as a principle of justice, although we shall not try to argue this important question here. Rather, our aim is to give a brief sketch of the conception of distributive shares implicit in the principles of justice which, it seems, would be chosen in the original position. The philosophical appeal of utilitarianism is that it seems to offer a single principle on the basis of which a consistent and complete conception of right can be developed. The problem is to work out a contractarian alternative in such a way that it has comparable if not all the same virtues.

II

In our discussion we shall make no attempt to derive the two principles of justice which we shall examine; that is, we shall not try to show that they would be chosen in the original position.[2] It must suffice that it is plausible that they would be, at least in preference to the standard forms of traditional theories. Instead we shall be mainly concerned with three questions: first, how to interpret these principles so that they define a consistent and complete conception of justice; second, whether it is possible to arrange the institutions of a constitutional democracy so that these principles are satisfied, at least approximately; and third, whether the conception of distributive shares which they define is compatible with common-sense notions of justice. The significance of these principles is that they allow for the strictness of the claims of justice; and if they can be understood so as to yield a consistent and complete conception, the contractarian alternative would seem all the more attractive.

The two principles of justice which we shall discuss may be formulated as follows: first, each person engaged in an institution or affected by it has an equal right to the most extensive liberty compatible with a like liberty for all; and second, inequalities as defined by the institutional structure or fostered by it are arbitrary unless it is reasonable to expect that they will work out to everyone's advantage and provided that the positions and offices to which they attach or from which they may be gained are open to all. These principles regulate the distributive aspects of institutions by controlling the assignment of rights and duties throughout the whole social structure, beginning with the adoption of a political constitution in accordance with which they are then to be applied to legislation. It is upon a correct choice of a basic structure of society, its fundamental system of rights and duties, that the justice of distributive shares depends.

The two principles of justice apply in the first instance to this basic structure, that is, to the main institutions of the social system and their arrangement, how they are combined together. Thus this structure includes the political constitution and the principal economic and social institutions which together

---

[2]This question is discussed very briefly in "Justice as Fairness," see pp. 138–41. The intuitive idea is as follows. Given the circumstances of the original position, it is rational for a man to choose as if he were designing a society in which his enemy is to assign him his place. Thus, in particular, given the complete lack of knowledge (which makes the choice one under uncertainty), the fact that the decision involves one's life-prospects as a whole and is constrained by obligations to third parties (e.g. one's descendants) and duties to certain values (e.g. to religious truth), it is rational to be conservative and so to choose in accordance with an analogue of the maximum principle. Viewing the situation in this way, the interpretation given to the principles of justice in Section IV is perhaps natural enough. Moreover, it seems clear how the principle of utility can be interpreted: it is the analogue of the Laplacean principle for choice uncertainty. (For a discussion of these choice criteria, see R. D. Luce and H. Raiffa, *Games and Decisions* (1957), pp. 275–98).

define a person's liberties and rights and affect his life-prospects, what he may expect to be and how well he may expect to fare. The intuitive idea here is that those born into the social system at different positions, say in different social classes, have varying life-prospects determined, in part, by the system of political liberties and personal rights, and by the economic and social opportunities which are made available to these positions. In this way the basic structure of society favours certain men over others, and these are the basic inequalities, the ones which affect their whole life-prospects. It is inequalities of this kind, presumably inevitable in any society, with which the two principles of justice are primarily designed to deal.

Now the second principle holds that an inequality is allowed only if there is reason to believe that the institution with the inequality, or permitting it, will work out for the advantage of every person engaged in it. In the case of the basic structure this means that all inequalities which affect life-prospects, say the inequalities of income and wealth which exist between social classes, must be to the advantage of everyone. Since the principle applies to institutions, we interpret this to mean that inequalities must be to the advantage of the representative man for each relevant social position; they should improve each such man's expectation. Here we assume that it is possible to attach to each position an expectation, and that this expectation is a function of the whole institutional structure: it can be raised and lowered by reassigning rights and duties throughout the system. Thus the expectation of any position depends upon the expectations of the others, and these in turn depend upon the pattern of rights and duties established by the basic structure. But it is not clear what is meant by saying that inequalities must be to the advantage of every representative man, and hence our first question.

III

One possibility is to say that everyone is made better off in comparison with some historically relevant benchmark. An interpretation of this kind is suggested by Hume.[3] He sometimes says that the institutions of justice, that is, the rules regulating property and contracts, and so on, are to everyone's advantage, since each man can count himself the gainer on balance when he considers his permanent interests. Even though the application of the rules is sometimes to his disadvantage, and he loses in the particular case, each man gains in the long-run by the steady administration of the whole system of justice. But all Hume seems to mean by this is that everyone is better off in comparison with the situation of men in the state of nature, understood either as some primitive condition or as the circumstances which would obtain at any time if the existing institutions of justice were to break down. While this sense of everyone's being

[3]For this observation I am indebted to Brian Barry.

made better off is perhaps clear enough, Hume's interpretation is surely unsatisfactory. For even if all men including slaves are made better off by a system of slavery than they would be in the state of nature, it is not true that slavery makes everyone (even a slave) better off, at least not in a sense which makes the arrangement just. The benefits and burdens of social co-operation are unjustly distributed even if everyone does gain in comparison with the state of nature; this historical or hypothetical benchmark is simply irrelevant to the question of justice. In fact, any past state of society other than a recent one seems irrelevant offhand, and this suggests that we should look for an interpretation independent of historical comparisons altogether. Our problem is to identify the correct hypothetical comparisons defined by currently feasible changes.

Now the well-known criterion of Pareto[4] offers a possibility along these lines once it is formulated so as to apply to institutions. Indeed, this is the most natural way of taking the second principle (or rather the first part of it, leaving aside the requirement about open positions). This criterion says that group welfare is at an optimum when it is impossible to make any one man better off without at the same time making at least one other man worse off. Applying this criterion to allocating a given bundle of goods among given individuals, a particular allocation yields an optimum if there is no redistribution which would improve one individual's position without worsening that of another. Thus a distribution is optimal when there is no further exchange which is to the advantage of both parties, or to the advantage of one and not to the disadvantage of the other. But there are many such distributions, since there are many ways of allocating commodities so that no further mutually beneficial exchange is possible. Hence the Pareto criterion, as important as it is, admittedly does not identify the best distribution, but rather a class of optimal, or efficient, distributions. Moreover, we cannot say that a given optimal distribution is better than any nonoptimal one; it is only superior to those which it dominates. The criterion is at best an incomplete principle for ordering distributions.

Pareto's idea can be applied to institutions. We assume, as remarked above, that it is possible to associate with each social position an expectation which depends upon the assignment of rights and duties in the basic structure. Given this assumption, we get a principle which says that the pattern of expectations (inequalities in life-prospects) is optimal if and only if it is impossible to change the rules, to redefine the scheme of rights and duties, so as to raise the expectations of any representative man without at the same time lowering the expectations of some other representative man. Hence the basic structure satisfies this principle when it is impossible to change the assignment of fundamental rights and duties and to alter the availability of economic and social opportunities so as to make some representative man better off without mak-

[4]Introduced by him in his *Manuel d' économie politique* (1909) and long since a basic principle of welfare economics.

ing another worse off. Thus, in comparing different arrangements of the social system, we can say that one is better than another if in one arrangement all expectations are at least as high, and some higher, than in the other. The principle gives grounds for reform, for if there is an arrangement which is optimal in comparison with the existing state of things, then other things equal, it is a better situation all around and should be adopted.

The satisfaction of this principle, then, defines a second sense in which the basic structure makes everyone better off; namely, that from the standpoint of its representative men in the relevant positions, there exists no change which would improve anyone's condition without worsening that of another. Now we shall assume that this principle would be chosen in the original position, for surely it is a desirable feature of a social system that it is optimal in this sense. In fact, we shall suppose that this principle defines the concept of efficiency for institutions, as can be seen from the fact that if the social system does not satisfy it, this implies that there is some change which can be made which will lead people to act more effectively so that the expectations of some at least can be raised. Perhaps an economic reform will lead to an increase in production with given resources and techniques, and with greater output someone's expectations are raised.

It is not difficult to see, however, that while this principle provides another sense for an institution's making everyone better off, it is an inadequate conception of justice. For one thing, there is the same incompleteness as before. There are presumably many arrangements of an institution and of the basic structure which are optimal in this sense. There may also be many arrangements which are optimal with respect to existing conditions, and so many reforms which would be improvements by this principle. If so, how is one to choose between them? It is impossible to say that the many optimal arrangements are equally just, and the choice between them a matter of indifference, since efficient institutions allow extremely wide variations in the pattern of distributive shares.

Thus it may be that under certain conditions serfdom cannot be significantly reformed without lowering the expectations of some representative man, say that of landowners, in which case serfdom is optimal. But equally it may happen under the same conditions that a system of free labour could not be changed without lowering the expectations of some representative man, say that of free labourers, so that this arrangement likewise is optimal. More generally, whenever a society is relevantly divided into a number of classes, it is possible, let's suppose, to maximize with respect to any one of its representative men at a time. These maxima give at least this many optimal positions, for none of them can be departed from to raise the expectations of any man without lowering those of another, namely, the man with respect to whom the maximum is defined. Hence each of these extremes is optimal. All this corresponds to the obvious fact that, in distributing particular goods to given individuals, those distributions are also optimal which give the whole stock to any one person; for once a single person has everything, there is no change which will not make him worse off.

We see, then, that social systems which we should judge very differently from the standpoint of justice may be optimal by this criterion. This conclusion is not surprising. There is no reason to think that, even when applied to social systems, justice and efficiency come to the same thing. These reflections only show what we knew all along, which is that we must find another way of interpreting the second principle, or rather the first part of it. For while the two principles taken together incorporate strong requirements of equal liberty and equality of opportunity, we cannot be sure that even these constraints are sufficient to make the social structure acceptable from the standpoint of justice. As they stand the two principles would appear to place the burden of ensuring justice entirely upon these prior constraints and to leave indeterminate the preferred distributive shares.

IV

There is, however, a third interpretation which is immediately suggested by the previous remarks, and this is to choose some social position by reference to which the pattern of expectations as a whole is to be judged, and then to maximize with respect to the expectations of this representative man consistent with the demands of equal liberty and equality of opportunity. Now, the one obvious candidate is the representative man of those who are least favoured by the system of institutional inequalities. Thus we arrive at the following idea: the basic structure of the social system affects the life-prospects of typical individuals according to their initial places in society, say the various income classes into which they are born, or depending upon certain natural attributes, as when institutions make discriminations between men and women or allow certain advantages to be gained by those with greater natural abilities. The fundamental problem of distributive justice concerns the differences in life-prospects which come about in this way. We interpret the second principle to hold that these differences are just if and only if the greater expectations of the more advantaged, when playing a part in the working of the whole social system, improve the expectations of the least advantaged. The basic structure is just throughout when the advantages of the more fortunate promote the well-being of the least fortunate, that is, when a decrease in their advantages would make the least fortunate even worse off than they are. The basic structure is perfectly just when the prospects of the least fortunate are as great as they can be.

In interpreting the second principle (or rather the first part of it which we may, for obvious reasons, refer to as the difference principle), we assume that the first principle requires a basic equal liberty for all, and that the resulting political system, when circumstances permit, is that of a constitutional democracy in some form. There must be liberty of the person and political equality as well as liberty of conscience and freedom of thought. There is one class of equal citizens which defines a common status for all. We also assume that there is equality of opportunity and a fair competition for the available positions on the basis of reasonable qualifications. Now, given this background, the differences to be justified are the various economic and social inequalities in the basic structure which must inevitably arise in such a scheme. These are the inequalities in the distribution of income and wealth and the distinctions in social prestige and status which attach to the various positions and classes. The difference principle says tht these inequalities are just if and only if they are part of a larger system in which they work out to the advantage of the most unfortunate representative man. The just distributive shares determined by the basic structure are those specified by this constrained maximum principle.

Thus, consider the chief problem of distributive justice, that concerning the distribution of wealth as it affects the life-prospects of those starting out in the various income groups. These income classes define the relevant representative men from which the social system is to be judged. Now, a son of a member of the entrepreneurial class (in a capitalist society) has a better prospect than that of the son of an unskilled labourer. This will be true, it seems, even when the social injustices which presently exist are removed and the two men are of equal talent and ability; the inequality cannot be done away with as long as something like the family is maintained. What, then, can justify this inequality in life-prospects? According to the second principle it is justified only if it is to the advantage of the representative man who is worst off, in this case the representative unskilled labourer. The inequality is permissible because lowering it would, let's suppose, make the working man even worse off than he is. Presumably, given the principle of open offices (the second part of the second principle), the greater expectations allowed to entrepreneurs has the effect in the longer run of raising the life-prospects of the labouring class. The inequality in expectation provides an incentive so that the economy is more efficient, industrial advance proceeds at a quicker pace, and so on, the end result of which is that greater material and other benefits are distributed throughout the system. Of course, all of this is familiar, and whether true or not in particular cases, it is the sort of thing which must be argued if the inequality in income and wealth is to be acceptable by the difference principle.

We should now verify that this interpretation of the second principle gives a natural sense in which everyone may be said to be made better off. Let us suppose that inequalities are chain-connected: that is, if an inequality raises the expectations of the lowest position, it raises the expectations of all positions in between. For example, if the greater expectations of the representative entrepreneur raises that of the unskilled labourer, it also raises that of the semi-skilled. Let us further assume that inequalities are close-knit: that is, it is impossible to raise (or lower) the expectation of any representative man without raising (or lowering) the expectations of every other representative man, and in particular, without affecting one way or the other that of the least fortunate. There is no loose-jointedness, so to speak, in the way in which expectations depend upon one another. Now, with these assumptions, everyone does benefit from an inequality which satisfies the difference principle, and the second principle as we have formulated it reads correctly. For the representative man who is better off in any pairwise comparison gains by being allowed to have his advantage, and the man who is worse off benefits from the contribution which all inequalities make to each position below. Of course, chain-connection and closeknitness may not obtain; but in this case those who are better off should not have a veto over the advantages available for the least advantaged. The stricter interpretation of the difference principle should be followed, and all inequalities should be arranged for the advantage of the most unfortunate even if some inequalities are not to the advantage of those in middle positions. Should these conditions fail, then, the second principle would have to be stated in another way.

It may be observed that the difference principle represents, in effect, an original agreement to share in the benefits of the distribution of natural talents and abilities, whatever this distribution turns out to be, in order to alleviate as far as possible the arbitrary handicaps resulting from our initial starting places in society. Those who have been favoured by nature, whoever they are, may gain from their good fortune only on terms that improve the well-being of those who have lost out. The naturally advantaged are not to gain simply because they are more gifted, but only to cover the costs of training and cultivating their endowments and for putting them to use in a way which improves the position of the less fortunate. We are led to the difference principle if we wish to arrange the basic social structure so that no one gains (or loses) from his luck in the natural lottery of talent and ability, or from his initial place in society, without giving (or receiving) compensating advantages in return. (The parties in the original position are not said to be attracted by this idea and so agree to it; rather, given the symmetries of their situation, and particularly their lack of knowledge, and so on, they will find it to their interest to agree to a principle which can be understood in this way.) And we should note also that when the difference principle is perfectly satisfied, the basic structure is optimal by the efficiency principle. There is no way to make anyone better off without making someone else worse off, namely, the least fortunate representative man. Thus the two principles of justice define distributive shares in a way compatible with efficiency, at least as long as we move on this highly abstract level. If we want to say (as we do, although it cannot be argued here) that the demands of justice have an absolute weight with respect to efficiency, this claim may seem less paradoxical when it is kept in mind that perfectly just institutions are also efficient.

V

Our second question is whether it is possible to arrange the institutions of a constitutional democracy so that the two principles of justice are satisfied, at least approximately. We shall try to show that this can be done provided the government regulates a free economy in a certain way. More fully, if law and government act effectively to keep markets competitive, resources fully employed, property and wealth widely distributed over time, and to maintain the appropriate social minimum, then if there is equality of opportunity underwritten by education for all, the resulting distribution will be just. Of course, all of these arrangements and policies are familiar. The only novelty in the following remarks, if there is any novelty at all, is that this framework of institutions can be made to satisfy the difference principle. To argue this, we must sketch the relations of these institutions and how they work together.

First of all, we assume that the basic social structure is controlled by a just constitution which secures the various liberties of equal citizenship. Thus the legal order is administered in accordance with the principle of legality, and liberty of conscience and freedom of thought are taken for granted. The political process is conducted, so far as possible, as a just procedure for choosing between governments and for enacting just legislation. From the standpoint of distributive justice, it is also essential that there be equality of opportunity in several senses. Thus, we suppose that, in addition to maintaining the usual social overhead capital, government provides for equal educational opportunities for all either by subsidizing private schools or by operating a public school system. It also enforces and underwrites equality of opportunity in commercial ventures and in the free choice of occupation. This result is achieved by policing business behaviour and by preventing the establishment of barriers and restriction to the desirable positions and markets. Lastly, there is a guarantee of a social minimum which the government meets by family allowances and special payments in times of unemployment, or by a negative income tax.

In maintaining this system of institutions the government may be thought of as divided into four branches. Each branch is represented by various agencies (or activities thereof) charged with preserving certain social and economic conditions. These branches do not necessarily overlap with the usual organization of government, but should be understood as purely conceptual. Thus the allocation branch is to keep the economy feasibly competitive, that is, to prevent the formation of unreasonable market power. Markets are competitive in this sense when they cannot be made more so consistent with the requirements of efficiency and the acceptance of the facts of consumer preferences and geography. The allocation branch is also charged with identifying and correcting, say by suitable taxes and subsidies wherever possible, the more obvious departures from efficiency caused by the failure of prices to measure accurately social benefits and costs. The stabilization branch strives to maintain reasonably full employment so that there is no waste through failure to use resources and the free choice of occupation and the deployment of finance is supported by strong effective demand. These two branches together are to preserve the efficiency of the market economy generally.

The social minimum is established through the operations of the transfer branch. Later on we shall consider at what level this minimum should be set, since this is a crucial matter; but for the moment, a few general remarks will suffice. The main idea is that the workings of the transfer branch take into account the precept of need and assign it an appropriate weight with respect to the other common-sense precepts of justice. A market economy ignores the claims of need altogether. Hence there is a division of labour between the parts of the social system as different institutions answer to different common-sense precepts. Competitive markets (properly supplemented by government operations) handle the problem of the efficient allocation of labour and resources and set a weight to the conventional precepts associated with wages and earnings (the precepts of each according to his work and experience, or responsibility and the hazards of the job, and so on), whereas the transfer branch guarantees a certain level of well-being and meets the claims of need. Thus it is obvious that the justice of distributive shares depends upon the whole social system and how it distributes total income, wages plus transfers. There is with reason strong objection to the competitive determination of total income, since this would leave out of account the claims of need and of a decent standard of life. From the standpoint of the original position it is clearly rational to insure oneself against these contingencies. But now, if the appropriate minimum is provided by transfers, it may be perfectly fair that the other part of total income is competitively determined. Moreover, this way of dealing with the claims of need is doubtless more efficient, at least from a theoretical point of view, than trying to regulate prices by minimum wage standards and so on. It is preferable to handle these claims by a separate branch which supports a social minimum. Henceforth, in considering whether the second principle of justice is satisfied, the answer turns on whether the total income of the least advantaged, that is, wages plus transfers, is such as to maximize their long-term expectations consistent with the demands of liberty.

Finally, the distribution branch is to preserve an approximately just distribution of income and wealth over time by affecting the background conditions of the market from period to period. Two aspects of this branch may be distinguished. First of all, it operates a system of inheritance and gift taxes. The aim of these levies is not to raise revenue, but gradually and continually to correct the distribution of wealth and to prevent the concentrations of power to the detriment of liberty and equality of opportunity. It is perfectly true, as some have said,[5] that unequal inheritance of wealth is no more inherently unjust than unequal inheritance of intelligence; as far as possible the inequalities founded on either should satisfy the difference principle. Thus, the inheritance of greater wealth is just as long as it is to the advantage of the worst off and consistent with liberty, including equality of opportunity. Now by the latter we do not mean, of course, the equality of expectations between classes, since differences in life-prospects arising from the basic structure are inevitable, and it is precisely the aim of the second principle to say when these differences are just. Instead, equality of opportunity is a certain set of institutions which assures

[5]See for example F. von Hayek, *The Constitution of Liberty* (1960), p. 90.

equally good education and chances of culture for all and which keeps open
the competition for positions on the basis of qualities reasonably related to performance, and so on. It is these institutions which are put in jeopardy when
inequalities and concentrations of wealth reach a certain limit; and the taxes
imposed by the distribution branch are to prevent this limit from being exceeded.
Naturally enough where this limit lies is a matter for political judgment guided
by theory, practical experience, and plain hunch; on this question the theory
of justice has nothing to say.

The second part of the distribution branch is a scheme of taxation for
raising revenue to cover the costs of public goods, to make transfer payments,
and the like. This scheme belongs to the distribution branch since the burden
of taxation must be justly shared. Although we cannot examine the legal and
economic complications involved, there are several points in favour of proportional expenditure taxes as part of an ideally just arrangement. For one thing,
they are preferable to income taxes at the level of common-sense precepts of
justice, since they impose a levy according to how much a man takes out of
the common store of goods and not according to how much he contributes
(assuming that income is fairly earned in return for productive efforts). On the
other hand, proportional taxes treat everyone in a clearly defined uniform way
(again assuming that income is fairly earned) and hence it is preferable to use
progressive rates only when they are necessary to preserve the justice of the
system as a whole, that is, to prevent large fortunes hazardous to liberty and
equality of opportunity, and the like. If proportional expenditure taxes should
also prove more efficient, say because they interfere less with incentives, or whatever, this would make the case for them decisive provided a feasible scheme
could be worked out.[6] Yet these are questions of political judgment which are
not our concern; and, in any case, a proportional expenditure tax is part of
an idealized scheme which we are describing. It does not follow that even steeply
progressive income taxes, given the injustice of existing systems, do not improve
justice and efficiency all things considered. In practice we must usually choose
between unjust arrangements and then it is a matter of finding the lesser injustice.

Whatever form the distribution branch assumes, the argument for it is
to be based on justice: we must hold that once it is accepted the social system
as a whole—the competitive economy surrounded by a just constitutional and
legal framework—can be made to satisfy the principles of justice with the
smallest loss in efficiency. The long-term expectations of the least advantaged
are raised to the highest level consistent with the demands of equal liberty. In
discussing the choice of a distribution scheme we have made no reference to
the traditional criteria of taxation according to ability to pay or benefits received;
nor have we mentioned any of the variants of the sacrifice principle. These standards are subordinate to the two principles of justice; once the problem is seen
as that of designing a whole social system, they assume the status of secondary

6See N. Kaldor, *An Expenditure Tax* (1955).

precepts with no more independent force than the precepts of common sense in regard to wages. To suppose otherwise is not to take a sufficiently comprehensive point of view. In setting up a just distribution branch these precepts may or may not have a place depending upon the demands of the two principles of justice when applied to the entire system.

THE WELFARE STATE VS. THE REDISTRIBUTIVE STATE
by Marc F. Plattner

In the course of the 1970's, the United States has been engaged in an intensifying public debate over the future of the welfare state. At the present moment, widespread concern about inflation, along with resentment against high taxes and "big government," is creating pressures toward a modest retrenchment in spending on social programs. We will probably be witnessing further efforts to make these programs less wasteful and more efficient, and even to eliminate some of the more unproductive and intrusive ones. But despite the hopes of some on the Right and the fears of some on the Left, these efforts are not likely to lead to the crippling or destruction of the welfare state; indeed, if successful, they will undoubtedly conserve and strengthen it.

During the past decade, however, there has also been another noteworthy development in the debate over the welfare state. This more subtle but nonetheless critical change, which has been promoted largely by academics and intellectuals on the Left, amounts to nothing less than an attempt at a fundamental redefinition of the very purpose of the welfare state. This new vision of the purpose—and the agenda—of the welfare state can be expressed in a single phrase: the redistribution of income.

Now it might appear that such a platform would be nothing new for American liberalism, but merely more of the same medicine it has been prescribing for many years. After all, the United States has had a progressive income tax since 1913, and an extensive set of social-insurance and welfare programs at least since the New Deal. In more recent years the scope of these so-called income-transfer programs has grown enormously, and therefore the United States is already redirecting a vast amount of income from its richer to its poorer citizens.

Marc F. Plattner, "The Welfare State vs. the Redistributive State," *The Public Interest,* no. 55 (Spring 1979), 28–48. Reprinted wth permission. Passages from Arthur M. Okun, *Equality and Efficiency, The Big Tradeoff* (Washington, D.C.: The Brookings Institution, 1975) reprinted with permission of the Brookings Institution, Washington, D.C. Passages from Chrisopher Jencks, *Inequality* (New York: Basic Books, Inc., 1972) reprinted with permission of Basic Books, Inc.

But while the principles of progressive taxation and of the welfare state have come to be almost universally accepted, it would be a serious error to infer that the American polity has ever embraced the idea of income redistribution. Properly speaking, a policy of income redistribution is one that is *explicitly* aimed at reducing inequality in incomes. And the legitimacy of this goal has never been endorsed by the American people or their elected representatives. The progressive income tax was generally justified, not as a means of channeling funds from the rich to the poor, but as a fair distribution of the tax burden according to the taxpayer's ability to pay. The rationale was not that after-tax income should be made more equal, but rather that there should be an "equality of sacrifice" among the citizenry in meeting the revenue needs of government. As Walter J. Blum and Harry Kalven Jr. argued in their classic study *The Uneasy Case for Progressive Taxation,* progressive taxation was originally able to become a "respectable idea in our society" precisely *because* it was justified on non-redistributive grounds.

Similarly, social-insurance programs were meant to provide a cushion against particular contingencies, and welfare and other antipoverty measures were intended to relieve those who were unable to provide for their own needs in a minimally acceptable fashion. But one can easily accept the principle of public insurance on the one hand and public charity or relief on the other without acknowledging the propriety of governmental efforts to promote the goal of greater equality of incomes. And, in fact, the United States has adopted an impressive array of policies that wind up transferring money from the rich to the poor, but it has never approved a policy of explicit income redistribution. J. R. Pole, in his recently published *The Pursuit of Equality in American History,* asserts, "Not until George McGovern became a Presidential candidate . . . was the question of income redistribution placed on any party's agenda for serious political consideration . . ." The fate of McGovern's "demogrant" proposal—and of his candidacy—shows how far the American public is from accepting the legitimacy of income redistribution.

TWO VIEWS OF TAXATION

The hostility of the American people to income redistribution is clearly recognized by the most intelligent and forthright of its proponents. A notable example in Christopher Jencks, whose *Inequality* is perhaps the most explicit attempt to discredit the principle of equality of opportunity that animated social-reform efforts in the 1960's and to put in its place the principle of equality of result, with income redistribution as its chief instrument. The final chapter of Jencks' book features the following conclusions:

> The crucial problem today is that relatively few people view income inequality as a serious problem. . . .

> If egalitarians want to mobilize popular support for income redistribution, their first aim should be to convince people that the distribution of income is a legitimate political issue. Americans now tend to assume that incomes are determined by private decisions in a largely unregulated economy and that there is no realistic way to alter the resulting distribution. Until they come to believe that the distribution of income is a political issue, subject to popular regulation and control, very little is likely to change. . . . We need to establish the idea that the Federal government is responsible not only for the total amount of the national income, but for its distribution. If private decisions make the distribution too unequal, the government must be held responsible for improving the situation. . . .
>   . . . [I]f we want substantial redistribution, we will not only have to politicize the question of income inequality but alter people's basic assumptions about the extent to which they are responsible for their neighbors and their neighbors for them.

It is doubtful whether Jencks' exhortations have had much of an impact on the thinking of most Americans. However, the redistributionist premise has made considerable headway among those directly involved in the discussion and formulation of public policy. Increasing attention is being paid to the distributional consequences of government policies and programs; there is a growing sense that the distribution of income is a proper political concern; and there is a marked tendency to view specific public policies as justified only if—whatever their other effects—they contribute to (or at least do not work against) a narrowing of income inequalities.

Consider the public debate about the propriety of some form of tax credits or deductions for parents paying college tuition for their children. A principal argument employed by the opponents of such a policy is that it would bring greater savings to those taxpayers in the upper half of the income spectrum and thereby make the post-tax distribution of income more unequal; moreover, it would result in some tax reduction even for tuition-paying parents who are at the very top of the income distribution. These overall distributional arguments are regarded by many as outweighing any specific considerations relating to the tax treatment of college tuition: whether, like homeownership, college attendance should be encouraged by Federal tax policy; and whether it is fair that two otherwise identical families (say, with incomes of $25,000) should bear the same tax burden if one is supporting two children in college (say, at a cost of $8,000 in tuition) and the other has no college expenses. In a wide range of other policy areas, there has been a similar tendency to give greater weight to overall distributional implications, especially where the tax system is concerned. Tax policy is increasingly viewed by public-policy experts as a way to redistribute income, rather than as a way to apportion the financial sacrifice citizens must make to support their government.

The distinction between these two conceptions of taxation is nicely illustrated by another quote from Jencks' *Inequality*: "Americans have a strong feeling that once they have 'earned' a sum of money, it is theirs to do with as they please. They view taxes as a necessary evil, not as an instrument for making the distribution of income more equal." This appraisal is surely correct. It is true that, insofar as Americans generally endorse the notion of the progressive income tax, they accept the view that the better off should contribute a somewhat greater proportion of their incomes than the less well off toward defraying the cost of public business. Yet, most Americans still adhere to the traditional conception of taxation, according to which citizens pay a share of *their own* income to provide for the *common* expenses. The redistributionist view, by contrast, implies that the income obtained by individuals is not their own but that of the society as a whole. Hence, in assessing the rate of tax on an individual the government is deciding not how much of his own income it will require him to pay, but how much of the society's income it will allow him to keep. And if it allows its more productive citizens to keep a more than equal share of the national income, this is only because the government has decided that allotting unequal shares will promote a more efficient and more productive national economy—not because the more productive citizen is in any way *entitled* to a larger income.

JUSTIFYING REDISTRIBUTION

How can the redistributionist position be justified? On this question Jencks is not very helpful. The only theoretical support he offers for his egalitarianism is a brief paragraph arguing that equal incomes "maximize the satisfaction of the population" (later followed by the somewhat inconsistent assertion that "need should play a larger role than it now does in determining what people get back from society"). But in any case, arguments or assertions about the *desirability,* in the abstract, of a more equal society cannot by themselves suffice to establish the *justice* of income redistribution. We could doubtless achieve many desirable things with other people's money, but this does not mean that we have the right to take it from them. To justify income redistribution (as distinguished from a fair distribution of the tax burden), it is necessary to show that individuals somehow do not have just title to the income they have earned— and that what individuals have "earned" (as Jencks would have it) therefore may rightfully be thought to belong to society as a whole.

Such an attempt to show that individuals do not have a valid moral claim to the income they have earned is made by Arthur Okun in his *Equality and Efficiency: The Big Tradeoff.* As the title of his work indicates, Okun is willing to allow the case for redistribution to be limited by the need for unequal incomes as an incentive for greater economic efficiency. Yet despite his moderate tone and his unabashed admiration for the efficiency of the market mechanism, Okun's arguments wholly undermine any moral basis for opposing the most thoroughgoing redistribution of income. He finds that "the ethical case for capitalism is totally unpersuasive," because he holds that the incomes that the market yields cannot be regarded as "fair" or "deserved."

Okun begins his discussion by citing the "so-called marginal-productivity theory of distribution," according to which a perfectly competitive market "will pay workers and investors the value of their contributions to output." He then points out that in the real world, various market imperfections prevent the distribution that would be yielded by a perfectly competitive market from being fully realized. At this point in the argument, some critics believe they have completely undermined the case for granting any ethical value to the distribution produced by real-world markets. Yet the critique founded on market imperfections implicitly assumes that marginal productivity is the true criterion of just distribution. Thus, the moral bearing of this critique seems to be, not that we should blithely override the distributional outcome of real-world markets, but that, in the interests of justice, we should strive to make those markets as competitive as possible.

Okun himself appears to realize the insufficiency of the critique based on market imperfections. Hence he proceeds to challenge the fundamental notion that rewards corresponding to contributions to productivity are fair or just. He launches this challenge by citing the problem of inequality of opportunity: The contributions that people are able to make are affected by the unequal material and cultural advantages that they derive from their family backgrounds; therefore, competition in the marketplace is unfair in the same way as a race in which the contestants are not assigned equal positions at the starting line.

The question of whether and to what extent inequality of opportunity vitiates the justice of unequal rewards is a complex and difficult one. But inequality of opportunity is not the fundamental ground on which contemporary advocates of redistribution like Okun choose to rest their case. And it is easy to see why. For just as the critique based on market imperfections implicitly assumes the justice of rewards distributed by a perfectly competitive market, so the critique based on inequality of opportunity implicitly assumes the justice of market rewards insofar as equality of opportunity prevails. That is, it assumes that once the starting positions for all contestants are made equal, justice requires that rewards be given according to how well one performs in the race. Hence this critique suggests that the best way to achieve economic justice would be through a strategy aimed at eliminating the factors that make for an unequal start (the strategy that animated much of the Great Society). Any attempt to correct for the effects of inequality of opportunity simply by redistributing income from high earners to low earners inevitably would unjustly penalize or reward many individuals—those who achieved high earnings despite lesser opportunities and those who wound up with low earnings despite greater opportunities. Moreover, *since even the wholesale elimination of inequality of opportunity would achieve only a relatively small reduction in the overall in-*

equality of income,[1] *the critique based on inequality of opportunity could in any case justify no more than a rather modest redistribution of income.*

Thus the full-fledged redistributionist must attempt to show that even if there were complete equality of opportunity, with every competitor enjoying an equal start, it would not be just to reward the swift and the determined for their superior performance in the race. And to do this it is necessary to explain why the two chief characteristics that enable some to "run" better than others—namely, superior ability and superior effort—do not entail a legitimate claim to the fruits of the successes they bring. Okun's discussion of the moral status of what he calls "natural abilities" is rather sketchy, but his view seems to be the following: People's natural abilities are the product of the genes they inherit from their parents; but these are in no way "earned" by individuals, and hence they cannot be regarded as deserved; therefore those who receive superior genes enjoy an undeserved and unfair advantage over their less fortunate fellows. From here Okun leaps to the conclusion that "society should aim to ameliorate, and certainly not to compound, *the flaws of the universe.* It cannot stop rain, but it does manufacture umbrellas. Similarly, it can decide to restrict prizes that bestow vastly higher standards of living on people with greater innate abilities" (italics mine).

It is worth stopping to consider for a moment the bizarre metaphysical doctrine that is expressed in this passage. The universe is held to be flawed because some human beings are born with greater innate abilities of various kinds than other human beings possess. The clear implication is that the universe would be much improved if the existing distribution of innate abilities were replaced by a situation in which the innate abilities of all human beings alike were reduced (or increased) to the level of the current mean. It is hard to believe that Okun would really consider such a condition of universal human mediocrity—where there were no great scientists, or artists, or economists, or athletes, or statesmen—preferable to the "universe" that actually exists. A more likely and more charitable interpretation of this passage is that Okun was led to overstate his position by a momentary excess of egalitarian zeal. A bit later in his discussion Okun cites John Rawls' elaboration of the "principle of redress." Indeed, by turning to Rawls we can see a much more coherent statement of the viewpoint that Okun is here trying to present.

John Rawls' *A Theory of Justice* is the most ambitious and sophisticated attempt to provide a theoretical justification for the redistributionist view. And the foundation of Rawls' entire theoretical structure is the premise that greater natural talent or ability cannot provide a moral claim to greater desert or re-

---

[1]Jencks and his colleagues offer the following conclusion: "Our best estimate is that family background explains around 15 percent of the variation in incomes. . . . This implies that even if America could reduce inequalities in opportunity to the point where they were no greater than those that now arise between one brother and another, the best-paid fifth of all male workers would still be making 500 percent more than the worst-paid fifth. We cannot, then, hope to eliminate, or even substantially reduce, income inequality in America simply by providing children from all walks of life with equal opportunity. When people have had relatively equal opportunity, as brothers usually have, they still end up with very unequal incomes."

ward. Unlike Okun, Rawls recognizes that the "natural distribution [of talents] is neither just nor unjust"; it is simply a "natural fact." What he stresses, however, is that "inequalities of birth and natural endowment are *undeserved*" (italics mine). Because these differences in natural ability are undeserved, they are said to be "arbitrary from a moral point of view." Instead of exclaiming against the "flaws of the universe," Rawls speaks more reasonably and precisely of the "arbitrariness found in nature" or the "arbitrariness of the world." But the conclusion he draws from this is essentially the same as Okun's: Since superiority in natural ability is undeserved and hence arbitrary, justice calls not for rewarding those endowed with superior ability but for compensating those endowed with lesser ability.[2] In short, the redistributionist view is based on supplanting an *ethics of reward* in favor of an *ethics of redress.*

EFFORT

Before examining the claim that the arbitrariness of the distribution of natural ability justifies an ethics of redress, let us first consider how Okun and Rawls deal with the other human characteristic that allows some men to make a greater contribution to productivity than others—namely, effort. Okun begins his discussion of effort sensibly enough:

> Differences in incomes that are associated with differences in effort are generally regarded as fair. If everyone were offered the same hourly wage rate and the opportunity to work as many hours as he or she chose, the resulting discrepancies on payday would be understandable. In fact, it would seem unfair for the person who takes more leisure to get just as much income. Leisure is a form of income and an element in one's standard of living; thus, a sacrifice of leisure must be compensated in other ways if fairness is to be achieved.

[2]It is worth noting that, despite the very different nature of his conclusions, Rawls shares to a surprising degree the premises of such notable champions of the free market as Friedrich Hayek and Milton Friedman. Like Rawls, Hayek and Friedman both assert that superior natural ability is undeserved and hence can generate no *moral* claim to superior reward. In part, they use this argument because they wish to defend inherited wealth by showing that inequality deriving from the inheritance of property is *no less* defensible than inequality deriving from the inheritance of superior natural ability. But in Hayek's case at least, this also points toward a further agreement with Rawls—namely, that the distribution of income in a market economy can in no way be understood as rewarding moral merit or desert. Rawls concludes from this that the market distribution lacks any ethical standing and thus should be overridden by government to promote greater equality. Hayek, while also holding that the market distribution has no ethical validity, opposes in the name of individual liberty any such attempt at governmental redistribution.

Hayek is quite explicit in asserting that the distribution of income in a "free society" cannot be defended in terms of correspondence between merit and reward, or indeed on the basis of any notion of distributive justice at all. (Hence Hayek's own defense of the free society is founded not upon considerations of justice, but upon considerations of freedom and efficiency.) I believe that this view is not only mistaken, but is bound to leave liberal capitalism morally disarmed in the face of redistributionist assaults like those of Okun and Rawls. This is not to deny, of course, that there are serious problems involved in attempting to provide a satisfactory moral justification for the distribution of income in a liberal society. But such a task, which would require a great deal more than a refutation of the redistributionist critique, far exceeds the scope of this article.

But he then proceeds to muddy the waters with his subsequent paragraph:

> Extra income for extra effort is unquestionably useful in providing incentives as well as fair compensation for parting with leisure. The two roles are hard to disentangle. When the fairness issue is viewed in a broad and searching context, some difficult questions arise. Shouldn't society be capable of tolerating diverse individual attitudes toward work and leisure? Would society really want to starve those who might conceivably have lazy genes? Suppose for a moment that incentives are not relevant. If the total input of effort were completely unaffected, would society want the beachcomber to eat less well than his fellow citizens, including others who do not work, such as children, the elderly and students on fellowships?

It is hard to find in this "broad and searching" view any principle that casts serious doubt on Okun's earlier contention that fairness requires greater rewards in return for greater effort (or a greater sacrifice of leisure). Society is likely to be capable of "tolerating diverse individual attitudes toward work and leisure" precisely to the extent that it is not expected to reward them equally. One hesitates to believe that Okun means his remark about "lazy genes" to be taken seriously; but in any case, the world has probably never seen a human being whose genes were so lazy that he chose to starve rather than to make an effort to earn a living. As for Okun's final question, all modern societies—capitalist, socialist, or whatever—do hold that men who possess the capacity and opportunity for productive (or otherwise useful) work yet refuse to perform it have no moral claim upon the society's resources. And he has offered no argument that would establish such a claim independently of work or effort.

Despite all the attention he gives to society's distribution of income and wealth, Rawls has almost nothing to say about the human effort that produces them. At one point, however, he puts forth a somewhat more refined version of Okun's "lazy genes" argument: ". . . [I]t seems clear that the effort a person is willing to make is influenced by his natural abilities and skills and the alternatives open to him. The better endowed are more likely, other things equal, to strive conscientiously, and there seems to be no way to discount for their greater good fortune." Consider the consequences of this claim that the willingness to make a greater effort is as undeserved as greater natural ability. For it would imply that greater effort, like greater natural ability, has no moral calm to greater reward; instead, according to the ethics of redress, lesser effort, like lesser natural ability, is entitled to be compensated (or, in effect, rewarded). Thus the person who works harder is entitled to nothing more, while the person who works less hard gains a greater claim over what others have produced. The moral absurdity of this view is transparent.

Rawls is able to deny the moral connection between effort and material rewards only *by ignoring the fact that income and wealth are not simply "there" to be distributed, but are produced in the first place only by human effort.* Labor or effort is the human cost of material benefits. And, all other things being equal, it is clearly unfair to distribute equal benefits to those who have borne unequal costs. So even a community that decided to apply the principle of redress in regard to unequal natural abilities would justly insist that equal rewards be allotted only on the basis of equal efforts. (In Okun's words, "If everyone were offered the same hourly wage rate and the opportunity to work as many hours as he or she chose, the resulting discrepancies on payday would be understandable. In fact, it would seem unfair for the person who takes more leisure to get just as much income.") And if such a community (whether a commune, or a kibbutz, or a political society, or persons in Rawls' "original position") determined to share its material benefits in common, it would undoubtedly require that its members also assume a fair share of the common labor.

NATURAL ABILITY

Neither Okun nor Rawls, then, succeeds in discrediting the proposition that those who are more productive because they make greater efforts deserve, all other things being equal, to enjoy greater material rewards. But now we must consider the claim of those who are more productive because they are blessed with greater natural ability. Let us take the case of two men living in what economists refer to as a "Robinson Crusoe economy" (and philosophers have called a "state of nature"). Now suppose that each of these men expends equal efforts in constructing a dwelling for himself; but due to their differing natural abilities as builders, one produces—and thus is able to live in—quite a comfortable habitation, while the other produces an adequate but less desirable shelter.[3] In such a case, wealth would be unequally "distributed" (by nature itself) according to "undeserved" differences in natural ability. Here is a clear instance of what Rawls means by the "arbitrariness found in nature." But what possible moral justification could there be for redressing this natural distribution, or holding that the less talented man is entitled to a share of the rewards earned by the more talented? And if such a justification does not exist in a "Robinson Crusoe economy," at what point of increased complexity in men's economic, social, or political relations does it suddenly become valid?

Rawls never answers this question with any precision; but by basing his doctrine on a version of the social-contact theory (an agreement that "free and rational persons concerned to further their own interests would accept in an initial position of equality as defining the fundamental terms of their association"), he implies that the crucial change comes about when men enter politi-

---

[3]This example is, of course, intentionally constructed in such a way that the man with lesser natural ability is not incapable of providing for his needs in a minimally acceptable fashion. This fits Rawls' argument for redistribution, which is based not on need but simply on inequality. If there were a case of genuine neediness—for example, if there were a third man in the neighborhood who was crippled and unable to build a dwelling for himself at all—it might be argued that the others would have a moral obligation to assist him. In that case, the individual's right to the fruits of his own labor would have to be balanced against his obligation to others. But this would in no way invalidate the general principle that the rewards that flow from superior natural ability are deserved.

cal society. The agreement that underlies a just political society, according to Rawls, will include adherence to the "difference principle," which as he formulates it specifies that "social and economic inequalities are to be arranged so that they are to the greatest benefit of the least advantaged . . ."

Now, Rawls says of the difference principle that it "represents, in effect, an agreement to regard the distribution of natural talents as a common asset and to share in the benefits of this distribution whatever it turns out to be." This "collectivization" of individual natural talents is obviously of material advantage to the less talented, but how can it be considered fair to the more talented? Rawls' answer essentially boils down to repeating his assertion that the more talented do not deserve their greater natural gifts in the first place; hence they have no cause for complaint. But why do these undeserved natural talents, whose consequences are unobjectionable in a state of nature, require rectification or redress in political society? The closest thing one finds to an answer to this question is the following passage:

> But there is no necessity for men to resign themselves to these contingencies [i.e., the arbitrary distribution of natural talents]. The social system is not an unchangeable order beyond human control but a pattern of human action. In justice as fairness men agree to share one another's fate. In designing institutions they undertake to avail themselves of the accidents of nature and social circumstance only when doing so is for the common benefit.

What Rawls seems to be saying here is that in political society men are not bound by the arbitrary dispensations of nature precisely because they have the power to alter them, or at least their effects. Men can collectively design the institutions and implement the conception of fairness that *they* choose. And that conception of fairness need not be based on a consideration of men as nature has actually made them; instead, it can and should be based on a consideration of men that abstracts from the differences that nature has established among them. Social justice cannot take its guidance from human nature. It must improve upon and correct nature, by taking a moral starting point which is above or prior to the arbitrariness of the real world.

Is it possible, however, for human justice ever to attain a starting point that is totally free of the arbitrariness of the world? Rawls himself is forced to confront this problem when he poses the question whether our conduct toward animals should be governed by his principles of justice. (For after all, is it not merely a contingent fact of nature that we are born human beings rather than members of some other species?) Rawls' answer is that human beings, as opposed to other living things, are entitled to equal justice because they possess the "capacity for moral personality." Having or not having this capacity is said to be the "only *contingency* which is decisive" in determining who is entitled to just treatment. Moreover, the common possession of this capacity by all men constitutes the basis of human equality, which thus is "supported by the general *facts of nature.*" At the deepest level of his own theory, then, Rawls in effect concedes the impossibility of wholly pushing beyond the limits imposed by brute natural facts. For the underlying human egalitarianism of Rawls' doctrine cannot itself escape being founded on what is arbitrary and contingent.

EQUALITY VS. THE FAMILY

We may say, then, that Rawls takes as the Archimedean point of moral reasoning that arbitrary natural fact which makes human beings equal to one another and superior to other living things; but he then arbitrarily refuses to grant any moral status to those arbitary natural facts that distinguish one human being from another. Yet Rawls and his fellow redistributionists fail even to draw the radical conclusions that their own premises imply. One good example of where a rigorous application of these premises leads is provided by the Greek comic poet Aristophanes in his *Assembly of Women (Ecclesiazusae)*. This play tells the story of the takeover of Athens by a female government, which establishes a new egalitarian order featuring a community of property, women, and children. But when it is objected that such a scheme will lead all the men to line up before the beautiful women and neglect the others, Praxagora, the female lawgiver, responds with a decree requiring that a man sleep with an ugly woman before being permitted to sleep with a beautiful one. This decree is an almost perfect embodiment of Rawls' difference principle, inasmuch as it stipulates that the naturally favored women may benefit only when their doing so benefits the disadvantaged as well.[4]

[4]There is at least one other discussion in Ancient literature of the application of the ethics of redress to sexual matters.In Book I of the *Histories,* Herodotus describes an "ingenious" custom of the Babylonians:

> In every village once a year all the girls of marriageable age used
> to be collected together in one place, while the men stood round
> them in a circle; an auctioneer then called each one in turn to
> stand up and offered her for sale, beginning with the best-looking
> and going on to the second best as soon as the first had been sold
> for a good price. Marriage was the object of the transaction. The
> rich men who wanted wives bid against each other for the prettiest
> girls, while the humbler folk, who had no use for good looks in a
> wife, were actually paid to take the ugly ones, for when the auc-
> tioneer had got through all the pretty girls he would call upon the
> plainest, or even perhaps a crippled one, to stand up, and then ask
> who was willing to take the least money to marry her—and she
> was knocked down to whoever accepted the smallest sum. The
> money came from the sale of the beauties, who in this way pro-
> vided dowries for their ugly or misshapen sisters.

With its emphasis on monetary compensation, this scheme is much more in the spirit of Rawls' own thinking. Moreover, the notion of monetary compensation for natural disadvantages suggests a whole new avenue for applying the ethics of redress. Those who are born blind, or crippled, or mentally impaired might be made the beneficiaries not merely of programs designed to meet their special needs but of monetary grants to indemnify them for the psychic pain caused by their undeserved misfortune. Society would then be organized as a kind of insurance scheme against Divine malpractice—an arrangement that would appear a logical outgrowth of Rawls' principles.

This Aristophanean conceit raises the question of why Rawls does not extend the application of the difference principle to the distribution of sexual rewards. If the distribution of natural gifts is to be regarded as a "common asset" whose benefits are to be shared by all, why should those human beings who are beautiful or otherwise well endowed be allowed to enjoy the "undeserved" sexual benefits that flow from those qualities arbitrarily allotted to them by nature? And why shouldn't those who have the misfortune to be born ugly be compensated according to the dictates of the "ethics of redress"?

And what about children, the products of sexual union? In a society composed of families, there are some couples that very much desire to have children but are unable to have any, while other couples enjoy an abundance of children. Why aren't the "undeservedly" childless couples entitled to be compensated for their arbitrary misfortune by being given some of the children of the more prolific? Again, why not go further still? Because of genetic inheritance, parents with greater natural advantages tend also to have children with greater natural gifts, and thereby to enjoy the greater satisfaction that more talented children often bring. Why not, then, distribute children in such a way as to eliminate the impact of this "undeserved" benefit? But even an impartial distribution of children among all sets of parents would leave those children who were placed in "better" homes underservedly and unfairly favored over those who were placed in "worse" homes. Only the abolition of the family as an institution for raising children would appear capable of meeting the Rawlsian standard of fairness.

At one point in *A Theory of Justice,* after noting that "the family will lead to unequal chances between individuals," Rawls explicitly poses the question, "Is the family to be abolished then?" His answer: "Taken by itself and given a certain primacy, the idea of equal opportunity inclines in this direction. But within the context of the theory of justice as a whole, there is much less urgency to take this course."[5] And of course Rawls chooses not to take this course. Like his fellow redistributionists, he does not seem to be disturbed by "undeserved" inequalities in the sphere of marriage and the family except insofar as these are productive of inequalities of income and wealth. And even where such inequalities of income and wealth do result, the Rawlsian strategy is not to attempt to eliminate their causes but rather to attempt to mitigate their effects (through redistribution). The hallmark of the radical rejection of inequality since Aristophanes has been the call for a community of property, women, and children. But despite the radical egalitarianism of their ethical premises, our present-day redistributionists want no part of communism. Not only are

---

[5]There is also a rather cryptic passage in *A Theory of Justice* in which Rawls indicates that the difference principle would call for an active eugenics policy. Since the implications of this passage are so unclear, it is difficult to tell to what extent the eugenics policy Rawls has in mind would lead to social regulation of marriage and childbearing.

they perfectly content to leave the "bourgeois" family intact, but they even shrink from advocating a community of property. Indeed, even their call for redistribution falls far short of a demand for equality of income or wealth.

EQUALITY VS. WEALTH

Why are our redistributionists so "moderate" with respect to their agenda for egalitarian political reform? The answer is to be found by investigating the principle that they accept as permitting (or requiring) a justifiable limitation on redistribution toward complete equality. In Okun's case, the opposing principle is clearly stated in the very title of his book—*Equality and Efficiency: The Big Tradeoff.* It is for the sake of economic efficiency that Okun is willing to stop far short of attempting to achieve complete economic equality. But why should we be so concerned about economic efficiency? Okun explains the justification for making this "tradeoff" as follows: "In pursuing such a goal [i.e., complete economic equality], society would forego any opportunity to use material rewards as incentives to production. And that would lead to inefficiencies that would be harmful to the welfare of the majority. Any insistence on carving the pie into equal slices would shrink the size of the pie." Thus economic efficiency is to be valued because it increases "the welfare of the majority." And welfare is to be measured, it appears, in strictly economic terms—a larger slice (in absolute terms) of "economic pie" constitutes greater welfare.

In fact, then, Okun's "big tradeoff" is really an exchange between equality and *wealth.* The pursuit of economic equality is to be compromised or abandoned when it would lead to unacceptable reductions in most people's wealth. But as Okun presents it, there is a strange imbalance between the two sides of his tradeoff equation. Equality is presented as an ethical principle, while efficiency (or wealth) is treated merely as a practical or pragmatic consideration. It is a curious sort of moral reasoning that allows practical considerations to be weighed equally in the balance with ethical ones. We would hardly approve of the conduct of an individual who was just only when acting justly was compatible with preserving his wealth. Why should we be any more approving of a society that acts in this way?

Here again we can find a more sophisticated justification of Okun's essential position by turning to Rawls. The grounds on which Rawls legitimizes stopping well short of complete economic equality are internalized in his "difference principle" (which forms part of his second principle of justice). As noted earlier, the difference principle requires that "social and economic inequalities are to be arranged so that they are to the greatest benefit of the least advantaged." What Rawls means by this is that departures from the standard of equal distribution of economic goods are permissible only if they make the least advantaged (i.e., poorest) man wealthier than he would be if the distribution were made more equal. The way an unequal distribution can achieve this result is by offering incentives that promote productivity and thereby increase the size of the society's total economic product. So for Rawls, as for Okun, economic justice ultimately comes down to a tradeoff between equality and wealth (though Rawls makes the focal point of the tradeoff the least advantaged members of the society rather than the majority or the society as a whole).

In the structure of Rawls' theory, the goal of maximizing individual wealth is actually prior to the goal of equality. For Rawls' principles of justice are conceived of as those principles that would be chosen in a hypothetical "original position" by "free and rational persons concerned to further their own interests." Through the device of a "veil of ignorance," Rawls imposes strict limits on the knowledge available to the parties in the original position, but one thing they do know is that they wish to maximize their share of certain "primary goods," including wealth. So from their vary inception, the Rawlsian principles of justice have as an essential aim the maximization of individual wealth. (The initial standard of equal distribution, and its subsequent modification to allow those inequalities that improve the economic position of the least advantaged, are supposedly chosen only because no one is allowed to have any indication of what his own position in the distribution will be, and thus no one wants to take a chance on being too badly off in the event that he should happen to come out at the bottom of the income ladder.)

The priority of the goal of maximizing individual wealth over the goal of economic equality is strikingly reflected in the practical consequences yielded by an application of the difference principle. Let us take the example of a society that enforces strict economic equality and where everyone has an income of $5,000. Now let us assume that by allowing some people to earn up to $25,000, we will increase productivity and total output to a point where even the poorest members of the society have an income of $6,000. And then suppose that by increasing the maximum allowable income to $1 million, we increase the income of the poorest members of the society to $6,100. Each of these steps *away* from economic equality would be justified by the difference principle. Indeed, that principle would justify the most enormous income inequality if it were to produce merely the tiniest increment in the income of the poorest class. So there can be no doubt that for Rawls (as for Okun) economic equality has only the most subordinate status when weighed against the maximization of wealth.

It is only in this light that one can properly appreciate the extraordinary role played in Rawls' theory of justice by economic incentives. Recall that Rawls absolutely refuses to allow that those who make a greater economic contribution *deserve* greater economic rewards. Yet his difference principle nontheless affirms that it is *just* to grant them greater economic rewards insofar as these serve as indispensable incentives to increase their contributions in ways that ultimately benefit the disadvantaged. In other words, according to Rawls justice requires that the more productive receive rewards *that they do not deserve.*

This points to the profound inconsistency that besets the redistributionist position in its attempt to embrace simultaneously both radically egalitarian ethical premises *and* economic incentives. To deny that individuals deserve to enjoy the fruits of their efforts and natural abilities is to deny that powerful principle of human justice which holds that each is entitled to what is his own.[6] It is hardly less radical a denial of the right to one's own than would be the taking away from parents of their own children. And as such, it entails the most extreme sort of invasion of the private sphere and the rights of the individual in the name of the public and communal good.

The denial of this principle would be understandable in a doctrine that, aiming at a profound transformation of human nature, sought to erase men's attachments to what is private and to refocus them wholly upon the public (whether in the benign manner of the Israeli kibbutz or the barbaric manner of Pol Pot's Cambodia). But this is surely not the kind of thing our redistributionists have in mind. Their devotion to maximizing individual wealth and their consequent championing of economic incentives are inevitably calculated to foster self-interest and attachment to private goods. In this light it is not surprising that Rawls turns out to be almost as great an admirer of economic efficiency and of markets as Okun is. The prevailing spirit of both of their doctrines is profoundly bourgeois and capitalistic. Indeed, one suspects that both their hope and their expectation is that a society structured in accordance with their principles would not be terribly different from the United States as it is today. They want all the benefits that come from a bourgeois liberal democratic order, but merely wish to improve upon it through a kind of egalitarian "fine-tuning" aimed at bringing about a more equal distribution of income and wealth.

INDIVIDUAL RIGHTS AND LIBERAL SOCIETY

Yet the moral basis of Rawls' and Okun's economic egalitarianism is incompatible with, and destructive of, the moral basis of a liberal society. The moral and political tradition that animates liberal democracy is founded on the notion that the rights of the individual are prior to the claims of society—indeed, that the protection of those individual rights is the very goal of political society. Liberalism does not merely recognize that principle of justice which holds that each man is entitled to what is his own; it seeks to extend and exalt this principle, imparting to the private sphere a sanctity far greater than it enjoys

---

[6]It is the right to what is naturally one's own that John Locke, the pre-eminent philosopher of liberalism, holds to be "the great foundation of property": ". . . [E]very man has a property in his own person; this nobody has any right to but himself. The labor of his body and the work of his hands, we may say, are properly his." This, of course, is precisely what Rawls and Okun deny. They would presumably correct Locke along the following lines: "No man has a property in his own person; this everybody has an equal right to along with himself. The labor of his body and the work of his hands, we may say, are properly the society's as a whole."

in any other political doctrine. Liberal society leaves each man free to devote himself to the pursuit of his own happiness; in particular, it promotes the pursuit of economic self-interest. In Locke's phrase, it aims "by established laws of liberty to secure protection and encouragement to the honest industry of mankind . . ." And the bedrock moral premise of a liberal society is that those who devote themselves to "honest industry" are entitled to reap—in the form of private property—the economic rewards that it brings.

By contrast, the redistributionist view, in holding that individuals do not deserve the economic rewards that are the fruit of their own talents and efforts, and that the goods produced by their "honest industry" are instead the "common asset" of society as a whole, totally undermines the moral foundations of private property, and therewith of liberal society. And the consequences of such a view are not merely theoretical ones. As Jencks makes clear, the redistributionist position requires that society "politicize the question of income inequality." For if individuals have no moral claim to the private property they obtain, it is up to the government to decide how it should be distributed. Now, it would be one thing if, under the new dispensation, the distribution of income and wealth were to be determined by a benevolent despot applying the "difference principle" and carefully weighing the longer-range benefits that would accrue from varying degrees of economic incentives. But in a democracy, distributional decisions will be the subject of the most intense political controversy, with each citizen in effect casting a vote about how large his own share of the society's income and wealth should be. And since the potentially adverse long-range effects of reducing incentives will necessarily remain speculative, there is likely to be a tendency to cut down the share of the better off first and worry about incentives later.

Moreover, if people really come to believe that no one deserves the income he earns, the case for incentives by itself is bound to look morally suspect, particularly when it is a question of increasing them. To argue that those who are already better off should be granted still greater incentives to make them produce more will then resemble arguing that the rich should be given a wholly undeserved bribe paid out of the pockets of the poor. Under such circumstances, it would not be at all surprising if the poor decided that even if their own incomes were to suffer (from the general loss of productivity), they would prefer this to paying so offensive a bribe. (One cannot extrapolate from the relative self-restraint shown by democratic governments in similar matters today, because that self-restraint is in large part precisely a product of the belief that individuals do deserve what they earn and that taxes are a necessary evil rather than a mechanism for redistribution.) In any case, just the uncertainty about the safety of one's wealth and the prospects of one's future income caused by the politicization of the distributional issue would be bound to have a deleterious effect not only on incentives but also on the general feeling of political and economic security enjoyed by the citizenry. In this sense, at least, the shelter of the private sphere would be severely threatened.

But this is far from being the only danger to the private sphere implicit in the redistributive ethic. Jencks says that in order to have redistribution we must "alter people's basic assumptions about the extent to which they are responsible for their neighbors and their neighbors for them." He presumably has in mind here primarily a heightening of people's feelings of mutual solidarity and benevolence. Yet so long as the maximization of people's wealth remains a fundamental goal of the society, it is likely that their feelings of reciprocal responsibility will take a less attractive form. For if the society's wealth is regarded as a common product of which everyone is entitled to a generous share, the economic well-being of each individual becomes directly dependent upon the behavior of his fellow citizens.

In the first place, this is likely to lead to heightened public concern about who is admitted to citizenship. It is one thing for a country to accept unskilled immigrants (say, Vietnamese refugees) when it is essentially up to them to "make it" economically on their own; but it is a very different matter if they are immediately and perpetually entitled to draw upon a sizable share of the society's resources. Similarly, fears about adding to the number of unproductive people in the society could lead to attempts to restrict childbearing on the part of those who are thought incapable of raising children to be useful contributors to the nation's wealth. Moreover, there would be a strong tendency for the public to impose some work requirements upon those living off the common wealth without making what it deemed an adequate contribution of their own efforts. Or there might be an attempt to regulate the ways in which the beneficiaries of redistribution spend their money (designed, for example, to make sure they do not buy luxury items while stinting on the needs of their children). Public money is seldom disbursed without any strings attached, and if everyone comes to be viewed as a recipient of society's benefactions, it is only to be expected that they will be subjected to greater public accountability regarding the details of their private lives. In short, it is difficult to see how the private sphere can retain its autonomy when wealth is regarded as communal. The practice as well as the premise of redistribution would be incompatible with liberal society as we know it.

A FINAL WORD

By way of conclusion, it is worth re-emphasizing the vital distinction between redistribution and social-welfare programs. Social insurance and assistance to the needy can be regarded as legitimate functions of the public sphere, properly supported by public revenues. The obligation of citizens to pay taxes to finance the legitimate expenses of government has never been doubted by the liberal tradition. Financing public-welfare expenditures with tax dollars in no way conflicts with the notion that people have a right to what they earn, and that their own property is genuinely private. But as social programs grow larger and more complex, it is all too easy to make the mistake of regarding redistribution as a logical extension of—or even simply a way of rationalizing—the welfare spending of the liberal state This is an error to which economists are particularly prone, given their penchant for focusing on economic effects (i.e., how much is being transferred to whom) rather than political principles (i.e., on what grounds the money is being transferred). Yet there is an immense gulf of principle between the welfare state and the redistributive state, which can be crossed only at the gravest peril to a liberal political order.

DISCUSSION QUESTIONS

1. What are the mutual obligations between business and stockholders, employees, consumers, and host communities?
2. "All's fair in love and war," and "Business is business." What circumstances, if any, might justify a different code of ethics for business than for the rest of society? Is the lower expectation of ethical behavior in business a reflection of a different ethical code or simply recognition of extenuating circumstances which make us more tolerant of unethical business behavior? If the latter, what are these extenuating circumstances? What do love, war, and business have in common?
3. How does the concept of "business ethics" relate to the concept of corporate social responsibility analyzed in the prior chapter?
4. Should multinational companies adapt their codes of ethics to the cultural mores of their host countries?
5. What would be the consequences of announcing that all students in this class will receive a "B" grade regardless of test scores? Ignoring these consequences, would this egalitarian grading system be ethical or fair?
6. Do we enjoy equality of opportunity in the U.S.? What is needed to obtain true equality of opportunity within the private market system?
7. Is the distribution of income and wealth in the U.S. fair? If not, how and to what extent should income be redistributed? Would such a redistribution have important implications for economic efficiency? If so, how should these consequences be balanced against equity goals?
8. Adam Smith wrote: "[the] late resolution of the Quakers in Pennsylvania to set at liberty all their Negro slaves, may satisfy us that their number cannot be very great. Had they made any considerable part of their property, such a resolution could never have been agreed to." Did Adam Smith consider the Quakers unethical? Did he consider them to be acting in their own self-interest?
9. Are businessmen motivated by self-interest? Are politicians, civil servants, and college professors motivated by self-interest? Are consumer activists and environmentalists motivated by self-interest? Do people behave differently in socialist or communist societies?
10. How does the treatment of corporate "whistle blowing" in the ethics of interdependence differ from its treatment in the Corporate Democracy Act proposed in Chapter 2?

ADDITIONAL READINGS

CARR, ALBERT Z., "Is Business Bluffing Ethical?" *Harvard Business Review* (January–February 1968), pp. 143–53.

GORDON, SCOTT, "The New Contractarians" *Journal of Political Economy,* 84, no. 31 (June 1976), 573–90.

LESSNOFF, MICHAEL, "John Rawls' Theory of Justice," *Political Studies,* 19, no. 1 (1971), 63–80.

MARX, THOMAS G., "Egalitarian Regulation and the Pursuit of Self-Interest: Moral Conflicts for Private Enterprise," *Business Economics* (September 1980), pp. 36–40.

MOORE, THOMAS, "Industrial Espionage at the Harvard B-School," *Fortune,* September 6, 1982, pp. 70–76.

RAWLS, JOHN, *A Theory of Justice.* Cambridge, Mass.: Harvard University Press, 1971.

SOMMERS, ALBERT T., "A Collision of Ethics and Economics," *Across the Board* (July 1978), pp. 14–19.

WUTHNOW, ROBERT, "The Moral Crisis in American Capitalism," *Harvard Business Review* (March–April 1982), pp. 76–84.

CHAPTER 8
POLITICAL
RELATIONSHIPS

Business-political relationships raise one of the most fundamental institutional issues in society. Here, we are not concerned with the effects of business decision making on "stockholder democracy," "industrial democracy," or "local democracy," but with the direct effects on political democracy itself. These relationships are extremely complex. To understand these relationships, one must appreciate the basic differences between market and political control mechanisms detailed in Chapter 1, and the implications of these differences for efficient resource use and the protection of individual liberties.

Business and government exercise controls over each other, and provide support to each other. The business-political relationship is truly a complex two-way relationship, though those who stand at either end of the street tend to see only the on-coming traffic. An isolated reading of Chapter 9 (Government Regulation) might lead one to believe that business supports government and that government controls business. This chapter makes it clear that the flow of controls and support is, indeed, two way.

While this chapter and the following one are closely related, this chapter is more fundamental in a policy sense. Chapter 9 is more concerned with the form of government regulation and the effects of regulatory decisions on business, whereas we are concerned here with how these decisions are made. It is from the analysis of this decision-making process that one must draw fundamental conclusions about the compatibility of private, business decision making and political democracy.

The analytical framework necessary for understanding the interaction of market and political controls, and the two-way flow of traffic between business and government, is provided in the seminal analysis of the "demand and supply" of regulation by Professor George Stigler, the 1982 Nobel Laureate in Economics.

The unique, coercive power of the state represents an important potential benefit to business as well as a threat, though the latter is emphasized, especially by business, in the regulatory literature in the following chapter. Business participation in the political decision-making process can best be understood as an effort to maximize benefits received from the state while avoiding potential threats. It follows that business may actively seek government intervention as well as its avoidance, and that a much more complex and mutually beneficial relationship exists between business and government than is commonly thought.

Two competing theories of government control of market decisions follow from Stigler's analytical framework. The public interest theory interprets regulation as an imposition on business in response to public demands. Regulations are implemented to correct perceived deficiencies in the marketplace resulting from monopoly, externalities, and a variety of safety, health, and consumer protection issues founded in misleading or inadequate market information, or consumer technical or psychological inabilities (or plain contrariness!) to evaluate complex information.[1] The private interest theory has two variants (Murray Weidenbaum adds a third in the next chapter). The "capture" theory contends that regulation was initially implemented to protect the public interest, but that over time the regulatory agency is "captured" by those it is regulating, and the original purpose is contorted to promote private rather than public goals. The economic version of the private interest theory of regulation states straightforwardly that regulation is in response to the demands of private interests who wish to utilize the coercive power of the state for economic gain.

Obviously, every regulation does not fit neatly into one category or the other. However, Professor Stigler reaches a provocative conclusion: ". . . as a rule, regulation is acquired by the industry and is designed and operated primarily for its benefit." These benefits include cash subsidies, control over the entry of new domestic and foreign competitors, price fixing, the promotion of complementary goods (e.g., airlines seeking subsidies for airport facilities), and the establishment of impediments to substitute goods (e.g., butter manufacturers seeking obstacles to effective margarine production or marketing).[2] These benefits are "purchased" with the things politicians need—votes and resources (campaign contributions, services, information, and employment). The

---

[1]Political controls are essentially a collective exit option—the individual does not have a viable exit option, but society does. The individual cannot escape pollution by not purchasing a motor vehicle (i.e., by exiting from the motor vehicle market) but society can, by collectively exiting from vehicles which generate excessive pollution.

[2]It is interesting to speculate that if business interests were successful in controlling entry and business critics were successful in controlling exit (e.g., through plant-closing legislation), the dynamics of the entire economic system would be brought to a halt.

effects of these "purchases" on the political system is the critical issue in the discussion of political action committees in the final reading in this chapter.

Professor Lindblom explains that businesses' effectiveness in the political decision-making process arises from the fundamental dependence of government on business for the provision of society's goods and services. In modern society, it is not Pharaoh, but businessmen who produce the goods and services demanded by consumers, and provide the jobs needed to secure full employment and social stability. In a political democracy business cannot be compelled to perform these vital economic activities. It must be induced, which means that government must basically give business what it wants to carry out these functions: ". . . they have to be given those indulgences, incentives, pleasures, rewards—whatever you want to call them—that will actively motivate them to do the jobs that we are counting on them to do." If government does not give business what it wants, production and employment decline, depression comes in and politicians go out. Because of this dependent relationship, Lindblom concludes that our democratic government is subject to two systems of control, a democratic system of controls (electoral politics) and an undemocratic system of business controls.

From these observations, Professor Lindblom concludes: "The large private corporation fits oddly into democratic theory and vision. Indeed, it does not fit." There are two theses underlying this provocative conclusion: the inadequacy of market controls over business decisions; and undue business control of political decisions. It is true the market system is an incentive system, but does that mean there are inadequate market controls, and that business get what it wants, or does competition among firms reduce the returns to business to the minimum levels necessary to cover the cost of the resources used? (I want a million dollars for the critical economic services I perform for society, but so far society has been able to obtain these invaluable services for a mere pittance.)

While there may or may not be undue business influence in political decisions, it is important to recognize that market controls over political (as well as business) decision making is in itself not incompatible with political democracy. Indeed, such controls may be essential to the preservation of political democracy. In Chapter 4, Professor Simon described political democracy as a system for the protection of individual civil liberties through the control of power, including the power of the elected majority. The control of that power is obtained through the decentralization of authority and an elaborate system of checks and balances. In his *Autobiography*, Thomas Jefferson wrote: ". . . it is not by the consolidation or concentration of powers, but by their distribution, that good government is effected." The market control system, which is the epitome of decentralized decision making, serves as a natural and vital check on the concentration of political power.

Thus, the coexistence and interaction of market and political controls over the use of the nation's resources provides another important system of checks and balances on the concentration of authority in any sector of society. A government which completely controlled the nation's economic resources would wield vast power over its citizens. In the following chapter, Arthur Okun writes:

> As a counterweight, the decentralization of power inherent in a private enterprise economy supplies the limitation of government that is essential to the survival of democracy. It is a remarkable uniformity of history that a fully collectivized economy has never produced a single free election or one free press. And that uniformity is not merely an accident or a coincidence. A collectivized economy entrusts government officials with the command over all of society's productive resources. It is natural for them to exercise that enormous power, which allows them to deprive dissenters of their livelihoods and to keep the view of the opposition out of the press and off the airways. Why should they put up with democratic processes that threaten their own status and power?

Thus, the private corporation and market control of business and political power may fit very well into a democratic society, indeed they may be essential to it.

Professor Lindblom also notes that business engages directly in electoral politics to supplement its control over the political process: "Businessmen are the most active, best financed, and best organized participants in electoral politics. . . ." These observations reinforce his conclusion that business has disproportionate power over the political process. Businesses' influence in electoral politics has been a hotly debated issue because of the rapid expansion of business political action committees (PACs) since the federal election reforms of the early 1970s. Professor Epstein traces the growth of PACs following these reforms, and how they have increased the role of labor and especially business in politics at the expense of individuals and political parties—an unintended result. The rapid growth of PACs raises several fundamental business-society issues: Will PACs alter the traditional foundations of business-political relationships; and will they fundamentally alter the balance of political power among competing social constituencies (business, employees, stockholders, and consumers)?

Political action committees trace their origins to labor PACs started because labor could not make political contributions from union dues. John L. Lewis established the first PAC, "Labor's Non-Partisan Political League," in the middle 1930s. In 1955, the merged AFL-CIO created "COPE" (Committee On Political Education), which became the model for all subsequent PACs. Labor PACs were soon followed by professional PACs such as the American Medical Association. Business made little use of PACs prior to the federal election campaign reforms in the early 1970s because, prior to that time, many businesses were barred from contributing to political campaigns because they were government contractors and businessmen could make very large individual contributions.

The Federal Election Campaign Act (FECA) was intended to reduce the political influence of large individual contributors by limiting their contributions and requiring public disclosure, and by allowing business and labor to establish PACs to raise and distribute political funds. These reforms were sponsored by labor to protect their PACs from potentially unfavorable court rulings against union-financed PACs. In protecting their PACs labor also opened the door for business. Labor took what it thought to be a calculated risk because of businesses' prior limited use of PACs. The 1974 FECA amendments, also sponsored by labor, allowed business as well as labor to form PACs even if they were government contractors. This again worked to the advantage of business since most businesses did have some government contracts. The 1975 decision of the Federal Election Commission in SUN-PAC allowed PACs to use general treasury funds for their activities, and allowed business and labor to solicit contributions from stockholders and employees. A 1976 FECA amendment basically limited businesses' solicitation of funds to "executive or administrative personnel," and basically limited union solicitations to its members.

The intent of this series of electoral reforms was to reduce the influence of individuals in political campaigns. While it has done this, it has substantially increased the influence of business and labor PACs, especially business PACs. The growth of PACs since 1974 is tabulated in Table 8-1.

The growth of corporate and nonconnected (single-issue or ideological) PACs has been the most rapid since 1974. The number of corporate PACs increased from only 89 in 1974 to 1,467 in 1982. Corporate PAC expenditures increased from $5.8 million in 1976 to $42.2 million in 1982 when corporate PACs outspent labor PACs for the first time. Nonconnected PACs increased from 110 in 1977 to 746 in 1982, while their expenditures increased from less than a million dollars in 1974 to $62.2 million in 1982, the largest expenditure among all the PAC groups. Labor PACs have increased only modestly in numbers, from 201 in 1974 to 380 in 1982, though expenditures have increased

TABLE 8-1   PAC Growth 1974-1982

TYPE OF PAC	NUMBER OF PACS		PAC EXPENDITURES ($/MILLION)	
	1974	1982	1974	1982
Corporate	89	1,467	5.8[b]	42.2
Labor	201	380	11.0	35.8
Trade/Membership/Health	318	628	23.8[c]	41.8
Non-Connected	110[a]	746	.8	62.2
Other	28[a]	150	1.1	5.7
TOTAL	746	3,371	42.5	187.7

[a]Data for 1977
[b]Data for 1976
[c]Data for 1978

Source: Adapted from H. E. Alexander, *The Case for PACs* (Washington D.C.: Public Affairs Council), p. 8 (table 1) and p. 10 (table 3). Used with permission of the Public Affairs Council.

substantially from $11 million in 1974 to $35.8 million in 1982. The number of trade-membership-health PACs nearly doubled between 1974 and 1982, and expenditures nearly doubled between 1978 and 1982. It is important to recognize that much of the trade-membership-health and "other" PAC expenditures and activities are business related.

In the 1981 to 1982 election cycle, 24.4 percent of all the funds raised by federal candidates came from PACs. Corporate PACs accounted for 7.6 percent of the total funds raised, and labor PACs for 5.6 percent. Business and especially labor PACs are split along political lines, but variations in contribution patterns reveal interesting differences in political strategy. Business wants to ensure access to all elected representatives because of its relative advantages in administrative politics; that is its ability to work with elected representatives, supplying information and developing policy positions. Labor, whose comparative advantage lies in electoral politics (getting out the vote) is much more intent upon getting the "right" candidate elected. Thus, we see that in 1982, 35 percent of corporate PAC money went to Democrats and 65 percent went to Republicans, while 94 percent of labor PAC money went to Democrats with only 6 percent going to Republicans. Other PAC categories split their contributions more evenly; for example, 43 percent of trade-membership-health PAC contributions went to Democrats and 57 percent to Republicans.[3] Overall, PACs have also strongly favored incumbents over challengers.

Table 8-2 lists the ten largest PAC contributors in the 1981 to 1982 election cycle.

None of the ten largest PACs in 1981–1982 were business PACs. All were trade-membership-health or union PACs. The larger business PACs are substantially smaller than the larger labor and trade-membership-health PACs, though there are many more business PACs.

TABLE 8-2   Ten Largest PAC Contributors 1981-1982

	1982 CONTRIBUTIONS
National Association of Realtors	$2,115,000
American Medical Association	1,737,000
United Auto Workers (UAW-V-CAP)	1,624,000
International Association of Machinists	1,445,000
National Education Association	1,183,000
National Association of Home Builders	1,006,000
Associated Milk Producers, Inc. (C-TAPE)	962,000
American Bankers Association	947,000
National Automobile Dealers Association	917,000
AFL-CIO Committee on Political Education	906,000

Source: Federal Election Commission.

[3]Herbert E. Alexander, *The Case for PACs* (Washington, D.C.: Public Affairs Council), p. 22.

Table 8–3 lists the ten largest corporate PACs in 1981–1982.

The contributions of the largest of the business PACs (Tenneco) were about half as large as the contributions of the tenth largest nonbusiness PAC (COPE) listed in Table 8–2. The identity of the ten largest corporate PACs is somewhat surprising and provides some insights into the nature of business participation in the political process and, perhaps, some support for Professor Stigler's private interest theory of regulation. Four of the largest ten business PACs are large government defense contractors for whom the coercive power of the state is a substantial source of revenue. Three of these companies are engaged in oil, gas, and energy operations which have innumerable business-political relationships which importantly affect their profitability. The remaining three (Chicago Mercantile, American Family, and Winn-Dixie) are importantly affected by either securities or insurance regulation or antitrust actions.[4]

The FECA amendments sponsored by labor in the early 1970s have clearly worked to their disadvantage. As a result unions may now seek further changes in the regulation of PACs to limit total contributions. They may also promote public financing of Congressional elections to remove altogether the influence of PACs from electoral politics. Public financing would clearly improve the position of unions because of their advantages over business in voter registration activities, member communications, and "getting out the vote" drives.

These reforms were designed to bring under-the-table contributions to the surface. But now that they have surfaced, many do not like what they see. For example, House members who voted to exempt dairy industry subsidies from budget cuts received an average of $1,600 from dairy PACs, while those opposed to these subsidies received an average of only $200.[5] Members of the con-

TABLE 8–3 Ten Largest Corporate PACs 1981–1982

	1982 CONTRIBUTIONS
Tenneco, Inc.	$454,150
Chicago Mercantile Exchange	319,072
Winn-Dixie Stores, Inc.	281,375
Harris Corporation	249,250
American Family Corporation	232,775
Fluor Corporation	223,200
Litton Industries, Inc.	218,550
United Technologies Corporation	204,275
Standard Oil Co. (Indiana)	193,327
Grumman Corporation	188,978

Source: Federal Election Commission.

[4]Winn-Dixie is controlled by the Davis family which also has a strong aversion to labor unions and big government.

[5]William H. Miller, "Corporate PACs on Trial," *Industry Week*, October 4, 1982, p. 42.

gressional committees reviewing the Clean Air Act received almost $730,000 in 1980 to 1981 from 93 companies found in violation of the Act.[6] While correlation certainly does not prove cause and effect, it may have enough effect to cause significant restrictions on future PAC activities.

Professor Epstein concludes that while PAC contributions do not currently account for alarmingly high percentages of total contributions (about 25 percent), this may only be "the tip of a possible iceberg." Less than a quarter of the largest firms have PACs, and there is great potential for additional spending by each one. The election reforms gave labor and especially business significant advantages over other social constituencies (consumers and stockholders) which could alter fundamental business constituency relationships. Any conjoining of business-labor interests would thus represent a powerful political coalition.

Proponents of business PACs argue that they enable many more individuals to participate in the political process in an effective, meaningful way—PACs allow many more "voices" to be heard. They also contend that competition among PACs is the most effective way to debate issues openly in a pluralist society. They also note that much of business PAC money is simply old wine in new bottles (former contributions by individual businessmen); that contributions by individual business PACs are much too small to create undue influence; and that PAC contributions are not increasing proportionately to other contributions.

PAC critics are concerned that Congress is becoming beholden to special PAC interests which are buying undue access and influence. Congress will be dependent upon business for campaign financing just as it is dependant upon business for the production of society's goods and services, according to Professor Lindblom. Critics also ask who represents the public's (consumer's) interest in this pluralistic competition among PACs.

At issue is the fundamental right of individuals to combine together to try to elect representatives who share their convictions, a right Alexis de Tocqueville believed as natural as the right to act individually: "The most natural privilege of man, next to the right of acting for himself, is that of combining his exertions with those of his fellow-creatures, and of acting in common with them. The right of association therefore appears to me almost as inalienable in its nature as the right of personal liberty. No legislator can attack it without imparing the foundations of society."[7] However, de Tocqueville also cautioned: ". . . I do not think that a nation is always at liberty to invest its citizen with an absolute right of association for political purposes; and I doubt whether, in any country or in any age, it be wise to set no limits to freedom of association."[8]

---

[6]*Ibid.*
[7]Alexis de Tocqueville, *Democracy in America* (New York: Pocket Books, 1972), pp. 74–75.
[8]*Ibid.*, p. 194.

THE THEORY OF ECONOMIC REGULATION
George J. Stigler

The state—the machinery and power of the state—is a potential resource or threat to every industry in the society. With its power to prohibit or compel, to take or give money, the state can and does selectively help or hurt a vast number of industries. That political juggernaut, the petroleum industry, is an immense consumer of political benefits, and simultaneously the underwriters of marine insurance have their more modest repast. The central tasks of the theory of economic regulation are to explain who will receive the benefits or burdens of regulation, what form regulation will take, and the effects of regulation upon the allocation of resources.

Regulation may be actively sought by an industry, or it may be thrust upon it. A central thesis of this paper is that, as a rule, regulation is acquired by the industry and is designed and operated primarily for its benefit. There are regulations whose net effects upon the regulated industry are undeniably onerous; a simple example is the differentially heavy taxation of the industry's product (whiskey, playing cards). These onerous regulations, however, are exceptional and can be explained by the same theory that explains beneficial (we may call it "acquired") regulation.

Two main alternative views of the regulation of industry are widely held. The first is that regulation is instituted primarily for the protection and benefit of the public at large or some large subclass of the public. In this view, the regulations which injure the public—as when the oil import quotas increase the cost of petroleum products to America by $5 billion or more a year—are costs of some social goal (here, national defense) or, occasionally, perversions of the regulatory philosophy. The second view is essentially that the political process defies rational explanation: "politics" is an imponderable, a constantly and unpredictably shifting mixture of forces of the most diverse nature, comprehending acts of great moral virtue (the emancipation of slaves) and of the most vulgar venality (the congressman feathering his own nest).

Let us consider a problem posed by the oil import quota system: why does not the powerful industry which obtained this expensive program instead choose direct cash subsidies from the public treasury? The "protection of the public" theory of regulation must say that the choice of import quotas is dictated by the concern of the federal government for an adequate domestic supply of petroleum in the event of war—a remark calculated to elicit uproarious laughter at

George J. Stigler, "The Theory of Economic Regulation," *The Bell Journal of Economics and Management Science*, 2, no. 1 (Spring 1971), 3–21. Reprinted with permission.

the Petroleum Club. Such laughter aside, if national defense were the goal of the quotas, a tariff would be a more economical instrument of policy: it would retain the profits of exclusion for the treasury. The non-rationalist view would explain the policy by the inability of consumers to measure the cost to them of the import quotas, and hence their willingness to pay $5 billion in higher prices rather than the $2.5 billion in cash that would be equally attractive to the industry. Our profit-maximizing theory says that the explanation lies in a different direction: the present members of the refining industries would have to share a cash subsidy with all new entrants into the refining industry.[1] Only when the elasticity of supply of an industry is small will the industry prefer cash to controls over entry or output.

This question, why does an industry solicit the coercive powers of the state rather than its cash, is offered only to illustrate the approach of the present paper. We assume that political systems are rationally devised and rationally employed, which is to say that they are appropriate instruments for the fulfillment of desires of members of the society. This is not to say that the state will serve any person's concept of the public interest: indeed the problem of regulation is the problem of discovering when and why an industry (or other group of like-minded people) is able to use the state for its purposes, or is singled out by the state to be used for alien purposes.

1. WHAT BENEFITS CAN A STATE PROVIDE TO AN INDUSTRY?

The state has one basic resource which in pure principle is not shared with even the mightiest of its citizens: the power to coerce. The state can seize money by the only method which is permitted by the laws of a civilized society, by taxation. The state can ordain the physical movements of resources and the economic decisions of households and firms without their consent. These powers provide the possibilities for the utilization of the state by an industry to increase its profitability. The main policies which an industry (or occupation) may seek of the state are four.

The most obvious contribution that a group may seek of the government is a direct subsidy of money. The domestic airlines received "air mail" subsidies (even if they did not carry mail) of $1.5 billion through 1968. The merchant marine has received construction and operation subsidies reaching almost $3 billion since World War II. The education industry has long shown a masterful skill in obtaining public funds: for example, universities and colleges have received federal funds exceeding $3 billion annually in recent years, as well as

[1]The domestic producers of petroleum, who also benefit from the import quota, would find a tariff or cash payment to domestic producers equally attractive. If their interests alone were consulted, import quotas would be auctioned off instead of being given away.

subsidized loans for dormitories and other construction. The veterans of wars have often received direct cash bonuses.

We have already sketched the main explanation for the fact that an industry with power to obtain government favors usually does not use this power to get money: unless the list of beneficiaries can be limited by an acceptable device, whatever amount of subsidies the industry can obtain will be dissipated among a growing number of rivals. The airlines quickly moved away from competitive bidding for air mail contracts to avoid this problem.[2] On the other hand, the premier universities have not devised a method of excluding other claimants for research funds, and in the long run they will receive much-reduced shares of federal research monies.

The second major public resource commonly sought by an industry is control over entry by new rivals. There is considerable, not to say excessive, discussion in economic literature of the rise of peculiar price policies (limit prices), vertical integration, and similar devices to retard the rate of entry of new firms into oligopolistic industries. Such devices are vastly less efficacious (economical) than the certificate of convenience and necessity (which includes, of course, the import and production quotas of the oil and tobacco industries).

The diligence with which the power of control over entry will be exercised by a regulatory body is already well known. The Civil Aeronautics Board has not allowed a single new trunk line to be launched since it was created in 1938. The power to insure new banks has been used by the Federal Deposit Insurance Corporation to reduce the rate of entry into commercial banking by 60 percent.[3] The interstate motor carrier history is in some respects even more striking, because no even ostensibly respectable case for restriction on entry can be developed on grounds of scale economies (which are in turn adduced to limit entry for safety or economy of operation). The number of federally licensed common carriers is shown in Figure 8–1: the immense growth of the freight hauled by trucking common carriers has been associated with a steady secular decline of numbers of such carriers. The number of applications for new certificates has been in excess of 5000 annually in recent years: a rigorous proof that hope springs eternal in an aspiring trucker's breast.

We propose the general hypothesis: every industry or occupation that has enough political power to utilize the state will seek to control entry. In addition, the regulatory policy will often be so fashioned as to retard the rate of growth of new firms. For example, no new savings and loan company may pay a dividend rate higher than that prevailing in the community in its endeavors to attract deposits.[4] The power to limit selling expenses of mutual funds, which is soon to be conferred upon the Securities and Exchange Commission, will serve

___

[2]See [7], pp. 60ff.

[3]See [10].

[4]The Federal Home Loan Bank Board is the regulatory body. It also controls the amount of advertising and other areas of competition.

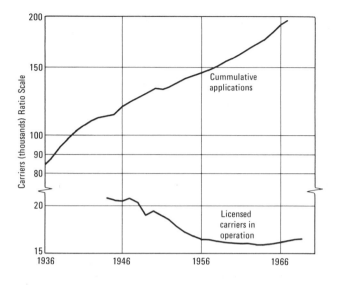

FIGURE 8-1 **Certificates for Interstate Motor Carriers**

Source: Table 5.

to limit the growth of small mutual funds and hence reduce the sales costs of large funds.

One variant of the control of entry is the protective tariff (and the corresponding barriers which have been raised to interstate movements of goods and people). The benefits of protection to an industry, one might think, will usually be dissipated by the entry of new domestic producers, and the question naturally arises: Why does the industry not also seek domestic entry controls? In a few industries (petroleum) the domestic controls have been obtained, but not in most. The tariff will be effective if there is a specialized domestic resource necessary to the industry; oil-producing lands is an example. Even if an industry has only durable specialized resources, it will gain if its contraction is slowed by a tariff.

A third general set of powers of the state which will be sought by the industry are those which affect substitutes and complements. Crudely put, the butter producers wish to suppress margarine and encourage the production of bread. The airline industry actively supports the federal subsidies to airports; the building trade unions have opposed labor-saving materials through building codes. We shall examine shortly a specific case of inter-industry competition in transportation.

The fourth class of public policies sought by an industry is directed to price-fixing. Even the industry that has achieved entry control will often want price controls administered by a body with coercive powers. If the number of firms in the regulated industry is even moderately large, price discrimination will be difficult to maintain in the absence of public support. The prohibition of interest on demand deposits, which is probably effective in preventing interest payments to most non-business depositors, is a case in point. Where there are no diseconomies of large scale for the individual firm (e.g., a motor trucking firm can add trucks under a given license as common carrier), price control is essential to achieve more than competitive rates of return.

Limitations upon political benefits.   These various political boons are not obtained by the industry in a pure profit-maximizing form. The political process erects certain limitations upon the exercise of cartel policies by an industry. These limitations are of three sorts.

First, the distribution of control of the industry among the firms in the industry is changed. In an unregulated industry each firm's influence upon price and output is proportional to its share of industry output (at least in a simple arithmetic sense of direct capacity to change output). The political decisions take account also of the political strength of the various firms, so small firms have a larger influence than they would possess in an unregulated industry. Thus, when quotas are given to firms, the small firms will almost always receive larger quotas than cost-minimizing practices would allow. The original quotas under the oil import quota system will illustrate this practice (Table 8-4). The smallest refiners were given a quota of 11.4 percent of their daily consumption of oil, and the percentage dropped as refinery size rose.[5] The pattern of regressive benefits is characteristic of public controls in industries with numerous firms.

Second, the procedural safeguards required of public processes are costly. The delays which are dictated by both law and bureaucratic thoughts of self-survival can be large: Robert Gerwig found the price of gas sold in interstate

TABLE 8-4   Import Quotas of Refineries as Percent of Daily Input of Petroleum (Districts 1-IV, July 1, 1959-Dec. 31, 1959)

SIZE OF REFINERY (THOUSANDS OF BARRELS)	PERCENT QUOTA
0-10	11.4
10-20	10.4
20-30	9.5
30-60	8.5
60-100	7.6
100-150	6.6
150-200	5.7
200-300	4.7
300 and over	3.8

Source: Hearing Select Committee on Small Business, U.S. Congress, 88th Cong., 2nd Sess., Aug. 10 and 11, 1964, [12] p. 121.

[5]The largest refineries were restricted to 75.7 percent of their historical quota under the earlier voluntary import quota plan.

commerce to be 5 to 6 percent higher than in intrastate commerce because of the administrative costs (including delay) of Federal Power Commission reviews [5].

Finally, the political process automatically admits powerful outsiders to the industry's councils. It is well known that the allocation of television channels among communities does not maximize industry revenue but reflects pressures to serve many smaller communities. The abandonment of an unprofitable rail line is an even more notorious area of outsider participation.

These limitations are predictable, and they must all enter into the calculus of the profitability of regulation of an industry.

An illustrative analysis.   The recourse to the regulatory process is of course more specific and more complex than the foregoing sketch suggests. The defensive power of various other industries which are affected by the proposed regulation must also be taken into account. An analysis of one aspect of the regulation of motor trucking will illustrate these complications. At this stage we are concerned only with the correspondence between regulations and economic interests; later we shall consider the political process by which regulation is achieved.

The motor trucking industry operated almost exclusively within cities before 1925, in good part because neither powerful trucks nor good roads were available for long-distance freight movements. As these deficiencies were gradually remedied, the share of trucks in intercity freight movements began to rise, and by 1930 it was estimated to be 4 percent of ton-miles of intercity freight. The railroad industry took early cognizance of this emerging competitor, and one of the methods by which trucking was combatted was state regulation.

By the early 1930's all states regulated the dimensions and weight of trucks. The weight limitations were a much more pervasive control over trucking than the licensing of common carriers because even the trucks exempt from entry regulation are subject to the limitations on dimensions and capacity. The weight regulations in the early 1930's are reproduced in the appendix (Table 6). Sometimes the participation of railroads in the regulatory process was incontrovertible: Texas and Louisiana placed a 7000-pound payload limit on trucks serving (and hence competing with) two or more railroad stations, and a 14,000-pound limit on trucks serving only one station (hence, not competing with it).

We seek to determine the pattern of weight limits on trucks that would emerge in response to the economic interests of the concerned parties. The main considerations appear to be the following:

(1)   Heavy trucks would be allowed in states with a substantial number of trucks on farms: the powerful agricultural interests would insist upon this. The 1930 Census reports nearly one million trucks on farms. One variable in our study will be, for each state, trucks per 1000 of agricultural population.[6]

---

[6]The ratio of trucks to total population would measure the product of (1) the importance of trucks to farmers, and (2) the importance of farmers in the state. For reasons given later, we prefer to emphasize (1).

(2) Railroads found the truck an effective and rapidly triumphing competitor in the shorter hauls and hauls of less than carload traffic, but much less effective in the carload and longer-haul traffic. Our second variable for each state is, therefore, length of average railroad haul.[7] The longer the average rail haul is, the less the railroads will be opposed to trucks.

(3) The public at large would be concerned by the potential damage done to the highway system by heavy trucks. The better the state highway system, the heavier the trucks that would be permitted. The percentage of each state's highways that had a high type surface is the third variable. Of course good highways are more likely to exist where the potential contribution of trucks to a state's economy is greater, so the causation may be looked at from either direction.

We have two measures of weight limits on trucks, one for 4-wheel trucks (X_1) and one for 6-wheel trucks (X_2). We may then calculate two equations,

$$X_1 \text{ (or } X_2) = a + bX_3 + cX_4 + dX_5,$$

where

X_3 = trucks per 1000 agricultural labor force, 1930,
X_4 = average length of railroad haul of freight traffic, 1930,
X_5 = percentage of state roads with high-quality surface, 1930.

(All variables are fully defined and their state values given in Table 7 in the appendix.)

The three explanatory variables are statistically significant, and each works in the expected direction. The regulations on weight were less onerous; the larger the truck population in farming, the less competitive the trucks were to railroads (i.e., the longer the rail hauls), and the better the highway system (see Table 8–5).

The foregoing analysis is concerned with what may be termed the industrial demand for governmental powers. Not every industry will have a significant demand for public assistance (other than money!), meaning the prospect of a substantial increase in the present value of the enterprises even if the governmental services could be obtained gratis (and of course they have costs to which we soon turn). In some economic activities entry of new rivals is extremely difficult to control—consider the enforcement problem in restricting the supply of domestic servants. In some industries the substitute products cannot be efficiently controlled—consider the competition offered to bus lines by private car-pooling. Price fixing is not feasible where every unit of the product has a different quality and price, as in the market for used automobiles. In general, however, most industries will have a positive demand price (schedule) for the services of government.

---

[7]This is known for each railroad, and we assume that (1) the average holds within each state, and (2) two or more railroads in a state may be combined on the basis of mileage. Obviously both assumptions are at best fair approximations.

TABLE 8–5   Regression Analysis of State Weight Limits on Trucks (*T* Values Under Regression Coefficients)

DEPENDENT VARIABLE	N	CONSTANT	X_3	X_4	X_5	R^2
X_1	48	12.28 (4.87)	0.0336 (3.99)	0.0287 (2.77)	0.2641 (3.04)	0.502
X_2	46	10.34 (1.57)	0.0437 (2.01)	0.0788 (2.97)	0.2528 (1.15)	0.243

X_1 = Weight limit on 4-wheel trucks (thousands of pounds), 1932–33
X_2 = Weight limit on 6-wheel trucks (thousands of pounds), 1932–33
X_3 = Trucks on farms per 1,000 agricultural labor force, 1930
X_4 = Average length of railroad haul of freight (miles), 1930
X_5 = Percent of state highways with high-type surface, Dec. 31, 1930

SOURCES: X_1 and X_2: *The Motor Truck Red Book and Directory* (11), 1934 Edition, p.85-102, and U.S. Dept. of Agric., Bur. of Public Roads, Dec. 1932 (13).

X_3: *Census of Agriculture,* 1930, vol. IV, (14).

X_4: A.A.R.R., Bur. of Railway Economics, *Railway Mileage by States,* Dec. 31, 1930 (1) and U.S.I.C.C., *Statistics of Railways in the U.S.,* 1930 (18).

X_5: Statistical Abstract of the U.S., 1932 (16).

2. THE COSTS OF OBTAINING LEGISLATION

When an industry receives a grant of power from the state, the benefit to the industry will fall short of the damage to the rest of the community. Even if there were no deadweight losses from acquired regulation, however, one might expect a democratic society to reject such industry requests unless the industry controlled a majority of the votes.[8] A direct and informed vote on oil import quotas would reject the scheme. (If it did not, our theory of rational political processes would be contradicted.) To explain why many industries are able to employ the political machinery to their own ends, we must examine the nature of the political process in a democracy.

A consumer chooses between rail and air travel, for example, by voting with his pocketbook: he patronizes on a given day that mode of transportation he prefers. A similar form of economic voting occurs with decisions on where to work or where to invest one's capital. The market accumulates these economic votes, predicts their future course, and invests accordingly.

[8]If the deadweight loss (of consumer and producer surplus) is taken into account, even if the oil industry were in the majority it would not obtain the legislation if there were available some method of compensation (such as sale of votes) by which the larger damage of the minority could be expressed effectively against the lesser gains of the majority.

Because the political decision is coercive, the decision process is fundamentally different from that of the market. If the public is asked to make a decision between two transportation media comparable to the individual's decision on how to travel—say, whether airlines or railroads should receive a federal subsidy—the decision must be abided by everyone, travellers and non-travellers, travellers this year and travellers next year. This compelled universality of political decisions makes for two differences between democratic political decision processes and market processes.

(1)   The decisions must be made simultaneously by a large number of persons (or their representatives): the political process demands simultaneity of decision. If A were to vote on the referendum today, B tomorrow, C the day after, and so on, the accumulation of a majority decision would be both expensive and suspect. (A might wish to cast a different vote now than last month.)

The condition of simultaneity imposes a major burden upon the political decision process. It makes voting on specific issues prohibitively expensive: it is a significant cost even to engage in the transaction of buying a plane ticket when I wish to travel; it would be stupendously expensive to me to engage in the physically similar transaction of voting (i.e., patronizing a polling place) whenever a number of my fellow citizens desired to register their views on railroads versus airplanes. To cope with this condition of simultaneity, the voters must employ representatives with wide discretion and must eschew direct expressions of marginal changes in preferences. This characteristic also implies that the political decision does not predict voter desires and make preparations to fulfill them in advance of their realization.

(2)   The democratic decision process must involve "all" the community, not simply those who are directly concerned with a decision. In a private market, the non-traveller never votes on rail versus plane travel, while the huge shipper casts many votes each day. The political decision process cannot exclude the uninterested voter: the abuses of any exclusion except self-exclusion are obvious. Hence, the political process does not allow participation in proportion to interest and knowlege. In a measure, this difficulty is moderated by other political activities besides voting which do allow a more effective vote to interested parties: persuasion, employment of skilled legislative representatives, etc. Nevertheless, the political system does not offer good incentives like those in private markets to the acquisition of knowledge. If I consume ten times as much of public service A (streets) as of B (schools), I do not have incentives to acquire corresponding amounts of knowledge about the public provision of these services.[9]

These characteristics of the political process can be modified by having numerous levels of government (so I have somewhat more incentive to learn about local schools than about the whole state school system) and by selective use of direct decision (bond referenda). The chief method of coping with the

[9]See [2].

characteristics, however, is to employ more or less full-time representatives organized in (disciplined by) firms which are called political parties or machines.

The representative and his party are rewarded for their discovery and fulfillment of the political desires of their constituency by success in election and the perquisites of office. If the representative could confidently await reelection whenever he voted against an economic policy that injured the society, he would assuredly do so. Unfortunately virtue does not always command so high a price. If the representative denies ten large industries their special subsidies of money or governmental power, they will dedicate themselves to the election of a more complaisant successor: the stakes are that important. This does not mean that every large industry can get what it wants or all that it wants: it does mean that the representative and his party must find a coalition of voter interests more durable than the anti-industry side of every industry policy proposal. A representative cannot win or keep office with the support of the sum of those who are opposed to: oil import quotas, farm subsidies, airport subsidies, hospital subsidies, unnecessary navy shipyards, an inequitable public housing program, and rural electrification subsidies.

The political decision process has as its dominant characteristic infrequent, universal (in principle) participation, as we have noted: political decisions must be infrequent and they must be global. The voter's expenditure to learn the merits of individual policy proposals and to express his preferences (by individual and group representation as well as by voting) are determined by expected costs and returns, just as they are in the private marketplace. The costs of comprehensive information are higher in the political arena because information must be sought on many issues of little or no direct concern to the individual, and accordingly he will know little about most matters before the legislature. The expressions of preferences in voting will be less precise than the expressions of preferences in the marketplace because many uninformed people will be voting and affecting the decision.[10]

The channels of political decision-making can thus be described as gross or filtered or noisy. If everyone has a negligible preference for policy A over B, the preference will not be discovered or acted upon. If voter group X wants a policy that injures non-X by a small amount, it will not pay non-X to discover this and act against the policy. The system is calculated to implement all strongly felt preferences of majorities and many strongly felt preferences of minorities but to disregard the lesser preferences of majorities and minorities. The filtering or grossness will be reduced by any reduction in the cost to the citizen of acquiring information and expressing desires and by any increase in the probability that his vote will influence policy.

---

[10]There is an organizational problem in any decision in which more than one vote is cast. If because of economies of scale it requires a thousand customers to buy a product before it can be produced, this thousand votes has to be assembled by some entrepreneur. Unlike the political scene, however, there is no need to obtain the consent of the remainder of the community, because they will bear no part of the cost.

The industry which seeks political power must go to the appropriate seller, the political party. The political party has costs of operation, costs of maintaining an organization and competing in elections. These costs of the political process are viewed excessively narrowly in the literature on the financing of elections: elections are to the political process what merchandizing is to the process of producing a commodity, only an essential final step. The party maintains its organization and electoral appeal by the performance of costly services to the voter at all times, not just before elections. Part of the costs of services and organization are borne by putting a part of the party's workers on the public payroll. An opposition party, however, is usually essential insurance for the voters to discipline the party in power, and the opposition party's costs are not fully met by public funds.

The industry which seeks regulation must be prepared to pay with the two things a party needs: votes and resources. The resources may be provided by campaign contributions, contributed services (the businessman heads a fund-raising committee), and more indirect methods such as the employment of party workers. The votes in support of the measure are rallied, and the votes in opposition are dispersed, by expensive programs to educate (or uneducate) members of the industry and of other concerned industries.

These costs of legislation probably increase with the size of the industry seeking the legislation. Larger industries seek programs which cost the society more and arouse more opposition from substantially affected groups. The tasks of persuasion, both within and without the industry, also increase with its size. The fixed size of the political "market," however, probably makes the cost of obtaining legislation increase less rapidly than industry size. The smallest industries are therefore effectively precluded from the political process unless they have some special advantage such as geographical concentration in a sparsely settled political subdivision.

If a political party has in effect a monopoly control over the governmental machine, one might expect that it could collect most of the benefits of regulation for itself. Political parties, however, are perhaps an ideal illustration of Demsetz' theory of natural monopoly [4]. If one party becomes extortionate (or badly mistaken in its reading of effective desires), it is possible to elect another party which will provide the governmental services at a price more closely proportioned to costs of the party. If entry into politics is effectively controlled, we should expect one-party dominance to lead that party to solicit requests for protective legislation but to exact a higher price for the legislation.

The internal structure of the political party, and the manner in which the perquisites of office are distributed among its members, offer fascinating areas for study in this context. The elective officials are at the pinnacle of the political system—there is no substitute for the ability to hold the public offices. I conjecture that much of the compensation to the legislative leaders takes the form of extrapolitical payments. Why are so many politicians lawyers?—because everyone employs lawyers, so the congressman's firm is a suitable avenue of compensation, whereas a physician would have to be given bribes rather than patronage. Most enterprises patronize insurance companies and banks, so we may expect that legislators commonly have financial affiliations with such enterprises.

The financing of industry-wide activities such as the pursuit of legislation raises the usual problem of the free rider.[11] We do not possess a satisfactory theory of group behavior—indeed this theory is the theory of oligopoly with one addition: in the very large number industry (e.g., agriculture) the political party itself will undertake the entrepreneurial role in providing favorable legislation. We can go no further than the infirmities of oligopoly theory allow, which is to say, we can make only plausible conjectures such as that the more concentrated the industry, the more resources it can invest in the campaign for legislation.

Occupational licensing.   The licensing of occupations is a possible use of the political process to improve the economic circumstances of a group. The license is an effective barrier to entry because occupational practice without the license is a criminal offense. Since much occupational licensing is performed at the state level, the area provides an opportunity to search for the characteristics of an occupation which give it political power.

Although there are serious data limitations, we may investigate several characteristics of an occupation which should influence its ability to secure political power:

(1) The size of the occupation.   Quite simply, the larger the occupation, the more votes it has. (Under some circumstances, therefore, one would wish to exclude non-citizens from the measure of size.)

(2) The per capita income of the occupation.   The income of the occupation is the product of its number and average income, so this variable and the preceding will reflect the total income of the occupation. The income of the occupation is presumably an index of the probable rewards of successful political action: in the absence of specific knowledge of supply and demand functions, we expect licensing to increase each occupation's equilibrium income by roughly the same proportion. In a more sophisticated version, one would predict that the less the elasticity of demand for the occupation's services, the more profitable licensing would be. One could also view the income of the occupation as a source of funds for political action, but if we view political action

---

[11]The theory that the lobbying organization avoids the "free-rider" problem by selling useful services was proposed by Thomas G. Moore [8] and elaborated by Mancur Olson [9]. The theory has not been tested empirically.

as an investment this is relevant only with capital-market imperfections.[12]

The average income of occupational members is an appropriate variable in comparisons among occupations, but it is inappropriate to comparisons of one occupation in various states because real income will be approximately equal (in the absence of regulation) in each state.

(3) The concentration of the occupation in large cities.

When the occupation organizes a campaign to obtain favorable legislation, it incurs expenses in the solicitation of support, and these are higher for a diffused occupation than a concentrated one. The solicitation of support is complicated by the free-rider problem in that individual members cannot be excluded from the benefits of legislation even if they have not shared the costs of receiving it. If most of the occupation is concentrated in a few large centers, these problems (we suspect) are much reduced in intensity: regulation may even begin at the local governmental level. We shall use an orthodox geographical concentration measure: the share of the occupation of the state in cities over 100,000 (or 50,000 in 1900 and earlier).

(4) The presence of a cohesive opposition to licensing.

If an occupation deals with the public at large, the costs which licensing imposes upon any one customer or industry will be small and it will not be economic for that customer or industry to combat the drive for licensure. If the injured group finds it feasible and profitable to act jointly, however, it will oppose the effort to get licensure, and (by increasing its cost) weaken, delay, or prevent the legislation. The same attributes—numbers of voters, wealth, and ease of organization—which favor an occupation in the political arena, of course, favor also any adversary group. Thus, a small occupation employed by only one industry which has few employers will have difficulty in getting licensure; whereas a large occupation serving everyone will encounter no organized opposition.

An introductory statistical analysis of the licensing of select occupations by states is summarized in Table 8-6. In each occupation the dependent variable for each state is the year of first regulation of entry into the occupation. The two independent variables are

(1)   the ratio of the occupation to the total labor force of the state in the census year nearest to the median year of regulation,

(2)   the fraction of the occupation found in cities over 100,000 (over 50,000 in 1890 and 1900) in that same year.

---

[12]Let n = the number of members of the profession and y = average income. We expect political capacity to be in proportion to (ny) so far as benefits go, but to reflect also the direct value of votes, so the capacity becomes proportional to ($n^a y$) with $a > 1$.

We expect these variables to be negatively associated with year of licensure, and each of the nine statistically significant regression coefficients is of the expected sign.

The results are not robust, however: the multiple correlation coefficients are small, and over half of the regression coefficients are not significant (and in these cases often of inappropriate sign). Urbanization is more strongly associated than size of occupation with licensure.[13] The crudity of the data may be a large source of these disappointments: we measure, for example, the characeristics of the barbers in each state in 1930, but 14 states were licensing barbers by 1910. If the states which licensed barbering before 1910 had relatively more barbers, or more highly urbanized barbers, the predictions would be improved. The absence of data for years between censuses and before 1890 led us to make only the cruder analysis.[14]

In general, the larger occupations were licensed in earlier years.[15] Veterinarians are the only occupation in this sample who have a well-defined set of customers, namely livestock farmers, and licensing was later in those states with large numbers of livestock relative to rural population. The within-occupation analyses offer some support for the economic theory of the supply of legislation.

A comparison of different occupations allows us to examine several other variables. The first is income, already discussed above. The second is the size of the market. Just as it is impossible to organize an effective labor union in only one part of an integrated market, so it is impossible to regulate only one part of the market. Consider an occupation—junior business executives will do—which has a national market with high mobility of labor and significant mobility of employers. If the executives of one state were to organize, their scope for effective influence would be very small. If salaries were raised above the competitive level, employers would often recruit elsewhere so the demand elastici-

---

[13]We may pool the occupations and assign dummy variables for each occupation; the regression coefficients then are:

size of occupation relative to labor force: -0.450 ($t = 0.59$)
urbanization $: -12.133$ ($t = 4.00$).

Thus urbanization is highly significant, while size of occupation is not significant.

[14]A more precise analysis might take the form of a regression analysis such as:

Year of licensure = constant
+ b_1 (year of critical size of occupation)
+ b_2 (year of critical urbanization of occupation),

where the critical size and urbanization were defined as the mean size and mean urbanization in the year of licensure.

[15]Lawyers, physicians, and pharmacists were all relatively large occupations by 1900, and nurses also by 1910. The only large occupation to be licensed later was barbers; the only small occupation to be licensed early was embalmers.

TABLE 8–6. Initial year of Regulation as a Function of Relative Size of Occupation and Degree of Urbanization

OCCUPATION	NUMBER OF STATES LICENSING	MEDIAN CENSUS YEAR OF LICENSING	REGRESSION COEFFICIENTS (AND T-VALUES)		R^2
			SIZE OF OCCUPATION (RELATIVE TO LABOR FORCE)	URBANIZATION (SHARE OF OCCUPATION IN CITIES OVER 100,000*)	
Beauticians	48	1930	−4.03 (2.50)	5.90 (1.24)	0.125
Architects	47	1930	−24.06 (2.15)	−6.29 (0.84)	0.184
Barbers	46	1930	−1.31 (0.51)	−26.10 (2.37)	0.146
Lawyers	29	1890	−0.26 (0.08)	−65.78 (1.70)	0.102
Physicians	43	1890	0.64 (0.65)	−23.80 (2.69)	0.165

Embalmers	37	1910	3.32 (0.36)	-4.24 (0.44)	0.007
Registered Nurses	48	1910	-2.08 (2.28)	-3.36 (1.06)	0.176
Dentists	48	1900	2.51 (0.44)	-22.94 (2.19)	0.103
Veterinarians	40	1910	-10.69 (1.94)	-37.16 (4.20)	0.329
Chiropractors	48	1930	-17.70 (1.54)	11.69 (1.25)	0.079
Pharmacists	48	1900	-4.19 (1.50)	-6.84 (0.80)	0.082

Sources: The Council of State Governments, "Occupational Licensing Legislation in the States," 1952 [3], and U.S. Census of Population [15], Various Years.

*50,000 in 1890 and 1900.

TABLE 8-7 Characteristics of Licensed and Unlicensed Professional Occupations, 1960

OCCUPATION	MEDIAN AGE (YEARS)	MEDIAN EDUCATION (YEARS)	MEDIAN EARNINGS (50-52 WKS.)	INSTABILITY OF MEMBERSHIP*	PERCENT NOT SELF-EMPLOYED	PERCENT IN CITIES OVER 50,000	PERCENT OF LABOR FORCE
Licensed:							
Architects	41.7	16.8	$ 9,090	0.012	57.8%	44.1%	0.045%
Chiropractors	46.5	16.4	6,360	0.053	5.8	30.8	0.020
Dentists	45.9	17.3	12,200	0.016	9.4	34.5	0.128
Embalmers	43.5	13.4	5,990	0.130	52.8	30.2	0.055
Lawyers	45.3	17.4	10,800	0.041	35.8	43.1	0.308
Prof. Nurses	39.1	13.2	3,850	0.291	91.0	40.6	0.868
Optometrists	41.6	17.0	8,480	0.249	17.5	34.5	0.024
Pharmacists	44.9	16.2	7,230	0.119	62.3	40.0	0.136
Physicians	42.8	17.5	14,200	0.015	35.0	44.7	0.339
Veterinarians	39.2	17.4	9,210	0.169	29.5	14.4	0.023
Average	43.0	16.3	8,741	0.109	39.7	35.7	0.195

Partially Licensed:							
Accountants	40.4	14.9	6,450	0.052	88.1	43.5	0.698
Engineers	38.3	16.2	8,490	0.023	96.8	31.6	1.279
Elem. School Teachers	43.1	16.5	4,710	(a)	99.1	18.8	1.482
Average	40.6	15.9	6,550	0.117(b)	94.7	34.6	1.153
Unlicensed:							
Artists	38.0	14.2	5,920	0.103	77.3	45.7	0.154
Clergymen	43.3	17.0	4,120	0.039	89.0	27.2	0.295
College Teachers	40.3	17.4	7,500	0.085	99.2	36.0	0.261
Draftsmen	31.2	12.9	5,990	0.098	98.6	40.8	0.322
Reporters & Editors	39.4	15.5	6,120	0.138	93.9	43.3	0.151
Musicians	40.2	14.8	3,240	0.081	65.5	37.7	0.289
Natural Scientists	35.9	16.8	7,490	0.264	96.3	32.7	0.221
Average	38.3	15.5	5,768	0.115	88.5	37.6	0.242

(*) 1-R, Where R = ratio: 1960 age 45-54 to 1950 age 35-44.

(a) Not available separately: teachers N.E.C. (incl. secondary school and other). = 0.276

(b) Includes figure for teachers N.E.C. in note (a)

Source: U.S. Census of Population, [15], 1960.

ty would be very high.[16] The third variable is stability of occupational membership: the longer the members are in the occupation, the greater their financial gain from control of entry. Our regrettably crude measure of this variable is based upon the number of members aged 35–44 in 1950 and aged 45–54 in 1960: the closer these numbers are, the more stable the membership of the occupation. The data for the various occupations are given in Table 8–7 (pp. 250–51).

The comparison of licensed and unlicensed occupations is consistently in keeping with our expectations:

(1)   the licensed occupations have higher incomes (also before licensing, one may assume),
(2)   the membership of the licensed occupations is more stable (but the difference is negligible in our crude measure),
(3)   the licensed occupations are less often employed by business enterprises (who have incentives to oppose licensing),
(4)   all occupations in national markets (college teachers, engineers, scientists, accountants) are unlicensed or only partially licensed.

The size and urbanization of the three groups, however, are unrelated to licensing. The inter-occupational comparsion therefore provides a modicum of additional support for our theory of regulation.

3. CONCLUSION

The idealistic view of public regulation is deeply imbedded in professional economic thought. So many economists, for example, have denounced the ICC for its pro-railroad policies that this has become a cliché of the literature. This criticism seems to me exactly as appropriate as a criticism of the Great Atlantic and Pacific Tea Company for selling groceries, or as a criticism of a politician for currying popular support. The fundamental vice of such criticism is that it misdirects attention: it suggests that the way to get an ICC which is not subservient to the carriers is to preach to the commissioners or to the people who appoint the commissioners. The only way to get a different commission would be to change the political support for the Commission, and reward commissioners on a basis unrelated to their services to the carriers.

Until the basic logic of political life is developed, reformers will be ill-equipped to use the state for their reforms, and victims of the pervasive use of the state's support of special groups will be helpless to protect themselves. Economists should quickly establish the license to practice on the rational theory of political behavior.

[16]The regulation of business in a partial market will also generally produce very high supply elasticities within a market: if the price of the product (or service) is raised, the pressure of excluded supply is very difficult to resist. Some occupations are forced to reciprocity in licensing, and the geographical dispersion of earnings in licensed occupations, one would predict, is not appreciably different than in unlicensed occupations with equal employer mobility. Many puzzles are posed by the interesting analysis of Arlene S. Holen in [6], pp. 492–98.

APPENDIX

TABLE 5   Common, Contract and Passenger Motor Carriers, 1935–1969[1]

YEAR ENDING	CUMULATIVE APPLICATIONS			OPERATING CARRIERS	
	GRAND-FATHER	NEW	TOTAL	APPROVED APPLICATIONS[3]	NUMBER IN OPERATION[2]
Oct. 1936	82,827	1,696	84,523	—	—
1937	83,107	3,921	87,028	1,114	—
1938	85,646	6,694	92,340	20,398	—
1939	86,298	9,636	95,934	23,494	—
1940	87,367	12,965	100,332	25,575	—
1941	88,064	16,325	104,389	26,296	—
1942	88,702	18,977	107,679	26,683	—
1943	89,157	20,007	109,164	27,531	—
1944	89,511	21,324	110,835	27,177	21,044
1945	89,518	22,829	112,347		20,788
1946	89,529	26,392	115,921		20,632
1947	89,552	29,604	119,156		20,665
1948	89,563	32,678	122,241		20,373
1949	89,567	35,635	125,202		18,459
1950	89,573	38,666	128,239		19,200
1951	89,574	41,889	131,463		18,843
1952	(89,574)[4]	44,297	133,870		18,408
1953	"	46,619	136,192		17,869
1954	"	49,146	138,719		17,080
1955	"	51,720	141,293		16,836
June 1956	"	53,640	143,213		16,486
1957	"	56,804	146,377		16,316
1958	"	60,278	149,851		16,065
1959	"	64,171	153,744		15,923
1960	"	69,205	158,778		15,936
1961	"	72,877	162,450		15,967
1962	"	76,986	166,559		15,884
1963	"	81,443	171,016		15,739
1964	"	86,711	176,284		15,732
1965	"	93,064	182,637		15,755
1966	"	101,745	191,318		15,933
1967	"	106,647	196,220		16,003
1968	"	(6)	(6)		16,230[5]
1969	"	(6)	(6)		16,318[5]

Source: U.S. Interstate Commerce Commission *Annual Reports* [17].

[1]Excluding brokers and within-state carriers.

[2]Property Carriers were the following percentages of all operating carriers: 1944-93.4%; 1950-92.4%; 1960-93.0%; 1966-93.4%.

[3]Estimated.

[4]Not available; assumed to be approximately constant.

[5]1968 and 1969 figures are for number of carriers required to file annual reports.

[6]Not available comparable to previous years; applications for permanent authority *disposed of* (i.e., from new and pending files) 1967-69 are as follows: 1967-7,049; 1968-5,724; 1969-5,186.

TABLE 6   Weight Limits on Trucks, 1932–33*, by States (Basic Data for Table 2).

STATE	MAXIMUM WEIGHT (IN LBS.)		STATE	MAXIMUM WEIGHT (IN LBS.)	
	4-WHEEL[1]	6-WHEEL[2]		4-WHEEL[1]	6-WHEEL[2]
Alabama	20,000	32,000	Nebraska	24,000	40,000
Arizona	22,000	34,000	Nevada	25,000	38,000
Arkansas	22,200	37,000	New Hampshire	20,000	20,000
California	22,000	34,000	New Jersey	30,000	30,000
Colorado	30,000	40,000	New Mexico	27,000	45,000
Connecticut	32,000	40,000	New York	33,600	44,000
Delaware	26,000	38,000	No. Carolina	20,000	20,000
Florida	20,000	20,000	No. Dakota	24,000	48,000
Georgia	22,000	39,600	Ohio	24,000	24,000
Idaho	24,000	40,000	Oklahoma	20,000	20,000
Illinois	24,000	40,000	Oregon	25,500	42,500
Indiana	24,000	40,000	Pennsylvania	26,000	36,000
Iowa	24,000	40,000	Rhode Island	28,000	40,000
Kansas	24,000	34,000	So. Carolina	20,000	25,000
Kentucky	18,000	18,000	So. Dakota	20,000	20,000

State			State		
Louisiana	13,400	N.A.	Tennessee	20,000	20,000
Maine	18,000	27,000	Texas	13,500	N.A.
Maryland	25,000	40,000	Utah	26,000	34,000
Massachusetts	30,000	30,000	Vermont	20,000	20,000
Michigan	27,000	45,000	Virginia	24,000	35,000
Minnesota	27,000	42,000	Washington	24,000	34,000
Mississippi	18,000	22,000	West Va.	24,000	40,000
Missouri	24,000	24,000	Wisconsin	24,000	36,000
Montana	24,000	34,000	Wyoming	27,000	30,000

*Red Book [11] Figures are reported (p. 89) as "based on the state's interpretations of their laws [1933] and on physical limitations of vehicle design and tire capacity." Public Roads [13] Figures are reported (p. 167) as "an abstract of state laws, including legislation passed in 1932."

'14-Wheel: The smallest of the following 3 figures was used:

(A) Maximum gross weight (as given in Red Book, p. 90-91).

(B) Maximum axle weight (as given in Red Book, p. 90-91), multiplied by 1.5 (see Red Book, p. 89).

(C) Maximum gross weight (as given in Red Book, p. 93).

Exceptions: Texas and Louisiana—see Red Book, p. 91.

'26-Wheel: Maximum gross weight as given in Public Roads, p. 167. These Figures agree in most cases with those shown in Red Book, p. 93, and with Public Roads maximum axle weights multiplied by 2.5 (see Red Book, p. 93). Texas and Louisiana are excluded as data are not available to convert from payload to gross weight limits.

TABLE 7 Independent Variables (Basic Data for Table 2 — Cont'd)

STATE	TRUCKS ON FARMS PER 1,000 AGRICULTURAL LABOR FORCE	AVERAGE LENGTH OF RAILROAD HAUL OF FREIGHT (MILES)	PERCENT OF STATE HIGHWAYS WITH HIGH-TYPE SURFACE
Alabama	26.05	189.4	1.57
Arizona	79.74	282.2	2.60
Arkansas	28.62	233.1	1.72
California	123.40	264.6	13.10
Colorado	159.50	244.7	0.58
Connecticut	173.80	132.6	7.98
Delaware	173.20	202.7	7.98
Florida	91.41	184.1	8.22
Georgia	32.07	165.7	1.60
Idaho	95.89	243.6	0.73
Illinois	114.70	207.9	9.85
Indiana	120.20	202.8	6.90
Iowa	98.73	233.3	3.39
Kansas	146.70	281.5	0.94
Kentucky	20.05	227.5	1.81
Louisiana	31.27	201.0	1.94
Maine	209.30	120.4	1.87
Maryland	134.20	184.1	12.90
Massachusetts	172.20	144.7	17.70
Michigan	148.40	168.0	6.68
Minnesota	120.40	225.6	1.44
Mississippi	29.62	164.9	1.14
Missouri	54.28	229.7	2.91
Montana	183.80	266.5	0.09
Nebraska	132.10	266.9	0.41

State			
Nevada	139.40	273.2	0.39
New Hampshire	205.40	129.0	3.42
New Jersey	230.20	137.6	23.30
New Mexico	90.46	279.0	0.18
New York	220.50	163.3	21.50
No. Carolina	37.12	171.5	8.61
No. Dakota	126.40	255.1	0.01
Ohio	125.80	194.2	11.20
Oklahoma	78.18	223.3	1.42
Oregon	118.90	246.2	3.35
Pennsylvania	187.60	166.5	9.78
Rhode Island	193.30	131.0	20.40
So. Carolina	20.21	169.8	2.82
So. Dakota	113.40	216.6	0.04
Tennessee	23.98	191.9	3.97
Utah	101.70	235.7	1.69
Vermont	132.20	109.7	2.26
Virginia	71.88	229.8	2.86
Washington	180.90	254.4	4.21
West Virginia	62.88	218.7	8.13
Wisconsin	178.60	195.7	4.57
Wyoming	133.40	286.7	0.08

(1) *Average length of RR haul of (revenue) freight* = average distance in miles each ton is carried = ratio of number of ton-miles to number of tons carried. For each state, average length of haul was obtained by weighting average length of haul of each company by the number of miles of line operated by that company in the state (all for class I RR's).

(2) *Percentage of state roads with high-quality surface:* Where high-quality (high-type) surface consists of bituminous macadam, bituminous concrete, sheet asphalt, Portland cement concrete, and block pavements. All state rural roads, both local and state highways systems, are included.

REFERENCES

1. ASSOCIATION OF AMERICAN RAILROADS, BUREAU OF RAILWAY ECONOMICS. *Railway Mileage by States.* Washington, D.C.: December 31, 1930.
2. BECKER, G. S. "Competition and Democracy." *Journal of Law and Economics,* October 1958.
3. THE COUNCIL OF STATE GOVERNMENTS. "Occupational Licensing Legislation in the States." 1952.
4. DEMSETZ, H., "Why Regulate Utilities?" *Journal of Law and Economics,* April 1968.
5. GERWIG, R.W. "Natural Gas Production: A Study of Costs of Regulation." *Journal of Law and Economics,* October 1962, pp. 69–92.
6. HOLEN, A.S. "Effects of Professional Licensing Arrangements on Interstate Labor Mobility and Resource Allocation." *Journal of Political Economy,* Vol. 73 (1915), pp. 492–98.
7. KEYES, L.S. *Federal Control of Entry into Air Transportation.* Cambridge, Mass.: Harvard University Press, 1951.
8. MOORE, T.G. "The Purpose of Licensing." *Journal of Law and Economics,* October 1961.
9. OLSON, M. *The Logic of Collective Action.* Cambridge, Mass.: Harvard University Press, 1965.
10. PELTZMAN, S. "Entry in Commercial Banking," *Journal of Law and Economics,* October 1965.
11. *The Motor Truck Red Book and Directory,* 1934 Edition, pp. 85–102.
12. U. S. CONGRESS, SELECT COMMITTEE ON SMALL BUSINESS. *Hearings,* 88th Congress, 2nd Session, August 10 and 11, 1964.
13. U. S. DEPARTMENT OF AGRICULTURE, BUREAU OF PUBLIC ROADS. *Public Roads.* Washington, D.C.: U.S. Government Printing Office, December 1932.
14. U.S. DEPARTMENT OF COMMERCE, BUREAU OF THE CENSUS. *United States Census of Agriculture, 1930,* Vol. 4. Washington, D. C.: U.S. Government Printing Office, 1930.
15. _____. *United States Census of Population.* Washington, D.C.: U.S. Government Printing Office, appropriate years.
16. _____, BUREAU OF FOREIGN AND DOMESTIC COMMERCE. *Statistical Abstract of the U.S., 1932.* Washington, D. C.: U.S. Government Printing Office, 1932.
17. U.S. INTERSTATE COMMERCE COMMISSION. *Annual Report.* Washington, D.C.: U.S. Government Printing Office, appropriate years.
18. _____. *Statistics of Railways in the United States, 1930.* Washington, D.C.: U.S. Government Printing Office, 1930.

WHY GOVERNMENT MUST CATER
TO BUSINESS
Charles E. Lindblom

It's almost a cliché, but when you fly over New York City, as I did recently on a beautiful sunny day, it is hard not to be impressed by the demonstration of man's handiwork laid out for miles below. The massive buildings of Manhattan are, of course, the most striking feature of the landscape seen from the air. But as you move away from the city, you pass over all kinds of industrial installations, and see that here too is a staggering human accomplishment.

Who did it? How did it happen? If we had flown Ramses or Amenhotep over this same landscape, these ancient figures would have been confident that no one could have built so elaborate a set of structures for carrying on the world's work other than some rich and powerful government, for in the largest part of the history of mankind that has been the story. As for the ancient monuments of Egypt, it was, of course, an enormously wealthy, powerful, and coercive government that built them.

Looking out, however, on that vast terrain of man-made achievement in the New York metropolitan area (or any one of many other metropolitan areas in this country or in Western Europe), you realize that these are not, on the whole, the products of government but the products of business enterprise. I do not in any way qualify the opinion that the institution called "business enterprise" has been of enormous consequence for the welfare of mankind. In the argument on business power that I am going to develop here, I shall not speak, as some critics of business do, of businessmen as "malefactors of great wealth," conspirators, or exploiters. Businessmen and their financial associates have performed the principal tasks of moving and shaking the Western world for many decades now, and that is an accomplishment for which they are justified in taking great pride.

***

My particular argument on business power is a simple one, put down in just a few steps.

1. The first step is that businessmen, as I have just implied, constitute one of the two great leadership groups in Western society. By "leadership group" I mean people who are in charge of important public functions, getting the big jobs done for society. The other group, of course, is the top level of government officialdom, both the bureaucracy and the legislative and executive branches.

2. Most of the big tasks of shaping and doing in our kind of society are entrusted to businessmen rather than government officials. The big tasks of producing and organizing the labor force, putting it to work and motivating it, paying out income shares—all these absolutely fundamental tasks of social organization—are largely in the hands of business.

3. Under the rules of these systems—the constitutional and traditional rules—these prodigiously important business officials cannot be commanded to perform their functions. You cannot command a businessman to produce; he is not simply a government official who takes orders from his hierarchical superior.

4. Instead, businessmen have to be induced to perform their functions, induced somehow by the income, prerogatives, indulgences, or autonomy accorded them.

5. What they have to be given as inducements in order to get them to do their job is very roughly speaking, whatever they need, *as a condition of being willing to do their job*. I don't mean that they get everything they want, but the character of their rewards is determined by what they want. If it is high income they want, that is what they must be given. If it is a chance to let their enterprises grow that they want, that is what they have to be given. If it is political responsibility, autonomy, discretion, or rights of consultation, that is what they must be given. In other words, they have to be given those indulgences, incentives, pleasures, rewards—whatever you want to call them—that will actually motivate them to do the jobs that we are counting on them to do.

6. The next step in the argument is that there is no more important function for government to perform than to see to it that business is offered the necessary inducements, whatever they may be. If they are not, we suffer unemployment, sluggish growth, or other kinds of economic disorder. These ills are not only deeply distressing to the population as a whole, but suicidal for public officials. That is because political leaders lose their positions if they cannot maintain a relatively healthy economy. It becomes essential in all Western-style systems that government accept the responsibility to indulge business. Political officials usually understand this elementary fact of life.

7. That being so, every democratic government is subject to two major methods of control: the democratic or electoral controls and the business controls. I therefore suggest that the business controls are in some sense extrademocratic, nondemocratic, or antidemocratic.

In most models of the democratic system—the ones we are taught in school and the ones that political theorists develop—democracy is a system in which officials at the top are controlled by the vote. Citizens mobilize extra powers because they have the vote—that is, they can organize into interest groups and undertake letter-writing campaigns to their congressman. But the basic or underlying control that we call democratic is the vote, which in principle achieves a kind of egalitarian sharing of authority through the one man–one vote rule.

By "business controls" I mean a quite different set of controls which simply do not appear in models of democratic government. These are the controls that lie in the hands of business simply because every government official knows that, unless he meets the needs of business, he is in trouble. These controls he must respond to even if they call, at times, for policies strikingly different from policies that are being signalled by voters through the electoral process. There is constant conflict between these business controls and democratic controls.

I am aware that the predominant opinion of businessmen is that the democratic controls usually win out, that electoral pressures and party politics constantly impose new regulations on business. The impression is overwhelmingly of a constant defensive fight to maintain a reasonable minimum of business independence so that they can get the job done. I suggest that businessmen look more deeply. They are indeed constantly and inevitably engaged forever in a fight for their prerogatives. But it is a fight on the edge of a battlefield most of which they long ago captured. The businessman commands almost all the field. A disproportionate business influence on government is so pervasive as to go unnoticed, however vigorously business goes on defending itself at the fringes.

I want, now, to add a supplementary point. In addition to business controls exercised not through the electoral process but through the practical necessity for government to meet the needs of business, businessmen also enter into the electoral process. When business makes one set of demands on government and the electoral process makes another, there has to be some way of resolving that conflict. Obviously, one way to do it is to try to bend the electoral controls so that they conform with the business controls. This is what business enters into electoral politics to do. Business spends heavily in party and interest-group activity. Businessmen are the most active, best financed, and best organized participants in electoral politics—all to move the electoral influences on government in the direction of the business influences. Given the marginal defeats they suffer, businessmen are the last to perceive that the effect of participation of business in electoral politics is to overwhelm, in organizational efficacy and in money spent, the activity of any other group.

I am not saying that this is an intolerable situation. I am not saying that we must undercut these business controls. I am simply saying that we live in a system in which, although we have created in our minds a vision of an egalitarian, democratic pattern of control over government, our vision does not take into account the special needs of business, and business's consequent disproportional power.

If you are skeptical about business power, let me offer some simple examples. If in my town of North Haven I were to want my local government to lower my taxes or offer me other favors, I would not bother to ask because it would be futile. But when a corporation came to North Haven some years ago to ask that certain streets be relocated, new traffic controls be established, and tax concessions be made, these benefits were granted. For it was understood that the corporation was, in effect, saying, "If North Haven will do what we want, we will locate a plant in North Haven, and there will then be new tax possibilities for the municipality and thousands of new jobs."

Here is another example: Last spring the *New York Times* announced that Mayor Koch would set up a new organization to attend to the needs of business because he fears the flight of business from New York City. His administration is determined to take special pains to find out how far he can go in giving business what it needs in order to keep business in New York City. If I were in his shoes, I would do the same thing. But note that this effort represents a degree of solicitous concern that is not matched by an equivalent concern for any other group.

***

Should anything be done about this state of affairs? I do not intend to discuss that question. Instead I would like to propose that businessmen consider thoughtfully the possibility that there is a genuine conflict between the two forms of control and that, consequently, there may be fundamental and persistent undemocratic elements in systems founded on private enterprise. I should like then to consider that political beliefs are therefore changing. In Harris polls during the years between 1965 and 1972, the number of people who said they repose confidence in business leadership in the United States dropped approximately 50 percent. We also see other signs that the American and Western-style systems are deeply under attack, abroad through the spread of Communist systems, internally through the spread of disaffection.

If businessmen want to understand the possibilities of maintaining our kind of a system for the future, I believe that they should reflect thoughtfully on the conflict between rising democratic aspirations in Western society and the privileged position of business. The two are inconsistent, difficult to reconcile.

AN IRONY OF ELECTORAL REFORM
Edwin M. Epstein

The 1970s have witnessed an explosion in federal regulation of the electoral process. When the Ninety-Sixth Congress deliberates the Federal Election Campaign Act Amendments of 1979, it would do well to keep in mind an important lesson of the three previous rounds in federal campaign legislation. The lesson is that campaign regulation, like regulation in other fields, often has unintended—and indeed ironic—consequences.

It is not an exaggeration to say that the Federal Election Campaign Act (FECA), enacted in 1971 and amended in 1974 and 1976, has legitimized the role of corporations and business-related groups in federal elections, greatly improving their position vis-a-vis labor and other social interests. The act has

Edwin M. Epstein, "An Irony of Electoral Reform," *Regulation* 3, no. 3 (May–June 1979), 35–41. Copyright 1979 American Enterprise Institute. Reprinted with permission.

also established the political action committee (PAC), labor's long-time and essential political mechanism, as the primary vehicle for business involvement in the electoral process. The irony is that, in each of the three legislative rounds, it was organized labor, not business, that brought about the key provisions relating to PACs. A further irony is that comprehensive campaign regulation has increased the role of organized "special" interests within the federal electoral process at the expense of political parties and individual contributors—surely a far cry from what reformers intended.

FEDERAL ELECTION REGULATION OF BUSINESS AND LABOR IN THE 1970s

A glance at recent history will help explain how these developments came about. Union experience with PACs dates to the mid-1930s when John L. Lewis established Labor's Non-Partisan Political League. Then, in 1955, the merger of the AFL and CIO brought with it the creation of the Committee on Political Education (COPE), the model for virtually all future political action committees. From the outset, national, state, and local units of COPE have not only raised and distributed funds, but they also served as the mechanism for coherent and comprehensive union activity in the electoral process, including voter registration, political education, and get-out-the-vote drives.

Business, however, did little with PACs before 1972. Actually, until the reforms in campaign financing laws of the 1970s, there was little need for business PACs: monies from business-related sources could legally enter the electoral arena in virtually unlimited amounts, in the form of individual contributions by wealthy persons affiliated with corporations and other business organizations. Thus, for example, the Business Industry Political Action Committee (BIPAC), formed by affiliates of the National Association of Manufacturers during the early 1960s, was a pale shadow of COPE.

The Federal Election Campaign Act of 1971 is the root of the PAC growth of the seventies. That act allowed corporations and labor unions (1) to communicate on any subject (including partisan politics) with stockholders and members, respectively, and their families, (2) to conduct nonpartisan registration and get-out-the-vote drives directed at these same constituencies, and (3) to spend company and union funds to establish and administer a "separate segregated fund" to be used for political purposes—that is, to set up political action committees.

The provision authorizing PACs was added to the bill on the House floor through an amendment drafted by the AFL-CIO. In this amendment, organized labor was seeking insurance against the possibility that the Supreme Court would uphold a court of appeal's ruling that the PAC organized by Pipefitters Local Union No. 562 was compulsory and union-financed rather than voluntary and member-financed, and was therefore illegal. Unions were, according to the AFL-CIO officials who helped draft the amendment authorizing PACs, taking a calculated risk. Since previous corporate electoral activity had been aimed at management-level employees rather than at shareholders and had focused primarily on fund-raising activities, few labor leaders thought companies would establish PACs. So they figured that the benefits from removing the threat to union political action committees would exceed the risks of giving business a virtual carte blanche to establish PACs. Though the new 1971 law provided the basis for the Supreme Court's reversal of the court of appeals in *Pipefitters* (1972), it nonetheless turned out to be a strategic error for labor in the longer term.

Corporate PACs played a relatively small role in the 1972 election. In addition to the fund-raising entrepreneurship of the Finance Committee to Re-Elect the President (which raised substantial sums from business sources), there was another reason. Many companies with government contracts were fearful of establishing political action committees after Common Cause, in a lawsuit against TRW Inc., questioned whether the authorization of corporate PACs was compatible with another section in the 1971 act that prohibited campaign contributions by government contractors.

Labor was also concerned with the Common Cause suit, because a number of unions were government contractors by reason of their federal manpower training and development contracts. Thus in the debate on the 1974 FECA amendments, labor led the successful campaign for a provision making it clear that corporations and labor unions with government contracts were *not* prohibited from establishing PACs. But, as in 1971, the effort backfired—in this instance because the overwhelming majority of government contractors are corporations. Thus, it has been business, not labor, that has been the major beneficiary of labor's effort.

The next chapter in our story begins with the Federal Election Commission's 1975 ruling in SUN-PAC, the most important advisory opinion in the commission's four-year history. In a 4–2 decision, the FEC held that Sun Oil Company could (1) use general treasury funds to establish, administer, and solicit contributions to SUN-PAC, its political action committee, (2) solicit contributions to SUN-PAC from both stockholders *and employees*, and (3) establish multiple PACs, each with separate contribution and expenditure limits, as long as the monies came solely from voluntary contributions. While it was the 1971 and 1974 amendments that provided the legal authority for business PACs, it was SUN-PAC that provided the imprimatur for the explosion in their size and numbers. In the six months following the FEC's decision, over 150 corporations established PACs, bringing the number in existence to nearly 300. Not surprisingly, labor groups vigorously denounced the SUN-PAC ruling and resorted once again to the Congress.

At the heart of Congress's concerns in drafting the 1976 campaign act amendments was rectification of the SUN-PAC outcome by establishing a new and politically acceptable balance between union and corporate rights in federal elections. Once again, lobbyists for the AFL-CIO and the United Auto Workers spearheaded the legislative effort. In the end, the bill, while hardly a complete labor triumph, was clearly more acceptable to labor than to business.

The nub of the compromise worked out was a provision limiting corporate PACs to soliciting contributions from stockholders and "executive or administrative personnel" and their families, while, as before, labor unions were limited to soliciting union members and their families. Twice a year, union and corporate PACs could make use of "cross-over" rights—that is, solicit the other's constituency by mail, using an independent third party as a conduit. Organized labor achieved a key objective when it was permitted to use payroll deduction plans ("check-offs") to collect from its members if the company PAC used that method with its stockholders or executive/administrative personnel. Finally, a "nonproliferation" provision was included: while a corporation (or union) could set up an unlimited number of PACs, all such affiliated committees were restricted to a contribution limit of $5,000 per candidate per election. This provision was designed to eliminate the establishment of multiple PACs by corporations seeking to take advantage of SUN-PAC ruling. Labor's triumph was only partial, however, since union and union-affiliated PACs were limited in the same way. Moreover, membership organizations, trade associations, cooperatives, and corporations without capital stock were explicitly authorized to establish PACs.

In summary, while the 1976 amendments restored part of what organized labor had lost in SUN-PAC, they gave the business community far greater running room in the electoral process than theretofore. Ironically, both business and labor exert a much stronger impact upon electoral politics today than reformers had envisioned or find acceptable.

CAMPAIGN 1978

Federal Election Commission statistics for 1976 and 1978 show the rapid expansion in numbers and activity by PACs in general and business-related PACs in particular. For those two years, the number of PACs rose from 1,242 to 1,938 and total spending by these committees rose from $30.1 million to $77.8 million. There were more corporate PACs than labor throughout the period but, in each campaign, labor PACs outraised and outspent their corporate counterparts. The situation was rapidly changing, however, for almost all of the increase in PAC funds was generated by nonlabor PACs—that is, corporate and "other." (See Table 8–8.)

In 1978 PACs contributed $35.1 million directly to congressional candidates, representing 18 percent of the $199 million these candidates received from all sources that year. Of this amount, corporate PACs donated some $9.8 million, favoring Republicans over Democrats ($6.2 million to $3.7 million) and incumbents over challengers and candidates for open seats (5.7 to 2.1 and 2.1);

TABLE 8-8   PAC Financial Data, Campaigns 1976 and 1978 ($ in millions)

	COMMITTEE TYPE			
	LABOR	CORPORATE	OTHER[a]	TOTAL BUSINESS ESTIMATED[b]
Number:[c]				
1976	303	450	489	695
1978	281	821	836	1,239
Number contributing to congressional candidates:				
1976	265	390	—	—
1978	211	697	551	973
Receipts (adj.):				
1976	$18.6	$ 6.8	—	—
1978	$19.8	$17.7	$43.1	$39.3
Disbursements (adj.):				
1976	$17.5	$ 5.8	$ 6.8 (est.)	$12.6 (est.)
1978	$18.9	$15.3	$43.6	$37.1
Contributions to congressional candidates:				
1976	$ 8.2	$ 4.3	—	—
1978	$10.2	$ 9.8	$15.0	$17.3

[a]Composed of all PACs classified by the FEC as No-Connected, Membership/Trade Association/Health, Cooperatives, and Corporations without Capital Stock.

[b]Includes figures for corporate PACs and for the half of "other" PACs (column three) that is assumed to be "business related" (see text), except that the figure for 1976 disbursements ($6.8 million) is for business-related PACs only (estimated by *Fortune*).

[c]Includes all PACs that engaged in activity during the two-year cycle.

Sources: FEC Report on Financial Activity, 1977-78, Interim Report (May 1979), FEC Disclosure Series No. 8 (1977) and 10 (1978), and *Fortune*, March 27, 1978.

and labor-affiliated committees donated $10.2 million, favoring Democrats over Republicans (9.7 to 0.6) and incumbents over challengers and open seat candidates (6.1 to 2.2 and 2.0).

Simple corporate-labor comparisons, while interesting, understate significantly the extent of business's electoral role. This is so because the FEC's classification scheme puts groups that are not explicitly business or labor into four separate categories—No-Connected Organizations (for example, Business-Industry Political Action Committee), Trade/Membership/Health (for example, National Association of Realtors), Cooperatives (for example, Associated Milk Producers, Inc.), and Corporations without Stock (for example, California Almond Growers Exchange). In 1978, as column three of Table 8-8 shows, the four categories accounted for 836 PACs and contributions to congressional candidates of $15.0 million. In those contributions Republicans were favored over Democrats ($8.7 million to $6.3 million) and incumbents over challengers and candidates for open seats (8.1 to 3.5 and 3.4). If we assume that only half the amounts raised, spent, and contributed to congressional candidates by the noncorporate, nonlabor PACs emanate from business-related committees—a very conservative estimate, indeed!—the receipts and disbursements attributable to business rise by over $21.5 million and contributions to congressional candidates by 7.5 million. Thus the totals for corporate and business-related PAC activity are those given in the fourth column of Table 8–8.

Based on these estimates, business and business-related groups out-raised and out-disbursed labor groups by almost two to one in 1978 and out-contributed them by almost 70 percent. Indeed several of the largest noncorporate business-related PACs, such as those of the National Association of Realtors and the National Automobile Dealers Association, out-raised, out-spent, and out-contributed (or matched) the two biggest labor committees, AFL-CIO COPE and UAW-V-CAP. These noncorporate business-related PACs, moreover, out-stripped even the largest company committees, Standard Oil of Indiana's and the International Paper Company's, by a factor of six to one.

The increase in PAC activity from 1976 to 1978 continued a trend. According to Common Cause, between 1974 and 1976 corporate and trade association groups had increased their contributions over two-and-one-half-fold ($2.5 million to $7.1 million), while labor groups had raised theirs by some 30 percent ($6.3 million to $8.2 million). It is thus no surprise that, between 1976 and 1978, corporate contributions to candidates more than doubled, while labor's contributions rose by 24 percent. Whatever measures one uses, it is apparent that business-related PACs (both of the corporate and noncorporate varieties) played a far more important role in 1978 than they had in any election theretofore.

Two caveats are necessary here. First, along with establishing PACs, corporations, unions, and other groups may advocate (in communications to their stockholders, managerial personnel, and members) the support or defeat of particular candidates, as long as they report such expenditures of $2,000 or more to the FEC. In 1976, sixty-six labor organizations reported spending slightly more than $2 million in internal communications, while only four corporations reported spending a total of $31,000. Second, the above figures do not include labor union spending for registration, get-out-the-vote, candidate logistical support, and general political education—activities that benefit labor-endorsed candidates and are considered by many political observers to be more important to a candidate's campaign than direct financial contributions. Michael J. Malbin estimates that, in 1976, organized labor at all levels spent almost two-thirds as much on these nonreportable items (and overhead) as its total reportable expenditures of $17.5 million (*National Journal*, March 19, 1977). In 1978, labor probably spent nearly $20 million for these items. While some national business groups (BIPAC, for one) and an occasional corporation have undertaken serious political education efforts, business has in general done very little in voter registration, get-out-the-vote, and non-candidate-related internal political communications. In these endeavors labor's expertise—and comparative advantage—remain most apparent.

THE BUSINESS PAC POTENTIAL

The explosion in total business PAC activity from 1974 to 1978 reflects mostly the rise in the number of corporate and business-related PACs. While labor's PACs increased some 35 percent, the number of corporate PACs expanded more than sevenfold and those affiliated with "other" interests expanded more than two-and-a-half times. Impressive as the growth in corporate PACs has been, what is astonishing is how few corporate PACs there are, given how many there might be. Contrary to popular opinion, only 41 percent of the corporations with PACs on September 30, 1978, were among the giants of American business, as measured by inclusion in any of *Fortune* magazine's 1978 lists.

Consider the bottom line of Table 8-9: of *Fortune's* top 1,000 industrials and 300 leading nonindustrials (1,300 firms in all), only 334 firms—26 percent—had a PAC as of September 1978. If we turn to the entire pool of potential corporate registrants, the figures are even more dramatic. The 823 corporate PACs active in the 1978 cycle represented only 22 percent of the 3,755 U.S. corporations with reported assets of $100 million or more (1974) and a meager

TABLE 8-9   PACs of Fortune-ranked Firms, by Firm Size, September 1978

SIZE CATEGORY (BASED ON 1977 REVENUES)		NUMBER OF PACs
Fortune's Top 1,000 Industrials:		
First 250		141
1st 50	35	
2nd 50	34	
3rd 50	30	
4th 50	25	
5th 50	17	
Second 250		52
Third 250		24
Fourth 250		7
Subtotal		224
Fortune's Leading 300 Nonindustrials (50 firms in each category):		
Commercial banking		25
Life insurances		6
Diversified financials		15
Retailing		15
Transportation		26
Utilities		23
Subtotal		110
Total, *Fortune's* 1,300 Firms		334

Source: FEC Report on Financial Activity, 1977-78, Interim Report No. 2 (September 1978).

3.4 percent of the 23,834 corporations with reported assets of $10 million or more. In short, the market for potential PAC formations is virtually untapped.

Moreover, in monies raised and donated, the 1978 operations of corporate PACs reveal just the tip of a possible iceberg. In 1976 only nine corporate PACs raised or spent more than $100,000, and in 1978 only six raised or spent more than $200,000.

Given the trend and the potential, there is no gainsaying that company committees give every promise of continuing to increase in numbers and in the distribution of their PAC funds. Surely by 1982, there could be 1,000 corporate PACs spending a total of some $50 million (an average of $50,000 apiece) and distributing $25–30 million directly to congressional candidates (assuming the present disbursement ratios do not change). My research suggests, moreover, that at least some companies will begin to undertake new forms of electoral involvement—automatic payroll deduction plans, nonpartisan registration and get-out-the-vote drives, and internal political communications among managerial level employees and shareholders.

Similarly, business-related (but noncorporate) associations are likely to increase both the size and vigor of their PAC operations. Here, too, the pool of potential registrants is large. For example, an estimated 1,500 trade and professional associations are currently headquartered in Washington, D.C., alone.

LABOR PAC POTENTIAL

On the labor side, on the other hand, the number of PACs is not likely to increase much from the high-water mark of 303 in 1976. The unions that are politically active have, in the main, been operating PACs for years. Moreover, according to FEC data, of the 303 labor committees active in the 1976 campaign, 42 raised and spent over 82 percent of labor's funds. If the 21 with receipts or expenditures of $50,000–100,000 are added in, we have nearly 90 percent of the union total. The remaining PACs represented either small unions or affiliates of large international unions (and, as such, were subject to the single contribution limit).

Labor's best opportunity for increasing its pool of voluntary political dollars lies in developing more productive fund-raising techniques. Very few unions, whether AFL-CIO affiliated or independent, have average contributions of a dollar per worker per year. If even that small amount were collected from each unionist, organized labor would raise some $19.4 million annually—or nearly $39 million biennially—from its U.S. members. This would almost double the amount generated by labor for campaign 1978 ($19.8 million) and would permit unions to contribute some $20 million directly to congressional candidates. Some unions are beginning to use payroll deductions (check-offs) to increase their per-member annual yield where this method is available through either reciprocal rights or collective bargaining. Others are considering direct-mail campaigns among their members—a technique used to good advantage by conservative groups and by the National Republican Congressional Campaign Committee.

COPING WITH UNINTENDED CONSEQUENCES

Certainly it is premature to suggest that labor's overall electoral effectiveness vis-á-vis business has been fatally impaired. Undoubtedly, some business-related PAC money is simply old wine in new bottles—funds that business had previously channeled into the campaign-financing process through company or associational officials or, on some occasions, sub rosa. But the rapidity and effectiveness with which the business community embraced the PAC was not anticipated by organized labor's political leadership. Nor did the leadership anticipate that the growth of business PACs would erode labor's position by providing alternative sources of funding for both congressional incumbents and challengers (particularly Democrats) who in the past were heavily dependent upon union monies for their campaigns.

It is hardly surprising therefore that, in the last Congress, the same labor representatives who were most instrumental in shaping the PAC provisions in the earlier campaign acts urged that PAC contribution limits be reduced from $5,000 to $2,500 and that partial public financing of House general election races be instituted. Arguably, the effect of the proposed halving of PAC contributions would be more cosmetic than real, since the great bulk of both labor and business contributions is in amounts of less than $2,500, yet it is noteworthy that union PACs gave more $2,500-and-over contributions in 1976 than did business. Labor apparently is willing to forego a short-run advantage from maintaining the higher limit in exchange for the longer-run benefit of forestalling the large corporate contributions that could come once company PACs have assembled truly substantial funds.

In addition—and for very similar reasons—organized labor is strongly backing the two public financing bills currently under consideration in the Congress (H.R. 1 and S.623). Many labor officials would like to have unions, corporations, and other interest groups wholly out of the business of making direct money contributions—through their PACs—to political candidates and party committees. They worry that direct business contributions could eventually far outstrip direct labor contributions and would prefer, therefore, to restrict business and labor involvement to those activities in which labor has the greatest comparative advantage—voter registration, political research and education, and get-out-the-vote endeavors.

A REMINDER TO CONGRESS

While the role of the individual contributor has been constrained by the Federal Election Campaign Act, union and particularly business electoral *potential* has been increased. The "reforms" of the 1970s have given both business and labor a distinct advantage over those social interests that have neither the legal right to use organization funds for PAC start-up and administrative costs, nor the requisite financial or organizational resources to emulate labor or business PACs. It is important to note here that, although business and labor are usually cast in the role of electoral competitors, frequently they in fact share sufficient political interests so that cooperation rather than competition can characterize their behavior. Joint labor-business geographical concerns or industry needs, or the opposition of a common foe (a militant environmental group) can mean coalition politics in which the two most powerful coalitions themselves join together. Arguably, one of the greatest potential challenges to the integrity of American electoral politics could arise from excessive harmony between powerful business and powerful labor.

The future of labor and business-related PACs is, however, uncertain. If *full* public financing of congressional elections should be adopted, business and labor would presumably shift their efforts from direct contributions to in-kind contributions and independent expenditures (assuming such activities remained legal). Labor, at least in the short run, would have a clear advantage here. Even without such a change, the future electoral roles of business and labor will be determined by what PACs actually do in the years ahead. If corporate and business-related PACs should raise $50 million per election biennium and contribute half that directly to federal candidates, and if labor PACs should achieve their $40 million goal, we might, indeed, reach a point where too much campaign money originates from these sources. This would be particularly the case if business and labor contributions were largely reinforcing—supporting incumbents (though different ones to some extent), doing little for challengers, and thereby perpetuating the congressional status quo.

Undoubtedly, the most important rationale underlying public regulation of corporate and labor electoral involvement has been to ensure that the power of wealth does not run roughshod over the people's will. In 1978, business and labor PACs provided 18 percent of the $199 million raised by congressional candidates. This percentage does not, in my view, amount to excessive interference in the political process or present the kind of threat to the body politic that would justify dramatic new regulation of electoral behavior. Nor shall we reach that point unless business or labor badly overplays its hand by misuse or overuse of its political action committees. The irony of all this is that organized labor unwittingly sowed the seeds that have borne the very fruit it sought to prevent—enhanced business electoral effectiveness—through business use of labor's favorite mechanism, the political action committee. It is a case in point that regulatory measures may have unforeseen consequences—which is something to be kept in the congressional mind.

DISCUSSION QUESTIONS

1. The airline and trucking industries have recently been substantially deregulated. Were these regulations primarily in the public or the industries' interests? What were the rationales for regulating, and more recently, for deregulating these industries?

2. Are professional licensing regulations for doctors, lawyers, barbers, plumbers, and taxi drivers designed primarily to protect public or private interests? How do these regulations protect the public interest? How do they promote private interests?

3. What is the basis for the "capture" theory of regulation? How are the regulators captured by the industries they are supposed to regulate? How can their "capture" be avoided?

4. Professor Lindblom writes in his article that businesses must be given "whatever they need, as a condition of being willing to do their job. I don't mean that they get everything they want, but the character of their rewards is determined by what they want." How would you evaluate Steven Kelman's moral arguments against competition among the states in Chapter 4 in the context of Lindblom's statement?

5. Professor Lindblom contends that market controls over government are "inconsistent, difficult to reconcile" with democratic aspirations. Do you agree with this position, or do market controls complement political democracy by limiting the centralization of decision-making power in the government? Would society be more democratic if government could order business (labor, consumers) to perform the economic functions it desired?

6. "Members of House and Senate committees reviewing the Clean Air Act received nearly $730,000 in 1980 and 1981 from 93 corporations found in violation of Clean Air Act emission standards."

   "House members who voted to exempt dairy-industry subsidies from sharp budget cuts this year have been given an average of $1,600 each by dairy PACs since January 1981. Those who opposed these subsidies got an average of only $200." [W. H. Miller, "Corporate PACs on Trial," *Industry Week* (October 4, 1982), p. 42.]

   Do PAC contributions result in undue favor for special interest groups in Congress? Should all Congressional elections be publicly financed to reduce the influence of political action committees?

7. Are businesses which seek special government assistance only acting in their self-interest? Are politicians who grant such special assistance acting in their self-interest? Who is acting in the public interest?

8. How do the basic political strategies of business and labor differ? What factors explain these differences?

9. Has the growth of business PACs increased the political influence of business relative to other interest groups (labor, consumers, etc.)?

10. Alexis de Tocqueville argued that freedom of association could not be abolished without impairing the foundations of democratic society, but that individuals

should not have an absolute right of political association. How does one strike the balance de Tocquevile is suggesting is necessary, or should individuals have an absolute right to form political associations?

ADDITIONAL READINGS

ALEXANDER, HERBERT E., *The Case for PACs*. Public Affairs Council Monograph. Washington, D.C.: Public Affairs Council, 1982.

DICKSON, DOUGLAS N., "Corpacs: The Business of Political Action Committees," *Across the Board*, 18, no. 10 (November 1981), 13–22.

KIEM, GERALD D., "Foundations of a Political Strategy for Business," *California Management Review*, 23, no. 3 (Spring 1981), 49–55.

MALBIN, MICHAEL J., "Neither a Mountain nor a Molehill," *Regulation*, (May–June 1979), pp. 41–43.

MARX, THOMAS G., "Political Consequences of Conglomerate Mergers," *The Antitrust Bulletin*, 27, no. 1 (Spring 1982), 107–33.

MILLER, WILLIAM H., "Corporate PACs on Trial," *Industry Week*, October 4, 1982, pp. 39–42.

WEIDENBAUM, M. L., "I'm All for Free Enterprise, but . . ." Whittemore House Lecture Series No. 7. St. Louis: Center for the Study of American Business, Washington University, 1982.

WERTHEIMER, FRED, "Of Mountains: The PAC Movement in American Politics." Paper presented at the Conference on Parties, Interest Groups and Campaign Finance Laws. Washington, D.C.: American Enterprise Institute, 1979.

CHAPTER 9

GOVERNMENT REGULATION

Government regulation of business is a fundamental business-society relationship of which businessmen are well aware. A third or more of an executive's time may be spent complying with regulatory requirements.[1] As Professor Weidenbaum observes:

> Entrepreneurial decisions fundamental to the business enterprise are increasingly becoming subject to governmental influence, review or control—decisions such as: What lines of business to go into? What products and services to produce? Which investments to finance? How to produce goods and services? Where to make them? How to market them? What prices to charge? What profit to keep?

These regulations are often the result of the debates over stockholder, consumer, and employee rights; social goals and responsibilities; political influence; and moral obligations analyzed in the preceding chapters. The surge of "new style," social (environmental, health, safety, and antidiscrimination) regulations since the 1960s is a direct reflection of government dissatisfaction with the market's inability to reconcile private and social interests and the business response to these social issues. At the same time, "old style" economic regulation (e.g., the regulation of prices, entry, and routes in the railroad, trucking, airlines, and communications industries) is being gradually eliminated in favor of greater reliance upon competitive market controls (85 percent of the

[1]Although this is a large portion of an executive's time, it does not appear to be any greater than the time European and Japanese executives spend on government relations.

federal regulatory budget is for social regulation and 15 percent is for economic regulation). These dual regulatory trends reflect both a reassessment of the market's relative strengths and weaknesses, and a shift in political influence from industries traditionally able to secure the coercive power of the state for their advantage to social interest groups now able to obtain regulation to promote their agenda.

The regulation of business represents the traditional, "external" control of business decision making by government. It does not attempt to alter the internal control of business decision making like corporate governance reforms or industrial democracy proposals. Rather, it mandates changes in the mix of private and public goods which business must produce (e.g., less steel and cleaner air). In *Taming the Giant Corporation*, Ralph Nader, Mark Green, and Joel Seligman argue that an additional massive infusion of federal regulation is necessary to correct the abuses of uncontrolled business power.[2] They recommend comprehensive federal chartering which would protect the interests of all constituencies affected by business decisions: a bill of rights for employees; a full-time outside board of directors for stockholders; deconcentration of oligopolistic industries for consumers; area impact statements for local communities; and greater information disclosure for taxpayers.

In the first reading, Professor Weidenbaum takes the completely opposite position that the costs of existing regulations are already excessive at $500 per capita, excluding the cost of regulatory disincentives to research and development and capital investment. He argues that it is the regulatory agencies which are exercising uncontrolled power over the allocation of the nation's resources. Weidenbaum advances a new version of the "capture" theory of regulation. According to Weidenbaum, the "new style" regulatory agencies have been "captured," not by the industries they regulate, (the original version of the capture theory) but by the "self-styled representative of the public interest who has succeeded so frequently in identifying his or her personal prejudices with the national well-being."[3] In a suggested additional reading, Senator Kennedy makes the very interesting observation that the regulatory agencies, rather than Congress, often wind up making social policy in an undemocratic way.[4] He wants to open up regulatory agency decision making to the public, and to include all affected constituencies in the decision-making process. This, of course, is reminiscent of the criticisms and proposed reforms of business decision making and, more than anything else, emphasizes the need to account for imper-

---

[2]Ralph Nader, Mark Green, and Joel Seligman, *Taming the Giant Corporation* (New York: W. W. Norton & Co., Inc., 1976).

[3]The "new style" regulatory agencies do not actually regulate specific industries. Environmental, safety, and health regulations cut across all industries in the economy. Thus, the social regulatory agencies are less subject to being captured by industry, and also have substantially broader power over the economy.

[4]Edward M. Kennedy, "Regulatory Reform: Striking A Balance," in *Reforming Regulation*, Eds. T. B. Clark, M. H. Kosters, and J. C. Miller, III (Washington, D. C.: American Enterprise Institute, 1980).

fections in political as well as economic instituions in the search for effective solutions to changing social priorities.

The reading by Arthur Okun (whose analysis of the trade-offs between ethics and efficiency were discussed in the Marc Plattner article in Chapter 7) suggests a need for a better mix of market and political controls over the nation's resources to achieve social goals more efficiently—to achieve them at less total cost to society. However, while favoring regulatory reform, Okun cautions against wholesale abandonment of existing regulations, especially in the safety, health, and environmental protection areas. Okun is primarily concerned here as elsewhere with the trade-offs between the efficiency values of the marketplace, and the humanitarian values of political democracy. Economists' strong preference for market decisions proceeds from their primary concern with efficiency, while those with a primary concern for equity and justice more often favor political over economic decision-making processes. Reflecting one of the primary ethical issues of Chapter 7, Okun argues that inequalities in income generated by an unregulated market system seriously obstruct the American ideal of equal opportunity. He concludes that we need ". . . to make the verdict of the market more humane and operations of our government more efficient." Under sufficiently competitive market conditions, Okun sees self-interest as an "engine of social welfare," in the spirit of Adam Smith and company. But he cautions that market limitations (monopoly, inequality, and harmful externalities) can make self-interest an obstacle to the achievement of social goals.

Weidenbaum and Okun both favor substantially replacing existing command-and-control regulations (product, performance, or technology standards) with market incentives (e.g., environmental taxes, pollution fees, marketable emissions rights, or subsidies for hiring the disadvantaged) to achieve social goals. Command-and-control regulations specify detailed rules and standards which business must meet. These rules often produce decidedly poor results. It they achieve their goals at all, they do so at substantially higher costs than necessary. Market incentives would leave greater decision-making control with business which, presumably, knows best how to achieve any goal (private or public) at minimum cost. We can be fully confident that self-interested businessmen will minimize the cost of meeting social goals if we allow them the flexibility to do so.

Command-and-control regulations are inefficient because they do not allow business the flexibility needed to allocate resources efficiently in complying with regulations, and do not provide incentives for the development of more effective regulatory compliance technologies. For example, U.S. motor vehicle emissions standards which require identical emissions reductions on every car are not cost-effective because they ignore differences in compliance costs among different cars, and prevent manufacturers from reducing emissions relatively more on vehicles where it is less costly to do so, and relatively less on vehicles where it is more costly to reduce emissions. The substitution of market incentives (e.g., emissions fees) for emissions standards would produce the same social result, but at less cost to society because manufacturers could allocate their resources to those vehicles where emissions abatement is most cost-effective.

The current regulatory approach also discourages long-range technological innovation because of the great risk of noncompliance (having to close down an entire operation), and because there are no market nor political rewards for exceeding the standards. The use of market incentives would encourage innovation by making it profitable (e.g., emissions reductions below the standards would either reduce the fees paid, or be banked, traded, or sold), and by making risk proportional to the degree of noncompliance (under the standards approach, a miss is as good as a mile).[5]

Greater use of market incentives also represents a response to social control loss, discussed in Chapter 1, resulting from the extensive amount of information regulatory agencies require to monitor and enforce command-and-control regulations. Market incentives internalize regulatory goals to the firm, largely eliminating the need for substantial information flows between the companies and regulatory agencies.

The heavy reliance upon command-and-control regulations also reflects government equity goals and, again, a strong political bias for the status quo. Emissions fess or taxes, for example, would apply to all pollution sources whereas standards can be applied selectively. The emission standards for *new* motor vehicles put the regulatory cost burden on higher-income, new car buyers whereas a gasoline tax would affect all drivers on the basis of miles driven (amount of pollution generated) rather than relative income. Thus, regulation, in some circumstances, may be designed to promote an equity goal at the expense of economic efficiency.

In other circumstances, we simply have the political bias for the status quo as succinctly described by Charles Schultze:

> The bias in pollution control is not so much in the law as in its execution. New investment has to meet stringent "new source performance standards." But when some community gets in trouble with pollution from its older steel plants, the EPA negotiates a compromise agreement with the firms involved. Being tough on old firms sometimes destroys identifiable existing jobs, while being tough on new investment means that potential jobs for unidentifiable people are lost. As a consequence, when the chips are down, "toughness" is reserved for the new, while the old is treated more gently.[6]

The economic efficiencies of market incentives, however, have encountered a host of ethical and political criticisms. For example, it is argued that environ-

---

[5]For additional analysis of the substitution of market incentives for command and control regulations, see Thomas G. Marx, "An Alternative Approach to Motor Vehicle Emissions Control," *Business Economics*, 17, no. 3 (May 1982), 17–22; and Bruce Yandle, "The Emerging Market in Air Pollution Rights:, *Regulation* (July–August 1978), pp. 21–29.

[6]Charles L. Schultze, "Industrial Policy: A Solution in Search of a Problem," *California Management Review*, 25 no. 4 (Summer 1983), 14.

mental taxes or pollution fees are a "license to pollute"; consumer and employee rights cannot be traded off for economic gains; and that it is immoral to place a dollar value on clean air, safe products, endangered species, or human life. Unfortunately, such trade-offs are unavoidable in a world of scarce resources. Those who argue that it is immoral to make such trade-offs are really saying that they wish to sacrifice any amount of alternative private and public goals necessary to achieve their preferred objectives. The trade-off is still made whether it is acknowledged or not. There is no free lunch, only who eats the meal and who picks up the tab.

Because of these inevitable trade-offs, Professor Weidenbaum, like most economists, is also a strong advocate of regulatory cost-benefit analysis. Cost-benefit analysis, like the substitution of economic incentives for command-and-control regulations, is an attempt to rely more on market controls rather than political controls in the regulatory area to improve resource allocation. Regulation should be carried to the point where its incremental cost and benefits are equal, and no further. This is the economist's formula for optimal private resource allocation, which, it is argued, applies equally to public allocative decisions. Caution is necessary, however, because of information biases encountered in regulatory cost-benefit analysis. A special concern is the fact that the cost data for the analysis come primarily from the regulated industry, which is not a disinterested observer. Indeed, neither the industries nor the regulatory agencies can be said to be impartial observers. The biased data problem can be a source of endless controversy, as is the case with proposed passive restraint requirements for automobiles. Auto manufacturers have estimated the cost of air bags at over $1,000 per car, while air bag proponents (including suppliers) have estimated the cost at about $200.[7] To resolve this long-standing issue, General Motors recently suggested that the Transportation Secretary retain independent consultants to study the cost of alternative passive restraint systems.[8]

Cost-benefit analysis comes in for its severest ethical criticism in life-saving situations where it requires placing a dollar value on human life. This issue, perhaps more than any other, illustrates the inextricable economic, moral, and sociopolitical conflict of values underlying business-society relationships. As the final reading by Thomas Marx notes, every decision affecting life-saving programs, implicitly or explicitly, carries with it an imputed value for the lives at risk since more lives could always be saved with additional expenditures. Society does not choose to preserve life at any cost. Doing so would require sacrificing the quality of life unacceptably. It is not simply a question of trading lives for dollars, but of trading longevity for the quality of life which can be improved through alternative uses of the resources needed to prolong life. Proponents of cost-benefit analysis argue that such explicit calculations can result

[7]Thomas G. Marx, "Conflicting Political and Economic Challenges In the United States Automobile Industry," *Journal of Contemporary Business,* 10, no. 3 (1981), pp. 1–13.

[8]"GM Urges New Study by the U.S. on the Cost of Air Bags for Cars," *The Wall Street Journal*, August 30, 1983.

in more rational decisions regarding the number of lives and the particular lives to be saved, and in more lives being saved for any given level of expenditures. However, these calculations also create political, moral, and social costs which must be factored into the cost-benefit formula.

Cost-benefit analysis in life-saving situations also surfaces the issue of free individual choice in, perhaps, its starkest form. Can individuals objectively assess the value of small reductions in the risk of premature death provided by public live-saving programs? Do they possess the necessary technical skills and psychological objectivity to do so? If not, individual preferences might have to be set aside in favor of collective choice. But what if the skills are present, but the commitment absent? Does the government have a paternal responsibility to set aside individual preferences for risk-taking? In these circumstances, government must balance its responsibility for protecting life with its responsibility for protecting individual civil liberties, the most basic of which is the right to choose. As stated by Thomas Jefferson, "The God who gave us life, gave us liberty at the same time. The hand of force may destroy but cannot disjoin them."

THE CHANGING IMPACTS OF GOVERNMENT REGULATION OF BUSINESS

Murray L. Weidenbaum

The rapid and pervasive expansion in government regulation of business which has been occurring in the United States in recent years is altering fundamentally the relation between business and government. To begin with, I suggest that the concept of a regulated industry has become archaic. We now live in an economy in which every industry is feeling the rising power of government regulation in each major aspect of its day-to-day operations. Virtually every company in the United States knows the impacts of a vast array of government involvement in its internal decision making.

If we could accurately measure the pervasiveness of government intervention, I doubt that we would find the economists' favorites—electric utilities and railroads—at the top of the list. More likely, we would encounter such giants of the manufacturing sector as automobile, aerospace, and chemical companies, with the oil industry and health services not too far behind. Because of the rapid proliferation of government regulatory activity in the past two decades, it is difficult to understand the totality of the process which is still under way. This presentation is an attempt to provide an overview.

The limitations of this paper should be noted. This is not an attempt to evaluate the worthiness of the regulatory programs themselves. Rather, the impacts are examined from the viewpoint of the business firm. The costs of business compliance with government regulation are a factor that properly enters any reasonable benefit/cost analysis of regulation. But surely it is only one factor among many that must be weighed in the policy process.

THE PERVASIVE IMPACTS
ON THE BUSINESS FIRM

It is hard to overestimate the rapid expansion and the great variety of government involvement in business now occurring in the United States. The major growth of governmental regulation is not in the traditional independent regulatory agencies, such as the Interstate Commerce Commission and the

Murray L. Weidenbaum, "The Changing Impacts of Government Regulation of Business," in *Public Policy and the Business Firm*, Proceedings of a Conference compiled by Rogene A. Buchholz (St. Louis: Center for the Study of American Business, Washington University, 1980), pp. 21–44. Reprinted with permission.

Federal Communications Commission. Rather, the expansion of government power over business is occurring by use of the operating bureaus of government—the Departments of Agriculture, Commerce, Energy, Health and Human Services, Interior, Justice, Labor, Transportation, Treasury, and via new operating units such as the Environmental Protection Agency. Table 9-1 shows that 85 percent of the budgets for federal regulation is assigned to social regulation and only 15 percent to the older forms of economic regulation.

A very substantial further expansion of regulation is in the government pipeline. Many of the laws passed in recent years are in the early growth stages of development. As the U.S. Council on Environmental Quality pointed out in a recent annual report, current estimates of the burden of regulation "do not yet include many costs associated with the hazardous waste section of the Resource Conservation and Recovery Act of 1976, the Toxic Substances Control Act of 1976, and 1977 Amendments to the Federal Water Pollution Control Act, and the 1977 Amendments to the Clean Air Act." For most of this legislation, the Council pointed out, EPA is still in the process of developing its final regulations, and the effects will not be felt until business and government begin to implement the regulations.

Similar patterns prevail in other areas. The Occupational Safety and Health Administration has recently issued a generic carcinogenic standard, which it has been estimated, will generate compliance costs greater than the total existing array of OSHA standards. The National Highway Traffic Safety Administration is pursuing mileage goals at a pace which will test the outer limits of the survival capacity of the relatively few American companies that still produce motor vehicles.

Indeed, when we attempt to look at the emerging business-government relationship from the business executive's viewpoint, we find a very considerable public presence in what historically have been private matters. No business, large or small, can operate without obeying a myriad of government restrictions and regulations. Entrepreneurial decisions fundamental to the business enterprise are increasingly becoming subject to governmental influence, review or control—decisions such as: What lines of business to go into? What products and services to produce? Which investments to finance? How to produce goods and services? Where to make them? How to market them? What prices to charge? What profit to keep?

Virtually every major department of the typical corporation in the United States has one or more counterparts in a government agency that controls or strongly influences its internal decision making. There is almost a "shadow" organization chart of public officials matching the organizational structure of each private company. For example, the scientists in corporate research laboratories now do much of their work to ensure that the products they develop are not rejected by lawyers in regulatory agencies. The engineers in manufacturing departments must make sure the equipment they specify meets the standards promulgated by Labor Department authorities. Marketing staffs must follow

TABLE 9-1 Expenditures on Federal Regulatory Activities (Fiscal Years, Millions of Dollars)

AREA OF REGULATION	1970	1971	1972	1973	1974	1975	1976	1977	1978	1979	(ESTIMATED) 1980	1981	% CHANGE 1970 to 1979	% OF 1981 BUDGET
Social Regulation														
Consumer Safety and Health............	$392	$593	$948	$1059	$1251	$1347	$1464	$1772	$2261	$2474	$2606	$2857	+531%	41%
Job Safety and Other Working Conditions......	62	104	124	227	310	379	447	492	544	642	742	800	+935%	12%
Environment and Energy..	85	146	493	585	759	967	1026	1047	1296	1517	1688	2217	+1685%	32%
Total Social Regulation..	539	843	1565	1871	2320	2693	2937	3311	4101	4633	5036	5874	+760%	85%
Economic Regulation														
Finance and Banking.....	106	123	134	142	158	186	211	240	273	296	294	352	+179%	5%
Industry-Specific Regulation............	125	151	166	140	203	220	251	286	297	318	377	384	+154%	5%
General Business........	96	105	120	133	153	169	199	225	245	271	316	327	+182%	5%
Total Economic Regulation	327	379	420	415	514	575	661	751	815	885	987	1063	+171%	15%
Grand Total...........	$866	$1222	$1985	$2286	$2834	$3268	$3598	$4062	$4916	$5518	$6023	$6937	+537%	100%
Annual Nominal Increase.		41%	62%	15%	24%	15%	10%	13%	21%	12%	9%	15%		
Annual GNP Deflator.....		5.1%	4.1%	5.8%	9.7%	9.6%	5.3%	5.5%	7.3%	8.9%	8.9%	8.8%		
GNP Deflator Index[1]....	100	105.1	109.4	115.7	127.0	139.2	146.5	154.6	165.9	180.7	196.7	214.0		
Total in 1970 $........	$866	$1163	$1814	$1976	$2231	$2348	$2456	$2627	$2963	$3054	$3062	$3242		
Annual Real % Increase..		34%	56%	9%	13%	5%	5%	7%	13%	3%	0%	6%		

Note: [1] GNP Deflator figures for years 1971-1977 are taken from Statistical Abstract of the United States, 1978. Figures for 1978-1981 are taken from the Budget of the United States Government, Fiscal Year 1981.

Source: Center for the Study of American Business

procedures established by government administrators in product safety agencies. The location of business facilities must conform with a variety of environmental statutes. The activities of personnel staffs are increasingly geared to meeting the standards of the various agencies concerned with employment conditions. Finance departments often bear the brunt of the rising paperwork burden imposed on business by government agencies.

In short, there simply are few aspects of business activities that escape some type of government review or influence. Moreover—and most important—the impacts of regulation go far beyond general requirements for corporate results; they increasingly permeate every facet of internal business operations.

Important internal adjustments are taking place in the structure and operation of the typical corporation. Each of the major business functions is undergoing an important transformation. These changes tend either to increase the overhead costs of doing business or to deflect management and employee attention from the conventional tasks of designing, developing, producing, and distributing new and better or cheaper goods and services. As Arthur F. Burns stated in his Frances Boyer lecture in December 1978, "As things stand, many corporate executives find so much of their energy is devoted to coping with regulatory problems that they cannot attend sufficiently to the creative part of their business. . . ."

The role of top management is undergoing a fundamental metamorphosis as it responds to the changing external environment. The outlook of key corporate executives is shifting from primary concern with conventional production and marketing decisions to coping with a host of external and often strange policy considerations, frequently motivated by groups with nonbusiness and non-economic priorities. Members of the senior management group may become as attuned to the desires of those new interests as to their traditional accountability to shareholders.

It is not surprising that numerous chief executives report that one-third or more of their time is now devoted to governmental and public policy matters—dealing with the many federal, state, and local regulations that affect the company, meeting with a wide variety of civic and special interest groups that make "demands" on the organization's resources, and increasingly participating in the public arena. Donald Rumsfeld, Chief Executive of a major pharmaceutical company and former Secretary of Defense, has described very personally the pervasiveness of government involvement in business:

When I get up in the morning as a businessman, I think a lot more about government than I do about our competition, because government is that much involved—whether it's HEW, IRS, SEC, FTC, FDA. I always understood the problem intellectually, but the specific inefficiencies that result from the government, injecting itself into practically every aspect of our business—that is something one can feel only by being here.

Some of the most fundamental impacts of governmental intervention are discernible in the research and development area, although the ramifications are likely to unfold only over a long period of time in the form of a reduced rate of product and process innovation. A rising share of corporate R&D budgets is being shifted to so-called defensive research, that is, to meeting the requirements of governmental regulatory agencies, rather than to designing products with greater customer appeal. The trend is most advanced in the automotive industry, where the head of General Motors' research laboratory has stated: "We've diverted a large share of our resources—sometimes up to half—into meeting government regulations instead of developing better materials, better manufacturing techniques, and better products. . . ." A similar trend is now occurring in the chemical industry, in response to a plethora of new laws and regulations, all ostensibly designed to yield a cleaner or safer environment. The government, via the regulatory process, is building what amounts to a "legal envelope" around existing technology. A former assistant administrator of the Environmental Protection Agency, Glenn E. Schweitzer, points out:

> Most research directors are clearly becoming more conservative in their approaches to new chemicals. They are not eager to become embraced in hassles with the regulatory agencies. . . .

The combined impacts of the rulings of EPA, OSHA, the Food and Drug Administration, and the Consumer Product Safety Commission are also altering major aspects of the manufacturing function of the typical American business firm. One result of the pressures for production processes to meet government environmental and safety requirements is that a major share of company investment—about one-tenth at the present time—is being devoted to these required social responsibilities rather than to increasing the capacity to produce higher quantities or an improved quality of material output, at least as conventionally measured. Coupled with the many factory closings due to regulation, the result of these socially-imposed requirements is a smaller productive capacity in the American economy than is generally realized.

Moreover, we cannot always assume that the loss of private productivity is offset by an improvement in some area of social concern. For example, Armco Steel Corporation was required to install special scrubbing equipment at one of its plants to reduce the emission of visible iron oxide dust. The scrubber does succeed in capturing 21.2 pounds per hour of the pollutant. However, it is run by a 1,020-horsepower electric motor. In producing the power for that motor, the electric utility's plant spews out 23.0 pounds per hour of sulfur and nitrogen oxides and other gaseous pollutants. Thus, even though Armco is meeting government regulations on visible emissions, the air is actually 1.8 pounds per hour dirtier because of the government's regulatory requirement.

Virtually every aspect of the marketing function of business is affected by government. Advertising and product warranties are now subject to increasing regulation by the Federal Trade Commission. Labeling and packaging is now regulated by the Federal Trade Commission, the Food and Drug Administration, the Consumer Product Safety Commission, and the Department of Agriculture. Motor vehicle producers must include mileage ratings in advertising; cigarettes must display statements about their probable link to cancer; appliances must be labeled according to energy usage; and processed foods must list ingredients in specified order. The most severe restrictions, however, relate to the increasing power of government agencies to refuse to permit the production of products not meeting their standards or requiring the recall of products already sold. The latter is a process which is often euphemistically referred to as "reverse distribution."

The primary thrust of many personnel departments has shifted from serving the staffing needs of their companies to meeting the requirements of and pressures from government agencies. Maintaining complete familiarity with applicable regulations, filling out agency forms, and preparing reports to the government literally have been elevated to major end products of this traditional corporate function. One astute observer of the Washington scene has pointed out the adverse albeit unintended impact of these regulatory activities: "It has become considerably more expensive to employ anyone."

It is finance departments that often bear the brunt of the almost insatiable demand for paperwork from government agencies. To an increasing extent, corporate finance units are reacting to external demands for information, rather than primarily meeting the corporation's own data requirements for internal planning, reporting, and control. This reflects the change in the focus of corporate decision making whereby a variety of outside organizations and considerations figure so actively.

Expansions in specialized staff operations often constitute the most direct company response to the widening role of government in business. Virtually every company is developing some capability to inform itself about and evaluate present and future government developments as they relate to its activities. Firms of substantial size generally maintain headquarters planning staffs and Washington offices, while smaller companies rely primarily on their trade associations and on Washington-based attorneys and consultants. In some cases, substantial changes are made in the corporate organizational structure. A major headquarters office on government relations may be established by a company, with direct ties to each of its operating departments, as well as offices in Washington and state capitals.

Professor Douglas North of the University of Washington contends that the key margin of decision making in our society today is access to government influence. As he describes the matter, the predictable result "is to shift the focus of the investment of resources into attempts to favorably influence the strategic government official or to prevent the enactment of governmental policies that will adversely affect the interest of groups." The point may be overstated. There are still many more opportunities for private undertakings. Moreover, the adverse public reaction to massive use of business resources in politics would, under present circumstances at least, be overwhelming. Nevertheless, North is indicating an important emerging development, especially in the case of the larger business organizations.

MEASURING THE EFFECTS
OF REGULATION

Let us take another look at the phenomenon of regulation. Government imposition of socially desirable requirements on business through the regulatory process may appear at first to be an inexpensive way of achieving national objectives. This practice would seem to represent no significant burden on the consumer. However, the public does not get a free or even a low-cost lunch when government imposes requirements on private industry. In large measure, the costs of government regulation show up in higher prices of the goods and services that consumers buy. These higher prices represent the "hidden tax" imposed on the public by government regulation.

First-Order Effects.   The phenomenon of the regulatory tax is most visible in automobile regulation. The newly produced automobile in the United States carries a load of equipment which the federal government has mandated must be installed, ranging from catalytic converters to heavier bumpers. All in all, there was approximately $666 in government-mandated safety and environmental control equipment in the typical 1978 passenger automobile. But examination of the visible costs, such as to the motorist, provides only the initial or "first-order" effects of government regulation.

Second-Order Effects.   It is the indirect or second-order effects that are truly huge—the various efforts involved in changing a company's way of doing business in order to comply with government directives. One indirect cost of regulation is the growing paperwork imposed on business firms: the expensive and time-consuming process of submitting reports, making applications, filling out questionnaires, and replying to orders and directives.

Government regulation can also have strongly adverse effects on employment. This fact has been demonstrated in the minimum wage area where teenagers increasingly have been priced out of labor markets. One study has shown that the 1966 increase in the statutory minimum wage resulted in teenage employment in the United States being 225,000 lower in 1972 than it otherwise would have been.

It is difficult, of course, to obtain an aggregate measure of the total cost involved in complying with governmental regulations. A pioneering effort along those lines was made at the Center for the Study of American Business at Washington University in St. Louis. We culled from the available literature the more reliable estimates of the costs of specific regulatory programs. Using a conservative procedure, we put the various dollar figures on a consistent basis and aggregated the results for 1976. The total annual cost of federal regulation was shown to be approximately $66 billion, consisting of $3 billion of taxpayer costs to operate the regulatory agencies and $63 billion (or twenty times as much) for business to comply with the regulations. Thus, on the average, each dollar that Congress appropriates for regulation tends to result in an additional $20 of costs imposed on the private sector of the economy.

If we apply the same multiplier of twenty (between the amounts budgeted for regulatory activities and the private cost of compliance) to the budget figures which are available for more recent years, we can come up with more current approximations of the private sector's cost of compliance. On that basis, the costs arising from federal regulation of business in the United States (both the expenses of the regulatory agencies themselves as well as the cost they induce in the private sector) come to a total of $121 billion in 1979, consisting of $6 billion of federal budget costs and approximately twenty times that amount in private sector expenses of compliance. That is a substantial hidden tax imposed by federal regulation, of about $500 per capita.

Third-Order Effects.   Yet, the most fundamental impacts of governmental intervention are what we can call the third-order or induced effects on the corporation. These are the actions that the firm takes to respond to the direct and indirect effects of regulation. These responses often include such negative actions as cutting back on research and development and on new capital formation because of the diversion of funds to meet government-mandated social requirements. The basic functioning of the business system is adversely affected by these cumulative impacts, notably in the reduced pace of innovation, the lessened ability to finance growth, and ultimately the weakening of the capability of the firm to perform its central role of producing goods and services for the consumer. These difficult-to-measure induced impacts may, in the long run, far outweigh the more measurable direct costs resulting from the imposition of government authority over private sector decision making.

For example, the government decision making process can have adverse effects on capital formation by introducing uncertainty about the future of regulations governing new processes and products. It is becoming increasingly difficult for American companies to move ahead with building any new energy facilities. A cogent example is furnished in the report by a task force of the President's Energy Resources Council dealing with the development of a new synthetic fuel industry.

The task force stated, for example, that a major uncertainty was the length of time that a project would be delayed pending the issuance of an environmental impact statement that would stand up in court. They noted that the cost of such delays—additional interim financing and further cost increases in labor and equipment—is an obvious potential hazard for any new project. The task force provided the following evaluation of the overall impact of government regulatory activity: "In summary, some of these requirements could easily hold up or permanently postpone any attempt to build and operate a synthetic fuels plant."

Consider the innovative product research and development that is not performed because corporate research and development budgets increasingly are being devoted to what is termed "defensive research." A number of companies report that they devote large and growing shares of their scientific resources to meeting regulatory requirements or avoiding running afoul of regulatory restrictions. One hidden cost of government regulation is a reduced rate of introduction of new products.

Where the impact of government is less dramatic, it may be no less profound. A significant but subtle bureaucratization occurs in the corporate activity that is undertaken. The Employee Retirement Income Security Act of 1974 (ERISA) has shifted much of the concern of the management of pension funds from maximizing the return on the contributions to following a more cautious approach of minimizing the likelihood that the fund managers will be criticized or sued for their investment decisions. It thus becomes safer, although not necessarily more desirable to the employees covered, for the pension managers to keep more detailed records of their deliberations, to hire more outside experts (so that the responsibility can be diluted), and to avoid innovative investments. The federal rules also tend to make the pension fund manager unwilling to invest in other than blue-chip stocks, thus depriving smaller, newer, and riskier enterprises of an important source of venture capital.

From such regulatory experiences, we can see that the nation is paying yet another price for the expansion of government power—the attentuation of the risk-bearing and entrepreneurial characteristics of the private enterprise system.

THE IMPLICATIONS
FOR ACADEMIC THINKING

It needs to be recognized that impetus for most of the expansion in government power over business is not being provided by the industries being regulated; generally they have shown minimum enthusiasm for EPA, OSHA, EEOC, ERISA, etc. If anything, they claim that the "benefits" to them of these regulations are negative. The pressures for the new style of regulation come, rather, from a variety of citizen groups concerned primarily with non-economic aspects of our national life—environmentalists, consumer groups, labor unions, and civil rights organizations.

To talk or write about the regulated industry "capturing" its regulators is, to put it kindly, a rather quaint way of viewing the fundamental shift in business decision making now taking place, the shift of power from private managers to public officials. Yet, the core of the economist's version of the "capture'' theory still holds—public policy tends to be dominated by the organized and compact pressure groups who attain their benefits at the expense of the more diffused and larger body of consumers. But the nature of those interest groups has changed in recent years. Rather than the railroad baron (a relatively easy target for attack), the villain of the piece often has become a self-styled representative of the public interest who has succeeded so frequently in identifying his or her personal prejudices with the national well-being. In contrast, the business firm, in performing the traditional middleman function, typically serves the unappreciated and involuntary role of proxy for the overall consumer interest.

The changing nature of regulation can be seen with reference to Figure 9-1. The vertical lines show the traditional relationship between the old-style of regulatory commission (the Interstate Commerce Commission, the Civil Aeronautics Board—while it is still in existence—etc.) and the specific industry that it regulates. However, the great bulk of the economy—the manufacturing, trade, and services sectors—is virtually exempt from that type of regulation.

In contrast, the horizontal lines show the newer breed of regulation—the EPA, OSHA, CPSC, etc. In the case of these relative newcomers to the bureaucracy, their jurisdictions extend to the great bulk of the private sector and at times to activities in the public sector itself. It is this far-ranging characteristic that makes it impractical for any single industry to dominate these regulatory activities in the manner of the traditional model.

Yet, in comparison to the older agencies oriented to specific industries, the newer regulators operate in a far narrower sphere. They are not concerned with the totality of a company or industry, but only with the limited segments of operations which fall under their jurisdiction. If there is any special interest

FIGURE 9-1   Variations in Federal Regulation of Business Industry or Sector of the Economy

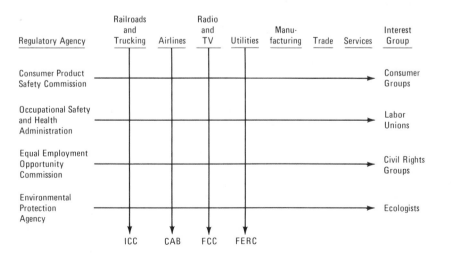

that may come to dominate such a functionally oriented agency, it is the one that is preoccupied with its specific task—ecologists, unions, civil rights groups, and consumer organizations.

Approaches to Regulatory Reform

Economists are prone to take measurements of economic phenomena. The numbers, of course, are not an end in themselves, but an input to decision makers. The measurement of the costs and related impacts that flow from government regulation is no esoteric matter. This information can be used in many ways. First of all, the cost data show the public and the government the economic importance that regulation has assumed, especially as measured by the large dollar of resources that are required to be devoted to meeting federal mandates.

Secondly, this information helps to shift the public dialogue onto new and higher ground. The pertinent policy questions are no longer, "Are you for or against clean air or safe products?" or other such absolutes. Increasingly, the public discussions are in terms of such less emotional and long-neglected questions as, "How well is the regulatory process working?" and, "Are there better ways of achieving the public's desires?"

Finally, the availability of information on the costs of regulation is an important step in reforming the regulatory process. The presence of the cost data inevitably leads to proposals for benefit/cost analyses, cost-effectiveness studies, risk-benefit evaluations, and similar analytical approaches to what in the past too often had been viewed as emotional issues. Hopefully, legislation reforming regulatory practices will mandate such analytical techniques and thus improve the cost—and benefit—data that are used in the regulatory process.

A new way of looking at the microeconomic effects of regulatory programs is needed. A parallel can be drawn to macroeconomic matters, where important and conflicting objectives are recognized and attempts to trade off are made (for example, as between economic growth and price stability). At the microeconomic level, it likewise is appropriate to reconcile the goals of specific government programs with national objectives. Environmental protection, product safety, and other regulatory efforts should be related to costs to the consumer, availability of new products, and employment. In part, this reconciliation can be made at the initial stages of the government process, when the president proposes and the Congress enacts new regulatory programs.

Benefit/cost analysis.   One device for broadening the horizons of government policymakers and administrators is the economic impact statement. Policymakers could be required to consider the costs (and other adverse effects) of their actions as well as the benefits. This is not a novel idea. In November 1974, then-President Gerald Ford instructed the federal agencies under his jurisdiction to examine the effects of the major regulatory actions on costs, productivity, employment, and other economic factors. President Carter has continued this effort, with some modifications.

This first step is subject to several shortcomings. Many of the key regulatory agencies—ranging from the Consumer Product Safety Commission to the Federal Communications Commission—are so-called "independent agencies," which are beyond the President's jurisdiction in these matters. Even in the case of the regulatory activities that come within presidential oversight, the agencies covered by the Executive Order are required only to examine the economic aspects of their actions; the weight they give to economic factors remains in their discretion—to the extent that Congressional statutes permit them to give any consideration to economic influences at all.

A broader approach is needed, one with a strong legislative mandate. In the fashion of the environmental impact statements (but without as much of the trivia), Congress should require each regulatory agency to assess the impact of its proposed actions on the society as a whole, and particularly on the economy. Much would depend on the "teeth" put into any required economic impact statement. Merely legislating the performance of some economic analysis by an unsympathetic regulator would serve little purpose beyond delaying the regulatory process and making it more costly. But limiting government regulation to those instances where the total benefits to society exceed the costs would be a major departure from current practice.

Government regulation should be carried to the point where the incremental costs equal the incremental benefits, and no further. Indeed, this is the basic criterion that is generally used to screen government investments in physical resources. Overregulation is not an emotional term. It is the economist's shorthand for regulation for which the costs exceed the benefits.

The critics of the analytical approach to evaluating government regulation tend to forget that benefit/cost analysis is a neutral concept. It gives as much weight to a dollar of benefits as to a dollar of costs. And in a broader sense, the estimation of benefits and costs need not be necessarily viewed in dollar terms. The costs as well as the benefits may at times properly be measured in terms of human life. For example, the Occupational Safety and Health Administration regulations may have a very high opportunity cost when they divert professional safety staffs of the companies from their traditional duty of training workers in safer procedures. The "benefits" of following the *Federal Register* may be far more illusory and surely fewer.

The implementation of benefit/cost analyses needs a great deal of attention. After all, a reluctant agency can merely go through the motions of studying the effects of its actions on the economy and proceed as it originally intended. An agency not directly involved in regulation—such as the General Accounting Office or the Office of Management and Budget—should set government-wide standards, concepts, and methods of performing economic evaluations of regulations, including the estimation of benefits and costs. The determination of the interest rates to be used in discounting future costs and benefits, for example, should not be a matter left to the judgment of the agency which is attempting to justify its own action. Where a dollar sign cannot be placed on the benefits, reliance can be placed on cost-effectiveness analysis, which is a search for least-cost solutions.

As a minimum, the Congress should endorse the kind of common sense that was embodied in the recent court decision which stopped OSHA from issuing new benzene regulations. The court's language is instructive: "Although the agency does not have to conduct an elaborate cost/benefit analysis . . . it does have to determine whether the benefits expected from the standards bear a reasonable relationship to the costs imposed by the standard."

The ability of the executive branch to change the basic regulatory system is limited. Each regulation is issued in accord with a law passed by Congress. Reform measures cannot simply be "proclaimed," they must be legislated. Many of the proposals to reform government regulation involve the "sunset" mechanism—the compulsory periodic review of each major regulatory program to determine whether it it worthwhile to continue it in the light of changing circumstances. This procedure would provide Congress with a formal opportunity to revise the underlying regulatory statutes or to determine that a given regulatory program is no longer needed and that the "sun" should be allowed to "set" on it. A benefit/cost analysis would provide a quantitative mechanism to aid in making those value judgments.

Budgeting as a management tool.   Greater attention should be given to the role of the budget process in managing regulation. In those cases where an agency's regulations generate more costs than benefits, the agency's budget for the coming year should be reduced, and perhaps vice versa. Because the appropriations for the regulatory agencies are small portions of the government's total budget, limited attention has been given to them in the budget process. In view of the large costs that they often impose on the society as a whole, greater attention is warranted to the reviews of their appropriation requests via a regulatory budget.

Changing attitudes toward regulation.   Fundamentally, regulatory reform is not a concern with technical measurements or administrative procedures. Rather, government decision makers need to take a very different view of the regulatory mechanism than they do now. Rather than relying on regulation to control in detail every facet of private behavior, the regulatory device needs to be seen as a powerful tool to be used reluctantly and with great care and discretion. Basically, it is attitudes that need to be changed. Experience with the job safety program provides a cogent example. Although the government's safety rules have resulted in billions of dollars in public and private outlays, the goal of a safer work environment has not been achieved.

A more satisfying answer to improving the effectiveness of government regulation of private activities requires a major change in the approach to regulation, and one not limited to the job safety program. Indeed, that program is used here merely as an illustration. If the objective of public policy is to reduce accidents, then public policy should focus directly on the reduction of accidents. Excessively detailed regulations are often merely a substitute—the normal bureaucratic substitute—for hard policy decisions.

Rather than placing emphasis on issuing citations to employers who fail to fill forms out correctly or who do not post the required notices, stress should be placed on the regulation of those employers with high and rising accident rates. Perhaps fines should be levied on those establishments with the worst safety records. As the accident rates decline toward some sensible standard, the fines could be reduced or eliminated. But the government should not be much concerned with the way a specific organization achieves a safer working environment. Some companies may find it more efficient to change work rules, others to buy new equipment, and still others to retrain workers. The making of this choice is precisely the kind of operational business decision making that government should avoid, but that now dominates many regulatory programs.

Alternatives to regulation.   The promulgation by government of rules and regulations restricting or prescribing private activity is not, of course, the only means of accomplishing public objectives. Codes of behavior adhered to on a voluntary basis can be effective. Moreover, government has available to it various powers other than the regulatory mechanism. Through its taxing authority, the government can provide strong signals to the market. Rather than promulgating detailed regulations governing allowable discharges into the nation's waterways, the government could levy substantial taxes on those discharges.

The use of taxation would be meant neither to punish polluters nor to give them a "license" to pollute. Rather, it would be using the price system to encourage producers and consumers to shift to less polluting ways of producing and consuming goods and services. Price incentives tend to force the environmental agencies to consider explicitly the cost of cleaning up pollution, while direct controls make it very easy to adopt extremely expensive if not unrealistic goals, such as zero discharge.

In the case of the traditional one-industry type of government regulation (as of airlines, trucking, and railroads), a greater role should be given to the competitive process and to market forces. Unlike the newer forms of regulation, the older forms of regulation are often mainly barriers to entry into a given industry, protecting existing firms from competition by potential new entrants. To date, none of the procedural reforms previously described has been enacted by the Congress. Perhaps the most significant single legislative action in the regulatory reform area in recent years was the law phasing out the Civil Aeronautics Board over a seven-year period.

With reference to consumer protection, an information strategy can provide a sensible alternative to compulsory product standards. For the many visible hazards that consumers voluntarily subject themselves to, the most important consideration in public policy is to improve the individual's knowledge of the risks involved rather than limit personal discretion. In their daily lives, citizens rarely opt for zero risk alternatives but trade off between speed and safety, for example.

The more widespread provision of information to consumers on potential hazards in various products may, in many circumstances, be far more effective than banning specific products or setting standards requiring expensive alterations in existing products. The information approach takes account of the great variety of consumer desires and capabilities. Interestingly enough, this approach often is favored in consumer surveys, although *not* by some of the most vehement representatives of the so-called public interest groups.

Any realistic appraisal of government regulation must acknowledge that important and positive benefits have resulted from many of the regulatory activities—less pollution, fewer product hazards, reducing job discrimination, and other socially desirable goals of our society. But the "externalities" generated by federal regulation do not justify governmental attempts to regulate every facet of private behavior. A reasonable approach to this problem requires great discrimination in sorting out the hazards that are important to regulate from the kinds of lesser hazards that can best be dealt with by the normal prudence of consumers, workers, and business firms.

The serious question, of course, is not whether government should deal with those market failures, but which techniques and approaches are most effective. To an eclectic economist, government regulation should be carried to the point where the incremental costs equal the incremental benefits, and no further. Those who are concerned that this approach justifies a considerable amount of government intervention in the economy may find some solace in the words of Friedrich von Hayek in his *Constitution of Liberty*:

> . . . a free market system does not exclude on principle . . . all regulations governing the techniques of production. . . . They will normally raise the cost of production, or what amounts to the same thing, reduce overall productivity. But if this effect on cost is fully taken into account and it is still thought worthwhile to incur the cost to achieve a given end, there is little more to be said about it. The appropriateness of such measures must be judged by comparing the overall costs with the gain; it cannot be conclusively determined by appeal to a general principle.

OUR BLEND OF DEMOCRACY AND CAPITALISM
Arthur M. Okun

In establishing a capitalistic democracy, the United States has built a society on two differing foundations. The capitalistic foundation attaches top priority to efficiency—operating through market incentives for getting the economic job done in the way that obtains the most useful output from our labor, capital, and natural resources. The democratic foundation, in contrast, emphasizes egalitarian and humanitarian values of cooperation, compassion, and fraternity.

Because our society rests on both of these foundations, we encounter creative tensions and uneasy compromises. As individuals, we attach different weights to the two sets of values, and we reach different conclusions on particular policy issues that define the scope of the marketplace and the scope of the political process. So, inevitably, we disagree and we debate. And the debates are often constructive. In the broad light of history, our nation has displayed remarkable ability to hammer out the needed compromises to balance the two value systems. We have generally avoided big polarizing ideological debates that might have rocked our institutional structure off its democratic and capitalistic foundations. Yet, the threat of polarization has always lurked in the background, and at times has become a clear and present danger.

The polarizers seem particularly hard at work today. By grasping at either the market or democratic value system and ignoring the other, one can readily indict our society for grave defects and grievous crimes. Those who march under the banner of democracy point to the ugly features of capitalism. Our economic contests are motivated by greed and allow the winners to ride roughshod over the losers. There is less nutrition on the tables of many of our poor than in the garbage pails of our rich. Our egalitarian political rights are sometimes contaminated by the power bought by money.

Those who wave the banner of market efficiency see a different set of specters: high tax rates that choke off initiatives; expensive government programs that fail to accomplish their goals; and a maze of regulations that impose large economic costs and that constrain individual liberty.

There is some truth in both of these diagnoses, but both are distorted and partial views that lead to fundamentally wrong and dangerous prescriptions. One would set laudable humanitarian targets and cripple the productive capability essential to hit those targets. The other would probably strengthen our productive capability, but in a manner that could destroy our social cohesion. Despite

Arthur M. Okun, "Our Blend of Democracy and Capitalism" *Across the Board* (March 1979), pp. 69–76. Reprinted with permission from *Across the Board*, published by the Conference Board, Incorporated, 845 Third Avenue, New York, N.Y., 10022.

the appeals of the polarizers, the vital center in American political and social attitudes typically prevails. These centripetal forces stem from the appreciation of the favorable features of both our capitalistic and egalitarian foundations, and from the recognition of their mutual limitations. I want to focus on some of the essential unifying principles that promote consensus—on the broadly shared ideas that help us to maintain our blend of democracy and capitalism.

THE MARKET AND THE GOVERNMENT NEED EACH OTHER

At bottom, most Americans know that our government and our private economy depend on each other. Many of the government's functions in promoting and regulating activity in the marketplace are not controversial; indeed, some are conducted so routinely that they tend to be taken for granted. And the same general, implicit acceptance applies to many of the contributions that our private economy makes to the vitality of our democracy. An explicit recognition and examination of these critical interdependencies helps to put into perspective the adversary relationships and the conflicting issues between the state and the market. The best antidote to polarization is the joint recognition that the pursuit of our human values depends on harnessing materialism and "greed," and that the conduct of our market activity relies on the restrictive legal powers of the state and its "bureaucracy."

Strikingly, the government needs the marketplace in two distinct ways—one as a support and one as a counterweight. As a support for government in a capitalistic system, the private economy is the goose that lays the golden eggs. The marketplace finances the public efforts to educate our youth, protect our shores, and aid our poor. The material resources required to fulfill the objectives of the public sector come from the tax base of a healthy, progressive, private economy.

As a counterweight, the decentralization of power inherent in a private enterprise economy supplies the limitation of government that is essential to the survival of democracy. It is a remarkable uniformity of history that a fully collectivized economy has never produced a single free election or one free press. And that uniformity is not merely an accident or a coincidence. A collectivized economy entrusts government officials with the command over all of society's productive resources. It is natural for them to exercise that enormous power, which allows them to deprive dissenters of their livelihoods and to keep the views of the opposition out of the press and off the airwaves. Why should they put up with democratic processes that threaten their own status and power?

On the other side, the marketplace depends critically on the government and on the exercise of its legal powers to make and enforce the rules of economic activity. The value of contracts, orders, promises to pay, and money itself stems from the power of politicians and bureaucrats to penalize the violators of the rules of the market game. Without the government as referee, there could be no game.

The property rights that are the essence of economic transactions are established and enforced by government in a way that necessarily restricts the actions of all citizens, not just those of the parties to a particular contract. Capitalism works only because the government authorizes the posting of millions of "keep-off" signs—not merely to thwart trespassing and theft in a narrow sense, but to establish ownership; to maintain trademarks, patents, franchises, and copyrights; and to clarify who has the right to sell any particular asset to someone else. The keep-off sign invokes the coercive power of the state: it prohibits some citizens from doing things that they would like to do. In enforcing such restraints, society draws a line between liberty and license, between legitimate access and trespass, between constructive and unconstructive freedoms. If our goals were truly maximum liberty in the sense of minimum coercion by the state, if we really wanted "laissez-faire," we would have a wasteland of chaos rather than a marketplace of economic activity.

Because we want an efficient and progressive economy, we ask the government to intervene in behalf of the marketplace in many ways. As a specific example, consider the joint stock corporation. Upon this inanimate entity the government has bestowed powers and rights normally reserved for human beings—and one outstanding right, eternal life, that is denied to all humans. This political invention has been enormously constructive; it has promoted the development of industrial capitalism and raised the living standards of the masses. The recognition of the corporation as a humaniod creation of the state illuminates a number of specific issues. Isn't it reasonable to expect corporate behavior to conform to our social norms? Is it obvious that a special tax on corporate income is inappropriate "double taxation"?

The government supplies private enterprise with physical and social as well as legal infrastructure. Obviously, public highways and airports have been essential to the development of our industries that manufacture and use motor vehicles and airplanes. Less obviously, public education has contributed much of the human capital employed in private business and has helped to establish a common language and common culture, which have been vital to American economic progress. In short, the successful private entrepreneurs and the successful public officials in our society owe each other a great deal.

THE COMPETITIVE MARKETPLACE IS GENERALLY THE BEST SYSTEM FOR ORGANIZING PRODUCTION

Every day for the past two centuries, our economy (as well as those of other advanced Western countries) has confirmed the validity of Adam Smith's theory of the "invisible hand." The competitive marketplace transmits signals to producers that reflect the values of consumers, offering profits for the production of those goods whose value to consumers exceeds their cost to producers. Profitability becomes the magnet that pulls resources into their most productive uses. Thus, in the competitive marketplace, economic self-interest becomes an engine of social welfare.

The market is such an impersonal, decentralized system that its contributions often go unnoticed. We take for granted that the goods we want are generally available in the stores; we don't award prizes for the continual decline in real costs of production generated by incentives for efficiency. And we do not applaud the flow of new products and new services that raise our standards of living.

Yet, when competition works, it creates values for the consumer far greater than the wealth it bestows on successful entrepreneurs and their financial backers. Clearly, an enormous social surplus was created by the dramatic transformation of energy use that Thomas Edison masterminded. We should all wish for a latter-day Edison who might do as much in the energy field today; and the whole country would gain even if he became 10 times as rich as the original Edison did.

To be sure, not every entrepreneurial success in the competitive marketplace represents a shared victory for the consumer. There are con games and rip-offs and deceptive marketing and fraudulent advertising. Because illegitimate business practices can poison the consumer's general confidence in the market, the government enhances the vitality of private enterprise when it can stamp out such practices. Beyond this range, we can all identify results of competitive marketing that seem regrettable and yet acceptable. In one class of such cases, firms operate not by serving the needs of consumers but by playing on their anxieties—for example, by making them worry about whether various parts of their bodies emit the "ideal" scent. I don't care for that smell in the marketplace, but I'd rather tolerate it than pass a law to deodorize it.

The main exceptions to the general presumption of competitive efficiency stem from the presence of vast economies of scale. Monopoly is the only way to capture the potential efficiencies of large-scale production in communication, in the transmission of gas and electricity, and in some areas of transportation. Yet, society simply cannot afford to entrust to a private monopolist the power to enforce scarcity and to collect a huge toll from the consuming public. So government intervention is required. The form of intervention chosen by the United States is different from that adopted by most other nations that regard themselves as capitalistic. They have generally nationalized these industries, while (with the exception of the Post Office) we have relied on the public-utility concept of regulation. The course we have chosen is complex, rigid, bureaucratic, and inelegant and imperfect in a hundred other dimensions. But when the defects of public-utility regulation are weighed against those of unfettered private monopoly and of nationalized operation, our strategy looks remarkably good.

Apart from economies of scale, all of the favorable implications of Smith's "invisible hand" depend on the presence of effective competition and are undermined by monopoly. For monopoly is the very antithesis of competition; it imposes a logic of scarcity rather than of productivity; it enforces rigidity rather than responsiveness, consumer exploitation rather than consumer sovereignty. Yet the very profit-seeking motives that make a competitive market tick also lead producers to try to eliminate competition by collusion, by blocking the entry of new competitors, or by gobbling up or squeezing out existing competitors. A century ago the United States wisely decided to outlaw the freedom to destroy competition, just as it had outlawed the freedom to break contracts and the freedom to trespass. For all its imperfections, our antitrust policy has served the marketplace well and has enhanced our long-run economic performance relative to that of other countries that tolerated collusion and cartelization.

Antitrust policy is confronted by a serious dilemma when monopoly emerges from a competitive race in which one firm has been so much more efficient than others that it grew rapidly in size and market share. Obviously, our regulatory policies should not penalize exceptionally good performance. But, also obviously, even when market share is obtained legitimately and constructively, it can subsequently be abused by practices that block the entry of competitors. In general, the bigness that comes from competitive success can be tolerated as long as new competitors have access to the market. To offer a particular example, I cannot share the concern of consumer groups in the Washington metropolitan area who decry the dominance of two food chains in the grocery business. With a huge number of competitors and extreme ease of entry, their large share of the market strikes me as a testimonial that they are doing something right rather than as a reason for suspecting that they are doing something wrong.

The government's role in preserving competition and curbing monopoly must adapt to changing developments in the marketplace. One important development in the past generation has been the vastly expanded scope of foreign trade. On the one hand, as long as this country pursues a liberal import policy, the presence of effective foreign competitors should permit some relaxation of antitrust policy. On the other hand, the emergence of multinational and state-sponsored corporations introduces new problems and issues. Monopoly has recently raised its ugly head in world markets through the formation of OPEC, the governmentally organized, multinational oil cartel. The world price of petroleum set by OPEC is a politically determined monopoly price, not a market-determined competitive price. Under these circumstances, the oil price in the United States is bound to be determined by government officials; the only question is how much of a role will be played by Sheiks and Shahs and how much by American Presidents and Members of Congress. A host of valid criticisms can be leveled against U.S. energy policy of recent years, but the charge that our government has interfered with a "free market" is not one of them. OPEC is not what Adam Smith had in mind! And that invalid charge can only weaken the strong case that can be made in favor of greater-profit incentives for U.S. energy production.

OUR DEMOCRACY SHOULD MITIGATE INHUMANE PENALTIES OF THE MARKET

The incentive system of the marketplace uses both a carrot and a stick, offering large rewards to the outstanding winners of the competitive race and imposing heavy penalties on some of the losers. The operation of the stick is often ugly—indeed, inhumane. The unmitigated verdict of the marketplace would condemn millions to deprivation. When our economy is depressed many skilled workers cannot find jobs. Even when our economy is prosperous there are not enough jobs to go around for the young and others who have not had the opportunity to develop skills. And there are never remunerative jobs for many with severe physical or emotonal handicaps. Small farmers are exposed to serious deprivation at the whim of nature. Technological progress exacts its toll; as we recognize Edison's contribution, we must also recognize that it indirectly destroyed the livelihoods of many owners, workers, and investors in the kerosene lamp business.

The cases of serious deprivation cannot be accepted passively or justified complacently in a democratic society. Even if the "losers" are all beaten in fair races, we must ask what is a fair penalty for a loser in a fair contest. And, unlike the citizenry of ancient Rome, we do not consider it fair to throw him to the lions!

In a fundamental sense, moreover, the contests *cannot* be fair over the longer run. Vast disparities in results—living standards, income, wealth—inevitably spawn serious inequalities in opportunity that represent arbitrary handicaps and head starts. In an unmodified market-dominated society, poverty becomes a vicious circle. The children of the poor are handicapped in many ways—their nutrition, their education, their ability to get funds to start businesses and buy homes, and their treatment on many of the hiring lines for both private and public jobs. Any commitment to a reasonable degree of equality of opportunity requires some correction of the glaring inequalities of results that an unmodified marketplace would decree.

Even more fundamental, poverty cannot be ignored by a society that proclaims democratic values, insisting upon the worth of all its citizens and the equality of their political and social rights. Our commitment to freedom of speech, equality of suffrage, and equality before the law rests on a broader com-mitment to human values that is violated by the persistence of economic misery in an affluent society. I cannot imagine how a sane society could decide deliber-ately to guarantee every citizen a fair trial before a judge and jury and at the same time permit some citizens to be condemned to death by the marketplace.

The record of history makes clear that capitalism has no built-in tenden-cy to correct the problem of deprivation and poverty, even though such a self-correcting tendency was predicted by many early advocates of a free market. In a particularly ringing passage, John Stuart Mill proclaimed that he would be a communist if he believed that deprivation and misery were inherent in capitalism. For nearly a century thereafter, America waited for Mill's implied prediction to come true. Then the Federal government began to intervene systematically to correct major areas of economic deprivation, producing evi-dence that Mill may indeed have been right. Deprivation and misery need not be inherent in a democratic capitalistic society *if* it uses its budgetary resources to eliminate them. Today, one-third of our Federal budget is devoted toward that end, largely through a reshuffle of progressive taxes into benefit payments. If not for that reshuffle, the number of Americans living below the poverty line would be at least double the actual figure.

This is an area of particularly vexing trade-offs. No objective dollar price tag can be placed on the benefit of reducing deprivation and misery; the valua-tion is a matter of individual judgment and ethical assessment, on which citi-zens will disagree. And with few exceptions, efforts to shift resources to the poor and disadvantaged have their costs. As I like to put it, society can trans-port money from rich to poor only in a leaky bucket. The leakages are of two distinct types: direct administrative and compliance costs of the tax and trans-fer programs; and indirect economic costs of the distortions of incentives to work, save, invest, and innovate. The cost of the leakages must be balanced against the benefits obtained from what is left in the bucket. A program can-not be damned just because it has some leakage, nor can it be blessed simply because something is left in the bucket. Correcting deprivation and preserving economic efficiency are both desirable goals, which unfortunately sometimes conflict with each other. Of necessity, we must live with compromises between the two. We cannot aid low-income groups to the point of destroying the incen-tive system of the market that marshals the effort and economic activity to fill the bucket. Nor can we tolerate kids with empty stomachs, adults selling ap-ples, and oldsters with begging cups in the name of a greater aggregate of real GNP. There are serious, legitimate grounds for debate and controversy among informed citizens about how much assistance should be provided and how it can be handled with minimum leakage. We need those constructive dialogues and debates, not ideological shouting matches, to formulate policies in this per-plexing and crucial area.

THE GOVERNMENT MUST LOOK AFTER
THE INTERESTS OF "THIRD PARTIES"

It is axiomatic that voluntary transactions in the marketplace are mutually advantageous to both the buyer and the seller—or else they would not be agreed upon by the two parties. But a transaction may harm some third parties whose interests are not reflected in the exchange decision. Only the political process can determine when the interests of third parties are sufficiently weighty to warrant protection.

In some cases the decision is easy. We would all object if our next-door neighbor sold his land for use as a garbage dump. And so zoning laws are enacted by which the government prevents indirect trespassing on our property rights. Similarly, we used the force of law to require vaccinations against smallpox, recognizing the strong interdependence of our exposure to contagious diseases. On the other hand, we do not require homeowners to grow pretty gardens nor do we ban activities that increase the likelihood of catching and spreading colds. In these cases our guide is not a general principle for or against government intervention, but rather a pragmatic weighing of costs and benefits. When the government does not intervene, the value of the unregulated activity—and the freedom to engage in it—is preserved for the participants, but the costs imposed on the nonparticipants are accepted. Regulation or intervention obviously reverses the balance sheet.

The complex environmental decisions that confront us today in the effort to control dirty air, dirty water, and unwarranted noise are similar to those posed by the nextdoor garbage dump or messy garden. Indeed, it is not obvious that the new problem areas are more vexing, in principle, than those of public health and urban land use that we now handle routinely. They evoke more controversy and divisiveness, in part because we have not shaken down our policies in these new areas, and in part because they are related to technological advances that are still fraught with uncertain consequences. Only recently has anyone had to worry about whether fluorocarbons should go into our air, whether nuclear power plants should be located in our suburbs, or supersonic transports should land at our airports. But, currently, those decisions have to be made—one way or the other. If they are left to the marketplace, the impact on third parties will be ignored and only the benefits and costs to producers and direct consumers will be reflected.

If, however, third party interests are considered through the political process, sometimes they will loom large enough to justify constraining the producers and consumers—thus increasing the scope of government regulation. If we continue to balance benefits and costs pragmatically, we must be prepared for some net increase in the range of third party protections as a by-product of technological advance. I do not welcome that prospect, but I believe it must be faced by improving regulation and collective rule-making, and not by disregarding the impact of technologically created interdependencies on the public at large.

GOVERNMENT ACTIONS MUST BE
SUBJECT TO THE TEST OF EFFICIENCY

I have emphasized that the competitive market gets its job done, but I have also identified some of its shortcomings—spawning monopoly, imposing inhumane penalties, and disregarding the interests of third parties. Any correction of those shortcomings must come through the operation of the government. But to score a net gain, the public sector must execute its tasks well. The government's cure must not be worse than the market's disease. In fact, Federal, state and local governments do carry out many of their traditional tasks with reasonable efficiency. But the record of performance on the additional tasks that the Federal government has undertaken in the 1960s and 1970s is disappointing.

One source of this disappointment was the veritable explosion of demands for new and complex services from the Federal government—improving neighborhoods, training the unskilled, cleaning up the air and the water, and rooting out discrimination and objectionable lobbying practices. Starting without a background of experience or a base of technological knowledge for the pursuit of these goals, we understandably encountered serious problems in trying to do so much so fast.

Some of the frustrations were not just a matter of the pace, but rather reflected the nature of the public sector and the political decision-making process. The public administrator cannot tune in to the market's signals; he does not get the guidance of the bottom line and the feedback of customer demand that make executives of competitive private firms perform efficiently.

Furthermore, the government suffers as a producer of services from a decision-making process designed to be painstaking and deliberate. Checks and balances of powers, and procedures to ensure due process and accountability are features of the political process for good reasons. They protect us against fraud, conspiracy, and capriciousness. But they also deprive us of flexibility, experimentation, and responsiveness in public administration, and they make political decision-making a costly process.

In addition, as Charles Schultze has explained in *The Public Use of Private Interest*, the pursuit of efficiency in the public sector is impeded by the rule of "we do no direct harm." The political process is generally intended to compensate losers and hence must avoid inflicting losses on citizens. But if it cannot inflict losses, it cannot follow those dictates of efficiency that require exercise of the stick (as well as the carrot). As Schultze notes insightfully, the rule was intended to protect citizens from arbitrary exercise of the powers of government, but it now works in practice mainly to extend the sphere of detailed state control. In order to avoid harming any minority, the government is busily adjudicating all kinds of competing claims, maintaining programs that have either failed or outlived their usefulness, and shunning the use of reward-and-penalty incentives.

A final impediment to efficiency is the greater weight attached to the interests of producers than to those of consumers, particularly in the Congress. In part, this imbalance is a corollary of "do no direct harm"; in part, it stems from the greater wealth and power of producer groups; mostly, in my judgment, it reflects an asymmetry of information and motivation. Every sugar producer knows how his Congressman votes on sugar legislation, while 200 million sugar consumers neither learn the facts nor care deeply enough to evaluate their Congressman on this particular dimension of performance. In principle, this imbalance can be rectified by organized consumer groups, but these generally find issues of health and safety more exciting than those of price supports, tariffs and quotas, restrictive labor practices, or tax shelters.

I doubt that there would be much serious disagreement with my assessment of the shortcomings of government performance in executing its new tasks or with my diagnosis of some of the contributing causes. But there is a highly significant controversy about the lessons to be learned from that record. Many conservatives see a confirmation of their convictions about how little the government can do constructively and a demonstration of the need to abandon some social goals. In contrast, to liberals and many centrists, the record is not only a keen disappointment but also a challenge for reforms to improve government efficiency. Those of us who take up that challenge realize that the tasks we set for government must be revised in light of what it can realistically accomplish at a price that the taxpayer can afford. Our past experience should allow us to kill some proposals on the drawing board, to nurture a selected few with more managerial effort, to follow up with a careful evaluation of results, and to phase out the failures.

I see a number of recent, significant, if still incipient, movements toward reform of government efficiency. First, the process by which priorities are weighed in the Congress has been changed for the better by the new budgetary process. With the establishment of the two Budget Committees and of the Congressional Budget Office and the institution of joint resolutions on the budget, our legislators now are facing up to the reality that the whole must equal the sum of the parts in the Federal budget. Second, "sunset" legislation is a promising procedure; if fully implemented, it should ensure that Federal programs do not keep going indefinitely by inertia. Third, despite the unrealism of the implied notion that every dollar of every program can be assessed anew each year, zero-base budgeting may bestow upon us 95-percent-base budgeting, which would be a genuine improvement over the traditional standard of 100 percent. Fourth, the newly enacted reform of the Federal civil service should strengthen carrot-and-stick incentives for our career public administrators.

Many policy-oriented researchers have advanced proposals for applying market-type incentives in public programs designed to correct the shortcomings of the market itself. Schultze's book developed that theme in detail and offered many examples of ways that rewards and penalties could be invoked to make private self-interest serve public purposes more effectively. These include the initiation of fees and subsidies for the curbing of pollution, greater dependence on liability insurance to meet safety and health objectives, the introduction of subsidies to private employers for hiring and training the disadvantaged and the handicapped. Currently, our elected officials are taking seriously proposals to invoke penalties or rewards through the tax system to help break the stubborn, ongoing wage-price spiral. This group of policy innovations calls for the government to apply the carrot-and-stick approach of the marketplace, as a partial substitute for the traditional command-and-control approach of the political process.

Efforts to improve performance in the public sector face many obstacles. Clearly, there is no built-in tendency for the government to become efficient any more than there is for the market to become humane. Indeed, I have noted several ways in which the political process creates inherent limitations on the efficiency of government as a producer of complex services. If we apply benefit-cost analysis rigorously, we will in many cases decide to tolerate market imperfections, rather than trying to correct them through public policy. But many tasks in our capitalistic democracy are going to be executed by government for better or for worse, and our common interest requires that they be done better.

Throughout this essay I have skipped over our serious and intriguing substantive economic problems—inflation and unemployment, poverty and productivity—in order to focus on the problem of polarization. In my judgment, that is a greater threat to our system than any of these substantive problems. And the character of that threat has changed. A decade ago it came mainly from the left—typified by the middle-class youths who emerged from their sports cars to condemn our society for its materialism and greed, for oppressing the masses, and for plundering the planet. Today, in my view, the main threat comes from the extreme right—from those who issue a blanket indictment against all government regulation and intervention, who redefine poverty as the "freedom to fail," and who basically ignore the values of democracy. The worst enemies of U.S. capitalism are a handful of its ardent proponents, who prescribe fiscal-monetary policies that would produce mass unemployment, regulatory policies that would flagrantly violate the legitimate interests of third parties, and "reforms" of government programs that would put vivid pictures of economic misery back on the front pages. The consequences of their program would swing the pendulum of public opinion far to the left. Because I do not believe that we will adopt their program, I expect capitalism to survive and thrive in the United States. And I expect us to continue to pursue the goals of democratic capitalism, striving to make the verdict of the market more humane and the operation of our government more efficient.

THE COST OF LIVING: LIFE,
LIBERTY, AND COST-BENEFIT ANALYSIS
Thomas G. Marx

More lives could always be saved if society spent more for kidney dialysis, cancer research, highway safety barriers, pollution controls, stringent plant safety standards, and the like. But society is not prepared to save lives at any cost—and it is also not prepared to admit this openly. Yet when decision makers choose not to fund particular life-saving programs, they are implicitly determining that the additional lives that would be saved are not worth the added cost. Because the amount of society's resources that can be allocated to such programs is limited, these implicit decisions affect the number of lives saved for any given level of expenditure. Because the population's exposure to risk varies by income, age, sex, race, occupation, and geographical location, these implicit decisions also have consequences for whose lives will or will not be saved.

The valuations of life implicit in the expenditures for different life-saving programs differ dramatically. For example, kidney dialysis treatment costs $270,000 per life saved; the Consumer Product Safety Commission's proposed lawn mower standards cost from $240,000 to $1,900,000 per life saved; and the Occupational Safety and Health Administration's coke oven emissions standard is estimated to cost from $4,500,000 to as much as $158,000,000 per life saved.[1] If society assigns an implicit value of $158,000,000 to a steelworker's life, why does it decline to provide mobile cardiac units, which could save a life for less than $2,000? Why do we spend millions of dollars to save one life on the factory floor when those same dollars could save numerous lives on the highway?

By explicitly addressing the consequences of life-saving decisions, cost-benefit analysis can significantly improve the effectiveness of life-saving programs. More lives would be saved, and decisions on whose lives are to be saved and how much money is to be allocated to life-saving programs would be more rational. The biggest challenge to cost-benefit analysis is the necessary explicit quantification of the value of the lives saved.

Two basic approaches, each with several variants, are used to quantify the value of life in cost-benefit analysis. The foregone-earnings method calculates the present value of lost future income resulting from premature death (excluding income generated by capital assets, which are unaffected by the death). The

"The Cost of Living: Life, Liberty, and Cost-Benefit Analysis," by Thomas G. Marx, is reprinted from *Policy Review*, no. 25 (Summer 1983), pp. 53–58. *Policy Review* is a publication of the Heritage Foundations, 214 Massachusetts Avenue N. E., Washington, D.C., 20002. Reprinted with permission.

[1]M. J. Bailey, *Reducing Risks to Life* (Washington, D.C.: American Enterprise Institute, 1980), p. 26.

rationale for this method is that it measures the loss of output to society from someone's premature death. The first variant of this approach measures society's loss as the reduction of net output, or production less the individual's consumption. The second variant focuses strictly on the individual, measuring only lost future consumption.

The net-output variant values only the individual's contribution to the rest of society, ignoring the fact that the individual is also a member of society who attaches some considerable value to living. In effect, this method views the individual as a machine, a slave whose only value is production for others. This method has not been used because of its unsavory policy implications: Calculations show that society would benefit from the early death of retirees, the handicapped, and others whose net future output is negative. The consumption variant recognizes the individual, but it also measures only his monetary losses and ignores the losses that his death would pose to other members of society.

ANOMALIES

The basic foregone-earnings approach has been used frequently, but despite its empirical manageability, it has serious limitations. It measures neither the value of a reduction in the risk of death provided by a life-saving program, nor the value of life in any meaningful sense. Life, after all, is not valued simply for the material goods and services it can produce. By ignoring all nonmonetary losses from premature death, this method greatly understates the value of life. The exclusive focus on monetary values also produces numerous anomalies with important policy implications—a rich man's life would be more highly valued than a poor man's, and a man's life would be worth more than a woman's. For example, studies show that the costs of saving a life by encouraging motorcycle helmet use are the same as those of a cervical cancer program—about $3,000. However, the benefits (that is, the value of the lives saved) figured on discounted future earnings are 55.6 times the cost for the motorcycle program and only 8.9 times the cost of the cervical cancer program.[2]

The second method of valuing lives is based more solidly on economic theory. A fundamental principle of economics is that the value of a good is determined by what individuals are willing to pay for it. An individual would, of course, pay any amount to prevent certain death. But what would he pay for a life-saving program that marginally reduced the statistical probability of premature death? The clear policy implication is that society should pay no more for a life-saving program than the benefiting individuals are willing to pay for it.

For example, if 5,000 individuals exposed to a risk were each willing to pay $200 for a live-saving program that reduced the probability of premature

[2]S. E. Rhoades, "How Much Should We Spend to Save a Life?" in *The Public Interest* (Spring 1978), p. 79.

death by 0.001, the government should fund this program only if its cost does not exceed $1,000,000 (5,000 x $200), which is what the program is worth to the individuals at risk as measured by their willingness to pay for it.

To this point, economists have been measuring only what individuals would pay for small reductions in the probability of premature death. In the aggregate, however, these individual decisions imply a value of life of $200,000, since the program will be funded only if its total cost doesn't exceed $1,000,000, or $200,000 per life saved. Society will not spend more than $200,000 to save the life of a member of this group.

The willingness-to-play calculation is conceptually straightforward. However, since these life-saving programs are not purchased in the market, individuals' willingness to pay for them must be inferred from market behavior or from survey data.

The converse of individuals' willingness to pay for small reductions in the risk of death is their willingness to accept compensation for small increases in the risk of death. And that can be determined from individual behavior in the job market, since employees are compensated for the disagreeable characteristics of their occupations, including the greater risk of death in hazardous jobs. Several studies have estimated the additional risks and compensation for employees in hazardous occupations from which willingness to pay for life-saving programs can be inferred.[3] For example, if the higher risk of death associated with the occupation is 0.002 and the additional compensation for this risk is $300, then society should not spend more than $150,000 ($300 ÷ 0.002) to save a life in this occupational group, since this is the amount the group itself is willing to accept.[4]

WHO BENEFITS?

A fundamentally different approach to estimating individuals' willingness to pay for reductions in the risk of death is based on direct surveys. For example, Jan Acton posed the following hypothetical question to a hundred Bostonians regarding ambulance services for 10,000 people: "In your area, there are about one hundred heart attacks per year. About forty of these persons die. With the heart attack program, only twenty of these people would die. How much would

[3]For example, R. Thaler and S. Rosen, "The Value of Saving a Life" in *Household Production and Consumption*, N. E. Terleckyj, Ed. (New York: National Bureau of Economic Research, 1976); and R. S. Smith, "Compensating Wage Differentials and Public Policy: A Review" in *Industrial and Labor Relatoins Review* (April 1979), pp. 339–351.

[4]A similar procedure for estimating individuals' willingness to pay for small reductions in risk from observations of market behavior is based on automobile seat belt use. The time and inconvenience costs of using seat belts are calculated and related to the reduction in risk from seat belt use. The cost individuals voluntarily incur to reduce the risk of death by using seat belts evidences their willingness to pay for small reductions in the risk of death. See G. Blomquist, "Value of Life Saving: Implications of Consumption Activity" in *Journal of Political Economy*, 87, No. 3 (1979), pp. 540–558.

you be willing to pay in taxes per year for the ambulance so that twenty lives could be saved in your community?''[5] The average response of $33 indicates that the value of this life-saving program to each individual is $16,500 (10,000 ÷ 20 × $33).

There are, however, several basic criticisms of valuing lives on the willingness-to-pay procedure. Its basic premise is that the beneficiaries of a government-funded program are better off, while those who bear the costs are, at least, not worse off, since in theory they could be compensated with the payments beneficiaries are willing to make. But for many life-saving programs there is no social transfer mechanism by which the beneficiaries of a life-saving program can actually be made to pay for it—despite their apparent willingness to do so. Therefore, those who bear the costs are worse off.[6]

For example, if chemical workers were willing to pay in aggregate $100,000,000 for reduced exposure to acrylonitrile and the cost of the reduction to society was only $90,000,000 dollars, willingness-to-pay criteria would sanction this life-saving program, since society could be reimbursed from the payments the chemical workers would be willing to make. Social welfare would be improved, since chemical workers would be better off while the rest of society would be at least as well off. However, because payments cannot actually be extracted from the chemical workers and the rest of society reimbursed, some members of society gain and others lose. Thus, no unambiguous statements can be made about improvements in social welfare.[7]

Another basic economic premise underlying the willingness-to-pay approach is that individual decisions ought to count. But opponents of cost-benefit analysis question whether individuals can assess the value of the reductions in risk of premature death provided by life-saving programs. Indeed, studies show that individuals systematically underestimate the likelihood of low-probability events.[8] The survey method in particular is criticized because the difficulty of valuing small reductions in risk is compounded by the hypothetical nature of the questions. Respondents who know that beneficiaries of the program will not bear the total cost might also overestimate or underestimate the

---

[5]S. E. Rhoades, *op. cit.*, p. 81.

[6]This, of course, is not a valid criticism when society in general benefits from the life-saving programs (e.g., medical research or improved national air-quality standards) so that there is no meaningful distinction between those who benefit and those who bear the cost. It should also be noted that the losses to those who bear the cost of the life-saving program are offset to some degree by their increased satisfaction from the reduction in the loss of other lives.

[7]Social welfare is measured against the criterion of Pareto Optimality. A distribution of resources is Pareto Optimal if no alternative distribution exists that would make at least one member of society better off without making another worse off. Nothing objective can be said about alternative distributions that benefit some members of society while making others worse off, since this involves interpersonal comparisons of utility.

[8]H. J. Otway, "The Quantification of Social Values," a paper presented at the symposium "Risk vs. Benefit Analysis: Solution or Dream," Los Alamos Scientific Laboratory, Los Alamos, N.M., February 1972; and H. Kunreuther, "Protection against Natural Hazards: A Lexicographic Approach," Discussion Paper No. 45, Fels Center of Government, University of Pennsylvania, 1974.

value of a life-saving activity, depending on the extent to which they would benefit from or bear the cost of that program.

Furthermore, say critics of the willingness-to-pay approach, the decisions
of individuals who voluntarily accept greater risks are not representative of
society's assessment of the value of life-saving programs. Individuals who
voluntarily accept greater risks may well be better able to cope with these risks,
or they may value their lives less. The approach thus ignores large segments
of the population who do not voluntarily take risky jobs.

The conceptual and empirical limitations to the various approaches to valuing lives have led critics to reject any use of explicit cost-benefit analysis for
evaluating life-saving programs. But economists, even though they disagree
about the best method, generally agree that all of the measures provide helpful
guideposts that would significantly improve existing decision-making procedures.
For example, Professor Zeckhauser concludes: "The search should be for significant insights, useful benchmarks and helpful guidelines, not unequivocal answers. Present procedures are sufficiently haphazard that even a much qualified
analytic approach can provide substantial benefits."[9]

THE MORAL QUESTIONS

The fundamental ethical criticism of explicit cost-benefit analysis is that it is
immoral to place a dollar value on human life. Critics of capitalism argue that
"human values are debased because people are goaded into placing market prices
on everything . . ."[10] To such critics, placing a dollar value on human life ex-
emplifies the immorality of the market system.

There is, however, a fundamental relationship underlying cost-benefit
analysis that is of mutual concern to economics and ethics.[11] Economics is concerned with the means of allocating scarce resources to achieve alternative private
and social ends. Ethics is concerned with the determination of right behavior.
There are two basic ethical approaches to making such a determination. Utilitarianism judges right behavior by the ends produced; deontology, the ethical
theory of moral duty, requires the means to be consistent with moral obligations. Bertrand Russell is undoubtedly correct when he states that in most circumstances both approaches are needed to determine what is right behavior:

---

[9]R. Zeckhauser, "Procedures for Valuing Lives" in *Public Policy*, 23, No. 4 (Fall 1975),
p. 462.

[10]T. Christoffel, D. Finkelhor, and D. Gilbarg, *Up against the American Myth* (New York:
Holt, Rinehart and Winston, 1970), p. 15.

[11]Two other approaches to the allocation of resources to life-saving programs essentially
deny this basic means-ends relationship and the consequent necessity for cost-benefit analysis. The
romantic approach denies the scarcity of resources (means) available to satisfy society's wants and
thus the need to choose among competing goals. The monotechnique method denies the existence
of competing social goals (ends) in advocating only the most technologically efficient alternatives
with little or no concern for cost.

In judging of conduct we find at the outset two widely divergent methods, of which one is advocated by some moralists, the other by others, while both are practiced by those who have no ethical theory. One of these methods, which is that advocated by utilitarians, judges the rightness of an act by relation to the goodness or fairness of its consequences. The other method, advocated by intuitionists, judges by the approval or disapproval of the moral sense or conscience. I believe that it is necessary to combine both theories in order to get a complete account of right and wrong. There is, I think, one sense in which a man does right when he does what will probably have the best consequences, and another in which he does right when he follows the dictates of his conscience, whatever the probable consequences may be.[12]

Within this means-ends context, it is clear that the ethical criticisms are against excessive reliance upon utilitarian justifications for cost-benefit analysis. The mistake of proponents of cost-benefit analysis is to emphasize the ends (efficient resource allocation) to the exclusion of deontological concerns for the means. If we could assess the moral implications of assigning dollar values to human life, we could determine whether improvements in allocative efficiency from cost-benefit analysis outweighed any offenses to human morality and dignity—what we may call demoralization costs. The circumstances that would be offensive include the following:

> If the lives at risk are identifiable individually or as a class. When used to value the lives of specific individuals rather than abstract, statistical lives, explicit cost-benefit analysis would deny the infinite value of life and also result in some lives being valued more highly than others, contradicting our fundamental belief that all persons are created equal.
>
> If there is a direct, predictable relationship between public expenditures and the loss of life due to an involuntarily incurred risk. By placing the individual's fate in the hands of society, explicit cost-benefit analysis here would unmistakably deny the infinite value of life.
>
> If the group at risk is economically or socially disadvantaged. People with pre-existing grievances are likely to perceive explicit cost-benefit analysis as calculated exploitation. Their fears would be compounded if analysis employed the foregone-earnings approach, which would assign them a lower value of life.

A failure to save known lives at risk because of cost considerations would be an admission that society is willing to sacrifice lives for dollars. Demoralization costs here would be intolerable. Imagine the moral impact on a society that witnessed the death of trapped mine workers because the cost of rescue exceeded the value of their lives or because it was determined that the resources could be more effectively used to broaden road shoulders on a busy highway.

In this and other, similar circumstances, such as air and sea disasters and kidney dialysis treatment, society is willing to allocate substantially more resources than it would allocate to programs that would save a greater number of unknown, statistical lives.

[12]Bertrand Russell, "The Elements of Ethics," in *Reading in Ethical Theory*, 2nd ed. W. Sellars and J. Hospers, Eds. (New Jersey: Prentice-Hall, 1970), pp. 9–10.

ALAS! POOR BOSWORTH!

When the risk is involuntarily assumed or very costly for the individual to avoid, as with workplace exposure to potential carcinogens or kidney disease, society's moral obligation to save lives is much greater than when the risks are voluntarily assumed, as in the case of lung cancer from smoking or a traffic accident from not wearing a seat belt. Cost-benefit analysis is not necessary in these latter circumstances because in assuming the known risk, the individuals themselves balanced benefits against costs. Society therefore does not have the same moral obligation to save those lives and, indeed, must weigh its responsibility for the safety of its members against its moral duty to preserve the individual's right to choose.

Both of those dimensions of demoralization costs—known identity of the victims and involuntarily incurred risk—are vividly illustrated by a fable spun by Steve Babson.[13] Babson strikingly reveals the moral turpitude of cost-benefit analysis with a supposed kidnapping of Barry Bosworth, former head of the Council on Wage and Price Stability and a proponent of cost-benefit analysis. Mr. Bosworth's kidnappers demand a $6,000,000 ransom. Unfortunately for Mr. Bosworth, that sum far exceeds his $1,400,000 discounted future earnings, the figure used by the council staff to value his life. Thus, "Our fable ends, and so, alas, does poor Bosworth."[14] Mr. Babson's point is that this fable illustrates what occurs routinely with the use of cost-benefit analysis to evaluate workplace safety standards, highway traffic safety, cancer research, kidney dialysis, or any other life-saving program.

Because of demoralization cost considerations, however, Mr. Bosworth would be saved. The identity of the victim is known, and the risks are completely involuntary and beyond his control. In such circumstances society is prepared to spend vast sums to save lives. Society, however, would not be prepared to spend such amounts to save Mr. Bosworth, and even less prepared to save statistical lives, from voluntarily assumed risks like smoking, careless driving, or mountain climbing.

The third instance that would generate large demoralization costs is if the people at risk are disadvantaged. A failure to allocate resources to sickle-cell anemia research, for example, would be unpalatable because of the economically disadvantaged status of blacks in addition to the known identity of the group (though not the individuals) and the involuntary nature of the risk.

Thus, demoralization cost considerations would weigh heavily against the use of explicit cost-benefit analysis to justify kidney dialysis programs, sickle-cell anemia research, and rescue operations, but they support its use for evaluating highway safety expenditures and treatment of smoking-related diseases. The recognition of demoralization costs thus provides a method for reconciling the

---

[13]S. Babson, "A Pound of Flesh" in *Technology Review* (November 1979), pp. 12–13.
[14]Ibid., p. 12.

fundamental means-ends conflict and a systematic basis for the eclectic use of cost-benefit analysis in life-saving situations.

ENTER POLITICS

The economic and moral conflicts over cost-benefit analysis in life-saving situations must be resolved through the political process. Political decision making differs from private decision making in several respects. The decisions affect the lives of others, they are binding on all, and they typically confer benefits on one group and costs on another. Since collective decisions must also reflect democratic pinciples of political equality, they must give greater weight to distributional justice than private market decisions, which emphasize economic efficiency. Because of these differences, society may not wish to utilize explicit cost-benefit analysis for public decision making. Professor Zeckhauser explains:

> Acceptance of the importance of process in life valuation has some discomforting implications, particularly for those who are trained to the use of analysis. We may find that we are spending $100,000 to save a life in one area, but sacrificing lives in others that could be saved for an expenditure of $10,000. The consequence is that with a reallocation of resources toward the latter area we could have both more lives and more money. Yet, if the decisions in the two areas were well accepted by the society, then it might be preferable not to change. Lives and dollars are sacrificed in return for more satisfaction with the way these decisions have been made.[15]

Economists may bemoan this trade-off, but given their acceptance of individual preferences elsewhere, they cannot object if society wishes to balance lives against satisfaction with the fairness and morality of the decision-making process as well as the cost of saving lives. Similar considerations of due process in the legal profession mitigate against the use of explicit cost-benefit analysis. Economists also quickly note, however, that since every life-saving decision carries with it an implicit valuation of life, explicit cost-benefit analysis is not inconsistent with accepted political values and decision-making processes. Robert Smith, for example, states: "It is more honest and useful to quantify these benefits explicitly than it is to pretend one is 'above' such a 'dollar-and-cents' approach and then value the benefits implicitly."[16]

Explicit cost-benefit analysis establishes the value of life in advance as a key variable in the decision. The outcome is then largely determined by the arithmetic. Implicit decision-making procedures are not based on such calculations. The decision makers are not aware of the implicit value assigned to the lives at risk until after the decision has been made: "The decision maker would

[15]R. Zeckhauser, *op. cit.*, p. 448.
[16]R. Smith, *The Occupational Safety and Health Act* (Washington, D.C.: American Enterprise Institute, 1976), pp. 36–37.

see himself as simply having made a deliberative judgment; the 'end effect' [cost-benefit] equivalency number did not play a causal role in the decision but at most merely reflects it.''[17] For example, the estimated cost (and implicit value) of $158,000,000 per life saved by coke emission standards or $625,000,000 per life saved by acrylonitrile standards did not enter into OSHA's evaluations of these programs.

MAKING SOCIETY SAFE

The same distinction exists for collective decisions based on individual willing-ness-to-pay calculations. An individual's willingness to pay for small reductions in the risk of premature death is also not based on explicit dollar estimates of the value of life. The value of life that these decisions imply is known only after the decisions have been made and aggregated. Thus, it can be reasonably argued that public decisions reflecting individuals' willingness to pay for reductions in risk are no more based on explicit dollars-and-cents estimates of the value of life than deliberative judgment procedures.

Because the allocation of resources to life-saving programs is decided by elected representatives, the private political costs and benefits to these decision makers also enter the debate. Explicit cost-benefit analysis has substantial costs for political decision makers when its use reduces their probability of reelec-tion by disgruntled (demoralized) voters. Politicians therefore eschew explicit cost-benefit analysis more than is justified by economic, demoralization cost, or process considerations. For example, Congress mandated that workplaces be "free of hazard" and specified "zero discharge" of pollutants into water-ways, not that water pollution be reduced until the marginal benefits equaled the incremental cost. Indeed, there is little mention of costs in any of the numerous regulations enacted throughout the 1970s.[18]

UNWARRANTED BIAS

Another political consideration is the role that private interest groups play. Be-cause the benefits and costs of life-saving programs fall on different sectors of society, private interest groups actively support programs from which they benefit regardless of total costs to society, while opposing other programs whose benefits exceed the costs. For example, the Oil and Chemical Workers Union has argued that "Congress mandated very specifically that the workplace should be free of hazards. It didn't say the workplace should be free from hazards

[17]S. Kelman, "Cost-Benefit Analysis, an Ethical Critique" in *Regulation* (January–February 1981), p. 40.

[18]W. Lilley III and J. C. Miller III, "The New Social Regulation" in *The Public Interest* (Spring 1977), p. 49.

only if the employer could afford it, or only if it wouldn't cost him too much money."[19] The United Steel Workers Union found it "despicable" that anyone should question coke-fume standards estimated to cost at least $4,500,000 per worker saved.[20]

Whether a life-saving program benefits the few while costing the many or vice versa, public policy is not likely to favor efficient allocation of resources. In the first instance—when benefits accrue to a small, identifiable group but costs are spread across society—the beneficiaries oppose explicit cost-benefit analysis. The general public tends to be indifferent to the cost of any particular life-saving program, even one that benefits the few, since when spread across society, the cost is small. Furthermore, the public is not easily organized for political action on such issues. Thus, there is unwarranted opposition and indifference to cost-benefit analysis.

In the second case—when society at large benefits from a life-saving program whose cost falls on a small group—those who bear the burden advocate explicit cost-benefit analysis, hoping to reduce their burden. The result here is a bias in favor of cost-benefit analysis.

A failure to reconcile significant differences in economic, moral, and political values has stymied progress toward more effective allocation of resources to life-saving programs. Proponents of explicit cost-benefit analysis have been slow to recognize the moral and political implications of their solution, and critics have been singularly unimpressed with allocative efficiency arguments. The predictable results have been, respectively, blanket endorsements and rejections of cost-benefit analysis. Cost-benefit analysis has become the rallying cry of regulatory reform; its critics see it as "the invention of those who do not wish to regulate, or to be regulated . . ."[21] Neither polar position is warranted.

Economic efficiency is a critical element in decisions when resources are inadequate to satisfy society's broad desires to protect life. However, the moral dimensions of life-saving decisions—the demoralization costs—are equally important. The methods for allocating resources must also preserve the social, moral, and political integrity of the collective decision-making process—concerns that must be distinguished from interest-group pressures.

ENDS AND MEANS

Progress toward more effective life-saving programs must be built upon greater recognition of the complex trade-offs of competing social values. Proponents of cost-benefit analysis cannot continue to exclude moral and political goals

[19]M. J. Bailey, *op. cit.*, p. 10.

[20]S. E. Rhoades, *op. cit.*, p. 75.

[21]B. K. Zimmerman, "Risk-Benefit Analysis: The Cop-Out of Governmental Regulation" in *Trial* (February 1978), p. 44.

from calculations of allocative efficiency. Opponents cannot push a life-saving agenda that ignores the economic consequences.

Professor Schultze explains why both are wrong. "Ends and means cannot and should not be separated. In the real world they are inextricably joined: we formulate our ends only as we debate the means of satisfying them. No electorate or politician can afford to turn over the crucial question of how social intervention is to be designed to supposedly apolitical experts."[22]

Ends and means, then, must be reconciled. Cost-benefit analysis can be neither advanced nor rejected as a general proposition. Each life-saving decision must give explicit consideration to both the ends sought and the means of achieving them. Gains in economic efficiency from explicit cost-benefit analysis must be weighed against demoralization costs and the social and moral acceptability of the decision. Only then will society benefit from more efficient allocation of resources to life-saving programs.

DISCUSSION QUESTIONS

1. What are the basic, minimum functions which government must preform in a private market economy?
2. Is government regulation of business generally excessive? In what areas should regulation be curtailed? Are there other areas where regulation should be expanded?
3. Is a third of a CEO's time too much to spend on public policy matters in today's society?
4. Would greater reliance on market-type incentives as opposed to command-and-control regulations improve regulatory effectiveness? What problems are encountered with the use of market-type incentives as a regulatory mechanism.
5. Should cost-benefit analysis be used to justify all regulations? Should the costs of regulations at least be calculated and made known to the public?
6. Professor Weidenbaum supports legislation making regulatory cost-benefit analysis mandatory. He states that cost-benefit analysis is a neutral concept that weighs a dollar of cost the same as a dollar of benefits. Others, however, caution against excessive reliance on cost-benefit analysis because of severe data limitations. Is cost-benefit analysis a neutral concept in actual practice?
7. Professor Weidenbaum suggests that voluntary industry codes of behavior may be effective alternatives to some regulations. Can society rely upon voluntary actions by the business sector to achieve social goals? Would such voluntary codes represent business acceptance of social responsibility or simply behavior consistent with businesses' best long-run interests?
8. Would a Corporate Federal Chartering Act create mutual obligations for business and its constituencies, or responsibilities for business and rights or entitlements for customers, employees, stockholders, and local communities? Would such an act create an ethical or political relationship between business and its constituencies?

[22]C. L. Schultze, "The Public Use of Private Interests" in *Regulation* (September–October 1977), p. 14.

9.   Should motorcycle drivers be required to wear safety helmets, or simply be informed of the risk of injury of driving without safety helmets? What factors might justify a mandatory safety helmet law?

10.   Is it immoral to place a dollar value on human life in making cost-benefit assessments of government regulations? Why would some economists consider it immoral not to place an explicit dollar value on human life when assessing government regulation?

ADDITIONAL READINGS

ARROW, K. J., "Two Cheers for Government Regulation," *Harper's* 262, no. 1570 (March 1981), 18–22.

BREYER, S., "Analyzing Regulatory Failure: Mismatches, Less Restrictive Alternatives and Reform," *Harvard Law Review*, 92, no. 3 (January 1979), 549–609.

COASE, RONALD H., "The Problems of Social Cost," *The Journal of Law and Economics*, 3 (October 1960), 1–44.

KELMAN, STEPHEN, "Cost-Benefit Analysis—An Ethical Critique," *Regulation*, 5, no. 1 (January–February 1981), 33–44.

KENNEDY, EDWARD, M. "Regulatory Reform: Striking a Balance," in *Reforming Regulation*, Eds. T. B. Clark, M. H. Kosters, and J. C. Miller, III, Washington, D.C.: American Enterprise Institute, 1980.

KIRKPATRICK, JEANE J., "Global Paternalism: The U.N. and the New International Regulatory Order," *Regulation* (January–February 1983), pp. 17–22.

KRISTOL, IRVING, "A Regulated Society?," *Regulation* (July–August 1977), pp. 12–13.

LILLY, WILLIAM, III, AND JAMES C. MILLER, III, "The New 'Social Regulation,' " *The Public Interest*, no. 47 (Spring 1977), 49–61.

MANNE, HENRY G., "The Parable of the Parking Lots," *The Public Interest*, no. 23 (Spring 1971), 10–15.

RUFF, LARRY E., "The Economic Common Sense of Pollution," *The Public Interest*, no. 19 (Spring 1970), 69–85.

SCHULTZE, CHARLES, L., "The Public Use of Private Interests," *Regulation* (September–October 1977), pp. 10–14.

CHAPTER 10
MANAGING CHANGING RELATIONSHIPS

The public affairs offices which sprang up in the 1970s in response to rapidly increasing social regulation of business are the most visible signs of business adapting its decision-making process to changing business-society relationships. Throughout the 1970s these offices attempted to mitigate the adverse effects of growing regulation upon their companies. For the future, they must shed this defensive mode for a more constructive posture. These offices are ideally situated to provide the corporate leadership needed to participate positively in the identification of critical social issues, the formulation of appropriate public policies, and the development of a broad social consensus on the appropriate role of modern business in a political democracy. Accomplishing these far-reaching goals will require a "vision" of the corporation and its role in society as Professor Post eloquently puts it:

> It should not be difficult for public affairs managers to think greatly of their function, for it is truly the frontier of modern management. I have no doubt that substantial progress will be made in further developing techniques and methods of public affairs management. But there is a need to think more broadly, as well as theoretically. Ultimately, public affairs professionals most possess and communicate a vision of the future that reflects a positive view of the role of the corporation within society.[1]

[1]James E. Post, "Public Affairs and Management Policies in the 1980s," *Public Affairs Review* (1980), p. 12.

In short, the challenge these offices face is the construction of new business-society relationships (relationships with stockholders, consumers, employees, communities, government, and other institutions) which rest solidly on the society's economic, moral, and political foundations.

If public affairs offices are to play this critical and pioneering role successfully, they will have to integrate public affairs issues into corporate decision making so that business strategies are in tune with the increasing global integration of economic and social demands. To date, public affairs offices have basically been Washington outposts, with the director of public affairs keeping track of new regulatory developments for the corporation. Professor Dickie's survey of corporate affairs offices in 400 corporations (90 percent of which have public affairs offices) reveals that public affairs offices have had more influence with government decision makers than with their own corporate policy decision makers. Their primary role has been to be the corporation's "eyes and ears" in Washington, and to communiate corporate concerns to Washington through business interest groups (e.g., The Business Roundtable), individual lobbying, and increasingly through political action committees.

For the future, public affairs offices must broaden their agenda to include all constituencies affected by corporate decision making, not just the federal government. As Professor Dickie notes: ". . . it is important that it [the corporate affairs office] also develop effective and multiple communications and interactions mechanisms with its other external stakeholders (community groups, employees, neighbors, customers and others)." The corporate affairs offices survey provided some evidence that this is already occurring.

In a suggested additional reading, Wallender and Lentz describe the greater complexity of the multinational public affairs function increasingly needed by large transnational corporations.[2] Different social constituencies and institutions, and relationships founded on different economic, moral, and sociopolitical theories confound businesses' interpretation of their role in foreign societies. Transnationals' experiences with marketing infant formula in less-developed countries, detailed in the following chapter, illustrate the complexity of the multinational public affairs effort.

The public affairs office must also help bring about some basic attitudinal changes among business policy decision makers. One of the most basic, and potentially most constructive, attitudinal changes required is for corporate decisions to be made in the context of broader social interests. Peter Drucker writes that Japanese leaders, especially business leaders, are ". . . expected to start out with the question 'What is good for the country?' rather than the question 'What is good for us, our institution, our members, and our constituents?' [3]

[2]H.W. Wallender, III, and A.B. Lentz, "Building the International Public Affairs Function," *Public Affairs Review,* 2 (1981).

[3]Peter F. Drucker, "Behind Japan's Success," *Harvard Business Review* (January–February 1981), p. 86. Copyright © 1981 by the President and Fellows of Harvard College; all rights reserved. Quoted with permission of the *Harvard Business Review.*

This is not to say that each constituency should not vigorously pursue its self-interest (and they do so in Japan), but it is to say that a disregard for broader social concerns by special interest groups is in no one's longer-run, self-interest. Drucker concludes: "Perhaps the Japanese model, under which both leaders and special interests derive their legitimacy from their stewardship of the national interest, might better serve the unavoidable pluralism of modern industrial society." [4]

The increasing integration of economic and social issues will require a new type of public policy business leadership for which the Japanese model may indeed be very useful. Professor Dunlop contends:

> The absence of effective leadership for the business community on many public policy questions—in consensus building and in dealing with other groups and governments—means that business enterprises forfeit almost entirely to politicians. The rapid expansion of government regulations in recent years and specifically government's penchant for rigid, bureaucratic "command and control" regulations, even when ineffective or counterproductive, have arisen in part from a lack of coherence and consensus within the business community about more constructive choices for achieving social purpose. [5]

The message from many quarters is the same. Business cannot thrive in a social vacuum. It is to its advantage, as well as society's, to help fill the social leadership void in a pluralist society. The public affairs office can play a leading role in identifying these broader national interests, and in helping formulate corporate policies consistent with these interests. But, in the future, business leaders will have to lead.

It is also essential to enlist the support of line managers for a truly effective public affairs program. Professor Sethi explains that public affairs has been primarily (exclusively?) a top management concern. Social concerns have not penetrated the domain of middle management decision making, especially operations management where the narrow focus of decision making is on profit-center performance. Middle managemenmt decisions, however, often have important social implications. Public affairs consciousness, therefore, must be present at all levels in the company. Professor Sethi recognizes that bringing about these changes throughout the corporation requires an extensive internal education program about the social consequences of business decisions, and a restructuring of internal reward systems to reinforce socially responsive decision making—two major challenges for the public affairs office. These operating profit centers are among the crowning achievements of the multidivisional corporate form which supplanted older functional organizations. Their narrow focus on and rewards for profitability are one of the primary sources of the

---

[4]*Ibid.*, p. 87. Quoted with permission of the *Harvard Business Review.*

[5]John T. Dunlop, "The Concerns: Business and Public Policy," *Harvard Business Review,* 57, no. 6 (November–December 1979), 100. Copyright © 1979 by the President and Fellows of Harvard College; all rights reserved. Quoted with permission of the *Harvard Business Review.*

multidivisional firm's superior performance. Making them socially responsive profit centers without sacrificing economic efficiency is a worthy challenge for top management, public affairs offices, and organizational specialists.

Finally, it is important to recognize that business competes in the market for ideas as surely as it competes in product markets, the labor market, and the market for corporate control. The development of the needed intellectual relationships with the rest of society is the unique province of the public affairs office which is responsible for communicating business policies to the public, and for bringing public views, issues, and concerns to the board room. Marina Whitman, vice president and chief economist for General Motors, interprets her job as an "economic bridge-builder" between General Motors and the rest of society:

> I interpret my role at General Motors as an ambassador for mutually beneficial exchange [of ideas] among the various elements of the total society of which General Motors is a part. . . . This role is becoming increasingly important with the growing complexity and interdependence among all aspects of society. There is virtually nothing General Motors does today that is not in some way affected by public policy.[6]

To bear the increasingly heavy and complex communications exchange necessary between business and society, these bridges will have to be constructed upon solid intellectual foundations.

[6]Marina v.N. Whitman, "Economics from Three Perspectives," *Business Economics*, 18, no. 1 (January 1983), 23.

PLAYING THE GOVERNMENT RELATIONS GAME: HOW COMPANIES MANAGE

Robert B. Dickie*[1]

In recent years industry after industry has recognized the importance of government policy in determining the shape of the playing fields on which businesses compete. Firms are increasingly learning how to make their case to government officials. In the 1960s and 1970s businesses were on the defensive. There is now evidence that businesses have advanced along a learning curve in handling their public affairs and government relations and that they will be much more effective, assertive, and self confident in the 1980s.

Indeed, the business community scored some remarkable successes in the 1980 elections and in the ensuing months. Pursuant to the President's promise to unshackle business from federal regulatory burdens, "regulatory relief" has been accorded to numerous industries. The steel industry expects to save millions of dollars annually by virtue of the postponement of noise abatement regulations. The auto industry was granted relaxed emission ceilings for heavy trucks and a delay in the requirement of seat belts that wrap around auto passengers automatically. In addition, Interior Secretary James Watts announced plans to speed up oil and gas leasing and to expedite strip mining proposals. The Association of Home Appliance Manufacturers anticipate that minimum efficiency standards for refrigerators, clothes dryers, air conditioners and other appliances will be dropped. Moreover, Congress approved faster tax writeoffs for the cost of new factories and equipment and was considering softening the rules against overseas payments. Indeed, some actions went so far as to precipitate complaints from businesses. Some oil executives feared that a speedup in oil and gas leasing would upset their capital spending plans, and the trucking industry resisted deregulation.[2]

In light of the importance of the changes, corporations were making unprecedented use of their government relations offices, and top executives have

Robert B. Dickie, "Playing the Government Relations Game: How Companies Manage," *Journal of Contemporary Business*, 10, no. 3 (1981). Reprinted with permission.

*Public affairs was defined to include "corporate external affairs" in the broadest sense. This would typically include media relations, government relations, community relations, and perhaps units dealing with specific interest groups. Only employee relations were not included in our definition.

[1]This article is based on research conducted with James E. Post, Edwin A. Murray, Jr., and John F. Mahon of Boston University.

[2]*Wall Street Journal*, July 16, 1981, p. 1.

been making considerable effort to influence government policy in a way favorable to their corporations. In doing this, they have been drawing on and using the organizational structures, contacts, offices and people which have been put in place over the past several years.

A STUDY OF HOW CORPORATIONS MANAGE PUBLIC AFFAIRS

The major structure used by most corporations has been the public affairs office. We have conducted a study of the public affairs function in American corporations. Public affairs departments have become an important new structural response designed to enhance communications between business firms and society. Despite their proliferation, relatively little was known about these offices, their functions, or their effectiveness.

Accordingly, we consulted published reports of the Conference Board, files and other information made available to us by the Foundation for Public Affairs, the Public Affairs Council, and the Public Relations Society of America. We then conducted several in-depth field studies, one function of which was to facilitate the development of a survey questionnaire designed to examine three areas. They were the management of government relations, the fit between public relations and corporate planning, and the impact of public affairs on management policy. The questionnaire was pre-tested, revised and sent to 1,000 large and medium sized companies from all sectors of American business.[3] Representatives of over 400 corporations completed the questionnaire, providing an excellent response rate of over 40 percent. This survey provides by far the largest data base ever assembled with regard to the management of external affairs in general and business-government relations in particular.[4]

The responses to the survey show that the vast majority (over 90 percent) of the companies have public affairs offices and that most of these were established since 1970. They also show that public affairs offices handle a broad range of functions, as shown in Table 10-1.

Clearly, government relations is among the most important functions, and the survey provided information and insights as to how this is handled.

[3]For more on our methodology, the reader is referred to: Edwin A. Murray, Jr., "The Corporate Public Affairs Function: Report on A Large Research Project," presented at AACSB Conference on Business Environment, Public Policy, University of Maryland, College Park, Maryland, July 14, 1981. Copy on file with the author and with the *Journal of Contemporary Business*.

[4]The questionnaire results are summarized in a report on Public Affairs Offices and Their Functions—Summary of Survey Responses, Public Affairs Research Group, School of Management, Boston University, March 1981.

Activity	Percentage of Respondents		
	Yes		No
Community Relations	84.9%		15.1%
Government Relations	84.2		15.8
Corporate Contributions	71.5		28.5
Media Relations	70.0		30.0
Stockholders Relations	48.5		51.5
Advertising	40.5		59.6
Consumer Affairs	38.5		61.5
Graphics	33.5		66.5
Institutional Investor Relations	33.5		66.5
Consumer Relations	23.8		76.2
Other	26.3		73.7

"Other" includes grass-roots lobbying and political action committees.

TABLE 10–1   Functions Handled by Public Affairs Offices

GOVERNMENT RELATIONS—INFLUENCING FEDERAL POLICY

Federal government relations is perhaps the most important area handled by public affairs offices, as 73 percent of the respondents maintain a significant involvement or presence in Washington. The type of Washington presence takes a number of forms. The most popular are trade associations (used by 68 percent of the respondents), frequent visits to Washington by senior executives (58 percent), and company offices in Washington (43 percent).

In recent years, there has been a proliferation of the means by which corporations—particularly large corporations—make their views heard in Washington. Executives have become less willing to rely on a single channel of communication. As a result they have been developing multiple mechanisms for dealing with Washington, allowing senior executives flexibility in deciding how to present the corporate position in Washington.

This is illustrated by the actions of a large bank. Traditionally it worked chiefly through its industry trade association and through a government relations specialist who handled not only federal but also state and local matters. While it continues to use its trade association from time to time, in recent years the industry has become more segmented in the way it views many legislative and regulatory proposals. As a result, the top officers are unwilling to rely as heavily as in the past on the trade association. In the past two or three years the bank has developed other ways of making its views known in Washington, working more frequently with ad hoc groups of other banks having parallel interests. It also comments directly on proposed legislation and regulation, even when its interests are not vitally at stake, in the belief that informed, thoughtful comment will enhance its credibility when an important issue is at stake. Also, the chairman and president are making more trips to Washington than ever before, now devoting the majority of their time to external affairs, including government relations. Although it does not now have a Washington office, the bank is considering opening one and has recently hired a second government relations specialist as well as a full time media relations professional. Thus, the top executives now have a number of alternatives among which they can choose for seeking to influence the federal government at either the legislative or regulatory level. Rather than being limited to one or two channels of communication, they have a variety of resources upon which they can draw, alone or in combination, depending on the circumstances.

The bank is not the exception but rather representative of an emerging pattern. Washington relations are increasingly handled on a professional basis and are consuming greater portions of top executives' time and attention. Companies are developing a broader range of abilities in handling these relations, no doubt reflecting the increasing importance to the private sector of federal policy.

One measure of the increasing prominence of Washington relations is that from 1975 to 1980, two thirds of all the Washington offices increased in size. Washington offices are generally fairly lean, as 93 percent of the companies reported having four or fewer professionals, although one Washington office has a professional staff of 50.

These Washington offices are supported by budgets which in 1979 ranged from $20,000 to $2 million per year, with a mean of about $250,000. Table 10-2 shows the budgeted level of expenditures.

In summary, the survey data shows that companies consider their Washington presence to be important and that they maintain that presence through trade associations, visits to Washington, and company offices in Washington. The latter are clearly growing in size and importance. One vice president for government relations stressed the importance of good relations

TABLE 10-2   Washington Office Budgets

BUDGET RANGE ($'000)	NUMBER OF COMPANIES	%	CUMULATIVE %
0 to 100	19	20.9	20.9
101 to 200	18	19.8	40.7
201 to 300	20	21.9	62.6
301 to 600	17	18.7	81.3
Greater than 600	17	18.7	100.0
	n = 91		

with the Congressional delegation and, in turn, with the Congressmen's respective political constituents, particularly in the headquarters' community. This particular company has generally enjoyed good relations with its Congressional delegation, chiefly as a result of the company's reputation as a constructive force in its community. This reputation enabled the company to find a more sympathetic ear in Washington than would otherwise have been the case.

Companies use a variety of activities to communicate their corporate policies, objectives and positions to the federal government. The most commonly used activity is regular correspondence (used by 89 percent of the respondents), lobbying (73 percent), and political action committees (70 percent). In ranking the importance of the various activities in influencing federal legislation, the respondents again ranked the same three activities at the top. For each activity we computed a mean rank on a one (lowest) through five (highest) scale of importance, which shows the average level of importance assigned by respondents to each activity. Table 10-3 sets forth the activities in descending order of importance.

As shown in Table 10-3, lobbying ranks considerably higher than all other ways of influencing federal legislation,[5] and PACs have considerable influence despite their youth. Our case studies confirm this. Although there were only eighty-nine PACs in 1974, the federal Election Law reforms of the mid-1970s led to an explosive growth of PACs since 1975, as shown in Table 10-4.

Thus, while PACs are a recent phenomenon, they are an important one,

TABLE 10-3   Perceived Importance of Government Relations Activities in Influencing Federal Legislation

	MEAN RANK*
Lobbying	4.4
Regular Correspondence	3.9
Political Action Committees	3.7
Employee Newsletters	3.3
Plant Visits	3.2
Issue Advertising	3.1
Economic Education Programs	2.9
Speakers' Bureaus	2.8

*Scale from 1 (low) to 5 (high).

[5] Not to be overlooked in the lobbying process is the influence of Congressional aides, on whom Congressmen often rely. The ten most influential forms of communication cited by legislative aides are, in order: spontaneous letters from constituents, telephone calls from constituents, the Congressional Research Service, articles in major daily newspapers, editorials in major daily newspapers, visits from constituents, articles in district daily newspapers, the Congressional Record, editorials in district daily newspapers and government publications. Orchestrated mail campaigns ranked 11th, according to a study conducted by the Institute for Government Public Information Research at American University. National Business, October 1981, p. 25.

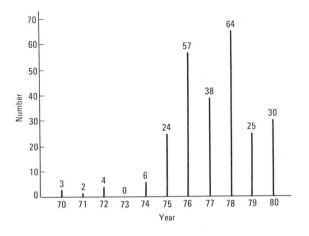

TABLE 10-4   Number of PACs Established Since 1970

being used by 70 percent of the companies. Their influence on the voting public was important in the 1980 elections and has sparked debate as to how powerful PACs will become.[6] Irrespective of the outcome of the debate, it is clear that PACs have become an important part of many corporate political strategists' repertoire.[7]

Broadly speaking, there are four types of tasks which those in the Washington office perform. *First,* they act as "eyes and ears," keeping senior management advised as to new developments, threats and opportunities. It is here that the Washington presence has its greatest influence (a mean rank of 4.0 on a 1 to 5 scale). The Washington presence has somewhat less influence in representing the company with regulatory agencies (a mean rank of 3.4) and in influencing proposed legislation (a mean rank of 3.3). *Second,* the Washington offices are occasionally expected to influence legislation or regulation after it is adopted. Here the influence was less (mean rank of 3.0), suggesting that once legislation or regulation has gone into effect the matter is turned over to other staff or line officers to handle compliance.

Executives at several of our research sites underscored the importance of the media in shaping public opinion and Congressional attitudes. Unfriendly treatment in the news media was thought to seriously impair corporate efforts to influence Washington policy, and vice versa. At least one executive spoke of the media as unfair at times, and others stressed the importance of managing relations with the media more actively. An increasing number of companies

---

[6]John R. Mulkern, Edward Handler, and Lawrence Godtfredson, "Corporate PACs as Fundraisers," *California Management Review*, Spring 1981, Vol. XXIII, No. 3, p. 49.

[7]See also Gerald D. Keim, "Foundations of a Political Strategy for Business," *California Management Review*, Spring 1981, Vol. XXIII, No. 3, p. 41.

have been hiring media relations specialists and providing training for top executives in handling such matters as television and radio interviews. Thus, Washington relations are part of the corporation's overall external affairs and are very much influenced by the corporation's public image, as shaped by the media.[8]

GOVERNMENT RELATIONS—INFLUENCING STATE AND LOCAL POLICY

Despite the tremendous importance of corporate relations with the federal government, the importance of state and local governments should not be overlooked. As one respondent observed, "In the 1980's, public affairs practitioners must realize that state and local government relations are as important as federal relations and they should revise their progams and strategies accordingly."

State and local governments have a tremendous impact on business through their taxing policies and legislation, particularly in certain industries such as insurance and utilities. Indeed most companies (60 percent) have one or more offices specifically designed to deal with state and local government relations, although most of these are staffed by five or fewer employees, and only 14 percent had budgets in excess of $500,000.

As in the case of handling relations with the federal government, regular correspondence and lobbying are the most popular means of communicating the corporate viewpoint to state and local government. They are considered by corporate management to be the most influential (lobbying having mean rank 4.3 and regular correspondence a mean rank of 3.7). Also like federal relations, companies reported using their state and local offices as eyes and ears to monitor developments at the state and local levels (mean rank 3.9) and only secondarily to represent the company to rule making agencies (mean rank 3.5) and to influence proposed legislation (mean rank 3.4).

INFLUENCE OF GOVERNMENT RELATIONS OFFICES ON CORPORATE POLICY

Importantly, government relations is not a one way street. Just as the corporation seeks to influence government policy, it is influenced by government policy. This occurs not only when laws and regulations are adopted, but also when they are being considered and when presidential or gubernatorial actions are being contemplated. Consequently, the corporate government relations offices often influence corporate policy.

---

[8]Keim, supra, "Foundations of a Political Strategy for Business," notes the distinction between public attitude and voting public attitude, suggesting that politicians—and therefore PACs—should focus more on the latter than the former.

Curiously, companies reported that even though the importance of their government relations offices had mean ranks of 3.3 to 3.5 in influencing proposed legislation and regulation at the federal and state and local levels, the same offices reported a mean influence on corporate policy of only 3.1. That is, these offices have more influence outside the organization than they did within it.

The influence of a government relations office on corporate policy varies depending upon the size of the company. In general, the larger the company (as measured by sales), the greater the influence of the Washington presence on corporate policy. We divided the reporting companies into five approximately equal groups according to size and then looked at the percentage of companies in each group which reported that their Washington office had an influence of 4 or 5 (on a 1 to 5 scale) on corporate policy. As Table 10-5 shows, the larger the company, the greater influence on corporate policy is likely to be.

We also found that the influence of the Washington presence on corporate policy is significantly affected by:

Regulation: Highly regulated companies (notably utilities) have more influential Washington presence than do other companies.

Consumer Product: The influence of the Washington presence on corporate policy of consumer product companies exceeds that of other companies.

Structure: Centralized companies' Washington presence is more influential than that of decentralized companies.

Planning System: Companies using long term (3–5 year) qualitative strategic planning have a more influential Washington presence than do companies using other types of planning systems.

In summary, the companies having the most influential Washington offices are the large companies in consumer oriented fields which are subject to

TABLE 10-5   Influence of Washington Presence on Corporate Policy

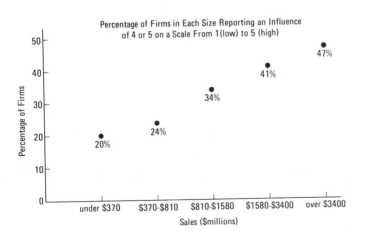

Percentage of Firms in Each Size Reporting an Influence of 4 or 5 on a Scale From 1(low) to 5 (high)

a high degree of regulation—defined to include price regulation. This is particularly true of companies using centralized structures and long range strategic planning of a qualitative nature. The case studies indicate that there are several reasons for this pattern. *First*, the large companies have the resources to develop sophisticated Washington offices; *second*, the high degree of regulation creates an incentive for them to do so; and *third*, being consumer oriented they must be particularly cognizant of their image and of the pressures to which elected officials will be subjected. In addition, *fourth*, the centralized structure lends itself more readily to the dissemination of the advice of the Washington office, whereas the diffusion of decentralized structures tend to dissipate staff efforts; *fifth*, the long term strategic planning places greater emphasis on qualitative inputs than do other planning systems. Other planning systems tend to be not only shorter term but also more confined to budgeting systems which merely extrapolate present trends into the future. A question which we have not answered is why utilities reported such a high degree of influence given that they are not regulated at the federal level and given that they are not large in comparison with other companies in the survey.

Virtually the same pattern was found with regard to state and local offices. The state and local government relations offices reporting the greater influence on corporate policy are large, highly regulated, consumer oriented, centralized, and using long range strategic planning.

The pattern with regard to size as a determinant of the influence of government relations offices was less clear at the state and local level than at the federal level. In general, the largest companies reported the greatest influence of their state and local offices on corporate policy. However, the smallest companies reported that their state and local offices had more effect on corporate policy than all but their largest counterparts. Table 10-6 shows the percentage of firms in each size category which reported that their state and local offices had an influence of 4 or 5 on corporate policy.

Again, the implication seems to be that the influence of state and local offices on corporate policy is greatest among the largest firms but is almost as great for the smallest firms. While there may be many explanations of this phenomenon, one of the most plausible is that the largest companies focus on state and local governments because they have the resources and sophistication with which to do it. The smaller companies focus their efforts on state and local governments because of the disproportionate influence that any particular state or local government may have on their business.

The case studies tended to confirm this interpretation. The smallest of the four companies, a utility (sales $150 million), devotes rather modest efforts to influencing Washington policy. On the other hand, the state government regulates the utility and top management devotes considerable effort to managing its relations with the regulatory body. At the other end of the spectrum, we studied a multinational chemical giant (sales $8 billion). Like the utility, energy costs and federal energy policy are tremendously important to it. Unlike the

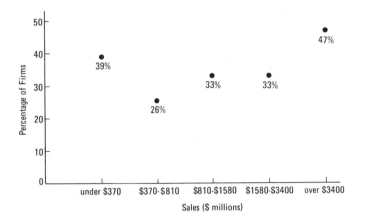

TABLE 10-6   Influence of State and Local Offices on Corporate Policy, Percentage of Firms in Each Size Reporting on Influence of 4 or 5 on a scale from 1 (low) to 5 (high)

utility, however, the chemical giant has a significant Washington presence, and apparently believes it could do something about federal energy policy. Not only does the company influence federal policy, but the Washington office has a considerable influence on corporate policy not only in the energy field but also in other areas, such as toxic waste. Nor is the chemical company too large to be concerned about state and local issues, for it has established regional offices specifically for the purpose of dealing with state and local governments and to manage emerging issues. This seems to suggest that the sophistication developed in dealing with Washington has been transferred to the offices handling state and local government relations.

DIRECTIONS FOR THE 1980s

Our survey asked corporations how they would characterize the public affairs movement of the 1970s and in what direction they see it moving in the 1980s.

More than 82 percent of the respondents gave optimistic responses. More perceived public affairs—including government relations—in the 1970s as responding to new pressures, chiefly from government, the major purpose being to fight immediate political battles by using lobbying and campaign contributions. The result was activity determined by individual issues as they came up, which companies handled on an ad hoc and reactive basis.

With regard to external affairs, the respondents reported that public affairs departments are becoming more mature and more realistic about what they can achieve. Companies will be more willing to work in coalitions—even with government—to achieve their objectives. The respondents expect companies to promote their own viewpoints more aggressively and less defensively in the 1980s in every forum, including government. Thus, public affairs will be more proactive by being more involved in formulating and implementing public policy.

Within the corporation, as public affairs in general—the government relations in particular—mature, the respondents expect that they will become more sophisticated and know more about their companies. As this happens, their credibility with top management will increase, and they will become more involved in day-to-day company decision making and corporate planning. Thus, their influence is thought by the respondents to be increasing both outside the corporation (including with government) and with top management.

Another way of looking at the responses described above concerning the 1970s and 1980s is that during the 1970s corporations were on the defensive. Feeling themselves to be under pressure from an increasingly hostile and unpredictable political environment, they responded by adding structure, among the most important of these being Washington offices and state and local government offices as well as public affairs offices. By 1981 these offices and their staffs have matured, with the result that they are more able to formulate strategies for themselves and their companies. That is, rather than putting out fires or copying other companies, they have developed the experience, sophistication and credibiltiy to develop strategies for the longer term, thus enabling themselves and top management to anticipate issues, take the initiative in framing issues, and generally find compatibility between the corporate and public objectives. Thus whereas strategy normally determines corporate structure, in the public affairs and government relations fields the initial corporate actions were structural, and the new structures are now shaping strategy. This is consistent with the finding that the influence of Washington offices, state and local government relations offices, and public affairs offices increases as companies use formal, long range strategic planning rather than planning of an informal, short term, or strictly budgetary nature.

While the business community has developed increasingly sophisticated and effective means of influencing federal, state and local government policy, it is important that it also develop effective and multiple communication and interaction mechanisms with its other external stakeholders (community groups, employees, neighbors, customers, and others). Our case studies and survey data indicate that this is indeed happening. To illustrate, the bank referred to earlier has developed a community development department with close ties to numerous communities and community groups, enabling it to identify and meet the banking needs of its community with more precision than had previously been the case. The larger computer firm which we studied has developed a highly sophisticated network of relationships to urban groups and is remarkably well equipped to monitor external developments. These cases are not aberrations; the survey data indicate that companies are generally becoming much more proactive and confident in handling external relations generally, as well as government relations in particular. The case studies and survey data suggest that a learning curve is at work and that companies have moved a significant distance along it in the past decade.

MOVING SOCIAL RESPONSIBILITY DOWN A PEG

S. Prakash Sethi

A survey of corporate leaders' public statements would reveal that most chief executives believe corporations have a social responsibility to community and society. And their statements are not just rhetorical; major corporations representing every segment of commerce and industry are involved in a wide variety of community activities.

Business's long-term commitment to an active social role also is evidenced by establishment of such units as corporate social responsibility offices, departments of social planning and analysis, public affairs or community affairs offices, and offices of social-issues management. Quite often these units are supervised by senior-level executives with direct access to the chief executive. Further, in many companies, boards of directors have set up directors' committees to oversee these functions.

Clearly, the recognition that business plays a vital role in American life, along with the realization that it cannot prosper and grow unless society also prospers and grows, has become one of top management's primary concerns.

Unfortunately, this concern for social responsibility has not yet penetrated the corporate hierarchy to line and middle management, especially managers who work in and are responsible for operating divisions in a company.

Talks with senior executives in a number of large companies reveal this to be a major problem, for without the cooperation and willing participation of line management, a corporation cannot deliver on its social contract. The result is erosion of its social legitimacy and, perhaps, greater public control and supervision of its activities. Integrating the notion of social involvement into the corporate ethos and making it part of a company's normal business operations is therefore a major challenge to top management.

LACK OF COMMITMENT

Corporations' failure to enlist the wholehearted support of line managers in social responsibility activites may reflect, in large part, senior management's inability to communicate effectively the rationale for and extent of its commitment. Lack of support also may reflect the absence of incentives that link rewards with social responsibility performance. It is important that we understand the reasons for the lack of line-management involvement and take steps to control and eliminate them.

Line executives have difficulty relating their roles and operational respon-

S. Prakash Sethi, "Moving Social Responsibility Down a Peg," *Public Relations Journal*, 38, no. 8 (August 1982), 25–27. Reprinted with permission.

sibilities to the corporation's social involvement. Lacking a clear-cut understanding of what the term implies, they tend to interpret it as a charitable gesture. Since line executives see themselves as "working in the trenches," they tend to assign a lower priority to directives on social issues. They view their jobs as primarily to insure that the economic activities of the company are carried out efficiently and profitably. To them, public relations and charitable contributions are strictly head-office concerns. Such attitudes are not limited to junior and middle-level managers, but also can be found among many senior managers.

Misunderstanding about what is meant by social responsibility is dangerous. The distinction must be made between a corporation's charitable activities and its involvement in the social arena. Although charitable contributions are important, their social impact is minuscule compared with that which a corporation can have as a consequence of its normal activities.

To say that a company must make a profit before it can do anything in the social arena is to focus on the wrong side of the equation. The most important issue for society is what the company does in the process of making profits rather than what it does with the profits once they have been earned. Thus, when we talk about the social responsibility of business, we are concerned with the social impact—both positive and negative—of everyday business activities.

Viewed in this light, line management clearly has a crucial role in a company's social impact. Top management may set overall policies, but it is the implementation that determines success or failure. A few examples will illustrate how line managements' decisions can have a significant impact on how a corporation is perceived by various publics.

New plants and other major capital investments can drastically change a community. A new plant brings in not only new jobs, but also new people, often different from those living in the community. A sudden increase in population may adversely affect the community's quality of life—services may be strained, pollution may increase to unacceptable levels, etc.

Examples of such impact are not hard to find. When Arco opened a new strip coal mine near Gillette, a quiet little town in Montana, it created a boom-town atmosphere that nearly wrecked the community. And Volkswagen's new auto assembly plant in Pennsylvania caused problems for the company because local people who were counting on jobs and training programs were disappointed when a significant number of skilled auto workers were imported from Detroit. Comparable upheavals occur when a company decides to close a plant, especially if it is the community's major employer.

Social impact of corporate activities is not limited to manufacturing or industrial companies. A decision to underwrite a loan for a manufacturing company with a strong reputation for union-busting tactics or for investment in South Africa could bring the underwriter firm significant adverse publicity and also might damage its good-corporate-citizen reputation with constituent groups. An insurance company's decision to invest in the construction of a major downtown hotel-office complex may be economically sound and may revitalize the downtown area. It also may hurt a lot of poor people if the need for new or widened roads through the inner city leads to demolition of their homes.

These consequences may be unintended, but their impact on the community is still significant. Quite often, the negative effects cause so much hostility and resentment that legal, political, and public pressure forces substantial modification or even abandonment of the projects after large sums have been spent. The point to remember is not that these projects should not have been undertaken, but that ignoring their social impact can significantly reduce the chances of success and add to immediate and long-term costs. An adverse public reaction can be extended to other programs and activities, so that the corporation winds up with a "bad guy" image.

FIRST-LINE DECISIONS

One point that often is poorly appreciated, if it is understood at all, is the extent to which even minor and often routine decisions taken at the lower levels of the corporate hierarchy can involve the entire corporation and have vast economic and social consequences.

For example, an insurance agent may decide not to write a homeowner's policy in a high-crime area, or a loan officer may deny a mortgage loan in a high-risk neighborhood. These decisions, although economically sound, also may reflect a racial or income bias, and can result in class-action suits, damages amounting to millions of dollars, and enactment of laws far more restrictive and damaging than a bad loan. Such adverse consequences might be avoided if local managers are sensitive to the impact their decisions have on the community, and base their decisions strictly on individual considerations rather than the general criteria of class or neighborhood prosperity or stability.

There are other instances where decisions at very low levels on, for example, hiring, firing and promotion can force companies into consent agreements with government agencies requiring drastic changes in record keeping and personnel policies.

PROGRAM STRATEGIES

A concerted effort must be made by all levels of management to educate employees about the importance of continually evaluating the social consequences of their activities. Such an information program needs constant reinforcement through communication, stimulation, and rewards to make social responsibility an integral part of employee thinking and thereby corporate philosophy. Following are some major strategies for an effective information program.

Long-range planning.   For major investment decisions, social-impact analysis should be integrated into long-range planning at the same time economic variables are being considered. Both affect profits and thus have a bearing on a company's investment strategy.

Social-accountability centers.   Social-impact analysis, to be credible, must be accompanied by after-the-fact evaluation. Impact of corporate decisions overlaps function areas, thus, evaluation should be carried out on a program basis. Further, accountability centers should be set up within or close to profit centers so that authority for administration and responsibility for analyses are easily delineated.

Performance measurement.   Performance measurement both at the individual and organizational-unit levels presents one of the most difficult problems in the social responsibility area. Despite decades of development work, we still do not have precise standards as do other organizational activities such as finance and accounting. What we do have are general standards that meet our specific needs in given situations. Thus, a modest approach to performance measurement is possible and likely to be quite productive.

Notion-of-learning curve.   Performance measurement is connected with performance goals. The initial step should be to set up broad goals and measurement criteria for individuals and organizational units in consultation with employees involved. No arbitrary quotas should be established—they are likely to cause resentment because employees might view them as unnecessary burdens.

Experience has shown that once employees are involved in the goal-setting process, desire to excel often drives them to exceed their goals. Moreover, we have found that the psychic satisfaction of doing good work often results in setting goals and targets that are far higher than management initially thought possible.

The notion-of-learning curve implies that, with experience, successive refinements in goal setting and performance evaluation are possible. To accomplish this, it is imperative that top management's social performance be consistent with its expectations of line managers. And top management must be willing to tolerate the mistakes of employees who are genuinely attempting to experiment with new approaches. Otherwise, innovation, boldness and learning are stifled.

REWARDS FOR EFFORTS

To develop organizational commitment for social-impact management, superior performance must be rewarded monetarily and by organizational recognition. Since we are talking about social impacts related to a line manager's everyday business activities, improved social performance means changes in the way activities have been traditionally performed, which entails risks, uncertainties and even trade-offs in the initial stages. Therefore, reward and recognition for successful implementation provides incentive.

DISCUSSION QUESTIONS

1. What types of changes in the mission, organization, and personnel of corporate public affairs offices will be necessary to transform these offices from defensive reactions against government regulation to positive, innovative efforts to help formulate effective public policy?
2. What types of chief executive officers will be required to run large corporations in the future? What type of education, training, skills, and experience will be required to enable these executives to perform effectively in an increasingly integrated economic and social society?
3. What are the basic functions of the public affairs office? How do these functions differ from the traditional activities of the "Washington Office?"
4. What special skills, training and experience will public affairs personnel require to deal effectively with public policy issues both within and outside the company?
5. Is a primary future role of public affairs offices to develop new business-society relationships? On what bases should these new relationships be formulated?
6. How can public affairs issues be integrated into corporate decision making? Can these issues be translated into "bottom line" numbers? How can better understanding of these issues be used to improve the effectiveness of the strategic planning process?
7. What special problems face the public affairs offices of large multinational companies? What type of skills and organization is needed to manage a multinational public affairs activity?
8. What is the value of the public affairs staff to the corporation?
9. Professor Sethi argues that corporate social responsibilities must also be the concern of operating managers if these programs are to be effective. What problems will be encountered in attempting to make operating managers perform in socially responsive ways? What does the experience with the subgoal pursuit problems of functionally organized business units suggest for the difficulty of making division managers exhibit greater social responsibility?
10. Should corporations publish an annual socioeconomic impact statement describing their total impact on society? What types of information should such a statement include?

ADDITIONAL READINGS

ASHLEY, WILLIAM C., "Strategic Planning: Impact of Public Policy and Environment," in *Public Policy and the Business Firm*, pp. 123–45. Conference proceeding compiled by Rogene A. Buchholz. St. Louis, Mo.: Center for the Study of American Business, Washington University, 1980.

DRUCKER, PETER. F., "Behind Japan's Success," *Harvard Business Review* (January–February 1981), pp. 83–90.

MACK, CHARLES S.,   "Ethics and Business Public Affairs," *Public Affairs Review* (1980), pp. 27–34.

POST, JAMES E.,   "Public Affairs and Management Policy in the 1980's," *Public Affairs Review* (1980), pp. 3–12.

STEINER, GEORGE A., HARRY KUNIN AND ELSA KUNIN,   "The New Class of Chief Executive Officers," *Long Range Planning*, 14, no. 4 (United Kingdom), (August 1981), 10–20.

STROUP, MARGARET,   "Issues Management," in *Public Policy in the Business Firm*, pp. 145–52. Conference proceedings compiled by Rogene A. Buchholz. St. Louis, Mo.: Center for the Study of American Business, Washington University, 1980.

TAVIS, LEE A., "Multinationals as Foreign Agents of Change in the Third World," *Business Horizons* (September–October 1983), pp. 2–6.

WALLENDER, H. W., III, AND A. b. LENTZ,   "Building the International Public Affairs Function," *Public Affairs Review*, 2 (1981), pp. 61–70.

CHAPTER 11

BUSINESS STRATEGIES AND SOCIAL RESPONSIBILITY

The two readings in this section were selected to illustrate how some companies have attempted to incorporate broader, moral, social and political issues into their internal planning process. These readings provide opportunities to apply many of the fundamental business-society concepts to concrete situations.

In the first reading, Sethi and Post analyze corporate responses to the infant formula controversy in less-developed countries. The "aggressive" promotion and marketing of infant formula in these countries, critics charge, leads to a reduction of more nutritious breast feeding, and to infant malnutrition and disease because infant formula is frequently diluted with impure water by low-income consumers in these countries. The marketing of infant formula, and a wide range of other consumer products, in less-developed countries raises even more complex social issues than in the U.S. The less-developed countries' lack of highly developed markets and informed consumers, upon which the efficiency and social legitimacy of private enterprise and free consumer choice rest, results in less market control over business decision-making authority and more concern for the individual's ability to evaluate alternative products. The fundamental issue of who is to exercise authority over the allocation of resources also becomes an issue of national sovereignty when a multinational corporation is operating in a foreign country.

The government apparatus for inspecting and regulating product quality and use in less-developed countries is also relatively primitive. The infant formula manfacturers, as well as many other producers of consumer goods for less-developed countries, are also large multinational companies owned and operated by stockholders and managers who perhaps espouse fundamentally

339

different ethical, cultural, and sociopolitical values from the MNCs' constituencies (customers, employees, and communities) in the less-developed countries where their products are marketed. For all these reasons, the fundamental economic, moral, and sociopolitical relationships between business and society may be substantially more complex in less-developed countries. The large multinational company may have to be prepared to accommodate very differing institutional relationships founded upon unfamiliar intellectual theories. Indeed, Richard Barovick refers to the infant formula controversy as ". . . a new *worldwide* war of ideas."[1]

These conditions may also create special ethical and social responsibilities for business. Is the producer responsible for product misuse in these circumstances? The more extreme asymmetry in the distribution of knowedge between manufacturer and consumer in less-developed countries may place a greater ethical responsibility on manufacturers to use their superior knowledge to promote the public welfare. Sethi and Post conclude: "We believe that the firm must be held responsible for any misadventure that arises as a consequence of the marketing efforts which it initiates. This does not serve to place on managers unlimited responsibility, but puts a premium on their efforts to foresee the public consequences of private action."

The authors interpret the companies' responses to the infant formula controversy within a corporate decision-making model which classifies business behavior according to its social legitimacy. Simple compliance with market demands and legal prescriptions (social obligation) obtains legitimacy from the law and from economics. But as Professor Boulding put it: "Economics is not enough." Legal and market compliance is necessary, but not sufficient to meet the rising demands of social legitimacy. Mitigating the adverse effects of business decisions on society (social responsibility) finds legitimacy in meeting social norms, values, and expectations. Finally, anticipating and preventing social problems (social responsiveness) acquires legitimacy by defining the corporation's proper role in society. The first mode captures the essence of the defensive posture most companies have assumed during the last decade, while the social responsiveness mode requires a "vision" of the positive role of business in society, and recognition of the need to formulate corporate policies consistent with broader national, indeed, international interests.

Anheuser-Busch's response to the public criticism of its adult soft drink illustrates more of the social responsiveness mode of decision making within the Sethi-Post framework. Anheuser-Busch resolved this issue by fundamentally changing its internal decision-making process prior to any threat of government intervention. Indeed, the government had approved the marketing of "Chelsea" as a soft drink, indicating that anticipating social issues is not a task which can be taken lightly. Though a soft drink by legal definition, Chelsea was pack-

[1] Richard L. Barovick, "Activism on a Global Scale," *Public Relations Journal* (June 1982), p. 29. (Emphasis added.)

aged and marketed as an adult beverage substitute for alcohol. The unforeseen social issue which emerged was that this product might precondition children, who could purchase Chelsea, towards alcohol consumption.

Anheuser-Busch sought to align its marketing of Chelsea with the broader social interests which were identified. Consumer and public interest representatives were brought into the internal decision-making process to assist in the identification, clarification, and resolution of the social issues raised by Chelsea. Jones noted that all parties benefited from this exercise in social responsiveness, but that: "The biggest winner, however, was the consumer who benefited from the exercise of democracy in the marketplace without footing the bill for governmental intervention." This experiment with a "mini-board of directors" for a specific social issue suggests one way to widen the board's social perspective without abandoning its traditional responsibility to stockholders.

PUBLIC CONSEQUENCES OF PRIVATE ACTION: THE MARKETING OF INFANT FORMULA IN LESS DEVELOPED COUNTRIES

S. Prakash Sethi and
James E. Post

The activities of multinational corporations (MNCs) in less developed countries (LDCs) have been justified on many grounds. The foremost among the benefits accruing to the less developed countries are the transfer of superior technology and management skills; the creation of jobs and of a broader economic base, and so, an improved standard of living; and the provision of superior goods at reasonable prices. These benefits are possible because multinational companies operate from a large base of resources, thereby exploiting economies of scale; and because MNC research and development facilities ensure superior products through in-house testing and quality control. The last point is quite critical in the case of a variety of products and services. The consumers in LDCs usually do not have either the information or necessary skills to evaluate the multitude of new products that are introduced by the MNCs. These products are quite often outside their cultural frame of reference, and so evaluation through comparisons with local products is not possible.

The small size of total demand makes it unattractive for more than one or two companies to compete for the market. Thus the role of competition in disciplining the suppliers and providing the consumers with necessary comparative information is limited. The LDCs are generally deficient in institutional mechanisms for inspection and regulation that would ensure the production and sale of products in a manner that serves public interest while also ensuring reasonable profits to the MNCs.

DIMENSION OF THE PROBLEM

At the aggregate level, the assumption that MNCs serve public interest in host countries through their activities in the private sector is largely supportable. However, at the level of the single company or industry in the single country, this is not necessarily so. Therefore, while a MNC may not have deliberately violated any laws, its normal activities in pursuit of self-interest may have untoward social consequences. All marketing activities of individual firms have second order effects that extend far beyond the boundaries of the parties to the immediate exchange. Quite often, these effects are far more pervasive in their collectivity than visualized by individual firms when making simple transactions. While the users of the product or those indirectly affected by it are unable to seek adequate remedy and relief in the marketplace, the cumulative effect of their dissatisfactions results in transferring the issue from the private to public domain. The solutions thus arrived at are essentially political in nature; are externally imposed; may be quite inflexible to accommodate specific peculiarities of the individual MNC operations; and, in the long run, may not be the optimal solutions for the MNCs or the LDCs involved.

This article focuses on a study of the infant formula foods by large MNCs in less developed countries to demonstrate the nature of second order effects of primary activities, the promotion and sale of infant formula foods. An analytical framework is presented within which one can compare the activities of different firms at different stages as the issue is gradually converted from private into public domain. Finally, some decision strategies are presented which companies might apply to similar situations. The basic questions raised are:

> To what extent should a firm be responsible for the undirected use of its products? Ought not the demand for a product the marketing of which is legal be the ultimate count in the MNC's decision to undertake its manufacture and sale?
>
> Under what circumstances should a corporation exercise self-restraint in advertising? Does the corporation have an obligation to promote only those products which it knows will be used correctly? Should a competitor's successful manufacture and promotion of a product influence a company to enter the market and utilize similar tactics?
>
> The operation of the market economy assures that the second order effects of a firm's activities are in the public domain and so must be handled by government agencies, leaving individual firms to pursue their self-interest unfettered by external considerations. Is it feasible or desirable for a MNC to assume a posture that is primarily market-oriented? What role can the LDC government be expected to play in this area? Should there be a government-directed choice of products a private corporation could manufacture? Finally, once a private market-oriented issue gets into the public domain, what changes should MNCs make to assuage society's demands?

INFANT FORMULA FOODS: THE INDUSTRY

Infant formula food was developed in the early 1920s as an alternative to breast-feeding. Sales rose sharply after World War II, and hit a peak in the late 1950s, following the 4.3 million births in 1957.[1] However, birth rates began declining

---

[1] Robert J. Ledogar, *U.S. Food and Drug Multinationals in Latin America: Hungry for Profits* (New York: IDOC, North America, Inc., 1975), p. 128.

in the 1960s, and by 1974 the annual number of births had declined to 3.1 million. The low birth rate caused a steep downturn in baby formula food sales.

The major U.S. and foreign companies engaged in the manufacture and marketing of infant formulas include Abbott Laboratories, which produces *Similac* and *Isomil* infant formulas through its Ross Laboratories division; American Home Products, which produces *SMA*, *S26*, and *Nursoy* infant formulas through its Wyeth Laboratories; Bristol-Myers, which produces *Enfamil*, *Olac*, and *Prosobee* through its Mead Johnson Division; Nestlé Alimentana, S.A., a Swiss multinational; and Unigate, a British firm. In their search for business, these companies began developing markets in third world countries, where population was still expanding, while baby food markets in developed countries were leveling off.

The international market for infant formula grew rapidly during the post-World War II era. Although a number of food companies had sold breast-milk substitutes in western Europe before that time, many of these products, made of evaporated milk or powdered milk, were not nutritionally equivalent to human milk, as are formulas. As prosperity returned to Europe and multinational firms expanded operations in Africa, South America and the Far East, infant formula became the "food of choice" for the children of expatriot Americans and western Europeans.

The large number of wealthy and middle-class persons able to afford infant formula in the U.S. and Europe made mass distribution and promotion of such products a widespread and acceptable phenomenon. In Africa, South America, and the Far East, however, the number of wealthy customers was fewer, and the size of the middle class was notably smaller. Local distributors were often used as a means of distributing the product. In an effort to expand sales, distributors, and sometimes the manufacturers themselves, began to promote the infant formula to broad segments of the population. This promotion reached the poor and those only marginally able to afford the product in less developed nations and produced the infant formula controversy.

Industry orientation.   Producers of infant formula products have two basic orientations which reflect the industry's historical approaches to product development. In the United States, the principal sellers of infant formula were founded after medical researchers produced an infant food substitute for mother's milk. By the late 1920s, Ross Laboratories, Mead Johnson, and Simulated Milk Adaptation (SMA) were in the business of producing and selling humanized infant formula. Through mergers and acquisitions, these firms eventually became part of large integrated pharmaceutical firms. SMA was acquired by Wyeth which in turn was acquired by American Home Products. Ross was merged with Abbott Laboratories, and Mead Johnson was acquired by Bristol-Myers. During the 1960s, a number of special "sick baby" formulas were produced by these companies for children with special dietary and health requirements. While the "sick baby" segment of the market is insignificant in comparison to the "well baby" segment (perhaps 2 percent of total sales volume), the existence of such specialized products is attributable to the pharmaceutical orientation of one segment of the industry and the research emphasis of both segments.

The second orientation in the industry is that of a food processor, and is characteristic of such firms as Nestlé and Borden. Both began in the sweetened and condensed milk business in the 1860s. Through the early decades of the 1900s, new uses were found for the canned milk products which Nestlé sold in Europe and Borden sold in the United States: one use to which they were put was infant feeding. This market segment expanded, but as medical research indicated that humanized infant formulas were nutritionally superior to canned milk for newborns, the food companies sought to retain their share of the infant food market by introducing infant formula products that were either developed internally (Nestlé as early as the 1920s), or whose rights were purchased from others (Borden in 1950s). The approach to the market of these firms was similar to that of other food companies. Sales were generated through heavy advertising, with a special reliance on mass media as newspapers, radio, and television. Brand identification was cultivated through advertising, with price sensitivity the key to preserving brand loyalty.

Business strategy.   After intense competitive battles, Ross Laboratories and Mead Johnson emerged as the winners in the United States market. By the 1960s, the two firms commanded approximately 90 percent of the domestic infant formula business (Ross's *Similac* 55 percent, Mead Johnson's *Enfamil* about 35 percent). So entrenched were these sellers in the domestic market that Nestlé, the acknowledged worldwide industry leader with 50 percent of the market, never attempted to penetrate the U.S. market.

With the leveling off in the U.S. birth rate in the 1960s, both Ross and Mead Johnson began to look outside the U.S. for major growth opportunities. This effort led Ross to industrialized nations with higher disposable income and prospects for market penetration. Canada and Europe became major foreign markets for Ross's *Similac*. Mead Johnson looked primarily to the Caribbean where export was relatively easy. Puerto Rico, Jamaica, and the Bahamas became important Mead Johnson export markets.

Wyeth Laboratories, never a major seller of infant formula in the United States, began to sell internationally before World War II. Following the war, the company's presence as a pharmaceutical manufacturer was the base from which infant formula was marketed by affiliates in Latin America, Europe, and Southeast Asia. Today, Wyeth probably accounts for close to 15 percent of worldwide sales. Table 11-1 provides a summary of the entry strategies of the

TABLE 11-1 Producer Orientation and Business Strategy

PRODUCER	INDUSTRY ORIENTATION	MAJOR MARKET	MAJOR AREA OF LDC MARKETS	BUSINESS STRATEGY
Bristol-Myers (Mead-Johnson)	Pharmaceutical	Domestic United States	Caribbean, Central America	Exports excess production from U.S. to nearby countries. Uses distributors. Has plant facilities in Philippines.
Abbot Laboratories (Ross Laboratories)	Pharmaceutical	Domestic United States	Rapidly developing African and Southeast Asian (e.g., Nigeria, Taiwan)	Exports from European plants; aimed at upper income market. Uses own sales force, limited use of distributors.
American Home Products (Wyeth Laboratories)	Pharmaceutical	Selective world markets (e.g., Canada, S. Africa)	Southeast Asia, Latin America, Africa	Exports as complement to drug sales. Uses Wyeth subsidiaries to market. Preference for regional/local production.
Nestlé	Food Processor	Europe, Africa, Latin America, Asia	Worldwide	Sells food products internationally. Established first milk industry in many nations & has full line local food processing plants.
Borden	Food Processor	Worldwide	Latin America, Caribbean	Food product marketed through distributors; participates in some joint ventures.

five MNC infant formula food manufacturers in the world. These are, however, not the only sellers of infant formula products. Multinational firms from the United Kingdom (e.g., Unigate), Denmark, France, West Germany, and Japan all sell modified infant formula or powdered milks which are used for infant feeding in LDCs. The pharmaceutical and food processor orientations, and the various business strategies discussed above are representative of the basic MNC approaches to the marketing of infant food products in LDC.

GROWTH IN INFANT FORMULA
SALES IN LDCS

Studies point to an increasing trend toward bottle-feeding in LDCs. In developing nations, breast-feeding has declined substantially and the length of the nursing period has shrunk from over a year to a few months.

Three important environmental factors[2] account for the shift toward bottle-feeding in LDCs. These are the sociocultural changes in developing countries, the changing attitudes of health workers and health institutions, and the promotional activities of infant formula manufacturers.

The sociocultural factors influencing change in infant feeding can be understood primarily in terms of urbanization, which has caused the westernization of social mores and the needs for mobility in employment. High income groups were the first to use infant formula, in imitation of western practices, and thus bottle-feeding came to represent a high-status modern practice. Low income groups tended to follow suit. Too, the breast has come to be viewed as a sex symbol, which has led to embarrassment in using if for nursing, and fear that nursing will make the appearance of the breast less desirable. Finally, there is the convenience aspect: most places of employment do not provide facilities for a nursing woman, so bottle-feeding of the infant may become a necessity for a working woman.

Health professionals—doctors, nurses, and clinic workers—and the policies of the hospitals and clinics often, wittingly or unwittingly, endorse the use of infant formula. Although much of this activity originates in the promotional efforts by baby food formula manufacturers to the mother, the endorsement may appear to come from the health professionals themselves. Nurses and social workers who staff hospitals and clinics may encourage the use of bottle-feeding. In many hospitals newborn babies are routinely bottle-fed whether or not the mother plans to breast-feed later. Hospitals and clinics receive free samples of infant milk and special plastic milk bottles which nurses distribute to mothers. These nurses may also distribute "vaccination cards" which advertise infant formulas, and baby care booklets which recommend bottle-feeding.

[2]Johanna T. Dwyer, "The Demise of Breast Feeding: Sales, Sloth, or Society?" in *Priorities In Child Nutrition,* report prepared for the UNICEF Executive Board under the direction of Dr. Jean Mayer (E/ICEF/L. 1328, March 28, 1975), vol. II, pp. 332–339.

INDUSTRY PROMOTION PRACTICES

Many observers claim that the infant formula industry's promotion is overly aggressive and has contributed to the decline of breast-feeding. The industry itself, however, feels that its promotion is generally responsible and performs a valuable function. Individual companies have concentrated on different promotional mixes, based on their orientation, i.e., pharmaceutical vs. processed foods; or depending on their market strategies, i.e., maintaining a dominant market position and protecting market share, or getting entry into new markets and increasing market share. Yet their impact from the public interest point of view is not very dissimilar. These practices can be summarized in the following categories:

Baby Food Booklets.   One of the major forms of promotion used by baby food companies is the information booklet. Some typical titles are *The Ostermilk Mother and Baby Book: Caring for Your Baby*, published by Ross Laboratories, and *A Life Begins*, published by Nestlé. These booklets are distributed free in maternity wards of public hospitals, clinics, doctor's offices, and by nurses. They provide information on prenatal and postnatal care, with special emphasis given to how babies should be fed. Many of these books are directed to illiterate or semiliterate women, using pictures to show correct or incorrect feeding methods.

Some baby food booklets, usually pre-1975 versions, describe and illustrate bottle-feeding without mentioning breast-feeding. However, as public concern rose over the possible harmful effects of bottle-feeding, promotional booklets began to discuss breast-feeding and to recommend "mixed feeding," in which the bottle is used as a supplement to breast milk. Examples of this type include Nestlé's *Your Baby and You*, which suggests "an occasional bottle-feed . . . if you cannot breast-feed Baby entirely yourself."[3] A Mead Johnson pamphlet states "More babies have thrived on Mead Johnson formula products than on any other form of supplementary feeding." Cow & Gate recommends its milk to "be used as a substitute for breast-feeding or as a supplement."[4]

In discussing the use of supplements for feeding the baby, these booklets often emphasize reasons to discontinue or diminish breast-feeding. Nestlé, for example, in *A Life Begins*, asserts that bottle-feeding must be substituted for breast-feeding if the mother is ill, if her milk is insufficient for the baby or of "poor quality," or if the mother's nipples crack or become infected. These booklets also suggest that breast-feeding should be diminished to include solid food into the baby's diet. The *Ostermilk Mother and Baby Book* advises introducing solid foods for babies a few weeks old or even earlier, while Cow & Gate suggests feeding its brand of cereal to the baby from two to three months.[5]

[3]Ledogar, op. cit., pp. 133–134.
[4]Ibid.
[5]Ibid., p. 142.

Other media practices.   Companies did promote their baby food products by advertising in magazines, newspapers, radio, television, and through loudspeaker vans. As with the baby care booklets, early advertisements usually did not mention breast-feeding: a magazine advertisement stated that Ostermilk and Farex products were "right from the start—the foods you can trust." Poster advertisements, often exhibited in hospitals and clinics, showed how to prepare baby formula, but gave only minimal attention to breast-feeding. Radio and television ads similarly emphasized bottle-feeding.

Free samples and gifts.   One of the most widespread promotional techniques is the distribution of free samples, and the offer of free gifts to users or potential users of baby food formula. These usually take the form of samples of formula or free feeding bottles, and may be handed out by nurses and salesmen at hospitals, clinics, or in the home. A survey in Ibadan, Nigeria, found that 9 percent of the mothers surveyed had received samples. These had been given in equal proportion to more affluent mothers and to those who could not afford baby food formula. A spokesman from Nestlé admitted that sampling in the Philippines cost about 4–5 percent of turnover.[6] Free gifts are less often used as an inducement to buy.

Promotion through the medical profession.   Hospitals and physicians are a logical focus for promotion and sales-related advertising. The users of artificial feeding products are sensitive to the "scientific" quality of infant formula, and physicians were the appropriate counselors to give advice. Also, hospitals are becoming increasingly popular as the site for birth, and the newborns are typically fed at the hospital for the first few days of their lives. The decision a new mother makes before birth to feed her child "Brand X" formula could be changed by the hospital's decision to feed infants "Brand Y" or the physician's recommendation to feed "Brand Z." As a marketing matter, prebirth advertising can create consumer awareness of a product; it cannot create sales. Sales creation occurs in the physician's office or in the hospital. For these reasons, the medical community has become the focal point for infant formula promotion in industrialized and developing nations alike.

In general, all promotional methods such as booklets, free samples, posters, and the use of salespeople are employed in the hospitals and clinics. In addition, the use of "milk nurses" and "milk banks" functions to associate baby food formula with the medical profession. "Mother-craft" or milk nurses are fully or partially trained nurses hired by infant food formula companies, and instructed by them in "product knowledge." Most nurses are paid fixed salaries plus a travel allowance, but some may receive sales-related bonuses. A number of hospitals allow milk nurses to speak to mothers in maternity wards

[6]Frances M. Lappé and Eleanor McCallie, "Infant Formula Promotion and Use in the Philippines: An Informal, On-Site Report," Institute for Food and Development Policy (San Francisco, California, July 1977). Lappé is the author of the new book *Food First*.

or clinics. Nurses visit mothers in their homes, and in some isolated areas, the milk nurses make formula deliveries. A 1974 study conducted by the Caribbean Food and Nutrition Institute found that Mead Johnson, subsidiaries of Nestlé, Glaxo, Ross Laboratories, and Cow & Gate all employed milk nurses in Jamaica. Mead Johnson employed twelve.[7]

Milk banks, usually set up in the hospitals and clinics that serve the poor, are sales outlets for commercial infant food formula. These banks sell formula at reduced prices to poor mothers. For example, at the milk bank at Robert Reid Cabral hospital in Santo Domingo, a pound tin of Nestlé's *Nido* is sold for 90¢, a 40 percent discount off the regular $1.50 price; Nestlé's *Nan* is sold for $1.35, a 33 percent discount off the regular price of $2.00.

Consumer behavior is directly tied to the influence of these promotional activities. It is generally accepted among marketers of infant products that new mothers are susceptible to advertising. During pregnancy, and immediately after giving birth, the mother is very anxious to use the "correct" product.[8] A number of consumer research surveys, including some proprietary studies by firms in the industry, have indicated that mothers will choose an infant formula based on the implied or actual brand endorsement of the hospital in which the baby was born, and will continue to use that product after discharge.[9] Through detailing, infant formula producers have been able to differentiate their products in the minds of physicians and achieve brand loyalty among the mothers of infants. Given the pharmaceutical orientation of some of the major companies that have developed infant formula in the United States, it is not surprising that the distinctive marketing competence of these firms resides in their ability to deal with health professionals. The success of this promotional strategy is evidenced by its firm entrenchment in the competitive conduct; and by what is more telling, the high priority which new entrants place on improving relations with physicians and hospitals.[10]

CRITICISM OF INDUSTRY PROMOTION PRACTICES

All forms of promotion used by infant formula companies have been criticized by different observers. In general, critics claim that most forms of advertising are misleading or use "hard sell" techniques to turn mothers away from breastfeeding.

[7]V. G. James, "Household Expenditures on Food and Drink by Income Groups," paper presented at seminar on Natural Food and Nutrition Policy, Kingston, Jamaica, 1974.

[8]*The American Druggist* (May 4, 1970).

[9]This has been acknowledged by industry executives and was a key point in the U.S. antitrust action brought by Baker Laboratories against Abbott (Ross) and Bristol-Myers in 1972.

[10]James E. Post, "The Infant Formula Industry: Strategy, Structure, and Performance," Working Paper, Management and Public Policy Research Program, Boston University, 1977.

Baby care booklets.   The main criticism of baby care booklets is that they ignore or de-emphasize breast-feeding. Critics feel that mothers reading these baby care booklets will be led to believe that bottle-feeding is as good or better than breast-feeding. Even if the booklet directly states "Breast-feeding is best," critics assert that the overall impression is still misleading. The new trend in these books toward promoting "mixed feeding," or the early introduction of solid food is also questioned. The La Leche League International, an organization which promotes breast-feeding, observed that:

> . . . the supplementary formula is one of the greatest deterrents to establishing a good milk supply, and frequent nursing is one of the greatest helps. You see, the milk supply is regulated by what the baby takes. The more he nurses, the more milk there will be. If he's given a bottle as well, he'll gradually take less and less from the breast, and the supply will diminish.[11]

In addition, the use of a bottle and overdiluted formula, even as a supplement, can cause infection and malnutrition in the infant.

Promotion through media.   The critics' objections to other media promotion is similar to their objections to the baby care booklets. They feel that even with the admission of the superiority of breast milk, media promotion remains essentially misleading in its encouragement of mothers to bottle-feed their children. A survey in infant feeding practices in Ibadan, Nigeria, revealed that of the 38 percent of 400 mothers who remembered having seen ads for formula, the majority recalled statements to the effect that the formula gives infants strength, energy, and power. None remembered having heard that breast milk is better for babies. In Nigeria, when ads for Ovaltine included the picture of a plump smiling baby, observers noted that there was a trend for mothers to feed their babies Ovaltine and water as a supplement.[12] This misinterpretation of ads is an obvious danger in a predominantly illiterate or semiliterate community.

Free samples and gifts.   Free samples of baby food formula and feeding bottles, as well as gift gimmicks, are considered a direct inducement to bottle-feed infants. The widespread distribution of these items shows an unethical lack of concern for either informing mothers about the superiority of breast-feeding or for determining whether mothers have the economic ability to regularly buy infant formula after the first samples.

Promotion through the medical profession.   Critics find the promotion of infant formula through the distribution of free samples and literature of the

---

[11]*The Womanly Art of Breastfeeding*, 2nd ed. (Franklin Park, Ill.: La Leche League International, 1963), p. 54.
[12]"Baby Food Tragedy," *New Internationalist*, p. 10; Mike Muller, *The Baby Killer: War on Want*, 2nd ed. (May 1975), p. 10.

display of advertising posters in hospitals and clinics especially dangerous. Dr. D. B. Jelliffe, head of the Division of Population, Family, and International Health at UCLA, called these promotional techniques "endorsement by association" and "manipulation by assistance." Jelliffe, along with many other critics, feels that companies providing hospitals and clinics with free samples and information on new developments in infant formula, as well as a barrage of advertisements, influence health care workers to favor and promote bottlefeeding to their patients. It is also argued that because mothers see posters and receive informational booklets and free samples at hospitals and clinics, they come to believe that the health profession endorses bottle-feeding. Thus, this type of promotion works two ways in influencing both the beliefs of professionals and the beliefs of mothers about the value of bottle-feeding.

The use of milk nurses also receives its share of criticism. Observers charge that the nurse uniform conceals the fact that the "nurses" are essentially salespeople who encourage mothers to bottle-feed. They assert that some nurses are paid on a sales-related basis, causing them to be even more eager to push for sales. In support of this belief, critics quote an industry man: "Some nurses will be paid a commission on sales results in their area. Sometimes they will also be given the added stick that if they don't meet those objectives, they will be fired."[13]

Milk banks.   Milk banks are used by companies to expand sales by encouraging bottle-feeding among the poor while still retaining the higher-income market. However, critics assert that the discount prices of the formula are still beyond the economic means of the people at whom the milk banks aim their services. For example, a milk bank in Guatemala City sells Nestlé products for $1.00 per tin, a discount of 80¢ to $1.00 from the regular price. A tin lasts only a few days when properly perpared. However, since the women buying milk there generally have household incomes of between $15 and $45 per month, they commonly buy fewer tins and dilute them. This starts the baby on a cycle of malnutrition and disease.

BUSINESS AND SOCIAL STRESS: AN ANALYTICAL FRAMEWORK

The manner in which all organizations, particularly large corporations, respond to social change is a matter of great public concern. Their economic actions necessarily involve social changes and may have such an impact on established behavioral patterns and underlying cultural values and beliefs as to cause tremen-

[13]Bristol-Myers Co., "The Infant Formula Marketing Practices," p. 13.

dous social stress. This is especially true in the case of LDCs. There is reason to believe that the effect of the modern corporation is even more profound in social and economic settings where there are fewer countervailing influences than exist in industrialized societies. These nations are in the process of becoming modernized and their is tension between the values of the old and the new, the technology of the past and the future, and the aspirations of the present with the traditions of the past. The modern coporation generally represents the new and the future. In such situations, it is not surprising that the impact of the corporation concerns those who care about the pace, the process, and the direction of development and change.

Infant nutrition is one area in which the complex interaction of changing social values, institutions, and technology has produced major changes in social habits. According to many public health and nutrition experts, there now exists a crisis of monumental proportions in LDCs as mothers abandon traditional breast-feeding practices in favor of bottle-feeding. In the view of some critics, the bottle has become a symbol of the most invidious intrusion of western technology into the lives and welfare of LDC populations. One might fairly conclude that the "great infant formula controversy" is one involving the politics of technology.

The objectives of MNCs and LDCs are not always congruent with each other. Nevertheless, there must be a common ground where the interaction between the two yield net benefits, both tangible and intangible, if any sustained cooperation is to take place. Conventional economic analysis shows direct costs and benefits of individual MNC-LDC cooperation, but usually overlooks social and political costs. These costs are difficult to calculate, as there is no common consensus of what they are or how they might be measured; and there is a fear that if these costs were specified, they could doom MNC projects. The cultural and sociopolitical costs are of critical importance. The long-range social acceptance on the part of the peoples in LDCs of MNC's investments depends on the decisions of MNC and LDC governments to taking these costs into account when developing economic projects.

The analytical framework presented in this section provides one method of examining the nature of the conflict, and also the adequacy of MNC responses, in terms of social relevance, so that comparisons over time and across industries and nations are possible. The framework consists of two components. The first deals with categorization of the types of corporate responses: these are defined not in terms of specific activities, but in terms of types of rationale applied in responding to social pressures. The second component deals with the definition of the external environment, or the context within which the corporate response is being made and evaluated. The emphasis is not on the specifics of a particular social situation or problem, but on the generalized external conditions created by a multitude of acts, by corporations, individuals, and social institutions, that are essentially similar within a given temporal and contextual frame.[14] The issue in terms of social responsiveness is not how corporations should respond to social pressures, but what their long run role in a dynamic social system should be. The corporation here is expected to *anticipate* the changes that are likely to take place. Corporations should initiate policies and programs that will minimize the adverse side effects of their present or future activities. Again, *while the activities relevant to social responsibilities are prescriptive in nature, activities related to social responsiveness are proactive, i.e., anticipatory and preventive in nature.*

THE EXTERNAL ENVIRONMENT

A distinction must also be made regarding the various external environments—physical, economic, and sociopolitical—within which a given corporate response to a set of social problems must be evaluated. This has been accomplished by describing the time between the emergence of a problem and its solution and ultimate elimination in four stages: the preproblem stage, the identification stage, the remedy and relief stage, and the prevention stage. There is some overlap among these categories because social problems do not fall neatly into discrete groups, nor can they always be solved in distinct successive steps.

The preproblem stage.   In the process of manufacturing and marketing, business firms are constantly engaged in a series of transactions with individuals and social groups. These transactions have certain direct and indirect adverse effects on the parties involved. The negative side effects may be the normal shortfalls found in any manufacturing activity, or they may pertain to actions by individual firms to cut corners either under competitive pressures or to increase short-run profits. Taken individually, each act or incident is not significant in its impact. However, when similar acts are performed by a large number of companies and continued over a long period of time, their cumulative effect is substantial. When that happens, a problem is born.

The preproblem stage is probably the longest of all the four. Most individuals and institutions respond to the problem passively. The effort is aimed at adaptation, and the problem is treated as given.

The identification stage.   Once a problem has become large enough, and its impact significant enough, there is a drive among the affected groups to de-

---

[14]For a further elaboration, discussion and application of this model, see S. Prakash Sethi, "Dimensions of Corporate Social Performance: An Analytical Framework for Measurement and Evaluation," *California Management Review* (Spring 1975), pp. 58–64; and S. Prakash Sethi, "An Analytical Framework for Making Cross-Cultural Comparisons of Business Responses to Social Pressures," in Lee E. Preston (ed.), *Research in Corporate Social Performance and Policy* (Greenwich, Conn.: JAI Press, 1978), in press.

fine the problem, identify its causes, and find the source. This is one of the most difficult stages in the whole process. Quite often the business entity could not have known of the problem because the technology for its detection did not exist. In most cases, direct linkages between cause and effect are all but impossible. The best that can be accomplished is to show through inference and weight of evidence that a given source was the major contributor to the problem. The definition of the problem may also involve the vested interest or value orientation of a particular group.

The remedy and relief stage.   Once the causal linkage has been established, there arises the question of compensatory and/or punitive damages to the affected parties. This stage is marked by an intense amount of activity by the parties to the conflict. An equally important role is played by courts, legislatures, and executive and administrative agencies of the government.

The prevention stage.   At this point, the problem has achieved maturity. The causal sources are either well-established or easily identifiable. The attempt is made to develop long-range programs to prevent the recurrence of the problem. These include development of substitute materials, product redesign, the restructuring of organizations and decision-making processes, public education, and the emergence of new special interest groups to bring about necessary political and legislative changes. It should be noted that the prevention stage is not sequential with, but generally overlaps, the problem identification and remedy and relief stages.

This stage is marked by considerable uncertainty and difficulty in making an accurate appraisal of potential costs and benefits. It is not uncommon to find a high degree of self-righteousness in the pronouncements of various groups, which may be long on rhetoric but short on substance. Groups tend to advocate solutions that favor their particular viewpoint, while understating the potential costs to those groups having opposing viewpoints.

DIMENSIONS OF CORPORATE SOCIAL PERFORMANCE

The development of absolute, universal norms of corporate behavior may not be possible or even desirable. Still, there must be some criteria that can serve as a guide for evaluating past and current performance, and for providing useful indicators in future activities. Corporations, like other social institutions, are an integral part of society and depend on it for their existence, continuity, and growth. Corporations constantly strive to pattern their activities—the nature of resources they use, the type of goods they produce, and the manner in which goods are distributed—so that they are in congruence with the goals of the overall social system. The quest for legitimacy by the corporation, and the questioning by its critics of the legitimacy of some of its actions, are the crucial issues in the concept of corporate social responsibility.

An effective way to evaluate corporate social performance is to use the yardstick of legitimacy. Given that both corporations and their critics seek to narrow the gap between corporate performance and its legitimacy, the social relevance and validity of any corporate action depends on one's concept of legitimacy. Legitimization involves not only corporate activities, but also includes the internal processes of decision making; the perception of the external environment; the manipulation of that environment—physical, social, and political—to make it more receptive to corporate activities; and the nature of accountability to other institutions in the system. The corporate behavior thus determined can be defined in three ways: as social obligation, social responsibility, or social responsiveness.

Corporate behavior as social obligation.   Corporate behavior in response to market forces or legal constraints is defined as social obligation.

The criteria for legitimacy in this arena are economic and legal only. The corporation satisfies the legitimacy criteria by competing for resources in the marketplace and conducting its operations within the legal constraints imposed by the social system.

This simplistic argument conceals more than it explains. Competition for resources is not by itself an adequate criterion. Corporations constantly strive to free themselves from the discipline of the market through increase in size, diversification, and the generation of consumer loyalty by advertising and other means of persuasion. Even in an ideal situation, the ethics of the marketplace provide only one kind of legitimacy, which has been rejected in times of national crisis or for certain activities deemed vital to the nation's well-being.

Nor can the legality of an act be used alone as the criterion. Norms in a social system are developed from a voluntary consensus among various groups. Under these conditions, laws may codify socially accepted behavior but seldom lead social change. *The traditional economic and legal criteria are necessary but not sufficient conditions of corporate legitimacy.* The corporation that flouts them will not survive, but the mere satisfaction of these criteria does not ensure its continued existence.

Corporate behavior as social responsibility.   Most of the conflicts between large corporations and various social institutions during the last two decades, in the United States and in other industrialized nations of the free world, fall into the category of social responsibility. Although few corporations have been accused of violating the laws of their nations, they are increasingly being criticized for failing to meet social expectations and to adapt their behavior to changing social norms. Thus, *social responsibility implies bringing corporate behavior up to a level where it is in congruence with currently prevailing social norms, values, and expectations of performance.*

Social responsibility does not require a radical departure from the usual nature of corporate activites or the normal pattern of corporate behavior. It is simply a step ahead—before the new social expectations are codified into legal requirements. *While the concept of social obligation is proscriptive in nature, the concept of social responsibility is prescriptive.*

Corporate behavior as social responsiveness.   The third stage of the adaptation of corporate behavior to social needs is in terms of social responsiveness. The issue in terms of social responsiveness is not how corporations should respond to social pressures, but what their long-run role in a dynamic social system should be. Again, while social responsibility-related activities are prescriptive in nature, activities related to social responsiveness are proactive, i.e., anticipatory and preventive in nature.

APPLYING THE FRAMEWORK

The analytical model described above can be used to better understand how social conflicts develop and firms respond. It can also be employed to predict the effectiveness of a particular corporate response at different stages of a conflict's evolution. In this section the framework is applied to the infant formula controversy. In the final section, a number of conclusions are drawn about marketing practices and social conflicts surrounding second-order impacts.

The infant formula controversy.   The first criticism of the industry and its promotional activities is traceable to the late 1960s when Dr. Jelliffe, Director of the Caribbean Food and Nutrition Institute in Jamaica, conducted his research. His findings and criticism culminated in an international conference of experts held in Bogata, Colombia, in 1970, under the auspices of the U.N.'s Protein Calorie Advisory Group (PAG). Out of this meeting, and the 1972 follow-up session in Singapore, came increased professional concern about the effects of commercial activity related to infant feeding. The PAG issued an official statement (PAG, Statement #23) in 1973 recommending that breast-feeding be supported and promoted in LDCs, and that commercial promotion by industry or LDC governments be restrained.

The first public identification of the issue occurred in 1973 with the appearance of several articles about the problem in *The New Internationalist*.[15] This, in turn, spurred Mike Muller to undertake a series of interviews and observations which were eventually printed as *The Baby Killer*, a pamphlet published in 1974.[16] The popularization of the issue resulted in a German translation of Muller's work published in Switzerland under the title, *Nestle Tötet*

---

[15]"The Baby Food Controversy," *The New Internationalist*, p. 10.
[16]Muller, op. cit.

Kinder (Nestle Kills Babies); and in a lawsuit by Nestlé against the public action group that published the pamphlet. A period of intense advocacy issued from the trial in the Swiss courts. Thus, between 1974 and mid-1976 when the case was decided, considerable international media coverage was given the issue.

The pressure began in earnest in 1975 when shareholder resolutions were filed for consideration at the annual meetings of the American infant formula companies. This pressure has continued, and several institutional investors such as universities and the Rockefeller and Ford Foundations have taken public positions which sharply question the responsiveness of the firms to the controversy. Church groups have led the fight, and have developed their own institutional mechanism through the National Council of Churches, the Interfaith Council on Corporate Responsibility, to coordinate shareholders' campaigns. At the LDC level, the government of Papua New Guinea recently passed a law declaring that baby bottles, nipples and pacifiers are health hazards, and their sale has been restricted to prescription only. The objective was to discourage indiscriminate promotion, sale and consumption of infant food formulas.[17]

Recently, institutions have acted to broaden their popular base by launching a grass roots campaign to boycott Nestle products in the United States. By linking public action groups throughout the U.S., the current campaign aspires to heighten First World pressure against the Third World's largest seller of infant formula foods.

Manufacturer responses.   The preproblem stage of the infant formula case existed prior to the 1970s. During this time, the adverse impacts on LDCs were not yet articulated. The MNC's response was of the social obligation type, answering only to prevailing law and market conditions. In effect, MNCs were free to conduct their business in ways most consistent with their own orientations and business strategies.

By the early 1970s the identification stage had been reached, as professional criticism grew and articles and stories began to appear in the mass media. The principal industry response to this professional concern was participation in the conference sponsored by PAG. Abbott (Ross), AHP (Wyeth), and Nestlé each sent representatives to these meetings as did a number of British, European, and Japanese companies. For most companies, this seemed to mark a decision point between *social obligation* and *social responsibility.* Only a few firms, notably Abbott (Ross), took steps to mitigate their negative impact in the LDCs. AHP (Wyeth), Borden, Nestlé and others did not follow suit until 1974, when first plans for the formation of an international trade organization were laid.

The remedy and relief stage seems to have begun in 1975, with the Nestlé trial in Switzerland and the shareholder resolutions filed in the United States.

[17]"Baby Bottles Banned in New Guinea," *The Dallas Morning News* (November 3, 1977), p. 8-C.

In November 1975, representatives of nine MNC manufacturers met in Zurich and formed the International Council of Infant Food Industries (ICIFI). Nestlé, AHP (Wyeth), and Abbott (Ross) participated in these discussions along with several European and four Japanese companies. Others, such as Borden and Bristol-Myers, sent representatives to the sessions, but chose not to participate actively or to join the council. ICIFI's initial directive was to instruct members to adopt a code of marketing ethics which obliged them to recognize the primacy of breast-feeding in all product information and labelling; to include precise product-use information; and to eliminate in-hospital promotion and solicitation by personnel who were paid on a sales-commission basis. For those companies that joined, the council seemed to mark a passage into *social responsibility* as efforts were undertaken to mitigate negative social impacts.

There was criticism of the ICIFI code from the beginning, and Abbott (Ross) withdrew from the organization, arguing that the code was too weak. The company then adopted its own and more restrictive code, which included a provision prohibiting consumer-oriented mass advertising. For ICIFI, the marketing code has been the most visible manifestation of concern for second-order impacts in LDCs. Additional criticism led to some incremental changes which strengthened the "professional" character of sales activity, but which have not yet proscribed all consumer-oriented mass advertising. Thus, ICIFI, the industry's mechanism for countering criticism and searching for means of addressing problems of product misuse in LDC environments, has been unable to reckon with any but the individual-level secondary impacts. Indeed, the critics continue to charge that the response at the user level has been insufficient.

Borden also moved from the social obligation to social responsibility stage. The company had shareholder resolutions filed with it in 1977. This filing perhaps facilitated a management review of promotional strategies in LDCs. In settling the resolution with the church groups before the meeting, Borden agreed to modify certain advertising and labelling of its powdered milk *Klim*; and to tightly oversee the marketing so as to minimize possible consumer misuse of the powdered milk product as an infant formula food. Separately, the company announced that it was withdrawing its infant formula *New Biolac* from two LDC markets in the Far East because it concluded it could not effectively market this product without extensive consumer advertising which was not permissible in the prevailing social-political environment.

As a public issue matures, companies may adopt actions which operate to prevent further growth in the legitimacy gap by minimizing or eliminating the underlying sources of criticism (the *prevention stage*). This has begun to occur in the infant formula controversy as both ICIFI and individual companies have taken action to prevent some of the secondary impacts discussed above. In 1977, Abbott (Ross) announced its intention to commit nearly $100,000 to a breast-feeding campaign in developing nations, and to budget $175,000 for a task force to conduct research on breast-feeding, infant formula, and LDCs. The company also announced a plan for a continuing cooperative effort with its critics in reviewing the situation. ICIFI has now also gone beyond its marketing code-of-ethics and has begun informally working with international health agencies to prepare educational materials, for use in LDCs, that would encourage breast-feedeeding and improve maternal and infant health care. The council is also involved in supporting scientific research of breast-feeding, infant formula products, and LDC environments.

Abbott (Ross) Laboratories' attempt to act in a way that will create positive impacts in LDCs signals a shift to a corporate *social responsiveness*. Granting that there is some danger of sending "double signals" to its sales force, the company seems to have adopted a posture that permits the sale of its products in appropriate circumstances, and assists the LDCs in encouraging breast-feeding where that is most appropriate.

Table 11-2 describes the patterns of responses, from social obligation to social responsiveness, in the evolution of the controversy from the preproblem to the prevention stage.

CONCLUSIONS

The infant formula controversy involves a social conflict of great complexity which illustrates the formidable involvement that can develop between an industry and the society in which it operates. First World products and technologies have consequences in Third World settings that cannot be ignored in the blind search for market opportunities. Artificial feeding, as a technology, and infant formula foods, as a product, have had a strong impact on LDCs in the past twenty years. Some, such as the provision of choices for consumers, have been intended; others have been unintended. Neither type can be ignored. To a number of those involved, the "action question" is now paramount: What is to be done and by whom? Certainly, firms in the industry, LDC governments, professional nutritionists, and public action groups throughout the world are pondering that very question.

There is a second, and perhaps more significant, question to be asked as well. Is it possible for a firm, much less an entire industry, to market its products in an ethically acceptable manner over a long period of time and in different social environments? This is the ultimate marketing question. Because public standards change, the answer lies not in a categorical yes or no. Rather it is to be found in the concerted efforts of a management that is sensitive to the ever changing agenda of public issues, to identify, assess and respond creatively to newly exposed expectations of corporate performance. The breakdown of the marketing concept occurs when managers to whom marketing strategy is entrusted become myopic, focusing on current markets rather than changing societal needs and expectations. The great infant formula controversy is an object lesson in marketing strategies gone awry.

The controversy surrounding infant formula foods is not an isolated case, unrelated to other industries or types of products. It is very likely "opening

TABLE 11-2 Socio-Political Dimensions of Infant Formula Foods Controversy: Patterns of Industry Responses (5 MNCs)

PATTERNS OF INDUSTRY RESPONSE	STAGES OF CONFLICT EVOLUTION			
	PREPROBLEM STAGE	IDENTIFICATION STAGE	REMEDY & RELIEF STAGE	PREVENTION STAGE
Social Obligation (Do what is required by law)	Bristol-Myers (Mead Johnson Division) Borden Nestlé American Home Products Wyeth Laboratories Abbott (Ross Laboratories)	Bristol-Myers (Mead Johnson Division) Borden Nestlé American Home Products (Wyeth Laboratories)	Bristol-Myers (Mead Johnson Division) Borden	Bristol-Myers (Mead Johnson Division)
Social Responsibility (Mitigate negative impacts)		Abbott (Ross Laboratories)	Nestlé American Home Products (Wyeth Laboratories)	Borden Nestlé American Home Products (Wyeth Laboratories)
Social Responsiveness (Promote positive change)			Abbott (Ross Laboratories)	Abbott (Ross Laboratories)

round" in the public questioning of the underlying legitimacy of marketing activity in societies where public needs are more important than private choice. It is not sufficient to say that any product which offers the consuming public a choice is acceptable in all societies. It is only by matching marketing activities to areas where genuine public needs exist, and by analyzing and assessing the primary and secondary impacts of products in particular social environments, that marketing strategies can remain viable in modern business environments.[18]

A senior executive of one of the infant formula manufacturers discussed above noted that much of the problem of infant malnutrition in LDCs was attributable to "misadventure" by the products' users—that is, a consequence of something the individual initiated. The fatal blow to that argument is the recognition that some actions of the marketer may have contributed to that consumer's misadventure. We believe that the firm must be held responsible for any misadventure that arises as a consequence of the marketing efforts which it initiates. This does not serve to place on managers unlimited responsibility, but puts a premium on their efforts to foresee the public consequences of private action.

It is clear that when a firm or industry ignores the second order effects of its actions, private conflicts between sellers and the customers become public controversies. Managers have the greatest discretion in dealing with conflicts at the earliest stages. But once an issue passes into the remedy and relief stage, and nonusers of the product are drawn into the controversy by proponents of change, the range of responses available to the firm becomes limited. This strongly suggests that managers ought to recognize public issues as quickly as possible, and move from the social obligation and social responsibility patterns of response into the proactive social responsiveness mode.

CHELSEA, THE ADULT SOFT DRINK: A CASE STUDY OF CORPORATE SOCIAL RESPONSIBILITY

Keith M. Jones

Following World War II, the pent-up needs of American consumers were unleashed in the domestic marketplace. An unending stream of new consumer products resulted, and the marketing concept was born. Simply put, the marketing concept argued that products existed solely to fill consumer needs. Products

Keith M. Jones, "Chelsea, The Adult Soft Drink: A Case Study of Corporate Social Responsibility," *Journal of Contemporary Business*, 7, no. 4 (1979), 69–76. Reprinted with permission.

[18]See James E. Post, testimony in *Marketing and Promotion of Infant Formula in the Developing Nations*, Hearings before the Subcommittee on Health and Scientific Research of the Committee on Human Resources, 95th Congress, Second Session, 23 May 1978, pp. 116–125.

were not purchased for their intrinsic value, but rather to satisfy a consumer need. The simple logic of the marketing concept was irresistible, so manufacturers began marketing their products instead of simply producing them.

Limits of the Marketing Concept

As the marketing concept flowered and consumer need research rivaled the aerospace program in detail, competition among manufacturers extended far beyond the characteristics of the product itself. Products were enlarged to become the "augmented product" of Theodore Levitt. The "augmented product" was articulated by Professor Levitt in his mid-60's best seller, "The Marketing Mode" as:

> . . . a new kind of competition that is in galloping ascendance in the world today. This is the competition of product augmentation: not competition between what companies produce in their factories, but between what they add to their factory output in the form of packaging, services, advertising, customer advice, financing, delivery arrangements, warehousing, and other things that people value.

As the augmented product achieved full dimensions, consumer needs to be fulfilled became increasingly complex: ego needs, status needs, and needs for conspicuous display of affluence. Ordering just a "scotch" whiskey for example was insufficient. Brand name scotch was required, and certain brands such as Johnnie Walker Black Label filled social needs that Johnnie Walker himself could never have imagined.

Product augmentation stretched the marketing concept to its furthest limits, and conflicts began to appear. Conflicts occurred between augmented products satisfying social needs and the larger role of the corporation in society. The need for convenient aerosol cosmetics conflicted with preservation of the environment. The stress and tension release provided by tobacco products conflicted with human longevity. The need for social lubricants conflicted with the social costs of alcohol abuse.

Marketing Concept Versus Social Responsibility

What happened to corporations whose pursuit of the marketing concept conflicted with their larger role as a responsible social citizen? Historically there were three consequences:

The product in question was publicly screened for social negatives.
The federal government was the screening agent.
The press had a field day at company expense.

There can be no doubt that the marketplace demands and deserves products free of social negatives. However, there is an alternative to coercive and often punitive governmental intervention. A corporation can self-screen its products by directly involving consumer opinion leaders. A case in point is the social screening of Chelsea, a controversial soft drink test-marketed by Anheuser-Busch. Rather than wait for governmental direction, Anheuser-Busch employed a unique approach to resolve a conflict situation—consumer participation.

The following discussion of the Chelsea experience consists of two segments. *First*, the Chelsea product and the controversy is briefly reviewed. *Secondly*, a step-by-step description of the social screening process is detailed.

CHELSEA, THE CONTROVERSIAL PRODUCT

Chelsea was the culmination of more than two years of consumer needs research which indicated that adults wanted a soft beverage with three characteristics:

Less sweet, drier taste
All natural ingredients
Social acceptability as an alternative to alcoholic beverages

The resulting product was a light blend of all natural apple, lemon, lime, and ginger flavors. Since Chelsea was pasteurized, no artificial preservatives were needed and it had no caffeine or saccharin either. Because Chelsea contained one-third less sugar than regular soft drinks, there were one-third fewer calories. To compensate for the body of sugar, a malt product was added which contained about one-half of one percent of alcohol fermented naturally. Like apple cider, ginger ale, and beer, Chelsea was a golden color with a frothy head.

An Adult Soft Drink

The product was reviewed by the Federal Bureau of Alcohol, Tobacco and Firearms (BATF) and the alcohol control boards of five test market states and was found to fit the FDA and state definitions of a soft drink. In summary, Chelsea was a natural, less sweet, adult soft drink.

Chelsea, The Augmented Product

To fulfill the adult need for a socially acceptable alcohol substitute, augmentation was required. *First*, a sophisticated package was selected with the sleek, thin shape and distinctive foil labeling an adult would expect. Next, Chelsea was priced higher than regular soft drinks to reinforce the "Cadillac" image of a natural, adult product. Finally, an advertising campaign was developed to communicate Chelsea as an extraordinary soft drink for extraordinary people aged 25 or older. Because Chelsea was "Not-So" sweet, "Not-So" heavy, "Not-So" artificial and "Not-So" ordinary as other soft drinks, the advertising slogan was the "Not-So" Soft Drink. Thus natural, less sweet Chelsea, with its packaging, pricing, and advertising augmentation entered into market test.

CHELSEA, THE CONTROVERSY

In Virginia test markets, Chelsea conflicted with the social concerns of several individuals and organizations. The Virginia Nurses' Association voted to boycott Chelsea. Seventh-Day Adventists condemned Chelsea as a contributor to the problem of alcohol abuse. Local educators, church groups and PTA councils even pressured store managers to remove Chelsea from their shelves. Press coverage of the Virginia controversy led to network television exposure and Chelsea became a national issue. Finally, respected national figures such as Senator Orrin Hatch (Chairman, Senate Sub-Committee on Alcoholism and Alcohol Abuse) and H.E.W. Secretary Joseph Califano publicly denounced the product and its manufacturer.

How Could A Natural Soft Drink Be So Controversial?

How could the first natural soft drink with less sugar and no chemicals or preservatives become so controversial? The problem was that although Chelsea was targeted for adults, it was by definition a soft drink, and therefore purchasable by children. Chelsea critics argued that children did not need a socially acceptable alcohol substitute because they could not consume alcohol in the first place. Reasonable people suggested that however unintended, the augmented product Chelsea was in conlflict with the social responsibility of a major corporation.

THE MANAGEMENT DECISION TO ACT

Corporations interpreting social responsibility as simple profit maximization may have done nothing at this point. It would have been easy to argue "tough-it-out" or "let the marketplace decide." Anheuser-Busch management, however, realized that action was required, and the process of social screening was initiated. Because the screening process had to be conducted objectively, without the pressure of time, and would intimately involve Chelsea critics, the first step was to defuse the controversy. Therefore all Chelsea manufacture, advertising and promotion was suspended on October 21, five weeks after test market start-up. The suspension was a signal to Chelsea critics that the company valued its social responsibility more than Chelsea profits.

DYNAMICS OF THE SOCIAL SCREENING PROCESS

The screening process is much easier to describe than to conduct. In essence the purpose of the process was to eliminate the conflict between corporate activity and larger social goals. At Anheuser-Busch the social screening process consisted of four steps:

Step I: Visible corporate commitment to social responsibility
Step II: Identification of the social issue
Step III: Active participation of consumer opinion leaders
Step IV: Public communication of screening results.

While the following discussion explores each step in detail, it should be pointed out that all four steps are intertwined in a continuous process and should not be considered as independent actions.

Visible Corporate Commitment

Effective social screening is impossible without commitment to social responsiveness at the highest levels of the corporation. Such commitment is not easy to demonstrate. It's not a matter of public relations, or of truth in advertising. It's not a matter of subsidizing the local symphony or of generosity during United Fund drives. It *is* a matter of ordering priorities. Corporate economic ends must clearly become subordinate to larger social objectives. Importantly, this ranking of priorities must be performed by top management. In the case of Chelsea, August A. Busch, III, chief executive officer and board chairman, made it perfectly clear that corporate responsiveness was a higher than profit and loss contribution.

Not only was this commitment made clear *inside* the corporation, but visible commitment was also communicated *outside* the corporation. For Anheuser-Busch, the October 21 public suspension of Chelsea manufacture, advertising and promotion conveyed this commitment.

Identification of the Social Issue

The best intentions are in vain if the corporate social screening process misidentifies or fails to identify the source of the conflict in question. With Chelsea, the basic social issue was not easy to pinpoint, and there were a few red herrings. The issue, for example, was not that children could purchase Chelsea. Restricting sales to minors would not have solved the problem. Nor was intoxication the issue (about 17 ten ounce bottles consumed in an hour would have been required for intoxication—more than a child's stomach capacity). The social issue in the Chelsea case was much more complex. The issue was one of social conditioning. Critics claimed that Chelsea could act to predispose children toward alcohol consumption because Chelsea product packaging and advertising suggested beer in some respects.

No quantitative data existed to refute or substantiate the predisposition claim, so its validity became a matter of opinion. Therefore, Anheuser-Busch consulted outside experts. Medical experts, religious leaders, authorities on alcoholism, and educators were involved. When their expert opinion confirmed that the "Stepping Stone" theory of Chelsea critics could be true, the required action was obvious. Those elements of the augmented product, Chelsea, which would act to precondition children had to be eliminated.

Active Participation of Consumer
Opinion Leaders

At this point, the executive might ask, "Who is running the company anyway?" Isn't the manager who invites outsiders into the decision making process abdicating his managerial responsibilities? Of course not. The consumer participants are only a sounding board, a miniboard of directors individually selected for expertise on the specific social issue identified in Step II. The corporate manager selects the outsiders, presents action plans to them, and is responsible for channeling their input in a manner which benefits the corporation. What about confidentiality? If the consumer participants exposed confidential information to the press or to competitors, wouldn't the whole screening process backfire? There was always such a risk. However, Anheuser-Busch felt the risk was outweighed by the benefit of articulate social input, and therefore selected consumer participants of demonstrated personal integrity who would respect confidentiality requests. The consumer participants included: the Director of Adolescent Medicine at a leading Virginia university, the Director of the Center for Research on Media and Children at the Wharton School of Business, members of the Virginia Nurses' Association, members of the Potomac Council of Seventh-Day Adventists and, of course, the staff of U.S. Senator Orrin Hatch. All of these individuals strictly adhered to our confidentiality requests and made significant contributions to the screening process. More specifically, each opinion leader was included in two tasks:

> Articulating social issues to be dealt with
> Previewing Anheuser-Busch's proposed action plan

In retrospect, the participation of outside opinion leaders was the key to successful social screening because through this process, the severest Chelsea critics became proponents of the revised product.

THE CHELSEA ACTION PLAN

Based on constructive consumer input, verified by independent market research, Anheuser-Busch revised Chelsea by eliminating those elements which could act to "predispose" children while preserving the original concept of a natural, less sweet soft drink for adults. Accordingly, the alcohol was virtually removed, the foaminess was dramatically reduced, the "Not-So" Soft Drink advertising was dropped, and the bottle was changed from clear to emerald green glass. Furthermore, the Anheuser-Busch name was reduced in size on the label and positioned behind "Soft Drink Division" in order to more clearly communicate soft drink identity.

The outside participants previewed the revised product and its augmentation support and offered their public approval. Now the stage was set to complete the social screening process and inform the public of the results.

PUBLIC COMMUNICATION OF SCREENING
RESULTS

When Step I (visible corporate social commitment) is sincerely taken, the responsible manager understands that the screening process is an integral part of augmented product marketing and not a public relations tool. Therefore, rather than use advertising or a major public relations program, Anheuser-Busch management chose to conduct a national press conference to communicate the screening results. On December 12, less than two months after the screening process was initiated, a socially screened Chelsea was announced at the National Press Club in Washington, D.C. More importantly, several key outside participants in the screening process (including Senator Hatch's staff, the Virginia Nurses' Association, and the Potomac Council of Seventh-Day Adventists) attended the press conference and issued public statements commending the new product and its manufacturer.

Defusing a Potentially Damaging
Situation

As a result, a potentially damaging situation was turned into one of those rare instances where all parties won. Chelsea critics won because they were able to change the marketing thrust of a major corporation. Anheuser-Busch won because new Chelsea more clearly fit consumer needs than the original product. The biggest winner, however, was the consumer who benefited from the exercise of democracy in the marketplace without footing the bill for governmental intervention.

THE CHELSEA EXPERIENCE: A SUMMARY

One of the most difficult challenges facing contemporary managers is the task of identifying those situations when the corporation's larger role as a social unit transcends short term profit motives. When such a situation does arise, responsible corporations require a process for resolving conflict. The Chelsea experience is offered as a case study of one corporation's process in action—the process of consumer participatory social screening.

Of course, the social screening process is not risk-free, nor is it appropriate in every conflict situation. Once initiated, the corporation is obligated to follow the process through. Once outside consumer opinion leader input is solicited, the corporation may forfeit the option of "doing nothing." Pursued to the extreme, the screening process could snowball management into socially positive actions that made poor business sense. In the Chelsea case, there was the possibility that the product and marketing revisions consisted of "throwing out the baby with the bath water." While it is still too early to tell if the

Chelsea screening was economically successful, one point is already clear: a corporation can regulate itself on social matters if it establishes a meaningful two-way dialogue with the consumer.

DISCUSSION QUESTIONS

1. What basic economic, moral, and sociopolitical factors in less-developed countries should be of concern to multinational corporations? How might the foundations for the social legitimacy of business decision making be different in less-developed countries? How can an international public affairs office help companies address these differences?

2. Do multinational corporations have special moral responsibilities for monitoring product use and marketing practices in less-developed countries where assumptions of market control, effective government regulation, and consumer rationality may be strained?

3. Were the infant formula marketing practices in the LDCs—including media advertising, free gifts, baby care pamphlets, milk nurses, milk banks, and hospital samples—socially irresponsible or unethical?

4. Should the infant formula manufacturers have better anticipated the social consequences of mass marketing baby formula in LDCs?

5. Anheuser-Busch opened its internal decision-making process to outside consumer interests in order to obtain expertise on the social issues created by Chelsea. These outside interests acted as "a mini-board of directors." Does this procedure represent a viable alternative to corporate governance proposals which would appoint special interest directors to the board? Should business open its internal decision-making process to special interest groups on a broader range of social issues? What are the advantages and risks of doing so?

6. Was Chelsea an "exercise of democracy in the marketplace"? Why was the exit market control option not satisfactory in this instance?

7. Has the growth of "augmented products" in advanced market economies increased the conflict between private and social goals?

ADDITIONAL READINGS

"Dayton/Hudson Corporation," in *Business Policy, Text and Cases*, 5th ed., pp. 510–32, ed., C. R. Christensen, and others. Homewood, Ill.: Richard D. Irwin, 1982.

HANSON, KIRK O., "The Effects of Fuel Economy Standards on Corporate Strategy in the Automobile Industry," in *Government, Technology and the Future of the Automobile*, pp. 144–60, eds., D. H. Ginsburg and William J. Abernathy. New York: McGraw-Hill, 1980.

JACOBS, BRUCE A., "Ross Labs Finds the Formula," *Industry Week*, December 8, 1980, pp. 71–74.

LEONE, ROBERT A., AND STEPHEN P. BRADLEY, "Federal Energy Policy and Competitive Strategy in the U.S. Automobile Industry," in *Annual Review of Energy* (1982), pp. 61–85.

MARGOLIS, HOWARD, "The Politics of Auto Emissions," *The Public Interest*, no. 49 (Fall 1977), 3–21.

MARX THOMAS, G., "Conflicting Political and Economic Challenges in the United States Automobile Industry," *Journal of Contemporary Business*, 10, no. 3 (1981), pp. 1–13.

"Mead Corporation," in *Business Policy, Text and Cases*, pp. 458–84, C. R. Christensen, and others.

MOORE, THOMAS, "The Fight to Save Tylenol," *Fortune*, 106, no. 11 (November 29, 1982), 44–49.